CW01216381

## PRAISE FOR *AGENT LINK*

"Raymond J. Batvinis is one of our great authorities on American counterintelligence. But he is not merely a scholar. He is himself a former FBI Special Agent, a gifted investigator who learned how spies operate by catching them. With his new book, *Agent Link*, he has brought to light an espionage tale that has been unjustly forgotten. William Weisband was a roguish American who became perhaps the most valuable double agent ever to work in the service of the KGB. Batvinis lays out the full story in all its noirish glory, presenting the reader with a gripping narrative full of character and incident. Hollywood, are you listening?"

— **Peter Duffy**, author of *Double Agent: The First Hero of World War II* and *How the FBI Outwitted and Destroyed a Nazi Spy Ring*

"I'm pleased that my friend Ray has followed the Weisband case, a case that I worked on for many years to its conclusion."

— **Robert Louis Benson**, former NSA historian

"I thought I knew the story of William Weisband, arguably the most damaging Russian spy in history, but it turns out I didn't have a clue. Ray Batvinis has unearthed FBI files that reveal for the first time how the hard-drinking, high-living Weisband wormed his way into the inner sanctum of American code breaking and gave away its most closely guarded secrets. And for his crime, he served less than a year in prison. Incredible!"

— **David C. Martin**, CBS News National Security correspondent and author of *Wilderness of Mirrors*

"This is an extremely important book about a very, very damaging counterintelligence failure long hidden by NSA and written by an experienced FBI Special Agent who is also a trained historian. A must read for anyone left in the US government seriously interested in counterintelligence."

— **Paul Redmond**, Chief of CIA Counterintelligence, retired

"*Agent Link* is more than a spy story. Weisband almost disappeared from the attention of historians and the appreciation of his important role in world affairs. Fortunately, Batvinis has countered this neglect by writing his deeply-researched, well-written, colorful, and valuable contribution to spy literature."

— **David Charney**, author of *NOIR: Proposing a New Policy for Improving National Security by Fixing the Problem of Insider Spies* and a psychiatrist who evaluated FBI spies Earl Pitts and Robert Hanssen and Brian Regan of the National Geospatial Organization

# SECURITY AND PROFESSIONAL INTELLIGENCE EDUCATION SERIES (SPIES)

### Series Editor: Jan Goldman

In this post–September 11, 2001, era there has been rapid growth in the number of professional intelligence training and educational programs throughout the United States and abroad. Colleges and universities, as well as high schools, are developing programs and courses in homeland security, intelligence analysis, and law enforcement, in support of national security. The Security and Professional Intelligence Education Series (SPIES) was first designed for individuals studying for careers in intelligence and to help improve the skills of those already in the profession; however, it was also developed to educate the public on how intelligence work is conducted and should be conducted in this important and vital profession.

1. *A Spy's Résumé: Confessions of a Maverick Intelligence Professional and Misadventure Capitalist*, by Marc Anthony Viola. 2008.
2. *An Introduction to Intelligence Research and Analysis*, by Jerome Clauser, revised and edited by Jan Goldman. 2008.
3. *Writing Classified and Unclassified Papers for National Security*, by James S. Major. 2009.
4. *Strategic Intelligence: A Handbook for Practitioners, Managers, and Users*, revised edition by Don McDowell. 2009.
5. *Tokyo Rose / An American Patriot: A Dual Biography*, by Frederick P. Close. 2010.
6. *A Woman's War: The Professional and Personal Journey of the Navy's First African American Female Intelligence Officer*, by Gail Harris. 2010.
7. *Handbook of Warning Intelligence: Assessing the Threat to National Security*, by Cynthia Grabo. 2010.
8. *Keeping U.S. Intelligence Effective: The Need for a Revolution in Intelligence Affairs*, by William J. Lahneman. 2011.
9. *Words of Intelligence: An Intelligence Professional's Lexicon for Domestic and Foreign Threats, Second Edition*, by Jan Goldman. 2011.
10. *Balancing Liberty and Security: An Ethical Study of U.S. Foreign Intelligence Surveillance, 2001–2009*, by Michelle Louise Atkin. 2013.
11. *The Art of Intelligence: Simulations, Exercises, and Games*, edited by William J. Lahneman and Rubén Arcos. 2014.
12. *Quantitative Intelligence Analysis: Applied Analytic Models, Simulations, and Games*, by Edward Waltz. 2014.
13. *The Handbook of Warning Intelligence: Assessing the Threat to National Security—The Complete Declassified Edition*, by Cynthia Grabo. 2015.

14. *Intelligence and Information Policy for National Security: Key Terms and Concepts*, by Jan Goldman and Susan Maret. 2016.
15. *Partly Cloudy: Ethics in War, Espionage, Covert Action, and Interrogation, Second Edition*, by David L. Perry. 2016.
16. *Shattered Illusions: KGB Cold War Espionage in Canada*, by Donald G. Mahar. 2016.
17. *Intelligence Engineering: Operating Beyond the Conventional*, by Adam D. M. Svendsen. 2017.
18. *Humanitarian Intelligence: A Practitioner's Guide to Crisis Analysis and Project Design*, by Andrej Zwitter. 2018.
19. *Handbook of European Intelligence Cultures*, edited by Bob de Graaff and James M. Nyce, with Chelsea Locke. 2018.
20. *Reasoning for Intelligence Analysts: A Multidimensional Approach of Traits, Techniques, and Targets*, by Noel Hendrickson. 2018.
21. *Counterintelligence Theory and Practice, Second Edition*, by Hank Prunckun. 2019.
22. *Methods of Inquiry for Intelligence Analysis, Third Edition*, by Hank Prunckun. 2019.
23. *The Art of Intelligence: More Simulations, Exercises, and Games*, edited by Rubén Arcos and William J. Lahneman. 2019.
24. *Weaponized Marketing: Defeating Radical Islam with Marketing That Built the World's Top Brands*, by Lisa Merriam and Milton Kotler. 2020.
25. *Shadow Warfare: Cyberwar Policy in the United States, Russia, and China*, by Elizabeth Van Wie Davis. 2021.
26. *The Academic-Practitioner Divide in Intelligence Studies*, by Rubén Arcos, Nicole K. Drumhiller, and Mark Phythian. 2022.
27. *The Handbook of Latin American and Caribbean Intelligence Cultures*, by Florina Cristiana Matei, Carolyn Halladay, and Eduardo E. Estévez. 2022.
28. *The Future of National Intelligence: How Emerging Technologies Reshape Intelligence Communities*, by Shay Hershkovitz. 2022.
29. *The Handbook of Asian Intelligence Cultures*, by Ryan Shaffer. 2022.
30. *Communicating with Intelligence: Writing and Briefing for National Security, Third Edition*, by M. Patrick Hendrix and James S. Major. 2022.
31. *The Handbook of African Intelligence Cultures*, by Ryan Shaffer. 2023.
32. *African Intelligence Services: Early Postcolonial and Contemporary Challenges*, by Ryan Shaffer. 2023.
33. *Ethics of Spying: A Reader for the Intelligence Professional, Volume 3*, edited by Jan Goldman. 2023.
34. *Agent Link: The Spy Erased from History*, by Raymond J. Batvinis. 2024.

35. *Lifting the Fog: The Secret History of the Dutch Defense Intelligence and Security Service (1912–2022)*, by Bob de Graaff. 2024.

To view the books on our website, please visit https://rowman.com/Action/SERIES/RL/SPIES or scan the QR code below.

# Agent Link

## The Spy Erased from History

Raymond J. Batvinis

ROWMAN & LITTLEFIELD
*Lanham • Boulder • New York • London*

Published by Rowman & Littlefield
An imprint of The Rowman & Littlefield Publishing Group, Inc.
4501 Forbes Boulevard, Suite 200, Lanham, Maryland 20706
www.rowman.com

86-90 Paul Street, London EC2A 4NE, United Kingdom

Copyright © 2024 by Raymond J. Batvinis

*All rights reserved.* No part of this book may be reproduced in any form or by any electronic or mechanical means, including information storage and retrieval systems, without written permission from the publisher, except by a reviewer who may quote passages in a review.

British Library Cataloguing in Publication Information Available

**Library of Congress Cataloging-in-Publication Data**

Names: Batvinis, Raymond J., author.
Title: Agent Link : the spy erased from history / Raymond J. Batvinis.
Description: Lanham : Rowman & Littlefield, [2024] | Series: Security and professional intelligence education series | Includes bibliographical references. | Summary: "Agent Link: The Spy Erased from History examines the life of Willaim Wolfe Weisband. It tells the story of his KGB recruitment and working with codebreakers at the top-secret Army Security Agency. The book reveals his motivations for spying, the extent of America's losses, how he was caught, and the consequences of his treachery"— Provided by publisher.
Identifiers: LCCN 2023054416 (print) | LCCN 2023054417 (ebook) | ISBN 9781538184899 (cloth) | ISBN 9781538184905 (paperback) | ISBN 9781538184912 (epub)
Subjects: LCSH: Weisband, William Wolfe, 1908–1967. | Espionage, Soviet—United States—History. | United States. Army Security Agency—Officials and employees—Biography. | Venona Project (U.S.) | Soviet Union. Komitet gosudarstvennoĭ bezopasnosti—Officials and employees—Biography. | Spies—United States—Biography.
Classification: LCC UB271.R92 W353 2024  (print) | LCC UB271.R92  (ebook) | DDC 327.1247092 [B]—dc23/eng/20240112
LC record available at https://lccn.loc.gov/2023054416
LC ebook record available at https://lccn.loc.gov/2023054417

*For Maura and Peter*

Sometimes the clues that should have been warnings are lost in a blur, only to be seen in hindsight. Caught in the need to move ahead, most people rush, like speeding trains, past the truths and half-truths tucked into the terrain they thought they knew.

Ann Hagedorn
*Sleeper Agent, 1*

In the realm of counterintelligence . . . there are many things one never knows for sure, even long after the battles have been fought.

Robert Lamphere
*FBI-KGB Wars, 31*

It's a scary business we're in, particularly in wartime because just a little shade of difference in judgement can mean a difference between losing a battle and winning a battle.

Frank Rowlett
*Oral History*

# Contents

| | |
|---|---|
| Acknowledgments | xiii |
| Reader's Note | xvii |
| Prologue | xix |
| Chapter 1: Lies | 1 |
| Chapter 2: Hotels | 9 |
| Chapter 3: Double Lives | 14 |
| Chapter 4: A Washington Committee | 24 |
| Chapter 5: Zero | 33 |
| Chapter 6: Radio School | 40 |
| Chapter 7: Pollock | 47 |
| Chapter 8: Failure | 52 |
| Chapter 9: Blerio | 55 |
| Chapter 10: Brooks and Werner | 62 |
| Chapter 11: Coos County | 71 |
| Chapter 12: Needle and Link | 79 |
| Chapter 13: Soldier | 86 |
| Chapter 14: The Farm | 95 |
| Chapter 15: European Theater of Operations | 101 |
| Chapter 16: Rendezvous | 107 |
| Chapter 17: Arlington Hall | 112 |

| | |
|---|---|
| Chapter 18: Settling In | 131 |
| Chapter 19: Disaster | 150 |
| Chapter 20: Disaster Times Two | 159 |
| Chapter 21: Top Secret—Cream | 172 |
| Chapter 22: Charter Member | 182 |
| Chapter 23: Mabel | 200 |
| Chapter 24: Jimmy's Place | 205 |
| Chapter 25: Top-Secret Glint | 211 |
| Chapter 26: The Big Stuff | 216 |
| Chapter 27: The Jewels in the Amber | 223 |
| Chapter 28: Strange Odyssey | 234 |
| Chapter 29: Vladimir Arrives | 239 |
| Chapter 30: Catastrophe | 246 |
| Chapter 31: Reckoning | 255 |
| Chapter 32: Face-Off | 263 |
| Chapter 33: Flight | 280 |
| Chapter 34: Aftermath | 296 |
| Chapter 35: Endgame | 302 |
| Chapter 36: Epilogue | 313 |
| Bibliography | 315 |
| About the Author | 325 |

# Acknowledgments

Writing a full-length biography is a challenge in itself. One made more onerous when researching the life of an obscure figure who produced no written record and left no paper trail behind for historians to follow. This is particularly so when delving into the life of a spy; one who led a treacherous double life and kept no diaries or other records that could expose his perfidy and land him in prison for life.

Some relief came about on July 4, 1966, when President Lyndon Johnson signed the first Freedom of Information Act (FOIA) into law. Nine years later in the wake of the Watergate scandal and President Nixon's historic resignation, Congress added real teeth to the law by ordering more frequent reporting of FOIA-available materials, shortening the agency response time to administrative appeals, and broadening the definition of agency to include all executive departments. The bill became law in February 1975 following congressional override of President Gerald Ford's veto.

I am grateful to our legislators for pushing this bill to a successful conclusion. Without it, I would have been denied access to the FBI files of William Weisband, Jones Orin York, and Elizabeth Bentley, and many other important materials. The rich secrets of the Venona Project and Weisband's National Security Agency file (it still took NSA fourteen years to fill my request) would remain locked away in a dusty government vault. Using these records as road maps, I was able to reconstruct the life of Weisband over the fifty-nine years of his life.

During five years of research for this book, I have encountered people who have helped in so many ways. One cannot list them all but my gratitude for their kindness is no less real and heartfelt. For special recognition I want to list the following.

A glimpse into Bill Weisband's KGB file in Moscow proved enormously useful for tracing the Russian side of the story. For that I have to thank former KGB officer-turned-journalist Alexander Vassiliev. In the late 1990s he got rare access to many important files on KGB operations and sources in

America during the 1930s and 1940s. Further appreciation goes to Professor Harvey Klehr of Emory University and John Earl Haynes, formerly of the Library of Congress, for assembling Vassiliev's notes into an easy-to-read online compendium known today as the "Vassiliev Notebooks."

Another special appreciation goes to David Thomas. Dave is a retired Defense Intelligence Agency analyst currently serving as a professor of Intelligence Studies at the Institute of World Politics in Washington, DC. Dave kindly gifted to me his complete collection of Comintern messages (all fourteen thousand of them), which I used to ferret out key details of Moscow's role in financing William Weisband's studies at the RCA Institute in New York City. I also want to thank Brian Belanger as well. Brian is the curator of collections at the National Capitol Radio and Television, a tiny gem of an archive located in Bowie, Maryland. It was there that I found brochures and other material describing the radio school courses and tuition costs. Ellen Hampton, an American residing in France, is recognized for her help in researching Alphonse Juin and the French Expeditionary Corps at the Service historique de la Defense at the Chateau de Vincennes, France.

Visiting the scene of the action is always a treat for a historian. One day I had the pleasure of taking in the full impact of the grand Senate Caucus Room located in the Russell Senate Office Building in Washington, DC, courtesy of Dr. Kate Scott. Kate is an assistant Senate historian who kindly allowed me access so I could get a sense of the 1934 Gerald Nye–led munitions hearings and the role Lydia Lee played in stealing committee's records. For my exploration of Jones York's yearlong disappearance into the unforgiving winter climes of northern New England, I tip my hat to Sean Flint with the US Fish and Wildlife Service for his help during my sojourn in the wilderness of Wentworth Location in Coos County, New Hampshire.

I was blessed to have the chance to interview the late Courtland Jones and Donald Walters, as well as Ellen Haring, daughter of Admiral Earl Stone. Over the years I have constantly picked the brains of Robert Louis "Lou" Benson and John Schindler, two NSA historians who did original groundbreaking research on the Weisband case. Particularly so to Lou for keeping this tale alive and his kindness in reading and commenting on the final manuscript. My thanks also to Dr. David Charney for taking time out of his busy schedule to read and critique my description of the KGB's recruitment of Weisband.

My gratitude goes to Sarah Bourne from the Prince George's County (Maryland) Historical Society as well as Dennis Campbell, historian for the Prince George's County Police Department, and Bill and Tania Ciminnetti for their reminiscences on Tania's father, Len Zubko. For their help and support I recognize Trina Yeckley with the Federal Records Center in New York; Rob Simpson, curator of collections, at the National Cryptologic Museum; Jamie

Parillo, director of the Saratoga Springs Historical Society, New York; Peter Duffy and Jim Whalen; Liza Mundy; Edward Chesnik; Bruce Craig; John Earl Haynes; Elise Amico; Scott Stephens with the National Oceanographic Administration; Paul Redmond; Robert Barbuto, Henry Flynn, and Dave Major for their friendship and assistance. As are Stavroula Stanos for her beautiful music and assistance with Jones York's musical pieces; my friends Jean Michel-Icard and General Jean Pierre Meyer, former chief of staff, Army of France; and Courtland Jones Jr. for allowing me permission to publish his father's photo. Further recognition goes to my friend and FBI historian Dr. John Fox; Dr. Christine J. M. Goulter, deputy dean and co-director of the Sir Michael Howard Centre for the History of War, Kings College, London; the staff of the New York Historical Society for helping me access the George B. Corsa Hotel Collection; Dr Arie Dubnov with the Department of History at George Washington University; Micha Broadnax with Mount Holyoke College Archives; Kevin Tankersley with the National Railroad History Society; Saratoga Springs, New York Historical Society collection curator, Jamie Parillo; Major Richard Green (US Army Ret.) of the US Army Signal Corps Officers Candidate School Association; retired FBI Special Agent Gerry Richards for his assistance with Weisband's photos, Jerry Seeper, retired *Washington Times* journalist for his wonderful copyediting work, Kathryn Armhein, granddaughter of Arlington Hall veteran Verner C. Aurell and Deborah Perkins, for photographic help. On Mabel Woody Weisband's early life in Del Rio, Tennessee, I want to thank Sidney Harrison, former mayor of Hot Springs, North Carolina, and Lisa Oakley and Vicky Bills of the East Tennessee Historical Society; Dr. Bob Hutton, associate professor of Appalachian Studies at Glenville State College in West Virginia; and most importantly, Vonda Blackwell, Mabel Weisband's half sister.

A certain special recognition goes to my dear friend Cynthia Kwitchoff. Cindy is a graphic web designer par excellence with a deep reservoir of great ideas for getting people's work out to the public. For twenty years she has managed my website, *fbistudies.com*. Over the course of researching and drafting this book, she was a constant source of moral support and most recently has supplied her reservoir of skills in preparing the photos for this book.

I also thank my publisher, Rowman & Littlefield, and Jan Goldman, editor in chief of the *International Journal of Intelligence and Counterintelligence*, for helping to arrange for the publication of my work.

Finally, and most importantly, there is Maryalice—a woman of boundless love, compassion, and joy, and the most important person in my life. Without her infinite patience and love, this book would never have become a reality. Words cannot adequately express my feelings of gratitude.

# Reader's Note

Over the seven-decade life of the Soviet Union, the government's principle foreign intelligence apparatus underwent eight name changes. For ease of reading, I refer to it throughout the book by its final name, "KGB" (Committee for State Security).

# Prologue

On the warm Tuesday morning of May 9, 1950, William Weisband, age forty-one and plumpish, with his dazzling young wife Mabel at his side, pulled his Buick Roadster away from his South Adams Street apartment in Arlington, Virginia, for the daily, fifteen-minute commute to work. The couple had met near the end of World War II when they both worked for the Army Security Agency. She had stayed on after the war because a government paycheck beat anything waiting for her back in small-town Tennessee. He had stayed because he was an agent of the KGB, a Soviet spy, perfectly positioned to give away some of America's most precious secrets and be handsomely rewarded in return. After stopping at the front gate to display their identification badges, the couple drove onto the grounds of Arlington Hall Station, a former girls' school that had been transformed into the top-secret nerve center of the US Army's code-breaking operations—first against Japan and, now that the Cold War had begun, against the Soviet Union.

Weisband was a Russian linguist assigned to a new and—even by Arlington Hall standards—deeply secret unit that was painstakingly breaking into Soviet codes and reading messages the Kremlin sent to its military, diplomatic, and espionage outposts around the world, revealing, among many things, the existence of a vast network of spies inside the United States and inside the Manhattan Project, which built the atomic bomb. For months as he helped translate the decoded cables from their original Russian into English, Weisband had felt the walls closing in, constantly worrying that one of the messages would reveal his own identity as a Soviet spy, but he had no inkling that before this day was out, he would be confronted by the FBI, which had finally—and too late—stumbled across his trail.

Weisband had long since warned his Soviet handlers that Arlington Hall had succeeded in breaking into their supposedly unbreakable codes. On a day known as "Black Friday" at the end of 1948, Moscow had suddenly changed all its codes, making all its messages once again indecipherable and strangling at birth one of America's greatest intelligence coups—a disaster of historic consequence known only to the select few who had access to what was delicately called "the Russian problem." Coming just eighteen months before the outbreak of the Korean War, Black Friday blinded the United States to any advance knowledge of Soviet intentions in a war that cost tens of thousands of American casualties.

It was all due to one man—William Weisband, whose freebooting lifestyle should have set off red flares long before he was in a position to do such serious and lasting harm. He was well known at Arlington Hall as a heavy drinker and malingerer with a high-stakes gambling habit who somehow on a government salary took Mabel on regular weekend getaways to New York City, staying at swank hotels, dining at upscale restaurants, and catching the latest Broadway show. How did such flagrant behavior slip through the security surrounding one of the most secret projects in the entire government? Why, even after he was finally caught, was Weisband never prosecuted for espionage? And why did US officials want the Weisband case to simply disappear into the fog of history never again to see the light of day?

After I retired from twenty-five years of chasing Soviet spies for the FBI, I filed a Freedom of Information Act request for all two thousand pages of the Bureau's files on the Weisband case. In 2002 I filed a similar request with the National Security Agency (NSA) for its file. Sixteen years later a package containing nearly one thousand pages appeared at my front door. Both sets of records now make up the spine of the story told here, much of it for the first time. Then I got lucky and came across information the FBI had never seen—notes taken from Weisband's KGB file in Moscow and published after the collapse of the Soviet Union. Weisband, one note read, had supplied "large quantities of highly valuable material"—so valuable that one week after he died the KGB delivered $40,000 in cash ($367,725 in 2023) to his long-suffering and still-loyal wife Mabel as final payment for his services.

This then is the saga of William Weisband, the Spy Erased from History.

## Chapter 1

# Lies

The Weisband story began in Russia. Israel Weisband, Bill's father, was a watchmaker, born in 1874 in the Russian Black Sea port city of Odessa. Sarah, his wife, three years younger than her husband, came from Kishinev, a city of 150,000, in what is now Moldava, part of the Pale of Settlement known as Bessarabia.

The young couple had already settled in Odessa when one of the most infamous pogroms in Russian history erupted in Kishinev on Easter Sunday April 9, 1903. For three days, rampaging mobs carrying makeshift weapons randomly attacked Jews in the street, destroying their homes and businesses. When it ended, fifty were dead and hundreds more were injured among a Jewish population of fifty thousand.

Adding to this debasement was "Bloody Sunday," a crisis that began early in the morning of January 9, 1905, as a peaceful march by workers and peasants demanding political rights descended on the czar's Winter Palace in St. Petersburg. As the surging throng grew rowdier, terrified security troops began shooting indiscriminately, leaving forty people dead and wounded. The killings were a watershed in Russian history. Suddenly the centuries-old compact between a distant, remote, Russian ruler and his millions of increasingly restless subjects was fractured. The ancient wall, one historian noted, that had protected the autocracy had been irrevocably "breached by the defeat in war" and by the blow rendered to the czar's personal prestige. Over the next year as further riots erupted across the empire, the scent of revolution began seeping into the military as well, the most notorious being the mutiny aboard the Russian battleship *Potemkin*, later dramatized in a Sergei Eisenstein film of the same name.

Desperate to ease the growing turmoil and regain some control, the hapless czar issued a series of reforms that only inflamed matters. Known as the October Manifesto, the new royal decree granted, for the first time, fundamental civil rights and political liberties to the masses along with a promise of constitutional freedoms and an elected parliament. Instead of easing pressures, the order unleashed new violence as centuries of seething ethnic and racial hatreds reemerged in what became known as the Revolution of 1905. Waves of savagery again broke out against Jews, students, intellectuals, and other national minorities in hundreds of cities, towns, and villages across Russia.

The port city Odessa, the country's fourth-largest metropolis, was not spared. It was an ancient city once occupied by the Ottomans and later founded by Catherine the Great as a Russian city in the eighteenth century. Known as the "Pearl of the Black Sea," it evolved over the years into a major Russian transportation and seaport hub. The principal languages of its more than four hundred thousand residents were Russian and Yiddish, with Jews composing about 35 percent of the population. More than a century later, the city's death toll and destruction from these pogroms still remains unknown. What is certain is that more than four hundred Jews and non-Jews were murdered, with another three hundred injured. Looters laid waste to sixteen hundred Jewish businesses, homes, and apartments as well. No other city in the Russian Empire in 1905 experienced a pogrom comparable to the one unleashed against the Jews of Odessa. One study called it a "primordial violence" that continued through to the Russian Civil War.[1]

In the wake of this nightmare, Russian Jews desperate to escape the violence began fleeing the country in droves. For Jews it was illegal to emigrate from Russia, as most had no passport and rarely traveled far from their villages. The journey was long and treacherous for families carrying little money and leaving everything behind. For most refuges heading west on foot was the best bet in the hope of crossing the Russian border into Austro-Hungary and on to the more peaceful environs of Western Europe. If they were lucky and could afford it, they headed for an Atlantic port city where they could arrange passage to America.

Sometime around 1906, Israel and Sarah joined this exodus. Instead of heading west, however, their odyssey took them south. The record is blank on their route of travel or whether they used the services of a smuggler along the way. What we can surmise, however, is that after boarding a ship at Odessa they crossed the Black Sea to Istanbul, where they arranged for passage through the Levant into Syria and on to Egypt, eventually settling in the tiny Jewish settlement in the port city of Alexandria.

It was there that Wolfe Weisband was born on August 28, 1908. He started his education at the St. Andrews School of Scotland, a school founded to both educate and convert Jewish youngsters to Christianity. Such conversions were rare, but the school did provide a good education for a much cheaper price than the English boys schools in Alexandria—the British Boys School (BBS) and the expensive and exclusive Victoria College. Wolfe remained there until graduation in 1923. For two years he attended Ecole Baron de Monasce.[2]

\* \* \*

After two decades living in Egypt, Israel decided to emigrate to America. While whole families could leave as a group this was rarely the case. The cost of ship passage for an entire family was prohibitive. Instead, one family member, typically of working age, would leave for America in the hope of finding employment. This laborious and time-consuming strategy, known as "chain migration," required the newcomer to work long, exhausting hours at some unskilled job for tiny wages in an effort to save enough funds to finance the next family member's ticket. It was a process that repeated itself over the years, sometimes decades, until an entire family was finally reunited in the United States.

Israel, Sarah, and Wolfe, age sixteen, sailed from Alexandria aboard the RMS *Adriatic* arriving in New York City on February 25, 1925. In the case of the Weisband family, an illegal hybrid of the chain migration principle was adopted. Wolfe's two older brothers, Shalom Alexander, who had changed his name to "Harold," born on November 8, 1902, and Mark, born on May 24, 1904, arrived ahead of their parents. Both boys first tried to enter the United States at New York as stowaways in November 1920. The attempt failed when they were discovered and sent back to Egypt. A second effort was a charm as they slipped off the ship at New York City (probably with a bribe) and quickly disappeared into the city's sea of humanity. Both soon found work, with Harold employed as a dental assistant and Mark at a local hotel. The problem, however, was the brothers' illegal status, which made it impossible for them to sponsor the family without throwing up red flags for immigration authorities.[3]

The easiest solution was to lie. Jacob Weisband, born in 1893 in Odessa, Russia, and a "nephew" of Israel, came to America eighteen years earlier. Jacob, who had arrived legally, was working with the Brooklyn and North River Road Transit System in 1925 while living in Manhattan's Lower East Side. In his application for entry, Israel Weisband falsely claimed that the family was sponsored by his "son," Jacob Weisband. When they arrived in New York, Jacob took them into his home, offering financial support while they looked for a place to live. When interviewed years later by the FBI, Jacob still felt a lingering sting of resentment over the shabby way Israel and Sarah treated him while guests in his home. They were always ungrateful for his daring and illegal act, he remembered. When they finally did find their own home and had no more use for him, he rarely ever heard from them again. He wryly told an agent that despite their own marginal circumstances during those early years, they still looked down their noses at him as the "poor relative."⁴

\* \* \*

The New York City of the so-called Roaring Twenties that Wolfe entered was a shock to his system in many ways. He was now in a world that was light-years ahead of the life he left behind in Egypt. Leaving a Muslim land governed by strict codes and rigid social mores must have felt like Alice falling through the rabbit hole and suddenly entering Wonderland.

On the eve of the First World War, America was the world's leading debtor nation, owing more than $3.8 billion. Five years later it had the world's number-one economy with New York City replacing London as the center of global finance. This dramatic transfer of wealth was due to American industrial power and military sales and loans to her allies, making it a creditor of Europe to the staggering extent of $12.9 billion. Interest rates on borrowed funds were at an all-time low, making loans easy to get and igniting a spirit of corporate and civic optimism that pervaded the country with a mythical sense that growth would continue forever. Over the seven-year period starting in 1922, American exports rose 26 percent while imports climbed only by 16 percent, setting a peacetime export record of $5.24 billion worth of goods—the same year the nation imported $4.4 billion in goods—a figure that was less than the $4.43 billion of 1926 and below the pre-war levels. By 1929, America's gross national product had hit $104 billion and the per-capita income was $857.

Meanwhile, American business began expanding, with new infusions of investment totaling $100 billion in capital equipment and bank loans of another $100 billion to foreign countries. Automobile production, a cottage industry at the turn of the century, exploded over the next three decades. By 1925, completely assembled Model T Ford cars rolled off the assembly line every ten seconds at Henry Ford's Highland Park plant, accounting for 10 percent of the nation's income and employing nearly four million workers. Investing in stocks and bonds, long the exclusive preserve of brokers and sophisticated experts, soon drew mainstream Americans who began purchasing shares on margins as low as 10 percent of the cost of the stock. The mid-1920s became known as the "Coolidge Prosperity" era, with President Coolidge touting "the chief business of the American people is business."⁵

The 1920s was also a decade of "consumerism." Before the First World War, purchasing on credit was discouraged. Most Americans believed in saving the full amount needed to buy that new appliance or home improvement. After the war, advertisers challenged this dogma with a new chant that buying on time was the right and moral thing to do for any knowledgeable consumer. Stores began to link large-scale purchases to long-term credit. By 1927, two years after Wolfe Weisband landed in the United States, 15 percent of all goods totaling $6 billion in value were bought on an installment plan. One scholar wrote years later that the tripling of household income after the war made millions of Americans members of the broad middle class. They now drove "Chevrolets purchased on time, wore clothes bought on credit and had radios, cigarette lighters, appliances, and medical care on easy payment plans. Should they die, their funerals could be provided with so much down and so much per month." Advertising also spawned a new magazine industry. *Time* published its first edition in 1923. H. L. Mencken's *American Mercury* appeared in 1924, followed a year later by the upscale *New Yorker*, which catered to so-called "caviar sophisticates."[6]

Consumerism even made its way into the world of popular culture. Motion pictures were the vogue, with the studios Famous Players–Lasky, RKO, and Paramount dominating the industry. Hollywood producers sold the American dream to Wolfe and millions of other eager moviegoers with handsome actors and their glamorous leading ladies draped in the latest fashions living in fabulous homes filled with expensive objects with no real explanation as to how they were acquired. For young men like Wolfe, fashion icons of the period such as Rudolph Valentino, Al Jolson, Douglas Fairbanks, and Charlie Chaplin filled the silver screen, setting new standards for what a well-kitted gentleman should wear.

The sixteen-year-old Wolfe was wild-eyed by New York City's new libertine lifestyle. It was the "Age of Excess" with nothing but "wonderful nonsense of all kinds." Lois Long summed up the decade with "tomorrow we may die, so let's get drunk and make love."[7]

Coco Chanel was fond of saying that fashion is not something that exists in dresses alone. "Fashion is in the sky . . . fashion has to do with ideas, the way we live, what is happening." The embodiment of this notion were the "Flappers"—women wearing long pants like men or, even more shocking, dresses that ended at the knees, revealing bare legs and lovely well-turned ankles. Because women now worked outside the home, dress hemlines rose first to mid-calf and then to the knee, creating a swank look that made it easier to hop in and out of the cars, or simply walk around. The new "Empire" waist dropped below the bustline between the breasts and the natural waist. By 1922 the plunge had dropped even further to the hips. Gone forever were formal tight-fitting corsets and crinoline.[8]

Along with dated dress wear, the new woman shed her tiresome long hair, choosing instead a smart-looking short bob for easy treatment and the fashionable look of the famous "Cloche Hat," which was all the rage. Wolfe witnessed another shattered taboo as women strolled arm and arm with men (or women) down crowded New York City avenues while smoking a cigarette. At local beaches his young head swiveled at the thousands of women lounging and swimming in one-piece bathing suits that exposed their legs and arms and shoulders.

New fashion meant new musical sounds and dances. It was the "Jazz Age," with such songs as "Ain't Misbehavin'" with Johnny Guarnieri on the piano and "I Love My Baby (My Baby Loves Me)," a 1925 hit performed by George Bruns and his Rag-A-Muffins. What began as a uniquely New Orleans African American sound quickly spread, taking root in jazz clubs across the country, most particularly New York City. The new sound spawned the careers of famed trumpeter Louis Armstrong, Count Basie, and the legendary Duke Ellington, who starred at the opening in 1927 of Harlem's famed Cotton Club. Wolfe and the youth of the 1920s rebelled against the traditional mores of previous generations, which many saw as a breakdown of traditional morality. It was the "devil's music," critics charged, with sounds and rhythms that promoted promiscuity.[9]

The 1920s also ushered in "café society." They were the so-called beautiful people with ambition and money to burn who became regulars at the city's posh haunts and restaurants—all in the interest of seeing and being seen. Nightclubs such as New York City's El Morocco and the Stork Club became hangouts for the in-crowd. Elegantly dressed couples performing ballroom routines on hotel dance floors were replaced by highly charged and sexually suggestive dances. The new craze had strange names like the "Fox Trot," "Charleston," and "Texas Tommy." Wolfe loved to dance and could often be found at local community centers for an evening of taxi dancing. "Taxi Dances" were egalitarian, and anyone could participate. By 1931, there were more than a hundred such dance halls in New York City alone, drawing between 35,000 and 50,000 customers per week. Taxi dancers were usually women between the ages of fifteen and twenty-eight from a poor or broken family, or a divorcee trying to support her children. Customers bought a ticket for a dime, which entitled him to dance with the woman for the length of a song and again and again as long as he bought more tickets. One study profiling typical customers in the early 1930s found them to be primarily Caucasian males who had immigrated from the European countries of Italy, Poland, and Greece, with Jews tending to predominate the scene. They were generally skilled or semi-skilled workers from the lower middle classes.[10]

Prohibition, the great social experiment starting in 1919 with the passage of the Volstead Act, outlawed the manufacture, distribution, and consumption of alcohol across America. But Wolfe Weisband could still get a drink if he knew where to look. There was "bathtub gin" and "bootleg liquor" sold at "Speakeasys" or gentlemen's clubs throughout the city, hangouts out of sight of the police where patrons spoke only in whispers. These were usually small operations with little more than a bar, a few chairs, and tables and rarely any entertainment. They operated with names like "O'Leary's," the "Bath Club," in the Bowery and one of the most famous, the "21" Club, which still stands today. Again, women were stepping out in the world with ownership of many of these places. One of them, Texas Guinan, a former screen and stage performer, and owner of the 300 Club and the El Fey, could be found nightly in one of her places greeting patrons with her famed line "Hey Suckers." Her two biggest competitors, also women, were Belle Livingston and Helen Morgan.[11]

Just blocks from where Bill would spend the next decade and a half stood the Ziegfeld Theater, a 1,600-seat palace, built on Sixth Avenue at 54th Street by the famed New York empresario Florenz Ziegfeld. "Flo," as everyone called him, was a larger-than-life figure from Germany who made a fortune with his Ziegfeld Follies, a spectacular stage revue modeled on the Follies Bergere of Paris. When Wolfe peeked in, he watched extravaganzas filled with lavish settings, sketches, and huge production numbers performed by a large ensemble of actors and actresses. The evening's signature moment was always Ziegfeld's finale, the famed Tableau Vivant, a full-stage spectacle with gorgeous vaguely undressed girls simply standing and sitting in statuesque poses in front of ogling audiences. They were the "best money could buy" Flo would tell everyone.[12]

For the newly arrived teenager, New York City was the place to be. And it wasn't long before he began putting his past behind him. First by shedding the name "Wolfe" and reinventing himself as "William" Weisband. He was in the magic kingdom—a place where anything seemed possible, and he wasted no time going after it.

## NOTES

1. Charles King, *Odessa* (New York: W. W. Norton & Co., 2011), 183.
2. New York Report, July 20, 1950. FBI file entitled William Weisband, 65–59095. Freedom of Information/Privacy (FOIPA). Hereafter referred to as "Weisband FBI file."
3. Ibid.
4. Ibid.
5. Dennis R. Shaughnessy, *The Business of America Is Business* (Boston, MA: Northeastern University Press, 2017), 210.
6. Lib Tietjen, "Let's Get Drunk and Make Love: Lois Long and the Speakeasy" (Blog Archive, Tenement.org).
7. Ibid.
8. No author, Gabriella Bonheur "Coco" Chanel, Biography online, Undated.
9. Nat Hentoff, "The Devil's Music," *Washington Post*, August 23, 1985.

10. Paul Goalby Cressy, *The Taxi Dance Hall* (Chicago: University of Chicago Press, 1932), 24.

11. Corey Creekmur, "It's Both Irish-America Month and Women's History Month so Meet Legendary 'Texas' Guinan," *Times Record News*, March 3, 1921.

12. Michael Kantner, *B'Way: The American Musical*, Public Broadcasting, Undated.

*Chapter 2*

# Hotels

Bill Weisband's first home was 568 Grand Street in the heart of the Lower East Side; a neighborhood where Jews mainly from southeastern Europe and Russia had been settling since the 1880s. Thirty years earlier the area south of Houston Street between Clinton and Columbia had housed more than eight hundred inhabitants per acre, making it the most densely populated spot on Earth. Over the ensuing years, this figure gradually declined. Yet in 1900 the 1.35 square mile space still had more inhabitants than the 444,000 square miles of Wyoming, Arizona, Nevada, and New Mexico. By 1910, it was more than three times as densely populated as New York City's most crowded neighborhood today.[1]

Tyler Anbinder, in a fascinating study of immigration and settlement history of New York City, addresses the concept of the "landsman"; a volunteer who aided newcomers in settling in and finding employment in the city. One such landsman, many years later, still had warm memories of his contributions. "Nearly everyone had a greenhorn guest or expected to get one soon. [We] were always occupied with looking for work for new arrivals" and taking "someone into your shop was considered the greatest good deed, almost the only good deed" that a person could perform for the recent arrival.[2] Another first was the transition from new immigrant to "new American," starting with the purchase of a new suit of clothes befitting someone entering the New York City workforce. "Everything had to be American," one historian noted, "if a greenhorn had any hope of getting that first job."[3]

Bill Weisband's landsman was his brother Mark, who got him a job starting the day after his arrival. Unlike millions of other immigrants before and after him, he had a head start. He spoke English and had years of education in schools where English was the primary language. He started as a typist at the Hotel Pennsylvania in midtown Manhattan where Mark was already working. When it opened in 1919, the hotel was the largest and most luxurious in the world. Located across from Pennsylvania Station and Madison Square Garden, the new palace ranked as the best that money could buy, with two thousand rooms linked to Gimbels Department Store by spectacular upscale shops lining the promenades. Its famed Café Rouge, where the beautiful people of the Roaring Twenties assembled nightly, hosted only the best entertainment, with marque performances by the Glenn Miller band, the Dorsey Brothers, and the Andrew Sisters. One reporter called it "the last word in the field of hotel construction."[4]

From that first job Bill bounced around for the next five years and, with two exceptions, was always chasing opportunities with New York City's newest and glitziest hotels. A year of typing at the Pennsylvania was followed by a brief period as a bookkeeper with the Metropolitan Life Insurance Company before returning to the Pennsylvania as a rack clerk. Then came a year as a billing clerk with the New York Edison Company before signing on as a night auditor with the newly opened twenty-seven-story Hotel Lincoln, just blocks from the Diamond District. Next came the Hotel Piccadilly in the city's Theater District followed by the New Yorker Hotel, which opened its doors in January 1930 with lush ballrooms, ten private dining rooms, five restaurants employing thirty-five master chefs, and an enormous barbershop with forty-two chairs.

Plans for a spectacular new hotel began in the mid-1920s with the selection of a site on Park Avenue between East 49th and East 50th Street. It was owned at the time by the New York Central Railroad Corporation, which appropriated ten million dollars to underwrite construction. Work soon got underway and on November 1, 1931, a new Waldorf-Astoria touting itself as the world's tallest and largest hotel opened for business. With it came the latest amenities to satisfy every comfort and pleasure the well-heeled visitor could imagine. There were sumptuous ballrooms, beauty shops, restaurants, smoking lounges, an assortment of swanky boutiques—all there to accommodate the locals and guests staying in one of its astonishing 2,200 rooms, each with a bath and private shower.

Tucked along the hotel's East 50th Street side, away from Park Avenue's busyness, was a simple private entrance monitored by an alert doorman twenty-four hours a day. Inside, an elevator whisked only the wealthiest guests to an exclusive cluster of suites known worldwide today as the "Waldorf Towers."[5] The two largest suites had eight or nine rooms made up of a bath, dressing room, large living room, galley-like entrance hall, library, separate study, and four bedrooms. Hotel officials leased a third of them on a long-term basis as private residences. Among the "Towers" more illustrious residents over the years were Herbert Hoover, who lived there for three decades after his presidency, and General Douglas MacArthur.

For evening entertainment there was the Starlight Roof. The legendary summers-only supper club located nineteen stories above Park Avenue was a symbol of elegance and sophistication that offered a steady diet of big bands broadcasting over radio to Americans around the country.

A month before the hotel opened, more than twenty thousand people filed through the front door in one day to ogle the new space and hear President Hoover broadcast to them from the White House through the marvel of radio. The nightly musical retinue featured the greatest entertainers of the era; none more identified with the hotel's glitz than the Empire Room's Xavier Cugat, an elegantly dressed, pencil-mustached Spaniard with slicked-back black hair, baton in one hand, chihuahua in the other, leading his band, the "Gigolos."[6]

Once again, a restless Bill was on the move for better pay and position. Departing the New Yorker for the new Waldorf-Astoria, he started as a charter member on September 26, 1931—one month before its grand opening. He was talented and knew what he was doing behind the scenes in the auditing end of the hotel business. At the time, the National Cash Register Company, maker of equipment for counting money and processing checks, was introducing new technology. Bill picked up on it quickly and was soon familiar with its use.

By 1931, Israel and Sarah Weisband had abandoned their poor relative, Jacob Weisband, and the Lower East Side for 80th Street across the East River in Brooklyn. They opened a small jewelry business repairing watches on the side and living above the shop. Over the next three years, both caught the entrepreneurial spirit and began investing in real estate. Israel bought property in Huntington, New York, on Long Island while Sarah acquired property in Brooklyn, which she later lost through foreclosure.

Barely age twenty-three when the Waldorf-Astoria opened, Weisband quickly became a "player." One friend from those days remembered Bill as always short of money—"financially embarrassed" in his words.[7] But it was the height of the Depression when no one had money. To make extra cash Bill began arranging for friends to spend a night or two at the Waldorf off the books. During those early days the hotel was never filled up and rooms frequently remained unoccupied for long periods of time. He would slip the key to friends and neighbors in exchange for extra tips. While Bill had no involvement in the family business, he routinely brought samples of jewelry with him to work for sale to co-workers.

Where Bill lived during this period was anybody's guess. Someone thought he was living with a woman in Greenwich Village. Others believed that he moved around, taking on the persona of a "playboy" with a penchant for drinking and entertaining women. He seemed constantly in a hurry, one person recalled, always bragging about some "babe on the string" and living a "Bohemian lifestyle."[8]

One of his girlfriends was Evelyn Crowder. Just eighteen years old at the time, she was working part-time at the Waldorf while attending college when they met. One day when she mentioned her difficulty with a French course, Weisband graciously offered to tutor her. Their tutorials developed into a romance marked by frequent dinner and dancing dates. Times were difficult in those days, she later recounted, but Weisband was always willing to spend despite being "hard-pressed" for money and only a meager Waldorf salary to depend on.[9]

Crowder was swept away by his "suave," sophisticated style and skill at handling people, "especially women." When they first met, she was living alone in a crowded rooming house, which she found inconvenient for entertaining guests. She soon got an apartment, to which Bill had a key. While they did not share the rent, Bill occasionally gave her five or ten dollars when she was short at the end of the month. Weisband was always enigmatic about his life and acquaintances, saying only that he and his mother shared an apartment in Brooklyn over the family jewelry shop. But Crowder had never been there and had only his word for this. The two of them spent many long hours alone in her apartment. She conceded that the two were lovers, but he never stayed overnight despite her many offers. On more than one occasion she urged Weisband to marry her, but he rejected the offers. Crowder believed he was only interested in "sharing me not marrying me."[10]

Another oddity was Weisband's numerous acquaintances but no mention of friends. Nor did he ever introduce her to them if he had any. There was a telephone in Crowder's apartment, but he never made calls nor received any. One time he casually asked her if he could invite friends to the apartment. She warily agreed, according to her FBI interview, as long as his "friends were not female friends." To her recollection none ever visited.[11]

Others described him as "affable" and likeable, with one calling him "extremely well-liked" by all who met him. His lighthearted personality marked by an ever-present smile aided him, according to one person, in controlling group activities with his "captivating" style and pleasant manner. His conversations were frequently littered with exotic tales about his early years in Egypt, his mother's Russian background, and an apocryphal story of his father's service as a "colonel in the British Army." A slight accent and ever-present aura of mystery only added to his allure, leading some to conclude that he was well educated—a belief he did nothing to dispel. Adding to this sense of mystery was the occasional hint of a brother who was experiencing some vague difficulty in New York that left his listeners eager for more details. They were never offered.[12]

Not everyone was taken in by Bill's charm. One Waldorf worker called him "irresponsible," always moving around with seemingly no fixed address. The FBI tracked down one woman, the sister of a girl he dated in New York, who outlined her suspicions of Weisband for reasons that she could never pinpoint. She basically "distrusted" him because of his "overbearing egotism" and brash conversation. Part of her resentment came from his constant efforts to flaunt a phony knowledge "on almost any topic," which he seemingly brought up every time they were together. In the end she told an agent he just came off as a "fake."[13]

One topic that repeatedly bubbled up to the surface was gambling. Many remembered him as a regular in penny-ante poker games played weekly while Waldorf workers stood around waiting for their pay envelopes. Others, however, confirmed Crowder's account that he was a "racetrack habitue" and a heavy gambler with lots of unexplained cash. Two decades later, when she sat down with the FBI for an interview, she was still puzzled by the fact that when they did go out it was always dining and dancing at different New York City hotels or day trips to racetracks on Long Island. Expenses that he could ill afford on his modest hotel salary.[14]

## NOTES

1. Tyler Anbinder, *City of Dreams* (Boston, MA: Houghton Mifflin Harcourt, 2016), 358–59.
2. Ibid., 369.
3. Ibid.
4. Nicole Saraniero, *The Hotel Pennsylvania's Uncertain Future*, Untapped New York, May 6, 2021.
5. No Author, *The Unofficial Palace*, The Towers, New York Residences, Undated.
6. Christopher Popa, *Xaiver Cugat: Passion for Life*, Library.com, April 2009.
7. New York Report, July 20, 1950, Weisband FBI file.
8. Ibid.
9. Miami teletype, May 22, 1950, and New York Report, October 10, 1950, Weisband FBI file.
10. New York Report, October 10, 1950, Weisband FBI file.
11. Ibid.
12. Ibid.
13. Ibid.
14. Ibid.

*Chapter 3*

# Double Lives

One of the most vexing and enduring questions asked by security and counterintelligence professionals is why a person decides to betray his country. What sparks such a sudden and reckless act that risks everything—arrest, imprisonment, and sometimes even death by stealing his nation's secrets and turning them over to a foreign power.

David Charney is a psychiatrist with a practice in the Washington, DC, area. In the late 1990s, having no background in counterespionage or counterintelligence, he was asked by defense attorneys for Earl Pitts, an FBI agent convicted of spying for the KGB, to evaluate their client. What Charney brought to this unique clinical challenge, however, was an impressive resume of professional experiences that was just as useful. As an air force officer and psychiatrist, he had served with the Strategic Air Command and later headed the Outpatient Clinic at Malcolm Grow Hospital at Andrews Air Force Base in Maryland; a position that included counselling NSA personnel. Later, in private practice, he counselled CIA personnel for a decade while acting as a consultant for the CIA's medical staff. All of which in his words offered an immersion into the "culture of the CIA."[1]

Charney's routine with Pitts called for weekly two-hour jail visits for a year with the goal of simply listening to him while he talked. During these sessions, Charney encouraged Pitts to unfold every detail of his life story, thus allowing his deepest thoughts and feelings to emerge over a gradually and methodically slowly one-hundred-hour-plus period of time. A few years later he applied this same methodology to two other spies, Robert Hanssen, another FBI agent, and Brian Regan, an employee with the National Reconnaissance Office. His career experiences coupled with the hours spent with these three American spies awakened him to what he today refers to as "inner lives" of American spies. Just as importantly, it also led Charney to rethink accepted Intelligence Community thinking about ideological and financial motivations for spying. From this emerged a groundbreaking study called the "Ten Life Stages of the Insider Spy."[2]

First, he points out that a spy is not born but rather "re-made" over the arc of his life. The descent begins in early life or the "sensitizing" stage when a child experiences difficulties and crises beyond his control. Such stresses can include, for example, long-term absences or abandonment by one or both parents, spousal abuse, parental abuse of a child, roller-coaster finances, the death of a parent, an alcoholic parent, and so on; all of which can, among a tiny percentage of the population, lead a person into making ill-advised or anti-social decisions later in life. Next comes the "Stress/Spiral Stage." This occurs when adult challenges pile up at the same time a person is beginning to compare himself with others; comparisons that diminish his own expectation of himself. "Much of how it goes" Charney writes "depends as much on external forces and blind luck. And for the unfortunates the going can get very tough." It happens to everyone, Charney explains, and no one is immune. For a tiny percentage of the population, it can be particularly problematic as the ever-mounting pile of troubles incrementally increases the pressure on a person, causing him in the end to "crack." Charney's work serves as a bellwether. When tracking the origins of a person's first moment of contact with an espionage service, Charney warns experts to look back six to twelve months for some type of crisis that prompted a spy to make the fateful decision. In some cases, this time period should be extended.[3]

Applying Charney's matrix one can closely approximate when Weisband made his decision to spy for the Russians. An analysis of Weisband's employment history for the Waldorf-Astoria years from 1931 to 1936 reveals some interesting facts. When he first began work with the Waldorf-Astoria, he had a white-collar position as a night auditor, a job with status he held until August 1933 when he was abruptly demoted to "night room clerk." This position remained steady until January 1936 when he was again demoted—this time to "junior room clerk." He held this job until his abrupt resignation from the Waldorf on September 15, 1936—during the heart of the Depression—five years after he started working there and one month after the sudden death of his father, Israel.[4]

Adding to the mystery of his decline in rank within the hotel's hierarchy was an accompanying reduction in salary as well. When he first started in 1931 as a night auditor, he was earning $32.50 per week, amounting to $1,625 per year. In 1932, it dropped to $30.90 per week, equaling $1,545 per year, followed by another drop from June 1933 to August 1933 to $29.25 per week, or $1,463 per year. That figure suddenly dropped again by a third, this time to $4.64 per day, for a yearly total salary of $1,114.[5]

As Bill's hotel career was in free fall, newly elected thirty-second president of the United States Franklin D. Roosevelt was wasting little time asserting himself on the diplomatic front. Within months of taking office, the president had begun negotiations to reestablish diplomatic relations with the

Soviet Union. Following a formal ceremony on November 17, 1933, William Bullitt found himself in Moscow as the new ambassador while veteran Russian diplomat Alexander Troyanovsky, formerly ambassador to Tokyo and vice-chairman of Russia's State Planning Commission, took up the reins as the Kremlin's man in Washington. As part of the agreement the countries opened consulates with the Russians, setting up in San Francisco and New York City. The New York consulate opened in 1934 when Ruth Pratt, a former congresswoman and wealthy New York socialite, leased her thirty-three-room, six-story mansion at 7 East 61st Street to the Russian government, just eight blocks from the Waldorf-Astoria.[6]

The consulate, known as the "Plant" in KGB parlance, quickly became the hub for Russian intelligence gathering across America. Heading operations was thirty-four-year-old Peter Davydovich Gutzeit, a Russian Jew, born in the Dnepropetrovsk Region, near the village of Berodayevka. Gutzeit joined the Communist Party as a teenager and later entered the Cheka, Lenin's brutal security and foreign espionage service. Arriving in New York in 1934 with his wife, Taisia, he took on the alias of "Peter Gusev," posing as an anonymous vice-consul handling mundane matters such as visa applications, replacing lost passports for Russian sailors, and the like.[7]

With no presence in the United States, recruiting and servicing of espionage sources and networks had fallen into disuse or had disappeared completely from lack of contact. "In past archives," one Moscow official recorded "we found certain people who had been connected with our work, but because of a lengthy interruption in our work, the connection with them was lost." Gutzeit's mission from the start centered on renewing contact with old sources and developing new ones—all for the purpose of building up productive spy networks stretching across the country.[8]

The New York station soon began reaching out to America's vast pool of scientists and engineers in a search for sources of technical intelligence. At the same time scientists and other sources then working in Europe were ordered to pull up roots and look for employment with US companies, where the pickings were brighter and nothing was off limits.[9]

Exactly when and under what circumstances Bill volunteered to work for the KGB still remain buried in classified Russian files. But it is reasonable to conclude that it occurred in 1934 just months after Gutzeit's arrival in New York. Moscow's new agent, whom they dubbed as "Link," was born. Weisband had no technical expertise of any value to the Russians nor any access to industrial secrets. But what he did have, in many ways, was more valuable—an ability to easily move around unnoticed without attracting the attention of counterintelligence authorities; a quality that made him ideal for the unique role of espionage courier. To be a courier first meant indoctrination into the world of *konspiratsiia*, loosely translated as "conspiracy"—Moscow's rigid security procedures that all agents in theory were required to follow without exception.[10]

To understand what Weisband had agreed to, certain lessons can be drawn from two of Moscow's most famous couriers during the 1930s. One of them was an American named Whittaker Chambers. Born and raised on Long Island, Chambers studied journalism at Columbia University before joining the American Communist Party. In the late 1920s he was recruited by the GRU, Russia's military intelligence apparatus, acting as a clandestine courier until his final break with communism in 1937. More than a decade later he penned *Witness*, his now famous memoir, in which he vividly recounts his spying experiences during those eventful years of his life. In rich detail he describes his complex, often nerve-wracking existence ferrying stolen documents—in his case between Alger Hiss, then living and working in Washington, and Chambers's Russian bosses in New York. For any courier, isolation and impersonal *konspiratsiia* was the essential element of life—they survived by this rule. Each KGB and GRU source knew others only by first names or aliases; friendships among members were discouraged. One American and longtime Russian courier named Alexander Koral had many contacts with Weisband yet knew him only as "Bill." As did two technical sources known only as Brother and Emulsion. The latter worked for the Eastman Kodak company. The reason was simple. Many sources maintained multiple pseudonyms. Chambers was known as "Bob" or "Carl" or "Eugene." There was always "danger," Chambers explained, "of their sharing [personal] information," which violated the "principle of separation." Such behavior placed personal loyalties over "loyalty to the apparatus."[11]

Another essential was ironclad adherence to the "chain of command." The imperative was to get the secret information from the originator to Moscow quickly in the most secure means possible. Any break in the chain could spell disaster for the entire network. To prevent such a possibility, only the head of the chain knew the true identities of everyone.[12] The second person in the chain knew only how to reach the third person and the third person knew how to reach the fourth and so on down the line. No one knew how to contact any higher member of the chain. As Chambers wrote:

> Thus, in theory, no subordinate knew how to reach his immediate superior at any point in the chain. If he were arrested, or defected, he could only reveal the identity of the man under him. The upper reaches of the chain were hidden from his sight, he simply did not know them.[13]

If arrested, the rule was to deny all charges, offer nothing, and profess innocence. Underground workers routinely required funds in order to operate. There were expenses for travel, meals, and payment to sources who had been recruited for money rather than on an ideological basis. Excessive drinking, which could loosen tongues and reveal dangerous information, would regularly lead to punishment for wrongdoers. Chambers once warned a contact, "If you do something wrong, we will find out." Chambers took it as a given that the underground apparatus had a cadre of personnel who did surveillance of other members.[14]

Moscow routinely called upon couriers to do more than just carry documents. Hede Massing, another important courier who, like Chambers, later abandoned the Communist Party, spent months recounting her life of espionage to the FBI. She described her unsuccessful attempts to recruit two State Department officers—Noel Field, who years later found sanctuary behind the Iron Curtain in Hungary, and Alger Hiss, who was already serving the GRU. In a memoir of her time as a spy, she related how she rented a room in New York across from a prominent journalist for use in monitoring his movements and contacts. Couriers needed eyes in the back of their head, Massing noted, constantly on the alert for someone shadowing her from a discreet distance. She survived on instinct or a "feel" for strangers trailing behind her that allowed for seamless adjustment of movements without alerting the followers. In the event of surveillance, couriers had to control emotions, never be flustered, never rush, be patient and keep nerves under control. A logical and verifiable cover story when the police suddenly approached was also mandatory. Fumbling for a plausible excuse under questioning could prove fatal. Like Chambers, she too emphasized decentralization as the "foremost principle" of conspiratorial work. Never was the site, time, or any reference to a meeting discussed over the telephone. Meeting times and locations were set at the previous meeting. If one person didn't show up, the other person knew to appear at the same site at the same time for the next three days. If the person still failed to appear, the other person would wait for a telephone call and then go to a previously arranged alternate meeting site. Massing, a genius at *konspiratsiia*, never mistook quiet for security. Her favorite meeting spots were always busy centers of activity like the New York Public Library or the downstairs lobby of the Radio City Music Hall—both in bustling midtown Manhattan. "The first commandment," she wrote, "is never must you come straight from home, your hotel, or wherever you live to a [meeting]. Always round about. Taxi, subway, bus, taxi—take plenty of time," and "don't spare expense."[15]

Other duties could include opening small businesses particularly around New York for legitimizing agents; searching for birth and death records for KGB use in acquiring legal documents for constructing legends for agents. Couriers also set up safe houses, mainly apartments, for secret meetings, transported funds to reimburse agents for expenses, smuggled agents in and out of the United States while acting as amateur psychologists by keeping a watchful eye for hints of disloyalty that could pose a danger to the network. In rare cases they even assisted in "wet affairs"; a KGB and GRU euphemism for assassinating agents suspected of traitorous behavior. Additional layers of security were ensured by the use of both "legal" and "illegal" networks.[16] A legal network was led by an intelligence officer like Gutzeit with diplomatic immunity that protected him from arrest and prosecution. An illegal network was usually managed by an intelligence officer posing as an American or immigrant. This particular cover offered anonymity and unfettered movement but with the accompanying danger of arrest for violation of US espionage laws if discovered.

So, just what did Weisband offer to the Russians when he began working for them? One important nugget of information derived directly from his work at the Waldorf. When construction began in 1929 a decision was made to install a train track below the hotel. Its purpose was to easily accommodate the private train cars of wealthy visitors wishing to slip in unnoticed by the general public. Track 61, as it was called, was a spur line that ran from a remote corner of Grand Central Station to a platform where guests could exit their railcars and take an elevator up to the main lobby.

Certainly, the most famous visitor to New York City in the 1930s was President Roosevelt. And one of the most closely guarded government secrets during his presidency was the lifelong polio that struck him in 1922, paralyzing him from the waist down. The American public was oblivious to the fact that FDR's ever-present jaunty smile and constant waving hid a stark reality that one incorrect step, even with the help of an aide, could leave the president sprawled on the sidewalk.

In the days before air travel became a routine of presidential life, Roosevelt traveled everywhere by train. For his first two terms he relied on *Marco Polo*, one of six train cars built in 1927 by the Pullman Rail Car Company. At seventy-four feet long, nine feet wide, and fifteen feet tall, it was the cream of long-distance travel, complete with an observation lounge where White House aides and a small retinue of Secret Service could relax, and the president could receive guests. Another railcar carried the president's limousine, a specially armored Pierce-Arrow.

On trips to New York City, the train left Washington from a secret rail siding under the building housing the Bureau of Engraving and Printing and then headed northeast crossing the Hudson River to Manhattan and into Grand Central Station, where specially briefed workers rerouted it to the Waldorf-Astoria. Under tight security and with no advance notice given to the public strolling along the sidewalk above, the president would be lifted into the waiting Pierce-Arrow for a short drive off the train and into a specially built eight-thousand-pound capacity elevator. The car, driver, and passenger were then lifted several floors to the grand ballroom of the Waldorf under the watchful eye of Secret Service agents and selected Waldorf officials. Roosevelt was then transferred from the car to a wheelchair and then a waiting elevator that would take him to the presidential suite; his home during his New York City stays. Hotels like the Waldorf were filled night and day with employees moving quietly about the building. It's axiomatic in the hotel business that the staff knows almost everything that is going on in the building. The presence of prominent guests in the Waldorf rarely went unnoticed among the workers. A presidential visit certainly would have gotten Weisband's attention. He could have briefed the Russians about Roosevelt's comings and goings and perhaps may have even had access to his suite as a room clerk. It is reasonable to assume that Weisband informed the Russians about the special track and the president's schedule along with tidbits of intelligence that he picked up from scuttlebutt and personal observations.[17]

The very nature of spying is designed to leave no paper trail for investigators or historians to follow. Only in the rarest cases have American spies kept any records documenting their espionage careers. Instructions were conveyed by word of mouth, which the spy was required to memorize. For their own safety, couriers kept no written record and carried nothing that could prove incriminating if they were ever stopped and searched.

So it was with William Weisband. Today we have no letters, notes, or diaries that would be useful for tracing his espionage career. What we do have, however, is something that offers us an insight into his work for the Russians during the 1930s. It comes from a woman who spent a good deal of time with Weisband and actually was a firsthand witness to his spying routine.

Her name was Patricia Grimes. She came to New York City in the early 1930s from Oregon, where she was born and raised. She was separated from her husband when Weisband met her at a local dance hall around Christmas 1937. Today we are fortunate that as a courier Weisband was routinely sloppy, committing a series of gross violations of the rules by drawing her into his espionage life. The two had been seeing each other for a while when Bill first confided to her about his special work for an "older man" who he never identified. His job was to contact "various persons for the purpose of delivering and receiving documents and packages" in accordance with instructions given to him by people he cryptically referred to as his "principals."[18] Grimes later told investigators that he didn't know the so-called contacts and just as often had never met them before. The meeting times, dates, and places were always prearranged in advance by his principals.

She remembered that she and Bill often drove around New York City when suddenly he pulled his car over to the curb, telling her to wait while he briefly met someone. He had some "secret" business to do, he told her, and she was not to look around or try to watch where he went or who he met. If he didn't return, she was to drive the car to her apartment building and wait for him to pick it up later. On other occasions when they were at her apartment, he would suddenly leave without a word, only to return an hour or so later saying he was doing some secret work. He made it a point to tell her never to be alarmed if he did not see her as often as she preferred but he would eventually contact her. Once when he was "moody" he told her that he may leave one day and she would never see him again. While never disclosing how much he was paid for his work, he did acknowledge that it was "ample" and would continue "indefinitely." As incomprehensible as it seemed, Grimes gradually came to realize that Weisband was working for the Russians.[19]

In one instance, Grimes's "personal relationship" with Weisband caused a crisis when he informed his superiors about her. His boss berated him for mixing *konspiratsiia* with pleasure, calling it dangerous behavior. It "caused an inquiry to be made," which, he told her, gradually subsided because he didn't tell them that he had "confided in her about his work."[20]

On another occasion he egregiously ignored another cardinal principle of *konspiratsiia* by taking Grimes deeper into his espionage world. It occurred one day when they drove across the George Washington Bridge into New Jersey for a visit with a young married couple living in a nearby farmhouse. Earlier that day the two of them went to a store where Bill purchased a set of expensive hand-painted crystal glasses as a gift for the couple. Years later, Grimes remembered that she was so impressed with them that she returned to the store and bought two of them for herself.

More than a decade later when interviewed by the FBI she could not remember the names of the couple they visited but recalled the strangeness of the encounter. As the visit went on, they became convinced that she was a member of Weisband's espionage ring based simply on a lapel pendant she was wearing that bore her initials.[21]

Grimes remembered Bill once returning from a meeting proudly patting his vest pocket. He said that he had with him an important document containing a secret formula for turning water into engine fuel. He was "elated" that he possessed such an item and could turn it over to his bosses. It was "very important," he bragged, and much desired "by any country that could get possession of it."[22]

One of the few Weisband sources we know about is "Smart," code name for Elliot Goldberg, an engineer for an oil equipment company in New York. Weisband's source for the water fuel formula may have been a KGB agent code-named "Octane." His name was Maurice B. Cooke. Cooke, who lived with his wife and daughter in New Jersey, was a chemical engineer born in 1893 and a graduate of Bucknell University in Pennsylvania. Later he worked for DuPont, the US Bureau of Mines, and Alco Products Company as the director of research.

Cooke worked for the New York station as an important industrial spy who came into the KGB's orbit in 1933 when he initiated a business relationship with Amtorg, the first trade representation of the Soviet Union in the United States. Over the years, he provided technical data from the Tennessee Valley Authority on phosphoric acid and "catalytic cracking" in return for $14,000 [$255,000 in February 2020], which he used to finance an affluent lifestyle that included at least five trips to Europe with his wife and daughter during the 1930s. When confronted years later by the FBI, he admitted turning over details about gasoline refining plants that he had stolen from his employer, M. W. Kellogg Company. He relied on a Leica camera to photograph masses of documents that he then turned over to Weisband on New York City street corners.[23]

Yet in addition to Emulsion, Brother, Goldberg, and possibly Cooke, Weisband handled another important source—one who has never been identified until now.

## NOTES

1. Dr. David Charney, Lecture, International Spy Museum/Smithsonian Lecture Series, Washington, DC, Undated, YouTube.
2. Dr, David Charney, NOIR, White Paper Studies, NOIR4.org.
3. Ibid.
4. New York Report, June 16, 1950, Weisband FBI file.
5. Ibid.
6. "Mrs. Ruth Pratt Sues to Evict Soviet Consulate," *New York Times*, January 1, 1947, 1.
7. Following the collapse of the Soviet Union in 1990, a rare window of opportunity opened up to get a glimpse into KGB foreign operations files covering the 1930s and 1940s. Seizing this chance the late American historian Allen Weinstein teamed up with Alexander Vassiliev, a former KGB officer turned journalist-historian, to examine these original records. What they produced was a monumental study of select Americans who spied for the Russians entitled *The Haunted Wood: Soviet Espionage in America—The Stalin Era*, published in 1999 by Random House. Some years later American researchers Harvey Klehr from Emory University and John Earl Haynes of the Library of Congress teamed with Vassiliev to incorporate Vassiliev's hundreds of pages of notes into a compendium identifying hundreds of other Americans working for the Russians. The result was *Spies: The Rise and Fall of the KGB in America*, produced in 2009 by Yale University. As part of this effort the entirety of Vassiliev's hundreds of notebooks containing original records from the file were translated and catalogued in what today is available online and called the "Vassiliev Notebooks."

They were broken down for easy reading as follows: Vassiliev Notebook Concordance (VNC), Odd Pages Translated (OPT), Vassiliev Black Notebook (VBN), Vassiliev Whit Notebooks 1 through 3 (VWN 1, VWN 2, VWN 3), and Vassiliev Yellow

Notebooks 1 through 4 (VYN 1, VYN 2, VYN 3, VYN 4), VWN -1–132. Manifest of SS *Majestic*, April 24, 1935, and Manifest of RMS *Queen Mary*, March 30, 1938, MyHeritage.com.

8. VBN 4.
9. Ibid.
10. VNC 250.
11. Whittaker Chambers, *Witness* (Washington, DC: Regnery Gateway, 1952), 284, 304.
12. Ibid., 285.
13. Ibid., 286.
14. Ibid., 297.
15. Hede Massing, *This Deception* (New York: Duell Sloan and Pearce, 1951), 78–81.
16. Ibid.
17. Sam Roberts, *Grand Central* (New York: Grand Central Publishing, 2013), 250–51.
18. WFO letter, June 29, 1950, Weisband FBI file.
19. Ibid.
20. Ibid.
21. The FBI conducted an extensive investigation to identify the mysterious couple with success. Ibid.
22. Ibid.
23. John Earl Haynes, Harvey Klehr, and Alexander Vassiliev, *Spies: The Rise and Fall of the KGB in America* (New Haven, CT: Yale University Press, 2009), 387–88.

*Chapter 4*

# A Washington Committee

At precisely 2:00 p.m. on September 4, 1934, the chairman's gavel slammed down, signaling to hundreds of assembled reporters and onlookers that the Senate Committee to Investigate the Munition Industry was underway. It would be the first of ninety-three such hearings spanning the next two years.

The site was the US Senate Caucus Room, a majestic, almost cathedral-like expanse flanked on two walls by twelve marble columns soaring up from a New Hampshire white marble floor and illuminated by two brilliant chandeliers suspended thirty-five feet overhead.

Built in 1904 as part of the Senate Office Building, it was originally planned as a conference room where forty-six senators could assemble for discussions of party strategy. Just eight years later, it held its first set of hearings when legislators, demanding answers, grilled a string of witnesses about the RMS *Titanic*, the White Star Line passenger ship that sank on its maiden voyage across the Atlantic, killing more than fifteen hundred passengers—among them a number of prominent Americans and one member of Congress.[1]

Heading the seven-member Munitions Industry panel was Gerald Prentice Nye, an obscure junior senator from North Dakota, then in his first full term. Born in 1892, the son of a newspaper publisher from the tiny Wisconsin town of Wittenberg, Nye skipped college after high school, striking out west for North Dakota where he, too, entered the newspaper business. From cub reporter, he steadily rose over the years to the position of editor by his early thirties.[2]

In 1925, Nye was propelled into national politics when North Dakota governor Arthur G. Sorlie appointed him to fill a Senate vacancy opened up with the sudden death of Edwin P. Ladd. From the start of his Senate career, Nye wasted no time strengthening his Midwest credentials. As an "appointed" senator eager for election in his own right, Nye began championing small shopkeepers, farmers, and consumers. In Nye, one observer noted, "American small-town life had a representative who would fight monopoly and privilege with indomitable courage and religious zeal."[3]

The choice of a Republican to head any Senate panel was a curious one. Congress was securely in the hands of "New Deal" Democrats with former New York governor Franklin D. Roosevelt occupying the White House for more than a year. Nye's journey to the chairmanship began on a snowy December afternoon in 1933 on Capitol Hill when George Norris, a Nebraska Progressive-Republican senator, met with a plain-looking thirty-eight-year-old Fort Wayne, Indiana, lobbyist named Dorothy Detzer.

To get an audience with such a powerful political fixture was no easy task, particularly for a woman. By the early 1930s, Detzer had become a rare but important figure in her own right among Washington's movers and shakers. Known half jokingly on the Hill as the "Lady Lobbyist," she could regularly be found stalking the hallways or posted at the House or Senate chambers doors hoping to waylay some unsuspecting member.[4]

Skipping college, Detzer had instead abandoned the United States for world travel, a decision that would determine the arc of her future life. First, she set off for Asia and then onto the Philippines, where she lived for two years before returning to Chicago, where she moved into the Jane Addams Hull House and took a job with the city's Juvenile Protective Association.

The end of World War I found her on the move again; this time as a relief worker with the American Friends Service Committee in war-ravaged Austria. Next came Russia's Volga Valley and confronting the horrors of the Russian Civil War for two years as a famine relief worker. In 1924, after returning to America and joining the Women's International League for Pacificism and Freedom (WILPF), she began championing a long list of causes, which included condemnation of war, inclusion of the Soviet Union into the family of nations, and leading an outcry for American neutrality. At the time of her conversation with Norris, she was the national secretary of the WILPF.

Prompting Detzler's drive for peace during the 1920s was a belief that the root cause of World War I was a cabal of greedy bankers and munitions manufacturers hungry for profits. For evidence she pointed to the mortality figures from the war. German and Austro-Hungarian forces killed more than 4.5 million French, Russian, and British soldiers, with their own losses topping three million. For millions more who survived, there were lasting scars left on unmarried women and the tragedy of widows and fatherless children. There was also a personal dimension to Detzler's sadness. She had a twin brother who survived the war only to die a few years later from the lingering effects of gassing.

What happened next was disillusionment. Americans, vainly struggling to answer this seemingly insoluble question, first sought comfort in the myth that international agreements would be a solution to permanent peace. These hopes were first boosted in 1922 when Germany and the Soviet Union normalized diplomatic relations after four years of uncertainty. World leaders rejoiced at the thought that two mortal enemies had agreed to "cooperate in the spirit of mutual goodwill in meeting the economic needs of both countries."[5] Three years later, in December 1925, the so-called Locarno Pact was signed, with the new states of Central and Eastern Europe settling territorial claims and normalizing relations with Germany. Guarantees were extracted from the new Weimar Republic that Germany would never go to war again with its neighbors. The capstone of the decade-long search for peace, however, came in 1928 with the signing of the "General Treaty for Renunciation of War as an Instrument of National Policy." Better known as the Kellogg-Briand Pact for Frank Kellogg, the US secretary of state, and Aristide Briand, the French foreign minister, sixty-two world leaders pledged never to turn to war as a solution for "disputes or conflicts of whatever nature or of whatever origin they may be, which may arise." The agreement was scheduled to go into effect on July 24, 1929, three months before the Wall Street financial collapse ushered in the worst economic calamity in world history.

These well-meaning vows abruptly faded in 1932 when Germany's election of Adolf Hitler as chancellor began a tragic chain of events that would lead to the century's second catastrophic war seven years later. Two years later Japan's departure from the League of Nations set Asia afire with its military invasion of Manchuria, a move that set the Soviet Union on edge and produced new tensions between Japan and the United States. In 1936, the Fascist forces of dictator Benito Mussolini invaded the helpless African nation of Ethiopia in a conflict that cost three-quarters of a million lives. That same year a series of left-wing elections and political assassinations launched a three-year civil war in Spain.

With the peace rationale now gone, bewildered Americans began looking for new scapegoats. From baseless conclusions emerged a convenient new theory: it posited the notion that powerful international bankers scheming with munitions makers had manipulated governments toward violence for the purpose of reaping enormous profits. Coining them "Merchants of Death," Detzer and her followers convinced themselves that industrialists, financiers, and even laborers and farmers profited from war in one way or another. Left to their own designs their greed would only continue the cycle of violence.[6]

Detzer called for nationalizing the munitions makers and placing tight restrictions on American bankers in the belief that such a national policy would eliminate future wars forever. But she needed proof, and it was in this spirit that she lobbied Norris for help in uncovering evidence that she was certain would reveal the truth.

The like-minded Norris eagerly threw his support for a resolution authorizing a committee to investigate Detzer's charges. As the two ran down a list of possible senators, Nye gradually emerged as the candidate. After months of parliamentary jockeying, Senate Resolution 208 passed on April 12,

1934. The excitement of supporters quickly dampened, however, when the new committee's operating budget was set at a miniscule $15,000, far less than the $35,000 requested. In addition to this fiscal cap, Nye was under pressure to complete the committee's work with the submission of a final report by the start of 1936. In the end, the committee was charged with gathering evidence on:

> firms, associations and corporations and all other agencies in the United States engaged in the manufacture, sale, distribution, import or export of arms, munitions, or other implements of war; the methods used in promoting or effecting the sale of arms, munition and other implement of war imported in to the United States and the countries of origin thereof, and the quantities exported from the United States and countries of destination.[7]

The new chairman's first order of business was forming a staff. In a few short weeks, Nye's core group of seven investigators were in place and setting out areas of responsibility. All of them, generally young, from varied backgrounds, with little or no investigative experience, were bound together by the common belief in the merchants of death.

First to be hired was Stephen Raushenbush. Then in his late thirties, Raushenbush was a determined social justice advocate with polished credentials as an investigator. A product of New York City, he was the son of Walter Rauschenbusch (the two "Cs" were dropped in the son's name), a well-known American theologian and Baptist minister. After completing Amherst College, Stephen Raushenbush joined the Ambulance Corps attached to the French army as a driver during World War I; a horrific experience that only reinforced his commitment to peace and just solutions to international problems.

After the war, he started a writing career with a series of muckraking exposes. First came *The Anthracite Question*, published in 1923, which examined abuses of miners in the Pennsylvania coal industry. Five years later came *Power Control*, his new study on the influence of public utility monopolies on household electric costs. After briefly teaching economics at Dartmouth College, he joined Pennsylvania governor Gifford Pinchot's administration as an economic advisor. Pinchot gave Raushenbush wide latitude to probe a broad range of social issues like child labor, predatory practices of the utilities industry, and old-age pensions. His one shortcoming, the absence of a law degree, was offset in Nye's view by a well-trained and resourceful mind as well as investigative experience. Raushenbush became both the committee's "chief investigator" and supervisor of the staff, and in a "very large sense constituted the committee, and generally directed its activities."[8]

Next on the list of hires was Robert Martin Wohlforth, a *Washington Post* reporter who had briefly attended Princeton University before entering the

US Military Academy in 1925. For the Nye committee he would lead the investigative team's New York City office. In a few short weeks, Nye's team of investigators was in place and ready for the day-to-day nitty-gritty work of gathering evidence.[9]

From the committee's opening moments, Moscow was keenly interested in its work. As early as September 1934, when the first hearing was held, secret directives were issued to Comintern outposts worldwide demanding as much information as possible about its progress. Begin "at once reporting from Washington while attaching the greatest importance to the deadening effect of industry" declared one such message.[10]

Leading the Russian charge in America was Earl Browder, a forty-three-year-old American born in Wichita, Kansas, and head of the Communist Party of the United States. The Kremlin's orders to Browder were simple and straightforward: Gather everything about the committee's work for Moscow's use in painting Germany and Japan as fascist imperialist predators linked with munitions makers in America and Great Britain. His mandate was to make the "largest utilization" of the committee's "disclosures of Japan and Germany's preparation for war."

> On account of the September numbers of the American papers, we suggest that the widest publicity and agitation should be given in the press to the WASHINGTON Senate disclosure regarding international armament capital. Unmask also especially the war-like roles of GERMANY and JAPAN. Direct the campaign especially in support of disclosure of war preparation of Japan and Germany. It is desirable to show up in a sensational and sharp manner, the particular crass type of the war profiteer and to describe the position of the workers in the armaments factories concerned. Draw special attention to the connection between the war industrial profiteers and members of Parliament. (? In the general BASLE) press. The campaign must be bound up closely with the fight against the transport of arms to JAPAN. Moscow to London. Moscow to Basel.[11]

One of Browder's first moves was seeking the help of New York newspaper columnist Ludwig Lore. The German-born Lore, who immigrated to the United States in 1903, had been recruited into the Communist Party in 1917 by Stalin's henchman, Leon Trotsky. Later he was appointed both secretary of the German branch of the Socialist Party and editor of its newspaper, the *New Yorker Volkszeitung*. Trotsky's break with Stalin prompted Lore's ouster from the party for what was termed "loreism," which claimed that his views were too liberal and reminiscent of a social democrat.[12] Undeterred, Lore remained an independent communist, turning to freelance journalism before joining the editorial board of the *New York Post*. There he began writing a regular column under the banner "Behind the Cables," which revealed details about the trans-Atlantic cable that brought European news to the United States with particular emphasis on the growing Nazi menace. At the time of the Nye committee hearings, Lore was a Comintern talent spotter and agent recruiter who handled four sources whose identities remain a mystery today.

Lore expressed an eagerness to assist Raushenbush even before the first gavel dropped. Responding to a letter from Nye seeking his help about foreign weapons sales by American manufacturers, Lore offered the committee "any material I have on the question." Days later Wohlforth extended Lore an invitation to meet with him in his Capitol Hill office when he next visited Washington.[13]

A separate Kremlin-directed approach involved one of the most important Moscow agents in America during the 1930s. The mystery man was a short, affable, and pudgy figure, with a dark complexion, bushy mustache and a ready smile for all. Over the years, his aliases included Joszef Peters, or sometimes simply J. Peters, Alexander Stephens, and John Pepper. Decades later a biographer wrote that his "greatest accomplishments consisted of the development of an underground apparatus and creation of an espionage operation in cooperation with Soviet intelligence organizations."[14]

He was born Sandor Goldberger in 1894 into a poor Jewish family in Csap, a tiny village in the northeast corner of the Kingdom of Hungary in the Austro-Hungarian Empire. After studying law, he committed to communism following four grinding years of war as an infantryman and later experiences with Hungarian prisoners of war coming back from Russia. He and his mother settled in the Yorkville section of Manhattan after emigrating to the United States in 1924. In keeping with the dictates of *konspiratsiia*, he soon dropped the name Goldberger for Joszef Peters; an alias he would use for avoiding police surveillance and as a demonstration of his communist loyalty.

Eventually Peters became a victim of his own success when Kremlin leaders ordered him to abandon the "open party" and move to the underground apparatus. Preparation for a new assignment began in 1931 with his travel to Moscow for a year of study at a special school managed by the Otdyel Mezhdunarodnoi Svyasi, or OMS, the Comintern's most secret department, responsible for worldwide coordination and control of subversive and conspiratorial activities. On his return to New York one of Peters first duties was to take control of Whittaker Chambers. The two men had previously known each other from their collaboration on propaganda issues years earlier when Peters was with the *Daily Worker* and Chambers was editing the *New Masses*, the party's monthly magazine.[15]

One source that Chambers handled was Alger Hiss, a young lawyer then assisting the Agriculture Department in the implementation of the newly passed Agricultural Adjustment Act. The high-flying Hiss had a bright future ahead of him in government. Born and raised in Baltimore, he attended Johns Hopkins University before entering Harvard Law School. There he served on the prestigious law review journal and became a protégé of Felix Frankfurter, a Harvard law professor, who would soon join the Supreme Court.

From the Agriculture Department, Hiss moved (probably under Peters orders) to the Nye investigative staff. Hiss's limited portfolio focused on examining the relationships between US aircraft manufacturers, the banking industry, and foreign governments. After several meetings, Hiss assured Chambers that his committee position was "so strong" that he could safely obtain confidential information from State Department files. Soon, however, Hiss was singing a new tune for Chambers. His access to State Department cables had been suddenly curtailed. New security measures had been imposed after complaints were raised by senior State Department officials and corporate leaders about the committee's poor handling of their sensitive data. One frustrated investigator writing to Raushenbush complained about his difficulties in dealing with the Wall Street financial giant J. P. Morgan Company. "Relations with Morgan have been growing more and more tense on the problem of prying stuff out of them" the letter stated, "making an increasing amount of delicate negotiations necessary."[16] So heated did committee access to Morgan company records become that attorneys for Morgan questioned the relevance of certain sensitive records for the investigation while demanding the drafting of "certificates of good character" signed by each staff member as a guarantee that the information turned over would not leak.[17]

In response to growing criticisms, Raushenbush began tightening security around the committee's growing collection of records. Orders were placed with a local Washington office supply company for sturdy filing cabinets equipped with special locks and bars that were secured at the end of each day. Adding to the locks and bars was a requirement that all of the committee employees sign loyalty statements of good character. To curtail leaks to the press, staff members were ordered to refer to corporations under investigation by code. The rudimentary system was based on a list of companies with a corresponding number for each one. For instance, the DuPont Company, the nation's leading gunpowder manufacturer, became "eleven," the number "four" was assigned to Curtiss–Wright Aircraft Company, while Bethlehem Shipbuilding Company was designated "twenty-eight," and so forth. Raushenbush took security seriously. In one case he fired a committee clerk who was assisting an investigator in examining Navy League records for becoming too chummy with a league official. Two weeks later investigators were surprised to find her working for that same official as a secretary.[18]

Hiss's access was further restricted in winter 1935 when a young whirlwind joined the staff. Josephine Joan Burns, then twenty-five, was the daughter of a New York City police inspector. Standing just 5'3.5", she was by her own admission something of a tomboy, with swimming, canoeing, skating, rowing, and playing basketball part of her regular routine. At Washington

Square College (a college within the New York University system), she made her presence felt as chairwoman of the Women's Athletic Association, editor of the women's sports journal and college yearbook, as well as membership on the student finance and social committees. On the academic side she was equally relentless. She learned French, studied history and political science, earning a Phi Beta Kappa key in the process. In 1930 she moved to Mount Holyoke College, completing her graduate degree in 1932 with a thesis on the relationship between the council and the assembly of the League of Nations. That same year, as a field secretary for the Women's International League for Peace and Freedom, she ventured off to Europe, spending the next few summers at the Zimmern School in Geneva, Switzerland, doing research for Manley O. Hudson, a Harvard Law School professor, then writing a book entitled *Permanent Court of International Justice*. Staying on at Mount Holyoke, Burns taught American government until she joined the Nye committee in February 1935. Backed by such impressive credentials, Raushenbush hired Burns as the committee's only female investigator. Her assignment from the start was ferreting through State Department records for any evidence of collusion between foreign governments and American industry.[19]

As Chambers later wrote in his memoir, "Officially or unofficially there was a ban against further release of confidential documents." Oddly, when Chambers showed his bosses the material that Hiss had removed from Nye committee files, they expressed a "complete lack of interest."[20]

Perhaps this strange KGB reaction concerning such an important Moscow priority sprang from other motives. For standing behind chairman Nye, as he slammed down his gavel, was a woman, ordinary in appearance, silently looking on.

## NOTES

1. Author wishes to express his appreciation to Dr. Kate Scott, assistant historian, US Senate, for taking me on a tour of the Senate Caucus Room and offering details of the hearings held there following the *Titanic* disaster. Author interview, June 3, 2018.
2. John E. Wiltz, *In Search of Peace* (Baton Rouge: Louisiana State University Press, 1963), 28.
3. Ibid.
4. Ibid., 34.
5. Gordon H. Mueller, "Rapallo Reexamined: A New Look at Germany's Secret Military Collaboration with Russia in 1922," *Military Affairs*, Vol. 40, No. 3 (October 1973): 109–17.
6. Wiltz, *In Search of Peace*, 21.

7. Ibid., 37.

8. Ibid., 49–51, "Nye Committee Held to Have Hindered Pre-War Unity," *New York Times*, February 4, 1948, 1.

9. In 1939 he was appointed to the antitrust division of the Department of Justice. Later during the Second World War, he headed an investigation of economic connections of the Nazis. In 1952 he became associated with a new publishing group that became Farrar, Straus and Giroux. He was its treasurer until he retired in the mid-1980s. Bob married Mildred E. Gilman in 1930. Mildred was a well-known writer, who prior to her death in 1994, produced a number of novels. He controlled the flow of information during the hearings by handing documents to senators when questioning witnesses. Princeton Alumni Weekly.

10. Author expresses sincere appreciation to Dr. David Thomas of the Institute of World Politics for supplying his complete collection of Comintern messages code-named MASK for examination. MASK Moscow to Basel, October 4, 1934, Nos. 218, 219, 302, 317.

11. MASK Messages, October 4, 1934, Nos. 218, 219, 302/171.

12. Haynes, Klehr, and Vassiliev, *Spies*, 155–56.

13. Ludwig Lore letter to Gerald Nye, May 22, 1934, Robert Wohlforth letter to Lore, May 24, 1934, RG 46, Box 11, General File, NARA.

14. Thomas Sakmyster, *Red Conspirator* (Urbana: University of Illinois, 2011), xiii.

15. At the time he started working with Chambers, he also took control of a loose collection of federal employees who met as a communist study group while at the same time stealing documents from government files. They were the so-called "Ware Group," named for Harold Ware, an American and veteran communist with ties to Moscow that extended back to his days as a collective farm worker in the new Soviet Union. Ware's years of emersion in Marxist–Leninist thought made him ideal for the task of radicalizing young idealists flocking to Washington to join the "New Deal" at the start of the Roosevelt presidency. Once again relying on his organizational skills, Peters sought order out of chaos by streamlining the unwieldy espionage/study group arrangement into two parallel networks with Chambers handling one of them and he the other as Sam Tanenhaus recorded "would penetrate the upper reaches of government." To make delivery of information safer, Peters gave Chambers a Leica camera and portable folding stand, both of which fitted neatly into a suitcase for easy storage and concealment. Chambers soon began making regular trips to Washington carrying the Leica camera and folding stand to photograph documents that he then returned to Peters in New York for passage to the Russians. Sam Tanenhaus, *Whittaker Chambers* (New York: Random House, 1997)96, 104.

16. Wiltz, *In Search of Peace*, 55.

17. Ibid.

18. Robert Wohlforth letter to Raushenbush, 8/3/1934, RG 46, Box 21, General File, NARA.

19. Micha Broadnax, archivist, Mount Holyoke College Archives, South Hadley, Massachusetts.

20. Chambers, *Witness*, 375.

*Chapter 5*

# Zero

Her KGB code name was "Zero."

Her journey to the Nye committee began around June 1934 following a conversation with Robert Wohlforth. How they initially met is unknown. Their paths probably crossed through journalistic connections. She quickly followed up with a two-page handwritten letter reminding him about their meeting and expressing interest in landing a job as a committee investigator. Her "training and experience," she stressed, qualified her to "take an active part in the research" and all she wanted was an "opportunity to show my worth." Curiously, her missive was devoid of specifics.[1]

She had been a student at New York's Columbia University, yet there was no mention of dates of attendance, major concentration, or degrees conferred. Details of her professional background were equally scant. For five years she worked as a reporter in New York with "newspapers-periodicals" and "ghost writing" articles for other journalists. She wrote feature articles (none of which she cited) and did copy writing; all "valuable experience"[2] that would prove useful to the committee's work. The only specifics were references to work on an "assignment desk" with Pictorial Press in New York City and arranging photo captions for World Pictograph News Service. Yet, here again, no dates of employment or names of supervisors were indicated. Closing her appeal, she minced no words about her motives for wishing to join the committee. "Wars are created for profit and munitions manufacturers for profit are out of preparedness—I should like to know who (shareholders Etc.) profit—and just what financial (direct or indirect) interests these persons might have in the countries to which munitions are being shipped?"[3]

What Wohlforth did not know was that the woman he met was not whom she claimed. She had introduced herself to Wohlforth as Lydia Lee yet she was, in fact, Lydia Levin or possibly Lydia Levinsky. A short, heavyset woman with thick black hair, Lee was born in New York City on November 2, 1902, to Isaac D. Levin, an itinerant dry goods dealer from Russia. His wife, Ida D. Kanevsky, was a homemaker from Austria. The couple had

33

another daughter, Eleanor, who would later marry and become Eleanor Rothenberg. Both children were raised in the Bronx and for a time Lydia attended Columbia University. In June 1929 she married Alex Millstone and had a child named after his father. After divorcing Millstone, she moved to Washington, where she disposed of Lydia Levin and Lydia Millstone and became Lydia Lee. Nearly a decade and a half later she married William Alger Heflin, who was born in 1910 in Washington, DC. The two probably met through their employment on Capitol Hill, where Heflin worked as a committee staffer with an assignment to one of the congressional inquiries into the Pearl Harbor disaster. The reason behind Lee's elaborate deception remains a mystery. Perhaps she was desperate to escape a bad marriage or had a simple desire to start a fresh life under a new identity. Anti-Semitism, like racial segregation, was rife in the nation's capital, which meant extraordinary difficulty securing government employment. Whatever the reason, Lee was hired to her undoubted dismay as a part-time clerk rather than as an investigator.

Today each political party has its own committee staff. When Lee started there was only a single non-partisan staff serving both parties on congressional committees. Then as now a committee clerkship was a "coveted" and well-paid (one hundred dollars a month for a full-time clerk) position that required performance at an exceptional level of service. Ubiquitous clerks moved silently behind the scenes with unchecked access to all materials and correspondence, preparing, transmitting, filing, and interpreting them with limited oversight. They had, as one Senate historian succinctly noted, "complete control."[4]

The 1930s was also an era with no thought given to background checks on employees applying for sensitive government jobs. The only criteria for hiring was an ability to handle the workload. Whatever the reason for her metamorphosis, she took full advantage of her colleagues' naivety and innocence. Wohlforth later conceded as much, acknowledging that he and his associates were "awfully green" about security and investigating, going so far as to admit that "some of us [were] pretty dumb."[5]

By the early fall of 1934, with her ever-present efficiency and helpfulness, Lee had become indispensable. Senate records suggest that she was working almost full-time and was assimilating well into the committee routine. In a letter offering a rare insight into Lee's growing responsibilities, Raushenbush extended regrets to Wohlforth that committee hearing transcripts destined for him in New York were being redirected instead to a group in London interested in setting up a similar inquiry.

> I am sorry I have to tell you that the set of galley sheets of the hearings which Miss Lee had assembled for you had to be deflected from you and sent to

England. A group of Englishmen who are interested in promoting the same kind of investigation for Great Britain that is now being made by this committee secured Senator Nye's O.K. for a set and since the only one available was the one intended for you, it had to be used. Miss Lee is going to try on Monday to get a special "dispensation" from the Printing Office for a set for you but she is not at all sure she can get it. She does have on hand some portions of the testimony and if you will let me know the cases in which you are especially interested, she will send them on to you, providing she can not secure the full set.[6]

Lee first began slipping committee documents to John L. Spivak, a left-wing journalist who probably numbered among the many observers packing the Caucus Room for the opening hearing. Spivak, then age forty-three, began his career as a police reporter in his hometown of New Haven, Connecticut. From chasing after homicides and burglaries, he graduated to Progressive-era muckraking with exposes about abuses in the coal industry and labor unrest in West Virginia. In *Georgia Nigger*, published in 1932, Spivak penned a vivid portrait of black prisoners laboring on chain gangs in the Deep South. Adding to his reputation were a series of essays he produced for *New Masses*, the Communist Party's monthly magazine, shedding light on Japanese agents in the United States and the anti-Semitic demagoguery of pro-fascist Catholic priest Father Charles Coughlin.

By 1934, under the code name "Grin," Spivak had been a Moscow Center agent for at least two years. The Kremlin found him a useful source of intelligence on Leon Trotsky, Stalin's nemesis, as well as of gossip about the latest goings-on in Washington.[7] Moscow was even more pleased to learn of his encounter with another Russian source, Frank Prince, code name "Courier," a self-styled expert on anti-Semitism and consultant to the House Committee on Un-American Activities known as the McCormick–Dickstein Committee. "We think it was good on our part that 'Grin' was connected with 'Courier,'" a Moscow official wrote, "[because] it is after all completely natural for 'Grin' to be interested in anything having to do with the work of the Nazis and anti-Semitism." Spivak began filtering tidbits gathered from his sources to Prince for the committee's assistance in exposing fascist groups and combating right-wing agitation around the country.[8]

When Spivak and Lee first crossed paths is unknown. What is clear, however, is that the stacks of documents she slipped to him from Nye committee files had caught Moscow's attention. "Grin has one agent [on the Nye committee]—Zero who gets large quantities of documents" and she "doesn't even know that she works for us." The rich troves an official reported, "go into detail," about the American chemical warfare industry, the division of the spheres of influence among the nation's largest arms producers, together with bribing methods, ties with intelligence agencies, and particularly the intelligence methods employed by the DuPont company against the USSR.[9]

Closely monitoring the Spivak-Lee relationship from New York was "Nord," a recent arrival from Europe sent by Moscow Center to take control of KGB illegal operations. Looking over the strengths and weaknesses of his new group, the ever-cautious Nord was undoubtedly pleased with Spivak's progress, with a lowly clerk quietly operating at the center of an important congressional committee. His bosses, too, were encouraged, viewing this connection as an important first step in meeting the Kremlin's goals for its American station. Stalin's growing fear of entrapment between Japan and Germany meant an increased demand for intelligence from America's far-flung listening posts around the world. "(Moscow Center) attach(es) serious significance to political work," Nord was warned, yet "we must simultaneously draw your attention to the fact that . . . in your country, the Nazis, along with Islanders (Japanese) and Whites (Anti-Stalinists and Monarchists) are taking measures to compromise our official agencies, in part by exposing our work."[10]

Accomplishing this mission required moles strategically placed within the most important cabinet departments of the new Roosevelt administration. On the top of Nord's list was the Department of State, with its analysis of Japanese intentions in China and Manchuria, and the growing Nazi crackdown on the German communist party and other leftist groups. As for the War and Navy Departments, the goal was acquiring the military appraisals of Hitler's growing Wehrmacht and Reichswehr advancements in new weapons systems.[11]

Such challenges were nothing new for the new station chief. Nord was born Boris Yakoleyvich Shpak in 1893 in the tiny village of Kovno Gubernia Lithuania. Later, after reinventing himself as Boris Bazarov, he joined the Communist Party and entered the secret police in 1921. Like all European illegals, he spoke multiple languages, including Russian, German, Serbo-Croatian, Bulgarian, and French. His espionage career began in 1924 as an agent runner in Bulgaria and Yugoslavia. Four years later, following an assignment to Moscow Center's Balkan Desk, he was posted to Berlin as the illegal resident. For the next six years, he ran operations across Germany and France under the nose of Nazi watchdogs while continuing his management of the Balkan line as well. According to historians Nigel West and Alexander Tsarev, Bazarov was a talented recruiter of sources. One of his important successes was Ernest Oldham, a cipher clerk with the British Foreign Office, who Bazarov recruited by posing as a menacing Italian communist named "DaVinci."[12]

As the supply of high-grade Nye committee information began piling up, Bazarov grew increasingly concerned about the Spivak–Lee security arrangement. While the journalist could easily receive information from Lee under less than secure circumstances, Spivak was not a trained agent handler. His misgivings were further strained over Lee's belief that the secrets she was feeding Spivak were for his use or possibly for the Communist Part of the United States of America (CPUSA).

With Moscow's authorization, Bazarov made the decision to move Lee from "indirect contact" through Spivak to "witting agent" status. As the day approached, the New York station informed Moscow that "in the next few days we will be taking Zero from Grin and including her in our network."[13]

The dicey mission of formally recruiting Lee was given to William Weisband. It was a critical move that begs the question—Why Weisband? He was a new recruit himself with virtually no experience dealing with agents.

Yet, was it a rash move, or something well thought out by a savvy and talented spy with years of experience behind him? In studying both Lee and Weisband, one can see faint outlines of Bazarov's thinking. In a number of important ways, Bill was well-suited for the assignment. Both he and Lee were Jewish and shared the Russian and Yiddish languages spoken in the homes of their youth. Both had familial ties with Russia. The two came from poor immigrant families with similar life experiences growing up on the teeming streets of New York City. Their close proximity in age, Bill then only twenty-seven, and Lee just six years older, would have been useful. After nearly a decade of experience dealing with all sorts of personalities at New York City's best hotels, Bill had grown into a handsome, well-turned-out man about town with a smooth, fast-talking charm and glib style that appealed to women. The fact that both were unattached may have also played a role in Bazarov's decision. Then there was the question of Lee's secret past. The Comintern apparatus routinely checked the background of its sources, a fact that may have alerted them to Lee's double life; a shared secret that gave Weisband a not-so-subtle leverage over her.

How he recruited her into Russian espionage is unknown. In 1935 Bill was still working the evening shift at the Waldorf-Astoria Hotel. Most likely they met when Spivak suggested to Lee that he had a friend who wished to meet her. The three then had a get-acquainted dinner together somewhere near Capitol Hill, with Spivak quickly excusing himself and leaving the two alone to chat. In keeping with the principles of conspiracy Weisband never revealed his true name or may simply have called himself "Bill." As Lee outlined her life and new committee duties, Weisband, softly oozing sincerity and interest, complimented her on her bravery and the importance of the information she had provided to Spivak. Then moving to the point of no return, he revealed that some of her information had made its way to Moscow, which found it vital to the country's safety and security. Steadily measuring Lee for any signs of alarm, Weisband stressed the need for greater security; so much so, that

Moscow wanted her to join their team working with Bill in a secret fashion. After absorbing the import of what she had heard, Lee probably had some thoughts of her own with queries about the nature of their future relationship; questions that Weisband parried so adroitly that within days Bazarov triumphantly signaled the Kremlin with a terse message; "Concrete outcome—Zero's recruitment."[14]

From that point Spivak was out of the picture. Instead, Weisband and Lee began meeting under clandestine conditions. A carefully prearranged schedule was established calling for Weisband's travel by train from New York City to Washington on a weekly or biweekly basis. Unlike today with metal detectors at building entrances a way of life, Lee came and went on Capitol Hill in the 1930s with no fear of random bag checks. They met in her tiny, rented room situated in a thirteen-hundred-square-foot row house on Kenyon Street, just a mile or so from Capitol Hill near the campus of Howard University. There Bill removed his Leica camera with its folding tripod from an ordinary suitcase that he carried with him. Filming would start and methodically continue until all of the documents removed by Lee were copied. The following day, as she returned them to the proper file in the committee office, Weisband carrying the film made his way to Washington's Union Station for the return train trip to Bazarov in New York.

From early 1935 to the end of the committee's life around February 1936, Lee continued to supply Weisband with everything that passed through her hands. Among the massive tranche of secrets were dispatches from America's commercial attaché in Berlin filled with sensitive details on American corporations "working to arm Germany." She lifted hundreds of "secret reports" authored by American consulate officials in Berlin, Stuttgart, and Czechoslovakia. There were also "copious notes" prepared by Josephine Burns taken from documents she reviewed at the State Department.[15] When not pilfering State Department documents, she expanded Moscow's range of knowledge with finished War and Navy Department analyses based on reports sent from American military officials in Berlin. Typically, they were filled with all sorts of details relating to German industrial growth and output, weapons manufacture, military war plans, preparations, and exercises along with carefully researched estimates of Hitler's growing military strength.[16]

As February 1936 rolled around and the Nye committee's life came to an end, Weisband grew anxious to move Lee into a position that would keep the secrets flowing. Efforts to get her into the Department of Justice failed as it did with the Department of State, which was "reluctant to admit new employees while doing everything it can to avoid hiring Jews."[17]

The spring of 1936 found Lee in the hunt for new employment and Bill turning to another mission that would have a profound effect on his future.

## NOTES

1. Lee letter to Wohlforth, 6/1/1934, NARA RG 46, Senate Special Committee to Investigate the Munitions Industry, Box 115, Washington, DC.
2. Ibid.
3. Ibid.
4. Scott, author interview, June 3, 2018.
5. Wiltz, *In Search of Peace*, 54–59.
6. No author but most likely Raushenbush, Undated, Box 21 NARA Munitions file. Letter to Wohlforth C/O Mr. Larson Remington Arms, Bridgeport, CT, from Washington, October 6, 1934.
7. Haynes, Klehr, and Vasiliev, *Spies*, 161–67.
8. VBN 15.
9. VBN 14.
10. VBN 20.
11. VBN 14, VBN 39.
12. Christopher Andrew and Vasili Mitrokhin, *The Mitrokhin Archive* (New York: Basic Books, 1999), 46.
13. VBN 43.
14. VBN 18.
15. Wiltz, *In Search of Peace*, 59.
16. VBN 25.
17. VBN 33.

## Chapter 6

# Radio School

In 1864, the First Communist International, known as the International Working Men's Association, was created in London by Karl Marx. A Second Communist International begun in Paris in 1889 ended with the Bolshevik Revolution in November 1917 amid outcries that it had succumbed to the whims of social democrats. The Third International, known as the "Comintern," was first led by Gregori Zinoviev. He was replaced in 1926 by Nikolai Bukharin when Stalin falsely imprisoned Zinoviev for ten years for complicity in the assassination of Sergei Kirov, Leningrad party boss and Stalin rival. In the years to come, both men met their fate at the point of a gun in the basement of Moscow's notorious Lubyanka Prison during Stalin's purges. By July 1935, Georgi Dimitrov, a Bulgarian Communist and Stalin toady, had replaced them as the new Comintern boss with his headquarters at 36 Mokovaia Street across Red Square from Stalin's office in the Kremlin.

To the world beyond Russia the Comintern projected an image of independence; a spiritual and ideological center of communism with the stated purpose of coordinating, supporting, and directing similar national movements worldwide. In fact, it was much more than that. Since its founding, Lenin and then Stalin had routinely used it along with the GRU and KGB for foreign espionage with well-vetted agents trained at a secret school in Moscow.[1]

Known officially as the International Lenin School (ILS), it first opened its doors in 1926 and operated continuously until its closing in 1938. Two American students at the school who later turned on the Russians were Morris and Jack Childs. Morris was Moishe Chilovsky, born in 1902 in Kiev, and he and his younger brother, Jakob, were the children of Josef and Nechame Chilovsky. The father, a Jewish cobbler by trade, suffered from pogroms that struck periodically throughout czarist Russia. Clashes with police led to repeated imprisonment and finally his exile to the United States, where he settled in Chicago. For several years he ran his own shoe shop, saving enough money for his family to come to the United States in 1911.[2] Morris left school at age fourteen to apprentice in his father's shop before taking a job as a messenger in the city's financial district. While taking night courses at the Chicago Art Institute, he discovered radical politics, which combined with reports about the czar's overthrow prompted him to begin studying Marxist-Leninism thought. When the various radical groups coalesced in 1919 into the United Communist Party of America, Morris became a "charter member." Over the next decade, Morris's party devotion underwent a dramatic shift from philosophical support to direct action. As a milkman and union agitator, he soon acquired the moniker "Red Milkman"[3] among fellow workers and customers for his outspoken militancy and proselytizing. Later he gave up work completely to devote himself full time to Communist Party work.

In 1929, Moscow ordered him to put the Party behind and travel to Moscow for special training. Equipped with a false passport identifying him as "Harry Summers," a Detroit auto worker, Morris Childs sailed for Europe and made his way to Moscow, where his passport was taken from him (he wouldn't see it again until he departed the Soviet Union) and he was ensconced in a hotel that would be home for the next two years.

Life at the ILS was an Orwellian experience. Students from around the world living side by side referred to each other only by assigned pseudonyms or first names. Courses ranged from the writings of Marx and Lenin to those more practical in nature. There was training in firearms and explosives combined with practical exercises in guerilla warfare tactics such as bank robbery, political violence, sabotage, and train hijacking. Students were also indoctrinated in espionage tradecraft techniques like secret meeting procedures, safe house operations, courier methods, and detecting and eluding police surveillance.

The centralized nature of the Comintern required a global communications network; one that dictated avoidance of detection by local police through the use of a clandestine radio system. Students at ILS spent countless hours hunched over a transmitter sending and receiving streams of practice messages until they became proficient in the use of International Morse code. Proficiency was also required in quickly assembling and disassembling radios under wartime conditions and moving equipment undetected from one safe house to another. Knowing how long to remain on the air without fear of interception was also crucial. All for the purpose of maintaining contact with Dimitrov after returning to their home countries.

In setting up his far-flung messaging system, the one thing Dimitrov had not counted on was a rather shy retiring former schoolmaster named John Hessel Tiltman. Born in London in 1894, Tiltman, a Scotsman, joined the British Army at the age of twenty. He began World War I as a commissioned officer in the King's Own Scottish Regiment serving in France from October 1915 until wounds forced his evacuation in May 1917. After the war, while assigned to British forces in Siberia, he took an interest in the Russian language and upon returning to London in 1920 began a course of study in Russian after joining British military intelligence. After a brief course in Russian diplomatic ciphers, he was dispatched to Samta, a city in India's west Bengal region, where he spent the next nine years decoding Russian messages. In 1931, having retired from the military, he entered civilian service with the Government Codes and Cipher School (GC&CS) as a cryptanalyst. Soon his code-breaking skills and years of experience were put to the test against the Comintern message system. Ever self-effacing and characteristically calling himself a "general purpose diagnostician," Tiltman successfully solved the mystery of Dimitrov's worldwide message system. Over the course of the operation, code-named "MASK," Tiltman and his band of code breakers cracked more than fourteen thousand radio messages sent between Moscow and clandestine radio stations operating in Great Britain and most European capitals, as well as in New York and Harbin, China.[4]

MASK messages ran the gamut. They often carried instructions regarding fraudulent passports and visas, paying couriers, and warning of danger from local police raids. Others incorporated general themes supporting Moscow's line of the day for use in local propaganda attacks. "Organize through student's organizations" one typical message demanded, "together with other non-Fascist student . . . involving prominent professors important university cities, large mass demonstrations solidarity students with heroic Chinese students struggling for freedom their people, under slogan—'Down with Japanese imperialism in China.' Send protest delegations to Japanese Embassy."[5] One message containing a stinging rebuke took American Communist Party leaders to task for failing to indicate a person's nationality on a false passport. "We informed you many times that when you apply for a visa it is necessary for us to know name or surname of passport, and also for what purpose the person is coming."[6] Disposition of funds smuggled into a particular country for party activities was also an issue. In August 1935, Dimitrov authorized payments totaling more than $1,200 ($23,085 in 2019) for travel expenses to Moscow of Communist youth delegates from the United States, Cuba, Mexico, and Canada. Another ordered the American party to send $1,990 ($37,200 in 2019) to the Canadian Communist Party to help its work. In May 1936 a cell in Vancouver, Canada, was told to provide dependents of a Lenin School student code-named "Wilson" $65 ($1,197 in 2019) and Toronto student "Lawrence" $26 ($479 in 2019) covering the months of April, May, and June 1936.[7]

International shortwave communications over many thousands of miles of varying topography and oceans were always a headache for the Russians. A common problem that often threw operations into chaos were disruptions and breaks in messages due to atmospheric conditions. Many times, messages weren't received at all; a problem that often required a receiving station to insist that it be resent, forcing extended and often risky airtime. "ABRAHAM. Practically impossible to read your signals on your present wave-length due to heavy interference WIF. Please try to increase frequency sufficient to clear WIF."[8]

Beginning in July 1935, Dimitrov began registering other complaints of a more operational nature. One message sent to Stockholm criticized a radio operator for his sloppy encoding skills; a problem that often arose due to repeated code changes sent out by Moscow. "NEW YORK cannot decipher many of our telegrams. Please communicate the numbers of telegrams which were sent by you on July 18th and 19th to New York, and which begin with groups RAJYKJYUVS and GUHEVRIPTA"[9] In another, Moscow wrote to Prague: "Your telegram in new cipher up to Number 70 and Number 37 and 38 in the old cipher received."[10] Another Moscow to New York message laden with frustration complained about having sent a message five times, causing "great numbers of messages waiting for transmission." As a remedy for this heresy, Dimitrov ordered the New York operator to activate his radio on a "daily" (in violation of basic security rules) basis to confirm receipt of messages in order to "save us useless repetition."[11]

One particular focus of Dimitrov's ire was an unknown American radio operator with the code name MORGAN. In a series of messages during November 1935, Moscow demanded to know why MORGAN had failed to "establish good connection" while questioning if he had correctly "deciphered all telegrams" sent through him. Adding to MORGAN's woes was another Moscow message two weeks later demanding to know why he could not listen for their communications on Saturdays and wondering if he had "overworked himself" listening for their transmissions one hour every day. Over the next several months, MORGAN's situation only worsened with complaints that transmissions to Harbin, China, were "not in order" and insisting on answers why Harbin "cannot communicate with you." After a week with no apparent response, Moscow again blasted the New York station; this time reporting Harbin's complaint that MORGAN's telegram address had been "cancelled." Explanations were demanded as to why "you did not inform us in due time" and along with reasons for MORGAN's "intolerably neglectful" behavior.[12]

Moscow was beginning to have difficulty not only with MORGAN but with other communicators as well. The reasons remain unclear today, but what is clear is that the idea of sending agents back to Moscow for radio training had either become insecure in light of the growing tensions in the world or there was simply a growing shortage of operators willing to do the work.

In either case, Moscow made a stopgap decision to remedy the problem by tasking its stations to find schools in their area where highly vetted and trusted agents could receive radio training. On March 9, 1936, Moscow sent a message to New York City, Stockholm, London, and Copenhagen demanding immediate answers to a series of questions in an attempt to solve this growing concern.

> In your country there are official and private wireless schools. It is desirable to find 5 to 7 tested and suitable party members, particularly from Youth, of suitable technical education to send to these schools, so that they may complete the full course. Expenses of the course to be charged to our account. In case the student's visit involves the giving up of his profession, we will bear the full expense of such a candidate. Report your practical proposals on this question, and as urgently as possible.[13]

In a separate communication to New York on March 23, 1936, Moscow posed a second series of questions. "What short term courses for radio operators are there in your country, and of what duration are they?" Were "private courses" a possibility and under whose control were they offered and operated? Worrying about US government registration, Moscow asked if the operator was then "registered somewhere" or required to work with the government. And, finally, what are the "conditions for admission and what are the fees asked for?"[14]

That same month, as messages flew between Moscow and New York and Lee's employment with the Nye committee ended, Bill suddenly enrolled at the RCA Institutes as a night student on Moscow's orders. RCA Institutes specialized in the emerging field of radio engineering. Located on the sixteenth floor of the Holland Plaza Building, it took up a city block at 71 Varick Street adjacent to the Canal Street subway entrance in Manhattan. The school was founded in 1919 by Guglielmo Marconi, a Nobel Prize winner and Italian engineer credited with inventing wireless telegraphy. According to its advertising brochures, the school was "devoted exclusively to instruction in Radio and Electrical Communications and associated electronic arts."[15]

The curriculum consisted of four terms a year, each about three months long with offerings in two programs. The first, a two-year program called the "General Course," required a total of eight terms with daily attendance both morning and afternoon from Monday through Friday. For part-time students, night classes were available for twenty terms spread over five years. A second and less comprehensive General Course, also available for day students, made up six terms with evening classes lasting sixteen terms for a period of four years. A second Commercial Radio Operating Course was also offered. It provided a "thorough knowledge of the radio industry as a whole"; completion of the program promised graduates success in the "U.S. Government commercial second-class radio telegraph and first-class radio-telephone operators license examination."[16] Such a license, the school trumpeted, would open doors to careers as a radio operator at commercial radio stations, aboard ships, in airports and aircraft, in police radio fields, and in point-to-point communication services.

For Weisband, like most students at the school, the costs were staggering. Tuition and supplies amounted to $225 ($3,700 in February 2019). Individual classes could also be taken for a cost of $225 paid at a rate of $9 per week ($161 per week in February 2019) for day students and $4 per week ($72 per week in February 2019).[17]

While still employed at the Waldorf-Astoria Hotel, Weisband started a Moscow-financed General Course as an evening student in March 1936, remaining continually enrolled until June 1937. Weisband also used some of Russia's funds to buy a new car just months before starting school in May 1936. When not working and attending to Lee, he was studying such technical topics as mathematics and physics, electrical engineering, applied acoustics and radio engineering. Following an unexplained five-month absence from December 1937 to April 1938, he reenrolled in the Commercial Radio Operating (CRO) course through February 1939, learning to send and receive coded messages at a rate of twenty-five per minute. In addition, he studied traffic procedures, US government laws and regulations, and computation tools. It appears that he completed the two-term CRO course and spent the remainder concentrating on Morse code skills as a day student. For reasons unknown he abruptly ended his studies without a diploma.

The records of RCA Institute offer insight into his frenetic and almost nomadic lifestyle during this time. They show him living at four different addresses: 342 68th Street, Brooklyn; 7617 54th Avenue, Brooklyn; 8320 5th Avenue, Brooklyn, in August 1938; and back at 7022 Ridge Boulevard, Brooklyn, in September 1937 and January 1939. Investigators later found a letter in the school's archives sent by Weisband. He claimed to be in Saratoga, New York, staying at a hotel called "The Spotswood." He was recovering from rheumatism, which would take a couple of weeks, and requested permission to take correspondence courses.[18] While the Kremlin paid Bill Weisband's full tuition, the record is blank as to whether Weisband ever acted as a radio operator communicating with Moscow.

Three months later his father, Israel, died suddenly in August 1936. A week later, after six years at the Waldorf-Astoria and three months as an RCA student, he quit his job.

It was still the height of the Depression, and he was now on the KGB payroll full-time, unencumbered by conventional employment and free to concentrate on his Russian-sponsored radio education and any other assignment the Kremlin might send his way.

One of them, as it turned out, was an escapade that would land him in jail.

## NOTES

1. Pavel Sudoplatov and Anatoli Sudoplatov, *Special Tasks* (Boston: Little Brown and Company, 1994), 51.
2. John Baron, *Operation SOLO* (Washington, DC: Regnery Press, 1996), 19.
3. Ibid.
4. "John H. Tiltman," *Cryptologic Quarterly*, October 28, 2011; John H. Tiltman, Oral History, December 11, 1978, National Security Agency, National Cryptologic Museum.
5. Moscow to US, No. 22–23, 1–16, 1936, 317–54.
6. Moscow to US, No. 198, 6/19/1935, 317/1.
7. Moscow to US, No. 305–6, 6-3-1936, 317/167.
8. London to Moscow to London, No. 27, September 26, 1935.
9. Moscow to Stockholm, No. 317, July 28, 1935, 318/29.
10. Moscow to Prague, No. 9, September 17, 1935, 318/51.
11. Moscow to US, September 21, 1935.
12. Moscow to US, Nos. 97–99, November 19, 1935, 317/47.
13. Moscow to Stockholm, Copenhagen, London, and the United States, Nos. 130–31, March 9, 1936, 321/257.
14. Moscow to US, No. 121, March 23, 1936.
15. Soviet military intelligence station in Shanghai starting in the late 1920s was run by Alexander Gurwich, an officer who had honed his skills while working in New York. During his stay he studied at the Radio Corporation of America, where he concentrated on the operation of long-range transmitters. Svetlana Lokhova, *The Spy Who Changed History* (New York: Pegasus Books, 2019), 183.
16. RCA Institutes Catalogue of Courses, 1937, Radio and Television Museum, Bowie, Maryland.
17. Ibid.
18. New York Report, June 16, 1950, Weisband FBI file.

## Chapter 7

# Pollock

It was a Thursday, November 3, 1938, when a sleep-starved Bill Weisband finally walked out of the Wadsworth Avenue police station in New York City after two nights in jail.

His legal headaches began two months earlier with a woman whom he seriously underestimated. Lillian Barrett was the manager at 183 Haven Avenue, an unpretentious apartment building situated four blocks east of Fort Washington Park, less than a mile south of the George Washington Bridge.

More than a decade later, Barrett could still describe her experience to FBI agents. She remembered Weisband's "dirty and disheveled" appearance as he casually approached her one day on the sidewalk in front of the building. He asked about available rentals and pointed to his luggage while claiming to have additional items stored at the local railroad station. Standing next to him was another stranger who Barrett remembered staring at her "malevolently" yet uttering not a word.[1] Weisband excused his friend's silence, telling Barrett that the man neither spoke nor understood English and all rental transactions would have to be conducted through him.

When she expressed concern over how the two men would maintain the place, Weisband quickly assured her that he planned to hire a cleaning lady. Barrett was suspicious but, absent any evidence and anxious to rent an available apartment, she made the deal. Weisband paid the rent flashing a large roll of bills that Barrett estimated in the thousands; she later described him as a "walking branch of the Treasury Department."[2] The next day she was surprised to see the two men exiting an automobile parked at the curb having thought they had arrived in the city by train.

To ensure that they kept their word about cleanliness, she visited apartment 10E "several times" over the next few weeks while the two men were out. Snooping around she discovered some unusual things that troubled her. None of the baggage they had told her about had been moved into the place. A check of the closets revealed new and expensive wardrobes. She thought it curious that the window shades were drawn "at all times" of the day and night. Scattered around on chairs and tables were racing programs, suggesting daily attendance at the racetrack. She also spied textbooks on codes and, from something Weisband said, she believed that he was a student at a radio school in New York.³

Barrett's periodic visits continued for the next six weeks until one day she surprised the two men as they were gathering their belongings in a hasty attempt to vacate. When she demanded the rent, Weisband turned on her, becoming abusive and refusing to pay. Frightened by his behavior she promptly called the police and had them both arrested. The cops later told her that Weisband had $350 ($6,449 in January 2020) in his pocket and had leased another apartment in the Jackson Heights section of Queens, New York.

After being released from jail, Weisband wasted no time starting damage control by reporting his predicament to his Comintern bosses. The stranger arrested with Weisband had been sent to the prison hospital at Ellis Island after the police learned he had illegally entered the United States. A day or two later, the man who claimed to speak no English found himself meeting with Isaac Shorr, one of the nation's top immigration and civil liberties lawyers.

The fifty-four-year-old Russian-born Shorr came to America at age twenty and soon found work as a cigarmaker while attending law school at New York University. Two years after graduation in 1913, he was admitted to the New York Bar. During World War I he served as counsel for the American Civil Liberties Union and in 1920 represented sixty clients caught up in Attorney General A. Mitchel Palmer's failed attempt to deport illegal aliens in what today is remembered as the Palmer Red Raids. Teaming with famed attorney Clarence Darrow in 1927, Shorr gained notoriety for his role in the acquittal of two anarchist tailors charged with murdering two Fascists named Nicholas Amaroso and Joseph Caruso.⁴

In 1924, Shorr joined the law firm of Joseph Brodsky, noted anarchist lawyer and chief counsel for International Labor Defense, the legal arm of the CPUSA. Brodsky was already recognized for his work as a defense lawyer in the so-called Scottsboro Boys case. A third firm member was a young partner named Carol Weiss King, who later gained her own notoriety for defending such prominent communists as labor leader Harry Bridges, Gerhart Eisler, and J. Peters.

Once in custody, Immigration and Naturalization Service (INS) officers identified the mystery man as John Francis Pollock. Investigation determined that he had previously been arrested for an expired visa and having been smuggled into the country on September 3, 1933, for $45 ($880 in March 2020).

Pollock was born in Ciobota, Russia, on March 7, 1907, to Frank Pollock and his wife, Katarina Vicrel. According to his INS testimony, he and his parents along with a sister, Malvina, arrived in Canada in 1915, settling there until his illegal entry into the United States in 1933. To the frustration of INS he refused to furnish any details of his time in Canada or his entry into the United States. He claimed he never worked for a living but rather lived with a woman for four years, again refusing to divulge any details about their relationship.

A decade or so later, the FBI displayed a photograph of Pollock to sources within the Communist Party and the Comintern. One of them, Louis Giberti, instantly recognized Pollock as a member of the Communist Party in New York around 1930. He described him as a highly skilled tool and die maker working in Pennsylvania who spoke English with an accent and was a talented public speaker. The two men worked together on a weekly basis, becoming well acquainted through the "Friends of the Soviet Union" (FSU).[5] Giberti told the FBI that at that time Friends of the Soviet Union was actively recruiting comrades in the United States with machine skills to send to the Soviet Union to work in factories in an effort to advance their economy.

A week after his arrest, Pollock's $500 ($9,100 in 2019) bond was posted when a woman calling herself "Lena Dietrich" approached Shorr with the funds. She gave her address as 135 Haven Avenue, across the block from Weisband and Pollock's safe house. INS investigators determined the address to be the office of J.A.B. Inc., a realty company that owned and operated a building at 735 West 172nd Street, which faced Haven Avenue. When questioned, Mr. James Bradley, president of J.A.B., explained that 135 Haven Avenue had always been the company's headquarters, and no one had ever resided there as a tenant. A check of the records for both addresses failed to show anyone named Lena Dietrich nor any employment for her. To further muddle matters, investigators found that Shorr was retained by an individual named "Hy Rosenberg," a friend of Pollock, whose address was interestingly listed as 41 Union Square, the same address as the Brodsky law firm.[6]

Upon examination by physicians at Ellis Island, Pollock was diagnosed as insane and released on the Dietrich-supplied bond on November 17, 1938. Shorr later told INS investigators that prior to Pollock's release he had made arrangements to send him to Silvercrest Sanitorium, a psychiatric facility located in Astoria, Long Island. When the date of his release came, however, Pollock, suddenly seeming "quite normal," expressed no interest in going to a sanitorium and instead was released to his home at 138 Haven Avenue. He was never seen again.[7]

Four years after Pollock's disappearance, Shorr was evasive when INS investigators again questioned him. He had heard nothing from him since his release nor did he know where Pollock was living. He suspected that Pollock had fled the country and would not be returning but had no details. As for the Dietrich-supplied bond, all he could remember was being approached by a woman claiming to be Pollock's common law wife. He did remember her name but his efforts to find Lena Dietrich had been equally futile.

Two years before his encounter with Mrs. Barrett, Bill had confidently strode into Brooklyn federal court planning to raise his right hand and swear allegiance to the United States as a new citizen. What Bill had not counted on was the presiding magistrate, Grover Moscowitz. As Weisband stood gaping in stunned silence, the fifty-one-year-old judge began rattling off a litany of offenses that would stall any dreams Bill had of earning his citizenship. It seems, the judge announced, that INS investigators had uncovered problems with his application. Over the past few years, Moscowitz told the packed court room, Weisband had willfully flaunted local laws by racking up multiple traffic violations and dozens of unpaid parking tickets. The judge demanded answers. In what one reporter characterized as a "tearful plea," Weisband played the victim, going on the offensive with vehement remonstrations against the judge and the charges.[8] The blame, he charged, should be directed not at him but rather his brother, who was the owner of the car, making him the responsible party. It was a ploy that Weisband would use again and again over the years to come when trapped in a self-made crisis. Clearly unmoved, Moscowitz ordered him to pay his fines before any citizenship application could be considered.[9]

One month after his arrest and Pollock's disappearance, a smiling Weisband was again in Brooklyn federal court standing before Judge Mortimer Byers. Having no record that Weisband was unemployed, nor his confrontation with Mrs. Barrett a month earlier, and the lies on his application about working as a hotel "room clerk," Byers signed the necessary forms on December 8, 1938, while congratulating him on finally earning his citizenship.[10] Bill then proudly raised his right hand, solemnly committing himself to the "principles of the Constitution of the United States and . . . good order and happiness of the United States."

Over the next two and a half years, Bill's steady pattern of shiftlessness, womanizing, spying, radio courses, gambling, and drifting from one brief hotel job to another held true to course. In 1939 he was fired after one day at the New York World's Fair for "sleeping" on the job. Then came another night auditor job at the Hotel Devon for six months, where he was remembered as "sleeping on occasions when he should have been awake" and blaming his fatigue on another unspecified day job.[11]

Then in May 1941, without warning, Moscow issued new orders to Link. Drop everything in New York, pull up roots, and move on to a new mission three thousand miles away.

## NOTES

1. New York Report, June 16, 1950, Weisband FBI file.
2. Ibid.
3. Ibid.
4. "Two Fascists Slain," *New York Daily News*, May 27, 1921.
5. New York Report, June 16, 1950, Weisband FBI file.
6. New York Report, June 16, 1950, Weisband FBI file.
7. Ibid.
8. "Thinks Washington Is Mayor, So Peddler Is Banned as Citizen," *Brooklyn Daily Eagle*, February 24, 1938.
9. Ibid.
10. NY Petition of Naturalization, 12/8/38, Federal Records Center, New York City, NARA.
11. NYO Report, June 16, 1950, Weisband FBI file.

## Chapter 8

# Failure

By all accounts he was a nice guy. A gentle soul who seemed to exist in another universe. Someone who would give you the shirt off his back and ask nothing in return. A sucker for a hard-luck story, he thought nothing of handing large sums of cash to strangers and then staying in touch with them to see how life was developing. His Cadillac, Pierce-Arrow, and two ancient Rolls-Royces rarely started. An amateur poet, he also composed lyrics for songs that he was convinced would top the Hollywood charts but, like everything else in his life, never amounted to anything.

Money was always a puzzle for him. What little income he earned soon vanished into one cockeyed scheme after another. It was his caprices and instability that drove his wife away, taking their only son with her. He rarely saw the child again. When life finally overwhelmed him, he simply reinvented himself under another name and disappeared without a trace only to resurface many months later. Friends and family gradually dismissed his mercurial behavior, viewing him as an anomaly. No one, however, could remotely fathom the dark side of his compartmented life, one he never allowed to surface. This strange little man was "Needle"—a code name assigned to him by the KGB as one of its most important spies among a large stable of important spies.[1]

Jones Orin York, or "Joe" or "Joy," as he was often called, the oldest of four children, was born in the town of Bushnell, Illinois, on August 5, 1893, to George York, a farmhand, and Myrtle, a homemaker. A childhood accident that twisted his knee joint inward left him with a distinctive limp that nagged him for the rest of his life. Standing barely 5'6" and weighing 155 pounds, he had an unimpressive countenance despite sporting a thin brown mustache and a goatee.

After finishing grammar school, he spent four years at Western Illinois State Normal School in Macomb, Illinois, about ten miles southwest of Bushnell. The school, later known as Western Illinois University, had a small student body studying to become teachers. For a year, the nineteen-year-old York also took correspondence courses through the International Correspondence School.

In 1914, Jones York made a fateful decision that would affect the rest of life. He left Bushnell heading west for California, where he moved in with a relative. For a time, he bounced from job to job, starting with Western Electric Company as a telephone switchboard installer. After striking out on his own in a failed grocery store venture, Jones turned to automobiles as a mechanic and salesman selling cars to returning World War I veterans. His marriage in 1915 to his hometown sweetheart, Alice McNeil, produced one child, a son named Gayle, born in 1918.[2]

\* \* \*

Jones York's passion for flying was boundless, yet he never learned to fly. He called himself an "aeronautical engineer" but had only a high school diploma.[3] Like countless other Americans caught up in the flying frenzy of the 1920s, York began taking flying lessons at a little airport near Glendale, California. Next came the York Aeronautical Engineering Company, an aircraft design firm he started in 1925. He then opened a school teaching aircraft ground operations at Long Beach, California, followed by solo lecturing and a resurrection of York Aeronautical Engineering. All ended in failure.

The cascading series of business defeats, no money, a wife and child to support, and no income produced a sense of failure that would remain a theme in York's life. When life became too overwhelming, he would suddenly, with no warning, and just the clothes on his back, flee California heading north. Eventually his journey took him to the vast Oregon wilderness, where he wasted away for months living in tents and self-built shanties. After a year of life in the rough, he would return to Los Angeles, facing the same woes compounded by no job, no money, and a wife who had despaired of his antics. Within months she left him, but not before securing a monthly alimony and child support settlement of $75 ($1,334 in 2017).[4]

York's descent into the world of spying soon came courtesy of a man who, it is said, recruited a generation of Americans working in the aviation industry. So skilled and successful was he as an intelligence officer that the SVR (Russian Foreign Intelligence Service) prominently displays his photograph today on a wall in its Hall of Fame.

**NOTES**

1. VBN 9–10.

2. Los Angeles Report, June 7, 1939, FBI file entitled "Jones Orin York, alias Joy York," number 65–2223, FOIPA.
3. Ibid.
4. Ibid.

## Chapter 9

# Blerio

Stanislav Shumovsky's KGB code name was "Blerio." He chose it in honor of the man he most admired—famed French aviator Louis Blerio, the first person to fly a plane across the English Channel from France to Great Britain.[1]

The eldest of four boys, he was born on May 9, 1902, to a Polish couple living in the Ukrainian city of Kharkov. His father's influential position as an accountant for the czar's treasury service opened doors for his sons, including a high-quality education at Kharkov's exclusive Gymnasium.

As something of a prodigy, Shumovsky excelled from an early age in science, mathematics, and linguistics, mastering French, German, Polish, and Ukrainian by his late teens. Czar Nicholas II's abdication in 1917 and Lenin's seizure of power soon ushered in a civil war that roiled across Russia for the next five years. The ensuing chaos and dislocation led the fifteen-year-old Shumovsky to join the Red Army. By 1922, as a hardened veteran and Bolshevik barely twenty years old with a new wife and daughter, he turned to a new passion for flying. Three years later he was a pilot with Red Army's 2nd Independent Reconnaissance Squadron, having made his first solo flight in a two-seater Polikarpov R-1 aircraft. The flying career he yearned for, however, soon came to a nearly deadly end when a crash left him with a permanent arm injury.

It was the mid-1920s with Stalin's Five-Year Plan to industrialize his country in full-swing when Stan left active military service (he remained in the reserves) to help advance the nation's modernization. The plan had a threefold purpose: creating an educated population, developing a modern industrial society, and securing Russia's borders from foreign threats. Achieving these ambitious goals required a small army of bright and educated young Russians to spearhead the effort.

As a new civilian, Shumovsky took up the challenge by signing on as an investigator in the armaments industry. His wide-ranging mission required assessment of the country's industrial ability to supply the armed forces with sufficient quantities of munitions under battlefield conditions over long time periods. Shumovsky's astute analysis exposing major structural flaws in the system caught the attention of Andrei Tupolev, one of Stalin's leading young aircraft designers, and a man who would gain world fame years later designing many of Russia's finest aircraft. So impressed was Tupolev with Shumovsky's findings that he promptly chose him to conduct a similar study of Russia's nascent aircraft industry.

At the time Tupolev, peering over the horizon, sensed that for Russia to achieve a state-of-the-art aircraft industry, young professionals like Shumovsky would have to study the successes of other countries and steal the knowledge for the Soviet Union. Shumovsky would be the prototype of a new intelligence officer; a bright, multilingual, sophisticated, well-educated, battle-hardened pilot capable of meeting with and wooing important Western capitalists. Shumovsky soon found himself living two lives: one in the world of aircraft, the other learning the art of espionage. For a full year he attended foreign intelligence school, absorbing the fine points of spying under the watchful eyes of instructors steeped in the art of surveillance, avoiding capture, assessing human weaknesses, and recruiting spies.

Shumovsky's spying career came to life on September 27, 1931, when he descended the gangplank of the SS *Europa* in New York along with seventy-five other Russian students. All were destined for America's finest universities. After a brief stay at the Hotel Lincoln (where Weisband had worked a year or so earlier), he boarded a Boston-bound train with twenty-two other Russian scholars. Six were destined for Harvard while Stan, and another fifteen, settled along the banks of the Charles River at the Massachusetts Institute of Technology (MIT)—his home for the next three years.

Shumovsky was one of thirty students chosen yearly for MIT's Course 16, the prestigious undergraduate aeronautics program within the mechanical engineering department. The challenges he faced were herculean. Lectures were conducted in English, a language he neither spoke, read, nor wrote. Absorbing the many foreign technical journals essential for course and laboratory work meant relearning French and German. Yet for Stan and the KGB, the task was well worth it; he was now nestled, as his biographer wrote, "among the world's finest aeronautical engineers" and "industry leaders as well."[2]

Photos of Shumovsky taken at the time reveal a tall, thin young man, ramrod-straight posture, his hairline as he approached his thirties already receding at the temples. Dressed in a dark, well-cut American-style business suit and tie, he conveys an intense and thoughtful countenance as he peers into the distance through rimless metal eyeglasses perched on a large nose. This makes sense, as his delicate mission called for "a first-class education necessary to be able to operate at the highest levels as a [scientific and technical] spy and aviation expert."[3]

Spotting and assessing potential candidates for espionage was mandatory. But risking capture by trying to recruit teachers or fellow students was out of the question.

In 1931, however, such an opportunity presented itself when a chance encounter, probably in a lecture hall, brought Stan into contact with a fellow student from Boston; a brilliant eighteen-year-old freshman named Benjamin Smilg.

Over the next three years, Shumovsky skillfully wormed his way into the Smilg family home. Ben was born in 1913, a year after his father, Harry, a forty-year-old leather cutter for a local shoe factory, and his thirty-eight-year-old wife Rebecca settled in Boston after arriving in America from Russia. Nearly a decade older than Ben, Stan probably recognized the hero worship of an American kid from a poor Jewish family living on the margins for a worldly older and sophisticated Russian military pilot who shared much in common with the Smilg family. Two decades later when the FBI finally interviewed Harry and Rebecca, they still remembered Stan fondly as their son's tutor and close friend; always open, jovial, and never "without a smile" during his many evenings and weekend stays at the Smilg home.

The fate of the Smilg family still living in Russia was always a central topic of conversation. Rebecca, in particular, appreciated Stan's frequent and solicitous offers of help from his Moscow associates in locating them. Fully aware of the dangerous game he was playing and unwilling to take any unnecessary chances, Shumovsky routinely kept his Moscow bosses informed of his progress in developing "Lever" (Smilg's KGB code name) as a potential long-term source. One KGB report described Smilg as a member of Shumovsky's group, whose immigrant Russian-Jewish "family has a very friendly attitude toward the USSR." It noted that after "graduating from high school thanks to exceptional abilities he was accepted at [MIT] for a free education, where [Smilg] was always one of the most brilliant students."[4]

After two years of intense assessment, Shumovsky risked all with a successful pitch to Smilg of cooperation with Russia based on a pull for the "old country" and its desperate need for assistance. Smilg eagerly accepted and began supplying aircraft secrets from the moment he graduated from MIT beginning with his first job at the Budd Corporation in Philadelphia, next at Glenn L. Martin Company, a major manufacturer of naval aircraft, and finally at Wright Field in Dayton, Ohio—the center of US military aircraft research and development.

Smilg pinpointed for Shumovsky Wright Field's importance. It was the "repository" for all types of aircraft data received from military attaches serving around the world. Wright also collected intelligence on the characteristics of German and Soviet aircraft shot down in Spain during the civil war. Blueprints and other proprietary technical data from American aviation companies were also held there as well under lock and key. One 1944 KGB report offered a hint of Smilg's contributions. "He provided materials on a dirigible, calculations on the vibrations of bomber assemblies, NACA materials." (NACA was the National Advisory Committee for Aeronautics, the predecessor to the National Aeronautics and Space Administration.)[5]

By the start of the 1930s, America had become for the Russians a benchmark for modern aircraft design and production. Such American aircraft pioneers as Donald Douglas and Jack Northrup were held as giants of the new science and technology of flight, with new innovations seemingly rolling out daily. Russian attitude toward this American phenomenon was summed up in an article published in Moscow.

> What accounts for the high level of American aviation technology? . . . The whole secret lies in excellent organization of scientific research and experimental work with results deployed through mass production. I state up front that the Americans have no rivals in this field. The Soviet Union must take special care to examine the American experience of research in aviation and apply it to the science of socialist planning.[6]

In the summer of 1935, Shumovsky's mentor, Andrei Tupolev, arrived in New York on a mission to examine this so-called American experience in aviation. Accompanied by his wife, Julia, and principal deputy Alexander Arkhangelsky, he set out by car from New York for what would be a ten-thousand-mile, three-month odyssey crisscrossing the full breadth of the United States. As none of them spoke English, they were accompanied on their tour by Shumovsky serving as translator. The previous year he graduated from MIT and was now working undercover for Amtorg while also an MIT graduate student working on a graduate thesis in aeronautical engineering. It was a dual cover that neatly fit with his espionage duties as well. Four years in America had familiarized him with Americans, the way they thought and their ways of doing things. His foremost quality, however, for Tupolev was the personal contacts he had made and cultivated with the nation's leading lights in aircraft development and production. Shumovsky was now forced to keep up a relentless pace serving both as the KGB's aviation expert and the main contact for TsAGI, the Soviet Center for Aircraft Design. Throughout 1935, Shumovsky traveled to California to represent Tupolev and at the same time with the goal of "cultivation of and recruitment of workers in the Douglas and Northrup factories."[7]

This was not Tupolev's first visit to America. In 1930, his travels took him around the country to dozens of aircraft factories and research centers where he carefully recorded the latest methods of production and insight into quality control and efficiency. For this visit Tupolev had ordered Shumovsky to lay out an exhausting itinerary that incorporated companies he had previously visited along with new ones that had sprung up over the previous five years.

Starting on Long Island with officials of Gruman Aviation, he went north to Boston for meetings with the MIT aeronautics faculty. The caravan of cars, seven in all, then headed west to Ohio, stopping at Wright Field in Dayton and on to the northwest for a tour of the Boeing Company plant in Seattle, Washington. From the Pacific Northwest they journeyed south hundreds of miles through Oregon and hugging the California coastline to Los Angeles. Waiting for them were Cal-Tech scientists along with a large cluster of Depression-burdened aircraft companies, struggling to stay profitable and eager to sell aircraft to anyone with money.

After thousands of miles of travel Tupolev, commanding a budget of $600,000, finally dipped into his purse to purchase two planes for $170,000. They were a DC-2 from Douglas and another civilian and military version of the same aircraft, the DC-2E, from the Northrup Company.

At the start of 1936 following Tupolev's return to Moscow, a group of Russian engineers arrived in Los Angeles to monitor the assembly of the two planes and oversee the implementation of requirements for Russian transliteration of aircraft service manuals and parts along with correct Cyrillic words properly etched on the planes' many dials and knobs, and so on. One of the changes they insisted on was the repositioning of machine guns on the wings of the plane. York had a major role to play in this change as he was working at the time with Douglas as an armaments engineer.

York met with the group regularly, and one of these anonymous Russian technicians who was fluent in English struck up an acquaintance with him that soon proved valuable for both Tupolev and the KGB. York soon found himself socializing with the Russian group and going out with them often for drinks and dinner. He later recalled one evening when he got so drunk that one of the group had to drive him home. York, having no sense of security, soon began opening up about his past in what Shumovsky's biographer described as "meaning of life" conversations. Over a steady diet of cocktails, he poured out more and more of his personal frustrations, filling in particulars about his failed marriage and business disasters. He described himself as an excellent engineer who was inadequately compensated for his work and ill-appreciated by management for his accomplishments. The Russians learned that in addition to his job at Northrup, he owned a company designing engines and fuselages. His business was causing him financial woes as well. The rapidly mounting costs of developing a new motor, then in the experimental stage, had dangerously overextended him, forcing him to take a bank loan for $500 ($10,661 in 2023) to "reorganize" York Aircraft Ltd., on a salary of $2,100 a year.[8]

Listening carefully and sympathetically to York's endless tale of woe was a Russian engineer named Bolayev. Although not an intelligence officer, Bolayev was still required to look for potential recruits. Soon he began sending York's complaints to Amtorg for passage to Shumovsky. In one report Bolayev noted that "(York) joined Lockheed and is designing a super high-speed air cruiser." He "designs all of the weapons for it." Over the next year while they worked side by side, the Russian carefully watched York's every move to ensure that he was genuine and not a plant by the local counterintelligence service.[9]

In the fall of 1936, the moment came for Moscow to make its move on York. Using the imminent departure of the Russian delegation at the end of their stay, Shumovsky arranged a celebration dinner to honor the occasion, making certain that York sat next to him. As the evening's festivities went on, Shumovsky chatted up York and in doing so skillfully engaged him in a lengthy conversation. By the end of the night, York had confirmed that his bosses don't "pay him enough and he wants to start his own business." When York brought up his new engine design, Shumovsky feigned interest, suggesting that he send the plans to Moscow for an opinion from specialists who work on similar things.[10]

During a two-week stretch in November 1936, Shumovsky staged a series of carefully calibrated lunches and dinners with York designed to tease out further insights while boosting his ego and increasing his sense of hope for a deal with the Russians. Venues were particularly important. They were always swank restaurants around Los Angeles such as the lavish Biltmore Hotel. Shumovsky always picked up the tab. These relaxed exchanges over cocktails and hearty meals, which tended to lower York's guard and loosen his tongue, produced deeper conversations allowing the intelligence professional to probe for what made York tick, what were his hopes and aspirations, was his behavior just an act conceived by American authorities to lure Shumovsky and the KGB into controlled operation that could lead to arrest. Most importantly, would York's personal and financial pressures push him enough to accept an offer to spy for the Soviet Union?

Finally satisfied that he had what he needed, Shumovsky began drawing his victim into a conspiracy. After some prodding using a business approach, York agreed to a "commercial" arrangement with the Russian government for further development of his new motor. They agreed that as he made progress, the blueprints and drawings would be sent to Moscow for review. Shumovsky gave the stunned York a down payment of $1,600 ($29,400 in January 2019) on the spot to defray the expenses for his work on the motor.[11]

Now that York had agreed, Shumovsky dropped the bomb that could result in his arrest when he also expressed interest in receiving Northrup company information. As York gasped, Shumovsky quickly stressed that initiatives like Tupolev's visit to California and the Russian delegation at Northrup and elsewhere were meant to protect Russia from Germany, which was threatening war for the second time in the last twenty years. Shumovsky assured York that his heroic efforts would be greatly appreciated and could result in the life or death of Stan's country. With the $1,600 hanging in the balance, York agreed, offering the rationalization for treachery as "some measure of cooperation on my part would eventually result in furthering my own ambitions, as well as strengthen [Russia's] position in relation to their location between Germany on the West and Japan on the East." Soon after this meeting Shumovsky confidently reported to Moscow that "Needle" initially "resisted but was ultimately convinced." As an offering York provided Shumovsky with the "mechanism for dropping bombs and reloading mechanism for machine guns."[12]

In January 1936, Shumovsky cemented the relationship over more dinners. It was around this time he made the decision to move York's meetings from the open to the clandestine. He told him that his busy schedule, which kept him busy crisscrossing the country, made it difficult to meet him on a regular basis. For his protection as well as Shumovsky's, he would introduce York to someone who would contact him and follow his progress on a regular basis.

## NOTES

1. Svetlana Lokhova, *The Spy Who Changed History*, 126.
2. Ibid., 115.
3. Ibid., 146.
4. Ibid., 141.
5. Lokhova, *The Spy Who Changed History*, 136–37; Haynes, Klehr, and Vassiliev, *Spies*, 369–70.
6. Lokhova, *The Spy Who Changed History*, 247; Haynes, Klehr, and Vassiliev, *Spies*, 369–70.
7. Ibid., 251.
8. Ibid., 249.
9. VBN 23.
10. Haynes, Klehr, and Vassiliev, *Spies*, 366.
11. LA Report, May 5, 1950, York FBI file, BVN 24.
12. Haynes, Klehr, and Vassiliev, *Spies*, 366.

## Chapter 10

# Brooks and Werner

Shumovsky was too high-profile to risk receiving secrets from an American spy. His dealings with important American business executives were vital for Moscow's rearmament agenda. With this in mind, Moscow Center assigned York to their illegal apparatus barely six weeks after his agreement to spy.

In the corner of a quiet Los Angeles restaurant one evening, Shumovsky introduced York to a mystery man known to the KGB as "Eduard."[1] Little about him was memorable. He was well-proportioned and in his mid-thirties with a stocky build: York thought he was a draftsman or a mechanical engineer. When he was nervous, which was often the case, he would complain about the pressures of underground work.

Eduard spoke English with a Slavic accent that sometimes caused him problems with American idioms. York still laughed years later when he confused "I sent him to hell" for "I told him to go to hell." Sometimes he bragged about his skill at recognizing the difference between educated and well-educated Russians from the way they spoke. York never knew his real name but knew him only as "Brooks," a professional in the world of *konspiratsiia* who spoke much but offered little about himself.[2]

"Eduard" or "Brooks" was Emanual David Locke, born in Odessa, Russia, in 1894. After landing in America in 1920 he was naturalized in San Francisco six years later while taking technical courses at the University of California. Locke joined the KGB as a courier in the early 1930s operating between California and New York. Moscow Center dispatched him to Harbin, China, in the guise of a salesman for a bogus business called American Products Company. Back in America in 1934, he was tasked to assess Bluma Karp, a Russian immigrant who settled with her family in New York. Naturalized in 1923, she found work as a translator for the Office of Naval Intelligence in Washington, DC, after graduating from Columbia University in 1929. A second assignment came from Lillian Scharnoff, an important Russian agent in New York. She connected him with Shumovsky in preparation for his return to California to handle York.[3]

The meetings between York and Locke were carefully scripted to avoid police detection. Monthly rendezvous occurred during daylight hours at Westlake Park on Wilshire Boulevard in the heart of busy Los Angeles. The park was named for Henricus Wallace Westlake, a Canadian physician, who donated the property to the city. The parkland with its large lake and meandering trails led strollers to a statue of Dr. Westlake, ideal for agent meetings. Future meeting dates and times were always set at a previous meeting to avoid confusion and unnecessary contact.

The basic pattern of their discussions was always the same. Brooks would first question York about his life and then stress the need for constant security. Following this casual chitchat, York handed Brooks a "bulky package" in an unopened manila envelope. Inside were blueprints, technical data, and penciled sketches on yellow-lined paper pilfered from his employer. York had little difficulty removing the documents, which he hid under his shirt or belt as he left work in the evening. Brooks, in turn, handed York an envelope filled with cash and a receipt for York to sign as "Rene" or "Orin."[4]

In the beginning, Locke never opened York's packages but merely passed them to Shumovsky in a time-consuming and dangerous procedure when he was in Los Angeles on business. In one case, York had a close call when he delivered what was later described as the "complete brochure for the engineering Section." Shumovsky was late getting it back to York, who had to return it to a file cabinet while co-workers hunted for it. Concerns arose again when company officials discovered the disappearance of documents from York's workplace for days and even weeks at a time. As a remedy, Shumovsky ordered Locke to photograph York's material. This, in turn, led to a new procedure calling for Locke to take the material from York, photograph it himself, and return the originals at the next meeting. Locke would hold the undeveloped film until his next meeting with Shumovsky, usually every three weeks or so in the busy lobby of the Biltmore Hotel in Los Angeles. To make matters even easier, Locke gave York a Leica camera with the serial number filed off so that he could photograph documents nightly and return them to the plant the following day.

Estimates by the FBI put York's monthly payments at $200 ($3,575 in 2018). Not to appear too mercenary, Moscow tried to show their appreciation for York's contributions in other more personal ways. Around Christmas of 1937, Locke surprised York with a gift waiting for him at the Southern Pacific Railway office at the Los Angeles train station. What York found was what he thought was a rare Bokhara rug. Only later did he learn that it was a "semi-antique Mahal or Hamadan rug."[5]

York clearly performed well for his Russian clients. From the start he supplied everything he could get his hands on, which certainly pleased Moscow. "Needle has a wonderful attitude toward his work," Locke wrote, and he "carries out all our assignments with precision and care. He is extremely happy with the work and has repeatedly expressed his warm feelings with regard to the Soviet Union."[6]

\* \* \*

Splashed across the front page of the June 21, 1938, edition of the *New York Times* was a sensational headline that screamed "Text of the Federal Grand Jury's Indictment of 18 Persons as German Spies." The lengthy four-column article singled out in rich detail a collection of charges brought by Lamar Hardy, US Attorney for the Southern District of New York, against three espionage agents accused of delivering US government secrets to Germany. One of them, a worker at the Seversky Aircraft Company in Farmingdale, New York, named Otto Voss, was then sitting in a New York jail awaiting trial. Voss had provided "information regarding the construction . . . and armaments of certain aircraft . . . being made and prepared by the Seversky Airplane Corporation." The charges against him were eerily similar to York's spying for the Russians.[7]

Three thousand miles away York continued his usual routine of walking through Westlake Park as he had done since his last meeting with Locke. This time he was startled to find someone else standing in front of the Westlake statue. As he approached, the stranger calling himself "Werner" greeted him with a friendly smile and a handshake. York cautiously took in his appearance. He was average height with a noticeably well-proportioned physique and a tailored business suit and tie. He was different from Brooks in that he spoke unaccented English, what he later described to the FBI as "normal American English."[8] York had no idea where he lived but noted his mentioning that he just arrived from New York. He joked that on the train he watched Nelson Eddy, the American actor, as he continually picked his nose.

Werner was different from Brooks in other ways as well. The professional way he carried himself combined with his relaxed manner and ease of conversation gave York confidence that he was in the hands of a professional in the spy business. Werner was open and friendly but, like Brooks before him, offered little except to say that he had been in Barcelona during the Spanish Civil War. When York inquired about Brooks, he learned that he had been sent elsewhere with no further details. The two men then got down to business, with Werner reminding him that good work meant good pay. Payments would continue to be made in cash in exchange for a signed receipt.

York's instincts regarding his new contact were fairly accurate. Werner was Zalman Franklin, a longtime Russian courier. He was a Milwaukee, Wisconsin, native, born in 1909, and a University of Wisconsin graduate who joined the Communist Party while in college. He had worked for a time as a laboratory assistant with the Tennessee Valley Authority while teaching chemistry at the University of Tennessee. In 1937 he dropped everything to travel to Spain to fight with the International Brigades against the forces of Francisco Franco. Returning to America he entered underground work as a courier using various aliases such as Irving Zalmond Franklin, Salmond Franklin, and Franklin Zelman. In between espionage operations he married Sylvia Callen-Caldwell, an American Communist, KGB code name "Satyr," and a key figure in Moscow's investigation of Leon Trotsky's widow, Natalia Sedova.[9]

During one of their first meetings, York requested funds for the purchase of a Leica camera for use in photographing documents. Most likely, he never mentioned the camera that Brooks had supplied him, which he pawned when he found himself short of funds.

Franklin intersected with York at a perfect moment for the KGB's hunt for American aircraft technology. At the time, General Henry H. "Hap" Arnold, a West Pointer, and pioneer in aviation warfare, was the head of the Army Air Corp. In February 1937, Arnold issued a top-secret bid for a competition to produce a plane that was unlike any ever built. His move was in response to the reality of a surging Japan and Germany in the race for advanced military aircraft and an America still hopelessly relying on World War I technology and in some cases, biplanes made of fabric and wood.

Arnold's challenge to American aircraft manufacturers was brief, clear, and demanding. Build a radically new fighter interceptor capable of reaching an unheard-of speed of 360 miles per hour and powered by a minimum fifteen-hundred- horsepower engine. The aircraft had to handle long-range missions with the ability to dive and climb rapidly to intercept bombers flying at twenty thousand feet. As if this was not enough, the winner of the competition had only eighteen months to complete construction and start test-flying a prototype.

Four months later, Lockheed won the contract, beating out rival firms Boeing, Curtiss, Vultee, and Consolidated. The plane, designated XB-38 ("X" for Experimental), would emerge as the fastest American fighter aircraft available at the start of World War II, revolutionizing the future of air combat in all theaters of the war.

The genius behind the XB-38, a kid from Ishperming, Michigan, near Marquette, would become a legend in aircraft design. He would go on to design the F-80, America's first operational jet fighter, and later at his Lockheed "Skunk Works," he would produce the XR 71 Blackbird and the U2, revolutionizing long-range, high-altitude photo surveillance. His forty-four-year career would be rewarded with the National Security Medal and the Medal of Freedom, the highest honor that a president of the United States can bestow on a civilian.

Clarence Leonard Johnson was born in 1910 to Swedish immigrants. One day after pummeling a bully in a schoolyard fight over the name "Clarence," kids began calling him "Kelly of the Emerald Isle."[10] The name "Kelly" stuck for the rest of his life. Johnson completed a three-year aeronautical engineering program in 1932 after only two years at the University of Michigan. Following another year to complete a graduate degree, he set out for California with a new job at Lockheed as a research engineer. Four years later he was the chief research engineer managing the XP-38 project.

The XP-38 would become the famous P-38 Lightning and the scourge of Japan and Germany's most advanced fighter aircraft. Johnson with justifiable pride called the plane the "most maneuverable fighter in the world." It "outclimbed, outran, outmaneuvered and outgunned any other aircraft by a factor of two."[11]

To meet Arnold's requirements Johnson and his team created a radically new design that would set the standard for the jet age to come. For the first time, an aircraft would have an all-aluminum structure, and instead of a single fuselage it would have a strange twin wing appearance with ailerons in the back.

It was unique in other ways as well. It abandoned the two wheels and a tiny guide wheel in the rear for a triangle undercarriage with two wheels that folded back into the nacelle and a nose wheel that folded into the fuselage. Maneuverability in tight turns at high speeds led to the installation of high-lift flaps with the XP-38, the first aircraft ever to have them. By the time they had pulled everything together, they had strung out the plane almost to the tail. What they then did was to extend the back tail another five feet and then add the tail.

It was a twin-engine aircraft that produced the characteristic twin-tailed appearance. It also had revolutionary counter-rotating propellers—a new and important feature that eliminated the tendency of the plane to turn to the right. The unusually quiet engine noise was due to the addition of another radical feature—turbo superchargers manufactured by the General Electric Company that boosted the power of the one-thousand-horsepower engines manufactured by the Allison Corporation. It had a prominent bubble canopy and a skin made of stainless-steel and smooth flushed rivets butt-jointed along the aluminum shin panels. With these additions the XP-38 was capable of reaching cruising speeds of four hundred and twenty miles per hour in level flight.

Such a radical new design required major modifications in weaponry. Arnold insisted that the new fighter interceptor carry an unprecedented one-thousand-pound weapons load for continued fighting capability over longer periods in the air. This meant repositioning the weapons from the wings to the nose of the plane for a point and shoot capability. The complication was that such a weapons repositioning had a dramatic effect on the plane's weight and balance, which impacted its performance.

York began working on the weapons system at Lockheed in June 1938, the same month he met Franklin for the first time at Westlake Park. All the evidence suggests that he had direct access to Johnson's blueprints and schematics because his task was to help design the armaments system for the craft. It did not take long for York to brief Werner on the aircraft and his new duties. Over time he began smuggling out sample cartridges and schematics of the tricycle undercarriage, which he steadily fed to Werner. As for the KGB they were delighted with his production, not to mention his "seriousness and discipline" in removing documents from his workplace. So valuable did York become that Moscow Center considered the formation of a special technical committee to analyze his information as it reached Moscow.[12]

As York busied himself designing weapons systems and photographing blueprints for the Russians, an uneasy sense overcame him that US counterespionage authorities may be closing in on him. A year earlier a disgraced Naval Academy graduate named John Semen Farnsworth had been imprisoned for passing secrets to the Japanese. He had been dismissed from the navy in 1926 after reports surfaced about his begging fellow officers and enlisted men for money to support an excessive lifestyle. After years in the shadows, he suddenly reappeared on the West Coast flashing large rolls of cash and reconnecting with old shipmates. Witnesses later testified that he routinely bought drinks and picked up dinner tabs at expensive restaurants around local navy bases. Farnsworth's sudden wealth and generosity was puzzling, yet when questioned, he deflected the conversation with vague responses. The Office of Naval Intelligence (ONI) soon started an investigation when word filtered back about Farnsworth's spending and his odd questioning about the US Navy's newest warships and weapons systems and the latest sea warfare tactics and doctrines. More ominous still were reports of his requests for blueprints and maps as well as codes and ciphers. After learning of the navy's inquiry, a now panicky Farnsworth rashly approached a local newspaper claiming that he was acting as "double agent" against the Japanese. His arrest soon followed when his claim was reported to the US Navy and FBI.[13]

In May 1938, the government drew even closer to York when an employee of Northrup, York's previous employer, conspired with his brother to make some money. His name was Karl Allen Drummond, and Vendee, his brother. Both were in debt, having lived beyond their incomes. Karl Drummond had quietly removed material while working as an inspector at the company's Inglewood aircraft facility. He and Vendee began shopping it around, first to the Japanese consulate in Los Angeles, and then to a Japanese ship captain. When they were rebuffed the two turned to a local Japanese lawyer, demanding two thousand dollars for 150 secret photographs and schematics.

The hapless duo became dejected when the lawyer agreed to take them for twenty dollars.

Their scheme was exposed when Vendee got cold feet and, fearing arrest, reported his brother to navy officials. On November 30, 1938, the arrest of the twenty-one-year-old Drummond was splashed across newspapers up and down the California coast reporting the sale of "aircraft photos . . . in various stages of construction embodying closely guarded secrets of design."[14] Over the next month while York looked on from the sidelines, Drummond went to trial. Two witnesses told a jury that the stolen documents were "secret" and outlined a plane then under development for two years. One expert testified that the information was sufficient, in his words, to permit "a clever engineer with a codebook to reconstruct such a ship." York must have been unnerved to learn that the government's key witness was Karl's co-conspirator, Vendee Drummond.[15] It took less than a month for Karl to receive the maximum two-year prison sentence for espionage and the loss of his citizenship.[16]

On December 16, 1938, just a week before Drummond's conviction, York was paralyzed to learn of the FBI arrest of Mikhail Nicholas Gorin and Hafis Salich. Both of them, now sitting in a Los Angeles County jail, were facing a high-profile prosecution handled personally by the US Attorney, Benjamin Harrison. The day following the arrest, M. I. Ivanushkin, Russian vice-consul in New York, flew to Los Angeles to ensure, he told waiting reporters, that Gorin was being "treated humanely."[17]

Gorin came to the United States with an initial assignment to Amtorg. Later he moved to Los Angeles as the head of Intourist, Moscow's official travel agency. Like Shumovsky, he, too, was a KGB officer in the hunt for intelligence sources on the US West Coast. In 1937, Gorin had a chance encounter with Salich, a Russian immigrant who first worked for the Berkeley, California, police department before moving on to the Office of Naval Intelligence. His secret work for ONI concentrated on the study of Japanese intelligence activities on the West Coast, giving him all-source access to navy, army, and FBI files.

The revelations about their spying activity came about by accident in 1938 when Gorin dropped off a suit for dry cleaning. After checking the pockets, a clerk found money and a suspicious note, which he turned over to the FBI. When interviewed by FBI agents, Salich admitted his gambling and the need for cash to support his habit. For more than a year he had supplied Gorin with ONI secrets in exchange for $1,700 ($30,800 in 2019). Salich justified his crime on the theory that Japan was a "common enemy" of both the Soviet Union and the United States, a claim eerily similar to York's justification.[18]

York had no illusions about Gorin's guilt. He knew of Gorin and was aware that he was just two steps away from him in the espionage chain.

While working for Brooks both men gradually became sloppy by ignoring adherence to the principals of *konspiratsiia* that protected secret operations. In times past, York, after meeting Brooks at Westlake Park, had driven Brooks to a particular Los Angeles neighborhood and dropped him off. The Gorin connection came about one day when a break in contact between Shumovsky and Brooks, for reasons unknown, forced Brooks to break in contact with York because of a shortage of funds to pay him. During this period York felt compelled to contact Brooks and, not knowing where he lived or how to reach him, he drove to the neighborhood near Harvard Street and San Marino Avenue in Los Angeles where he previously dropped Brooks off. Spotting Brooks's car parked on the street, he placed a note on the windshield with a request to contact him. While there he wandered into a nearby apartment house at 3316 San Marino Street in Los Angeles where Gorin lived with his thirty-two-year-old wife, Natasha. In the lobby York found the name "Gorin" on the tenant directory. As he stood looking at it, he recalled Brooks having once slipped by mentioning the name "Gorin" in conversation with him. York couldn't find Brooks that day but suspected that he lived in the same building as well.[19]

Gorin's arrest was too close to home for York. His fear only grew at the thought that both Brooks and Werner had been spotted by the FBI delivering his stolen information to Gorin at the Soviet sub-consulate in Los Angeles. Even more chilling was the likelihood that Brooks and Werner delivered the documents to Gorin's home, which was now being searched by the FBI.[20]

York's terror soon morphed into paranoia when he began seeing things that weren't there. He believed he was being followed and in danger of being murdered. On one occasion he thought someone had tried to drive his car off the road. He could confide in no one about his dilemma, and a growing sense of isolation only added to his worry. He hoped that he could alleviate his fears at his next meeting with Franklin scheduled for one day at the end of 1938. Franklin had been religious in his contacts with York and appreciative of his work. So much so that at their last get-together in early December 1938, he gave York a Patek Philippe pocket watch that he claimed he had purchased in Europe. After an agonizing few weeks, York showed up at the Westlake statue on the appointed day and time. After several hours of waiting, Werner failed to appear.

York's worst nightmare had now come true. Gorin was in custody facing espionage charges and possibly talking to the FBI. Werner had failed to appear. Perhaps he and maybe Brooks had been arrested and were telling all. Perhaps the FBI would soon be knocking on his door as well. As York's world squeezed in ever tighter, he knew what he had to do.

## NOTES

1. VBN 13.
2. Los Angeles Report, May 3, 1950, York FBI file.
3. Manifest for SS *Santa Clara*, October 3, 1936, MyHeritge.com; VBN 13; Los Angeles Report, June 27, 1956, York FBI file.
4. Los Angeles Report, May 3, 1950, York FBI file.
5. Ibid.
6. VBN 23.
7. "Four Nazi Spies Given Two to Four Years," *Washington Post*, December 3, 1938, 1.
8. Los Angeles Report, May 3, 1950, York FBI file.
9. Haynes, Klehr, and Vassiliev, *Spies*, 76.
10. Clarence L. Johnson with Maggie Smith, *Kelly* (Washington, DC: Smithsonian Books, 1985), 5.
11. Ibid., 77.
12. VBN 30.
13. Raymond J. Batvinis, *Origins of FBI Counterintelligence* (Lawrence: University Press of Kansas, 2007), 37.
14. "Plane Worker Held by US as Spy for Japan," *New York Herald Tribune*, December 1, 1938.
15. "Spy Suspect Found Guilty," *Los Angeles Times*, December 23, 1938, 1.
16. At his sentencing the judge removed his American citizenship remonstrating Drummond that his treachery carries with it "great opprobrium" because it strikes at the bases of our national life—loyalty. "Spy Given Two Years," *Los Angeles Times*, December 24, 1938, A-1.
17. "Soviet Aide Tells Purpose of Trip to See Spy Suspect," *Los Angeles Times*, December 12, 1938, 4.
18. Ibid., Batvinis, *Origins of FBI Counterintelligence*, 53–54.
19. Memorandum entitled Jones Orin York, July 3, 1952, York FBI file.
20. Los Angeles Report, May 3, 1950, York FBI file.

*Chapter 11*

# Coos County

The package arrived at the Lockheed offices on February 4, 1939. Inside was the "secret pass" Jones York wore on his work shirt and a brief letter explaining that stress and a need to recover his health had forced him to quit his job six days earlier.[1]

Three thousand miles away, York had arrived in New York City with a desperate plan to find his old benefactor, Stanislav Shumovsky. Having burned through the last of the funds that Werner had paid him, York sold two spy cameras before settling into a cheap rooming house. Over the next few days between wandering around the city and visiting tourist sites, he found the address of Amtorg Trading Company, Shumovsky's cover business. Taking a huge risk of being caught, the Russian spy walked into Amtorg's midtown headquarters one morning explaining that he wished to speak with his old friend, Stan. York was dismayed to learn that Shumovsky was in Moscow and would not be returning. Suspecting a lie, York then made his way to a nearby Western Union office, where he sent a telegram to Shumovsky at Amtorg and then waited for two days for a response that never came.

Alone and with no idea what to do next, he decided to move again. Boarding a bus, York headed north to Lake Champlain with a vague notion of crossing the border and disappearing into Canada's northern wilderness. This idea, too, quickly evaporated when immigration officers refused the penniless visitor entry fearing that he could become a ward of the state. With a second plan now squashed, a hapless York again changed direction; this time heading east on foot. Over the next few weeks, he walked one hundred or so miles across the state of Vermont, turning north toward Maine. After even more days of hiking, his journey ended in New Hampshire's Coos County, where towering snowdrifts blocked further progress. Working his way around the county, he finally found Wentworth Location. More than a year later local residents still recalled the threadbare bowlegged stranger limping through knee-high snowpacks with only a sled, tent, rifle, and a few blankets.

Today the Wentworth Location remains as it was when York first arrived there with its vast densely forested wilderness hugging the edges of the White Mountains and the Great North Woods. Its name derives from George Wentworth, a wealthy Portsmouth, Rhodes Island, farmer and speculator who purchased the land in 1797. Over the centuries the site passed through a series of owners before coming into the possession of Dartmouth College more than a hundred years ago. Aside from logging, the area's only other revenue source is guiding services for out-of-town fishermen and hunters eager to bag a moose, which are abundant in the region. Winters are brutal with heavy snowfalls, temperatures hovering in the twenties with dips into single digits a common occurrence. Even today it is accessible by only one or two barely paved roads. The many dirt trails connecting the local population to the outside world are nearly impassable in winter with mountainous snowdrifts and deep ruts as hard as iron. If York wanted to disappear, he certainly found a perfect spot. For the past 150 years, the population of this unforgiving region has been steadily declining from sixty-seven in 1850 (the first year that census figures are available) to twenty-eight in 2020.

York was lucky enough to meet a good Samaritan who offered the use of a shed to protect him from freezing to death. After a few weeks he built his own Rube Goldberg–type shanty, which he occupied for the next year.

Local residents remembered him well but could offer little to enlighten FBI agents when they later began poking around and asking questions. He gave his name as "Robert L. DuBois," an aviation engineer.[2] He was friendly, enjoyed talking about a lot of things while carefully avoiding details about his life. One person remembered conversations with him about foreign affairs, particularly the "Russian situation" when the Soviet Union and Germany signed a nonaggression pact. But again, no details were given. Flat broke when he arrived, he survived on occasional day jobs shoveling gravel for local road crews and transient farm labor. He had no contact with the outside world as Wentworth Location had no phone service. Checks at the local post office produced no evidence that he ever received mail or sent any letters or packages.

\* \* \*

York was right to suspect that he was under investigation. As it turned out, shortly before his departure from California the FBI had started looking at him after unearthing his connection with Gorin. Agents visited his father in the hope of locating him, but he could offer no idea where York had gone. Bemoaning his son's situation, George York described him as a "moody," undisciplined soul, incapable of managing money or keeping a budget.[3] His life was a constant flitting from one fantasy to another in the hope of striking it rich with his music and poetry or latest invention or investment. Yet, in the end all he ever achieved was a string of unpaid bills and defaulted loans to creditors, friends, and family members.

The interview with George York proved invaluable for investigators. As Jones York languished in New Hampshire, what began in February 1939 as an opaque portrait of his life gradually crystalized into sharp and disturbing relief by year's end.

One of the earliest insights came interestingly from a hitchhiker York picked up less than a year earlier. As they drove along a discussion about airplane technology ensued, prompting York's passenger to recount his idea for a plastic glue for fabricating airplane propellers; a technology he hoped would one day become profitable. Over the ensuing weeks the two met often, with York extending him $200 and on numerous occasions thereafter $10, $20 to help him along.[4]

In July 1938, when this person suddenly became ill, York encouraged him to move to a better house in Los Angeles, giving him $100 to cover the move. In appreciation, the guy offered York a half interest in anything he developed. In the end, however, York lost interest in the project and never received anything for his investment. When interviewed by the FBI in the spring of 1939, the person, who had not seen nor heard from York for eight months, confirmed that since their first encounter York had supplied him with nearly $500 ($9,175 in December 2019).

Further inquiries revealed that while working for the Douglas Company in December 1936, York deposited $1,200 ($22,000 in December 2019) into his bank account. A month later he rented an apartment for $125 a month ($2,250 in December 2019). The apartment was in a private home, nestled behind a tree-lined wall on Doheny Drive, in the exclusive Trousdale Estates neighborhood of Beverly Hills, California. Just blocks away was the famous Greystone Mansion built in 1929 by oil tycoon Edward L. Doheny.

The Doheny rental led the FBI to a married couple, Lois and Donald Smith. They were Californians whose acquaintance with York went back more than seventeen years. Like York, Donald Smith, a badly crippled paralytic, was an inventor who had spent a decade working on a new idea for an automobile carburetor. The two friends had kept in touch over the years in connection with developing Smith's device into a commercial venture.[5]

When the deal for the Doheny dwelling was made, York asked the Smiths to move in with him and act as caretakers with Mrs. Smith doing the cooking and housework. Over time, the Smiths remembered, York began acting strangely starting with a room that he always kept locked and off limits to everyone. In the evening he brought home stacks of blueprints, sketches, and documents from work, taking them directly to his room and closing the door. He spent hours there every night, sometimes until four in the morning, and on weekends. On the few occasions the couple caught glimpses of him, he was bent over his desk sketching, drawing, or typing with a jerry-built camera and lighting system for oversized blueprints right next to him.[6]

York received odd telephone calls day and night from individuals speaking heavily accented English. Afterwards he would insist that the Smiths leave the apartment while three men visited him. They routinely took the blueprints and paid him for them. York referred to one of the strangers, Smith recalled, as the "New York payoff man." Other times, after receiving a call, York immediately left only to return later flush with cash. When questioned by Smith, York described the contacts as his "principals."[7]

Four months after the Doheny rental, another property transaction revealed a new feature of York's personality. It was a rented penthouse apartment on Sunset Boulevard in the heart of Hollywood's movie industry with a monthly cost of $125 ($2,250 in December 2019). He soon installed some furniture, a piano, and a woman named Dorothy Mayhew. Having first met Mayhew through a mutual friend, York learned that she wrote music. Over time, he began pressuring her to move into the apartment, where they could collaborate on new songs that they could then publish. His idea, Mayhew later recounted, was to use the penthouse apartment as a "front" that would easily catch the attention of Hollywood music moguls and lead to big money for them both.

The couple worked on new songs in the evenings while York worked at Northrup and spied during the day. Mayhew, never keen on the penthouse scheme, believed it to be an expensive and harebrained notion from the start. Yet, after his repeated entreaties she soon found herself pounding away on a piano composing music set to his lyrics. The relationship was business with no romance, and he continued to live at the Doheny house with the Smiths. In the end, they produced a number of songs, none of which amounted to much and one which was copyrighted by Mayhew and "Joy York" entitled "A Knight of the Open Way."[8]

Still another woman remembered him coming by her apartment in the evening. For hours he would sit silently not saying a word while listening to the radio. Suddenly he would get up and leave without a goodbye. On other occasions the two simply went out for dinner at a nearby restaurant or dancing at some nightclub.

At the same time that he was busy slipping secrets to the Russians, sketching and photographing documents at the Doheny residence, and writing songs on Sunset Boulevard, York also found time to buy a home in one of Los Angeles's toniest neighborhoods. Palos Verdes Estates, a 3,200-acre plot on the Palos Verdes Peninsula overlooking the Pacific Ocean, was a new master-planned community designed by Frederick Law Olmsted Jr., America's premier architect. Houses could not just be built. A community art jury passed judgment on everything from size and shape of the home to construction details, slope of the roof, and materials to landscape features like fences, shrubbery, and hedges. York chose a three-story home on swanky Del Monte Drive complete with a three-car garage to hold his many cars. Relying on the $1,200 December 1936 deposit as a down payment, he took out a $7,600 mortgage ($131,000 in December 2019). As more and more questions were asked, details of his suspicious behavior began piling up. So much so that by June 1939 the Los Angeles FBI office reported to Washington that York had "apparently expended considerable (sp) more than he had earned at airplane factories" as well as "mysterious calls" from unknown foreigners.[9]

\* \* \*

A year of life as a hermit in the middle of nowhere freezing in an unheated hut was about all that York could take—even for someone hiding from the law. By January 1940, the bedraggled and penniless vagabond was on the move again—this time back home to California. Supplied with fifty dollars wired to him by his father, York boarded a bus headed west. By the end of the month, he was back where he started, living with his father and once again on the prowl for his special source of income.

Not long after York repeated his Amtorg New York ploy with a desperate approach to the Russian consulate in Los Angeles. Suspicious of York's motives, a wary Russian official listened intently to his tale of espionage, aircraft secrets, and Shumovsky before taking his name and address and handing him a Russian citizenship application to complete and return. For the next few weeks, as York sat at home waiting, KGB officials carefully digested his message. Satisfied that it was safe, orders were issued for Franklin to once again head west to reestablish contact with one of Moscow's most important industrial spies.

\* \* \*

When York got back to California, FBI agents were waiting for him. One day in February 1940, after contacting the FBI's Los Angeles office, agents sat down to interview him in his father's home. Over several hours of conversation York spun a story that, while hanging close to the truth, was a study in denial, evasion, and casual dismissal of difficult questions.

His sudden disappearance from California was easily explained by his overwhelming personal problems. He had serious financial troubles. Chief among them, a nagging ex-wife demanding alimony and child support. His divorce decree had saddled him with monthly payments that were more than a year in arrears. Then there were the relentless pressures of work with increasingly long hours working on the XB-38 project. Coupled with management demands for more overtime and increasing production targets, his nerves had been strained to the breaking point.

As the agents sat listening, he described his travel to New York City. His hope of solving his financial problems, he told them, rested on making a big score with the sale of a large collection of poems he had written over the years. When not spending time at the Museum of Natural History, he wandered around Manhattan making cold calls and pitching ideas to different publishing houses, including the Alfred A. Knopf Company. As he knew no one in New York, he stayed in a rooming house but could not remember the address. In addition to the poem story, York surprisingly produced another bizarre explanation for his disappearance. He claimed that someone or group was trying to harm him. "I feared bodily harm" he explained, "and thought (I) was being followed."[10] Next, he pointed to an attempt on his life while he was driving when a car forced him off the road. When asked by agents if he reported the incident to the police, he demurred saying he could not identify the vehicle, nor why his attackers would want to hurt him. After a year in New Hampshire living a "hermit life," he wired his father for funds to cover his bus fare back to California.

He flat out denied any spying or knowledge of Gorin. Yes, he had a relationship with the Russian government, but it was perfectly legitimate. It began in 1935 or 1936 when he met an aviation delegation from Moscow led by Stanislav Shumovsky during a visit to the Northrup plant where he was working at the time. On his own, he approached them with a project for an aircraft engine he was designing in the hope of selling it to them. York prepared a collection of sketches for their review, which he gave them during meetings at local restaurants. Later when they returned with encouraging suggestions for modifications, York quit Northrup to devote himself full time to the project, which he pursued "over a period of years until October 1938."[11] York cleverly downplayed Shumovsky's involvement with claims that "the group" gave him $1,500 ($28,765 in December 2019) to offset his expenses. The initial payment was $500 ($9,590 in December 2019) with lesser amounts that "they" spread over the next few years. In the end he breezily dismissed the whole thing claiming that no sale was ever made. When asked about Smith's term of "principals," he waved it off as merely referring to the Russian group.[12]

Agents then pressed him on huge disparities between his income for the years he worked for Northrup, Douglas, and Lockheed and large expenses for cars, rental properties, and his Palos Verdes home. Without missing a beat, York pointed to 1933, the year of his first disappearance. He boasted that he had saved $6,500, which he kept in cash denominations of 5-, 10-, 20-, and 100-dollar bills in a special hiding place. As incredulous agents sat listening, he described $5,000 as proceeds from the exchange of gold he had mined in northern California while the remaining $1,500 represented careful savings over the past six years. When confronted with his failure to file taxes in 1938 and 1939, he denied owing taxes. As for the gold—it was mined in such minimal amounts that it wasn't subject to tax. At the conclusion of the interview, his confidence now restored, York assured the FBI that he was not connected with any "subversive movement or isms of any kind," and "would die fighting for the United States."[13]

\* \* \*

Two weeks after the FBI interview, Franklin appeared unexpectedly at his door. He was anxious to see York and wanted to know where he had been for the past year. This was Franklin's second trip to California on a York mission in less than a year. When contact was lost in December 1938, the Russians made the risky decision of sending him to California in February 1939 to look for him. Over several weeks he spoke with a number of contacts with no luck. On one occasion when he risked approaching York's ex-wife, she suggested that he had simply vanished and may have fled the country.

York told Franklin that he was terrified when Gorin was arrested as he knew of him and his involvement in York's spy operation. Franklin's failure to make their last meeting confirmed his suspicion, forcing him to leave California in a panic. His flight to New York and failed effort to reach Shumovsky and stay in New Hampshire were also reviewed.

Franklin then explained that his failure to appear at their last meeting in December 1938 had nothing to do with Gorin's arrest. Rather, it was caused by a wrestling injury that landed him in a hospital. York then outlined his interview with the FBI. No mention was made of Shumovsky nor his years of espionage with the Soviets. He then gloated over his recent hire by Northrup Aircraft Company and his readiness to resume work for the Russians. Franklin agreed and later reported to Moscow that York was "again in position to obtain information for the Soviets."[14] This was an important meeting as the Werner–Needle relationship was once again in business. Franklin then gave him $150 ($2,750 in December 2019) to buy another Leica camera to begin photographing documents.

After a year of meetings with York, Franklin showed up in May 1941 with startling news. This would be their last meeting. Now for a second time he would be turned over to a new handler. As York watched, Franklin removed a photo of Shirley Temple, famed child movie actress of the 1930s, from his pocket. After ripping it in half he gave one piece to York. Urging him to be patient, York was told to expect contact in the near future, probably a woman, who would produce the other half of the Temple photo as confirmation of authenticity along with the date of birth of York's mother. After a few brief pleasantries, the two then parted with a handshake.[15]

York's only job now was to wait.

## NOTES

1. Los Angeles Report, June 7, 1939, York FBI file.
2. Los Angeles Report, August 13, 1940, York FBI file.
3. Los Angeles Report, December 6, 1939, York FBI file.
4. Ibid.
5. Los Angeles Report, June 7, 1939, York FBI file.
6. Ibid.
7. Ibid.
8. Ibid.
9. Los Angeles Report, August 13, 1940, York FBI file.
10. Ibid.
11. Ibid.
12. Ibid.
13. Ibid.
14. "Needle" was approached by the FBI. "'Center' Doesn't Trust Him," VBN 102. VWN-1, 113.
15. Los Angeles Letter to Director, April 11, 1950, York FBI file.

*Chapter 12*

# Needle and Link

It was June 1941 when the strategic balance across the globe had suddenly shifted with Hitler's launching of Operation Barbarossa, a surprise military blow along a one-thousand-mile front against his former ally, Josef Stalin. Over the following weeks, Moscow reeled in shock, as a million German troops backed by armored vehicles and aircraft rolled across Russia's western landscape swallowing up the Red Army with ease.

That same month York received an unexpected visit at his door from someone he did not recognize. The mystery man didn't identify himself, but York knew who he was. The two men shook hands as they cautiously took each other's measure. Wasting no time, the two halves of the Shirley Temple photo were matched, and an agreement was quickly made to meet again. A day or so later at Westlake Park, York, as he had done so many times before, casually meandered along the paths making his way to the Westlake statue. Waiting for him was his new contact man—a relaxed and smiling Bill Weisband.[1] This was the first of many meetings that would continue for the next fourteen months.

With their identities now confirmed, Bill skipped small talk. York, he said, was to concentrate on the business of spying. Moscow was not interested in his descriptions of the many military bases springing up throughout California. His job was to supply aviation secrets. To focus his new source, Bill pulled out a shopping list of Moscow's demands filled with details of aircraft designs, developments in radar, new armaments and weaponry, and breakthroughs on the latest electrical devices being installed in planes. When York complained that he had no camera (he had probably pawned his last one), Bill supplied him with funds to purchase one capable of producing high-quality images.[2]

Before long, York found himself operating a German-engineered and -built Contax III camera complete with the latest Sonar PL5 lens—ideal for snapping clear images of documents under difficult lighting conditions. Now with his delivery system to the Russians restored, York resumed the carefully

79

crafted routine of removing documents from his workplace, photographing them at home, and returning them to the proper filing cabinets the following morning. As for the undeveloped film cannisters York delivered to Weisband, they passed to an official at the Soviet vice-consulate in Los Angeles and then on to San Francisco, where Soviet consul Gregory Kheifets (a KGB officer) prepared them for shipment to Moscow.[3]

In a break from the past routine of meetings at Westlake Park, Weisband made a sudden change in procedure. Rather than conspicuous encounters in a public park, which could attract attention, the two soon began dining at different restaurants and bars around Los Angeles. One, the famed and often crowded Garden of Allah Hotel, located on the busy corner of Sunset Boulevard and Crescent Heights, was originally the private estate of Russian actress Alla Nazimova. The popular eatery, brimming with lush foliage, was set off by a large swimming pool in the shape of the Black Sea. Over the years the complex added luxury housing that drew such Hollywood luminaries and literary personalities as Greta Garbo, Orson Welles, Ernest Hemingway, and Dorothy Parker. As a bustling tourist site, it was perfect for two spies, posing as friends sharing a casual meal, to exchange secrets in plain sight of throngs of passersby. The Florentine Gardens was another excellent meeting site. A busy nightclub converted in 1938 into a dinner theater, it served mainly working-class types. There one could dine on Italian fare while an emcee barked out nightly names of such famous acts as the Mills Brothers and Sophie Tucker.

One of Weisband's first stops after arriving in Los Angeles was a modest house along Bencia Drive in one of the city's quieter suburban neighborhoods. When he knocked on the door a woman answered. She was Vivian Cubarkin, wife of Victor Cubarkin. She had never met him and was puzzled when he first appeared. In his usual jaunty manner, he introduced himself as Bill Weisband. He had just arrived in California, he said, and "Stan" suggested he look up the Cubarkins. Stan, it turned out, was Stanislav Shumovsky. The couple often entertained members of the local Russian community in their home and soon began including Bill in their soirees. It was the start of a long-lasting friendship that would have profound consequences for Weisband years later.[4]

Victor Cubarkin, then age thirty-seven, was a "supervisor of tools" with Douglas Aircraft Company for more than twenty years. He was a native of California born to Russian immigrant parents and raised in San Francisco. Vivian was a bookkeeper with a local poster company. For seven years, Cubarkin had been on the FBI's radar screen for suspected membership with the California Communist Party. One ONI source reported that he was a member of one of the party's "higher units" on the West Coast and had often posted bail for party members arrested for protesting. Another reported his attendance at a dinner in 1936 when he leveled support for agricultural workers in the hope that they would become "revolutionists." One source recalled his agitation activities in the San Francisco area in the past, referring to him as an "anarchist type." Still another source told investigators that Victor had spent some of his early years in the Soviet Union and was a soldier in the Red Army. That same informant opined that Cubarkin could not be considered reliable in the event of a national emergency and would be a "security risk" if hostilities erupted with the Soviet Union.[5]

The Cubarkin connection with Shumovsky originally began with a banquet held at the Biltmore Hotel by Douglas Aircraft honoring a group of Russian pilots who made a record-setting flight from Siberia to California. Because Victor spoke Russian, he had a prominent place at the head table, where he joined Shumovsky in conversation. They quickly became friends, with Stan often a guest at the Cubarkin home.

* * *

Weisband soon obtained a job as a night desk clerk at the magnificent Miramar Hotel in Santa Monica, California. The resort opened in 1928 on the site of an old hotel in existence since the mid-nineteenth century and was "famed for its dignity and the wondrous beauty of its location on the lofty Santa Monica palisades commanding sweeping views of the ocean coastline." The job came to him through Joe Gray, an old friend from the hotel business in New York City then working as Miramar's manager. Gray even supplied him with a hotel room for a week or so until he got settled on his own. Despite Gray's generosity Bill remained true to form regarding his work habits and dealing with his bosses. Years later he told the FBI that while he did quit his job, Miramar management was "undoubtedly pleased" when he left as their relationship had become "unsatisfactory."[6]

By then he had replaced the 1939 Ford that he had acquired in New York with a new Hudson bought at a Hollywood dealership. The sleek new four-door maroon sedan quickly raised eyebrows when skeptical Miramar co-workers began questioning how he could afford such an expensive vehicle on a $125 monthly clerk's salary. When pressed he gave only vague references to "big deals" he was pursuing through unnamed "big shots." To anyone who would listen, Bill claimed that he bought the new car and arranged his work schedule for road trips across the California desert to the Las Vegas gambling dens while taking daytime courses at the University of California. Bill's large rolls of cash, always on display, and a constant source of gossip, were occasionally useful when co-workers found themselves short at the end of a week and in need of a loan. At the same time the KGB was making monthly payments to him of $2,400 ($43,000 in January 2019).[7]

Bill's romantic life took an uptick a month before the Pearl Harbor attack when Pat Grimes suddenly appeared at the Miramar Hotel. Still unattached and having quit her job, she abandoned New York and drove her brother's car across country alone to California to meet him. For the first few days she, too, stayed at the Miramar, this time courtesy of Bill, and then again through Bill found a more permanent residence. Around Thanksgiving in 1941 the two left for Pendleton, Oregon, to visit her family. Grimes remembered him as relaxed, carefree as always, and with plenty of cash despite the loss of his Miramar job. When questioned he breezily brushed off Grimes's concerns, not with talk of big shots and big deals, but rather the continued payment for his "extra activity namely meeting people here and there on street corners."[8]

One of the first things he did after returning from Oregon was to find a new job. In a sharp departure from the past, he applied to Lockheed Corporation perhaps in an attempt to duck the draft board. His move may also have had to do with orders from Moscow to learn more about Lockheed advancements on the P-38 fighter plane and the final preparations for the first flight of the new XP-47, a second-generation fighter prototype based on the P-38 Lightning design. By the start of 1942, Lockheed was turning out P-38s by the thousands with new technologies and modifications underway all the time.

His employment application revealed a unique insight into just how brazen Weisband could be. In what would become standard corporate practice for hiring new employees, Lockheed officials checked his resume before making any job offer. In it he listed a Lockheed employee as a reference. Weisband had telephoned the person one day asking to use his name, saying he had been referred to him by a mutual friend. When later questioned by investigators, the employee emphatically stated that "in no way did he know William Wolf Weisband."[9]

While in California, Weisband resided for a time in a mansion situated on a bluff overlooking the Pacific coastline in the Pacific Palisades region of Los Angeles. He got the room through a contact and lived there for some months because the owner wanted a man occupying the house for security. One woman later told the FBI that after showing her around the estate, she came away believing that Bill had the "run of the place."[10] Like most of his opportunities, however, this one too was squandered when he was unceremoniously evicted after the owner unexpectedly appeared early one morning to complain about his excessive telephone bills only to find a woman in his room.

Bill loved to dance. One source who knew him during his Los Angeles period recalled that he was part of a "loosely knit group" of dance enthusiasts that moved from one hotel to another over a period of eight months. One typical nightspot was the elegant Biltmore Hotel on Pershing Square in downtown Los Angeles. On other occasions the group gathered in Bill's room at the Hotel Clark (in February 1942 he had obtained a job and residence at the Hotel Clark in downtown Los Angeles), where they regularly partied, drank, and listened to records on his phonograph player through all hours of the night.

\* \* \*

York's steady supply of high-quality secrets remained excellent throughout his relationship with Weisband. Two years earlier the Norwegian government had sent a purchasing commission to California made up of navy and army air corps specialists intent on inspecting a new plane under production at Vultee Aircraft Company. It was supposed to replace Norway's biplane fleet, which had become obsolete. Plans for the purchase were soon scrapped, however, when company officials conceded that they could not fit the plane with floats as required by the Norwegians. Instead, the delegation turned to Northrop, ordering twenty-four planes that became known as the N-3PB. Over the next twenty months Northrop engineers set to work redesigning an existing plane with new modifications. No one noticed York standing around the floor of the plant watching and studying the new armament systems that were being designed and installed along with cameras in the rear of the plane and changes in instrumentation and radios. All twenty-four were delivered to the exiled Norwegian Navy Air Service in November 1941, just months after York and Weisband first met.

During York's time with Werner, Northrop was also experimenting with a radically new top-secret aircraft design. It was the XB-35, the Flying Wing Experimental Heavy Bomber, forerunner of today's B-2 Stealth bomber. It was one massive aluminum wing three times heavier than a World War II B-17 Flying Fortress with a larger wingspan. From the cockpit enclosed in a distinctive bubble canopy, the pilot controlled four Pratt and Whitney engines mounted along the back edge of the aircraft, which produced an unheard of thrust of three-thousand horsepower. Using a few easy steps, the pilot could engage the plane's new electrically activated trim flaps, elevons, and landing flaps, which were uniquely arrayed along the trailing edge of the wing. Its eight ordnance bays with a carrying capacity of 10,000 pounds of bombs was unlike any conventional bomber in development at the time. In the first months of contact with Weisband, York worked on Project MX-140, as the bomber program was called, from the trial-and-error development stage through to the initiation of a contract with the Army Air Corps.

\* \* \*

By the summer of 1942, with secret plans underway in Washington for the invasion of North Africa, the War Department had a pressing need for more troops. Bill, now thirty-four years old, received a draft notice ordering him to report for duty on September 2, 1942. In those closing days of August, Weisband, like millions of other American men, began readying himself for military life. First to go was the Hudson that he owned for a year. Next, he informed the Clark Hotel management, who promised him his job when he returned.

Most importantly, however, was a final meeting with York at the Garden of Allah. Weisband was leaving immediately for a new assignment, Bill explained, but where was not stated. A fourth handler would soon contact him. All that York knew was that it would most likely be a woman. The procedure would follow the original track of Brooks and Werner with initial contact by telephone followed by a rendezvous at Westlake Park. The mystery woman would identify herself to York by asking about his "violin."[11]

Before he left there was one more chore to perform. A final evening with Patricia Grimes. Over a quiet dinner the two ate and drank as they reminisced about times past and the future of two people facing the uncertainties of a world at war. They had grown close over the last four years. While they had been lovers, Grimes had no illusions about marriage with Bill. Yet both shared the long-standing secret of his sudden disappearances, the rendezvous with strangers on street corners, the furtive exchanges of packages and envelopes that Weisband passed to his unnamed "principal."[12]

Looming over the evening was an unspoken anxiety that Bill was stepping into the unknown with no control of his life nor what lay ahead. So, Grimes was surprised when Bill, with all of these powerful life-or-death emotions swirling between them, suddenly grew nostalgic, almost sad. Lamenting the loss of his "secret" work, Bill voiced a hope that one day, after the war, if he survived, it would all begin again.[13]

## NOTES

1. Los Angeles Report, June 19, 1950, Weisband FBI file.
2. Ibid.
3. Ibid.
4. Los Angeles Report, August 8, 1950, Weisband FBI file.
5. Undated memorandum, NSA FOIPA.
6. "Miramar Hotel Holds Tradition of Early Days," *Los Angeles Times*, January 22, 1928, B2. Los Angeles Report, August 8, 1950, Weisband FBI file.
7. Los Angeles Report, June 19, 1950, Los Angeles Report, August 8, 1950, Weisband FBI file.
8. Los Angeles Report, June 19, 1950, Weisband FBI file.
9. Los Angeles Report, August 8, 1950, Weisband FBI file.

10. Ibid.
11. Los Angeles letter to Director, April 4, 1950, Weisband FBI file.
12. Los Angeles Report, August 8, 1950, Weisband FBI file.
13. WFO Reports, April 24, 1950, and June 2, 1950, Weisband FBI file.

*Chapter 13*

# Soldier

Fort MacArthur overlooks San Pedro Bay at the entrance of Los Angeles Harbor just miles from Terminal Island at Long Beach. The fortification named for General Arthur MacArthur, a former military governor of the Philippines and father of General Douglas MacArthur, was constructed in 1914, three months after the start of World War I.

Bill Weisband's military career began at Fort MacArthur when Local Draft Board #243 at Santa Monica, California, drafted him into US Army service on September 1, 1942, which is the same time General Dwight Eisenhower was finalizing preparations for landing thousands of American GIs on the beaches of North Africa.

What followed were three days of processing and testing before his dispatch one hundred miles north to Gardner Field, a flat, dusty army base near the farming town of Taft. Named for Major John H. Gardner, a World War I flying ace, the airfield was built in January 1941 to serve as the War Department's Western Flying Training Command for basic flight training for army pilots. For the next four months Private William W. Weisband, as one of the newest members of the Signal Corps, sat at a teletype machine relaying coded messages between Gardner Field and the War Department in Washington. In January 1943, bags packed, he headed east with orders to report to the heart of America's code-breaking establishment.

* * *

The hero of twentieth-century American cryptology and cryptanalysis was a genius named William Friedman. One longtime colleague, summing up the opinions of most of the American code-breaking community decades after his death, called him the "dean of modern American cryptologists, the most eminent pioneer in the application of scientific principles to cryptology who laid the foundation for present-day concepts."[1]

Curiously, Friedman and Weisband shared some things in common. Both were Jewish and born with the first name "Wolfe." Like Weisband's mother, Sarah, Friedman's father was Rumanian and also born in the city of Kishinev, probably while Sarah Weisband was still living there. In 1892, a year after Friedman's birth, the family emigrated to America, settling in Pittsburgh, where Wolfe changed his name to "William." While his father ran a sewing machine company and mother tended to the house, Bill Friedman was on his way to graduating with honors from Pittsburgh Central High School in the class of 1909. A year later he enrolled in the tuition-free Michigan Agriculture College with ideas of becoming a farmer. A growing interest in science led him to abandon agriculture for Cornell University and a 1914 degree in genetics. Friedman's plans for graduate study ended abruptly when a larger-than-life character named George Fabyan entered his world with an offer of work.[2]

"Colonel" Fabyan, as he preferred to be called (it was simply an honorific), had a master-of-the-realm physical presence about him and a great desire to be "somebody."[3] In a photo taken in 1916, one sees a ramrod-straight barrel-chested figure, well over six feet tall, sporting a thick mustache and beard, clad in a white peasant shirt and knee-high jodhpurs. His vast wealth, estimated at the time at three million dollars ($100 million in 2019) came from Bliss Fabyan & Company, the family's New England textile business, one of the leading fabric producers in the world.

Eschewing a Gilded Age lifestyle of golf, yachting, and glittering entertainment, Fabyan poured his fortune into three hundred acres along the Fox River in Geneva, Illinois. Situated a few miles west of Chicago, the Riverbank Laboratories, as he dubbed it, was an odd amalgam of a private home, which he called "the Villa," a working farm, and a science campus. It was home to all varieties of researchers conducting experiments, both legitimate and whacky, under Fabyan's watchful eye. "Some rich men," he once told an interviewer, "go in for art collections, gay times on the Riviera, or extravagant living, but they all get satiated. That's why I stick to scientific experiments, spending money to discover valuable things that universities can't afford. You can never get sick of too much knowledge." His goal, as he told it, was the creation of a "community of thinkers."[4]

Manning Riverbank Laboratories were one hundred and fifty men and women who, when not thinking, toiled away in a collection of research buildings dotting the property. There was, for instance, an acoustic center with an ultra-quiet test chamber used for the development of new technologies that would one day make cities more livable. Eliminating city noise referred to as "racket ogre" from machines and crowds was a major goal of Fabyan.[5] In the biology building, technicians froze cows, pigs, and sheep and then sliced them into thin strips in order to examine their anatomy.

Some of the work conducted at Riverbank was certainly scientifically questionable, not to mention unethical. Fabyan's so-called posture experiments were performed on "wayward girls" between the ages of eight and ten provided by the Illinois State Training School for Delinquent and Dependent Girls.[6]

It was a need for a geneticist to help improve grains and livestock on his farm that led Fabyan to Cornell and Friedman. The two men met, and the immigrant turned geneticist, then age twenty-three, abandoned school and started work at Riverbank in June 1915.

Friedman's introduction to the world of codes and ciphers began one day when he joined a group chasing a wild theory that the colonel wanted to prove. Like many before him Fabyan was convinced that the plays written by the Elizabethan bard, William Shakespeare, were actually the work of Sir Francis Bacon, England's legendary philosopher and scientist. To prove it, a carefully selected team was chosen to study Shakespeare's known manuscripts for evidence of Bacon's cipher signatures in the hope of exposing him as the true author. The research involved photographing documents and then enlarging the original texts to make the work easier. Friedman was drawn into the project because he was handy with a camera.

One of those Shakespeare researchers was a young woman assigned to collating the material. Elizabeth Smith, from the neighboring state of Indiana, was born in 1892 and arrived at Riverbank with a degree in English literature from Michigan's Hillsdale College. William and Elizabeth soon met and developed a lifelong fascination with cryptology and each other. It didn't take long before Friedman abandoned genetics and jumped knee-deep into the science of cryptology as Fabyan's new head of the Department of Ciphers. Decades later Friedman still vividly remembered the moment he made his career choice. "When it came to cryptology something in me found an outlet." The same could be said for his feelings for Elizabeth. As David Kahn wrote, "In May of 1917 they were married and started the most famous husband and wife team in the history of cryptology."[7]

A month before the couple's marriage, America entered the First World War. As the only active cryptology operation in the country, Riverbank was soon on the receiving end of encrypted German messages sent from both the War Department in Washington and the British War Office in London. Friedman, having quickly solved the initial batch, was soon deluged with more and more coded cables, which he solved in record time. By the fall of 1917, the successful twenty-eight-year-old geneticist turned code breaker found himself teaching a course in basic cryptography to a classroom of army officers. The teaching curriculum, however, required textbooks and other course materials that, for the most part, did not exist at the time. Remedying this problem forced Friedman to turn author. The eight monographs he produced launched a cryptologic writing career that would span the rest of his life, creating the most important body of literature in the history of cryptologic studies.

By the spring of 1918, Friedman was in an army uniform with the rank of captain bound for France and service with a military intelligence detachment. Back at Riverbank after the war he continued to refine his thinking by exploring new theories of cryptology and cryptanalysis (a word he coined that remains in use today). Like he did earlier, he committed his new theories to print, starting with "A Method of Reconstructing the Primary Alphabet from a Single One of the Series of Secondary Alphabets," and later his masterpiece, "Methods for the Solution of Running Key Ciphers and Index of Coincidence"—what David Kahn calls "the most important single publication in cryptology."[8]

His importance to cryptology in the twentieth century was gradually becoming monumental. Before Friedman, Kahn writes,

> cryptology eked out an existence as a study unto itself as an isolated phenomenon neither borrowing from nor contributing to other bodies of knowledge, Friedman led cryptology out of this lonely wilderness and into the broad rich domain of statistics. He connected cryptology to mathematics. The sense of expanding horizons must have resembled that felt by chemists when Friedrich Wohler synthesized urea demonstrating that life processes operate under well-known chemical laws and are therefore subject to experimentation and control and leading to today's vast strides in biochemistry.[9]

Having outgrown Fabyan and Riverbank, the Friedmans packed up their few belongings and headed east for Washington, DC, and the start of what would be remarkable careers for both. Waiting for William was a position with the War Department constructing new and stronger cryptosystems for the Army Signal Corps. His initial arrangement as a contractor soon morphed into a permanent position—one that would continue for the next thirty-five years. After two years on the job his unmatched talents and successes were rewarded with a promotion and the momentous title of "Chief Cryptanalyst of the Signal Corps in Charge of the Codes and Cipher Compilation Section, Research and Development Division, Office of the Chief Signal Officer."[10]

William worked at the west end of Washington's Great Mall, in a tiny office located in the so-called Munitions Building, a squat collection of temporary structures hastily built during World War I to meet War Department needs. Over the next nine years, cryptologic duties were divided between Friedman, a code-maker, and Herbert Yardley, an American from Indiana, leader of the "Black Chamber"; a polyglot group of code breakers who succeeded in cracking some of the most important encrypted foreign message traffic since its founding during World War I. When Yardley's operation shut down in 1929, the army consolidated both the code-making and code-breaking functions in 1930 under the Signal Intelligence Service with Friedman as its first director.

As the threat of global war loomed ever larger in the 1930s, Friedman turned his attention from teaching a handful of civilian cryptologists to the larger challenge of producing skilled military cryptologic specialists by the thousands. Friedman discouraged loners from applying, fearing they would be incapable of working with others in a coordinated manner. In a perfect world he hoped to recruit men possessing certain unique qualities. First, was the completion of a broad general education together with demonstrated competence in as many practical fields of knowledge as possible. Experience with large libraries full of works of current literature was also essential. An ideal candidate, Friedman believed, should possess a "rather unusual mental faculty . . . of inductive and deductive reasoning of a type that derived from the study of natural sciences like chemistry, physics, or biology." Other sciences such as philology, linguistics, and mathematics were also "excellent." In the end, he concluded that success in code-breaking and overcoming unknown ciphers was a matter of perseverance, careful analysis, intuition, and most of all—luck. Drawing on the words of an old miner, Friedman once wrote that luck trumps all just like "gold is where you find it."[11]

Fort Monmouth, situated about one hour south of New York City near the New Jersey shore, was the most important military communications and electronics research site in America. It sat on the grounds of the former Fort Monmouth Racetrack built in 1870. When it opened in May 1917, it was called "Camp Little Silver" after the nearest town. Three months later it was renamed "Camp Alfred Vail" for a New Jersey scientist who helped Samuel F. B. Morse invent the telegraph.[12] In August 1925 the name changed again to Fort Monmouth in honor of the Continental Army soldiers who fell at the battle of Monmouth. Four years later following the consolidation of the Signal Corps laboratories in Washington and New York, Fort Monmouth became the center for all army electronic research and development.

Over the years, scientists at Fort Monmouth had pursued a stream of experiments and new technologies to advance American war-fighting capability. An early study of meteorology using radio gear attached to balloons launched into the atmosphere produced data on upper winds and temperatures. There were also top-secret experiments in long-distance radar detection, which saved thousands of lives during World War II. So secret was this new technology that the entire operation was moved off-site to a hotel in a nearby town to shield it from prying eyes. The same year America entered World War II, Fort Monmouth scientists produced the SCR 510 portable FM radio. Carried on a soldier's back, it communicated tactical battlefield information back to senior commanders. So successful was the system that it was later recognized as one of the five most important technologies of World War II.[13]

War Department officials originally envisioned Fort Monmouth as a center of education in the emerging field of radio engineering. As such it was soon holding classes in new combat arts such as radio intelligence, combat photography, meteorology, and even carrier pigeons. During the interwar period, as military budgets sunk to all-time Depression lows, training and research were drastically slashed. As war clouds grew darker over Europe in the late 1930s, however, scientific work at Fort Monmouth rebounded.

On July 9, 1940, just weeks after the collapse of France in the face of the German army, Fort Monmouth experienced another first when the chief signal officer of the army directed the creation of a course in cryptography for *enlisted men* [italics added]. It was a pioneering venture with only a dozen soldiers assembled in a classroom for a week of lectures. Ten months before the Japanese attacked Pearl Harbor, Fort Monmouth added a new military radio intercept school to its array of duties, becoming in the words of one GI who passed through it, the "West Point of the Signal Corps."[14]

Qualifications for cryptographic training were set fairly low by the army. One only needed a high school education, sound eyesight to meet the strain of cryptographic work, a desire to undertake the work, and an interest in mathematics. The army insisted that candidates possess "unquestionable loyalty, integrity," and excellent character. Preference was given to "native-born citizens who have no intimate connections with foreigners in the United States or foreign countries." Emphasis was also placed on finances and spending habits in order to "render unlikely (the candidate) succumbing to temptation from these sources."[15]

Over the next year, with memoranda flying back and forth, General George C. Marshall, the army chief of staff, authorized the start of officer candidate schools (OCS) to meet the growing need for leaders at the lower ranks of the officer corps. On July 1, 1941, the training of new officers began for Infantry, Field Artillery, and Coastal Artillery at Fort Benning, Georgia, Fort Sill, Oklahoma, and Fort Monroe, Virginia. This was accompanied by schools for Armor, Cavalry, Engineers, Medical, Ordnance, Quartermaster, and the Signal Corps at Fort Monmouth.

How did Weisband make it into the Signal Corps? William P. Bundy was an American officer who later served at Bletchley Park, England's wartime code-breaking headquarters. Bundy recalled that the Signal Corps took a "completely democratic approach" when it came to recruiting potential cryptographers. "Everybody who had visible talent or aptitude whatsoever for electrical work or communications in the technological sense" and who had achieved a certain minimum test score in the appropriate categories of the General Classification Test was sent to "Crypt School" at Fort Monmouth. Friedman's course was used at Fort Monmouth as well as in a special ROTC cryptography program at the University of Illinois that served to spot talent. It was really a matter of finding someone with the right sort of mind as opposed to education and even the connection between talent and certain vocations. A 1944 US Army study noted that "no particular background of training" was "concretely indicative of cryptanalytic ability." Likewise, there were cases of high school graduates who showed a surprising aptitude for difficult cryptanalytic assignments. On the other hand, many individuals with five or six years of specialized university training were strangely limited in their aptitude for this type of work. As one observer put it, "civilian occupations or training told little about who would do well in the job."[16]

Starting in January 1943, William Weisband became a member of class 43–20, which began a four-month course of study at the Signal Corps Officer Candidate School, part of the Eastern Signal Corps Training Center (ESCTC). He was one of 1,550 officer candidates and nearly 20,000 enlisted men selected for this highly competitive program. Recruits arrived with vastly differing degrees of code-breaking proficiency and skills. Many had become interested in codes and ciphers as children after reading Edgar Allen Poe's famous tale *The Gold Bug*. While many had no previous experience, others were surprisingly talented, having had some instruction in civilian life.

William Weisband's Russian-financed RCA Institute career placed him in this last category. Upon induction he had taken the Army General Classification Test (AGCT), which measured both intelligence and aptitude. Based on the results, men were divided into five classes, from highest to lowest. Although all arms and services were supposed to receive the same proportion of men from each category, those with needs for high technical proficiency were quick to put in claims for high scorers. The Signal Corps fared well, with 39 percent of the men assigned to its training centers from March to August 1942 coming from Classes I and II; by 1943, that number jumped to 58 percent.[17]

At thirty-four years old, he was more than a decade older than the average draftee. In addition to speaking German, French, and Arabic, he arrived with strong typing skills along with a high degree of proficiency in Morse code and radio experience. Signal Corps leadership originally insisted on forty-eight weeks of training to produce a proficient cryptanalyst. The bitter lessons learned during the North African campaign reduced this requirement and kept doing so up until the last year of the war.

Army studies showed that for efficiency of learning, instructors could teach only twelve to fifteen students in a class. As demands from theater commanders for cryptographic specialists grew more pressing, advanced students, like Weisband, found themselves acting as "assistant instructors" responsible for grading student exam papers and tutoring weaker classmates.

As a Signal Corps OCS student, he had a hybrid training schedule. After being rousted out of his bunk at the crack of dawn, he stood for roll call followed by breakfast. He then made his way across the post to a bland set of barracks-like structures repeatedly altered over the previous three years to accommodate new classrooms for the ever-expanding number of students needed for wartime code work. For the remainder of the morning, he studied the fine points of officer leadership before returning to the mess hall at noon for lunch. The Friedman-designed curriculum was arranged to produce what the army termed "expert cryptanalysts" in a hurry.[18] When not drilling and marching, he sat in a classroom listening to lectures or laboring over worksheets full of incomprehensible numbers or letters. His course list included elementary and advanced cryptography followed by military cryptanalysis and features of the new top-secret International Business Machine (IBM) tabulator designed to speed up the process of breaking codes on an industrial scale.

Throughout his training, Weisband relied on the collection of Friedman-produced monographs. Securing codes required study of *Elements of Military Cryptography* followed by *Advanced Military Cryptography*. For code-breaking he carried with him *Elements of Cryptanalysis*: a top-secret textbook on the science of code-breaking filled with taxonomies of key terms, principles, and phenomena. From its first publication in 1923, David Kahn has written, it was a remarkable work that "guided the development of all American cryptology since then."[19] After mastering the basics, he received *Military Cryptanalysis*, Friedman's monumental four-volume series that incorporated everything he knew about code-breaking in 569 pages. So secret were these monographs that the NSA only declassified them in 2009, more than a half century after Weisband read them.

Bill also studied "Monoalphabetic Substitutions," "Simpler Varieties of Polyalphabetic Substitution Systems," "Varieties of Aperiodic Substitution Systems," "Transposition and Fractioning Systems," and "Opportunities Afforded by Studying Errors and Blunders Made by Enemy Cryptographer." The first step in the equation of determining the language of the enemy was the easiest. Next the cryptanalyst had to determine the general cipher system used by the enemy; a task that Friedman called "difficult, if not the most difficult step in its solution."[20] Once Bill and his classmates determined the correct cipher system, their third challenge was the reconstruction of a key to a code system that they had never seen. The key was critical in order to guide, control, and modify the various stages in the analysis of the general cipher system. When all of these steps had been successfully accomplished, the plaintext, for instance German, would emerge and then was passed to a linguist for translation. The final step required an analyst to incorporate the decoded and translated message traffic with information gathered from other sources of intelligence to produce a finished report for higher commanders.

In truth, what Weisband experienced was a difficult and demanding four months of training in a highly specialized discipline in which many of his classmates washed out. Weisband had made it. On April 24, 1943, a grinning Bill Weisband was honorably discharged as a corporal and then commissioned as Second Lieutenant William Weisband with the Signal Corp moments later. The KGB agent code-named "Link" was now amazingly one step closer to the heart of American code-breaking.

He had no orders yet and where he would go next remained a question mark.

## NOTES

1. Lambros Callimahos, "The Legendary William F. Friedman," *Cryptologic Spectrum*, Vol. 4, No. 1 (Winter 1974): 17.
2. David Kahn, *The Codebreakers* (New York: Scribner, 1986), 371.
3. Ibid., 370.
4. Jason Fagone, *The Woman Who Smashed Codes* (New York: Harpe-Collins, 2017), 24.
5. Ibid.
6. Ibid.
7. David Kahn, *The Codebreakers*, 371.
8. Ibid., 376.
9. Ibid., 383–84.
10. Ibid., 385.
11. William Friedman, "Military Cryptology," vol. I, p. 1. This was top secret at the time and was not declassified until the twenty-first century.
12. David Kahn, *The Codebreakers*, 384.
13. "History of Fort Monmouth," Virtual Tour and History of Fort Monmouth, CECOM, History Office, Fort Monmouth, New Jersey.
14. Thomas Arnold, Veterans History Project, Library of Congress, Washington, DC.
15. William Friedman, "Military Cryptology," vol. I, p. 1. This was top-secret at the time and was not declassified until the twenty-first century. NCM.
16. Stephen Budiansky, *Battle of Wits* (New York: Simon & Schuster, 2000), 138–39.
17. "History of Fort Monmouth."
18. Ibid.
19. Kahn, *The Codebreakers*, 385.
20. William Friedman, *Military Cryptanalysis* (Washington, DC: Government Printing Office, 1942), Volume I, 8.

*Chapter 14*

# The Farm

Just weeks after the Pearl Harbor disaster, the War Department received an odd telephone call from a Virginia man extending an invitation for someone to visit his home. He was the longtime owner of a farm tucked along a sleepy road about thirty miles west of Washington in the remote Fauquier County countryside.

Days later after a lovely lunch, a Signal Corps officer was shown into a backroom where a shortwave radio was displayed before him. To his amazement, the officer learned that at any time, day or night, the farmer could clearly listen to messages broadcast from Berlin, Germany. Tests conducted at Vint Hill Farms, as the site was called, soon revealed that it sat atop unique geological formations creating an acoustical anomaly. Like the US Navy's signal interception site at Two Rocks Ranch near Petaluma, California, the farm's location made it ideal for collecting international radio transmissions. A week later US Army lawyers knocked on the farmer's door with a check for $127,000 and orders to immediately vacate the property.[1]

Over the next year, a horde of army radio intercept operators descended on Vint Hill Farm, now known as top-secret "Monitoring Station Number One." In an odd twist the farm, together with Two Rocks Ranch, became the military's most important site for intercepting "Japanese" diplomatic messages.

By the spring of 1943, Monitoring Station Number One had been converted into a specialized training center called the Advanced Radio School (ARS) when the intercept staff moved to Asmara, Eritrea, where atmospheric conditions for signal collection were far better.[2]

Second Lieutenant William W. Weisband reported to ARS in June 1943. Days earlier he had passed through Arlington Hall Station, the new headquarters of the army's cryptologic program, where his travel orders were reviewed and a special identification badge was issued. With processing complete he next met with ARS's officer in charge. His qualifications for advanced cryptologic training were examined and student duties laid out. Weisband's eligibility for a security clearance allowing access to top-secret

## Chapter 14

materials also underwent a final determination. Security, which was taken very seriously by the Signal Corps, had steadily eroded over the previous year under the pressure of getting people cleared. In a letter sent to one potential recruit, Captain Lawrence Safford, a veteran code breaker and pioneer in building the navy's cryptanalyst program, spoke to the ideals of both his own service and the army on the importance of security.

> We can have no fifth columnists, nor those whose true allegiance is to Moscow. . . . Pacifists would be inappropriate as would candidates from persecuted nations or races—Czechoslovakia, Poles, Jews, who might feel an inward compulsion to involve the United States in war.[3]

Before leaving Fort Monmouth, Weisband had completed a two-page "Loyalty Check Sheet." The top portion of page one contained two questions to be executed by the candidate's commanding officer. The first was a confirmation that army intelligence had ensured that he had been "thoroughly investigated to verify his loyalty." The second, essentially the same as the first, alerted an investigator that the purpose of the investigation concerned "cryptographic duties." Page two listed biographic data with previous addresses, civilian employment, and relatives in foreign countries, along with "arrests, indictments, convictions except for traffic violations," and so forth. When completed the results of the investigation were returned to the director of training at Arlington Hall. No record of Weisband's investigation exists. Nor is there any evidence that his birth in Egypt and arrest with John Pollock in 1938 were ever checked or considered. With both boxes on the questions marked off, one of Moscow's best sources boarded a bus that carried him to Vint Hill Farms with a new security clearance in hand.[4]

On October 5, 1942, just weeks after Weisband's army induction, the Cryptologic Division of the Signal Corps became the Army Security Agency (ASA). Previously part of the Signal Corps, ASA was responsible for fighting the communications war against Japan while responsibility for cracking German communications rested with the British. Weisband now found himself working for ASA.

The pivot point in the global struggle came in the spring of 1943. At Stalingrad, Russian forces had ended Hitler's dream of Eurasian conquest at a cost of nearly two million casualties. The North African campaign launched while Weisband was still at Gardner Field had officially ended on May 22 in what historian Rick Atkinson called "an unqualified victory."[5] Allied forces now held strategic dominance of the Mediterranean with control of port facilities and airfields stretching from Casablanca on the Atlantic coast to Alexandria, Egypt, on the Suez Canal. Americans were also on the move in the Pacific. Japanese forces, now on the run but still a formidable enemy, had been bludgeoned at Guadalcanal and at Papua in New Guinea, as well as the Bismarck Sea in February 1943. A month earlier American forces had landed on Attu Island in the far-off Aleutians. On April 18, 1943, thanks to Allied cryptology, New Guinea–based US pilots flying P-38 Lightnings shot down the plane carrying Admiral Isoroku Yamamoto, the mastermind of the Pearl Harbor attack, killing all on board.

Hitler's Kriegsmarine was also facing oblivion. A year earlier swarms of German submarines, operating in so-called "Wolfpacks," were sinking Allied shipping in the Atlantic at a rate of one ship every eight hours. Now these numbers had been drastically reduced thanks in large part to the skill and determination of British code breakers in cracking the German *Enigma* naval cipher.

As May became June the accelerating pace of fighting in all theaters was putting increased manpower pressure on the already strained resources of the Signal Corps. To address the growing demand a memorandum entitled "Establishment of a Signal Corps Replacement Pool" was signed authorizing the creation of a reservoir of officers trained in various cryptologic specialties. The initial complement had a maximum capacity of 100 officers (later jumped to 150) under the command of the Military Personnel Branch. It had authority to change the assignment of any pool officer at any time without the concurrence of the commanding officer. This arrangement, however, was short-lived as one official later wrote due to the "scarcity and great demand for this type of officer." As to what training specialty they received—that was dictated by the growing demands flowing into the Pentagon from theater commanders around the world.[6]

As part of the replacement pool, Weisband was about to undergo crash training as a radio traffic analyst (RTA). Radio traffic analysis was virtually unknown to American military leaders before Pearl Harbor. "Traffic analysis was not part of the Army lexicon until World War II" as one writer delicately put it.[7]

This suddenly changed on the afternoon of December 8, 1941, when swarms of Japanese aircraft destroyed General Douglas MacArthur's entire air fleet of B-17s and P-40s on the ground at Iba Field west of Manila and Clark Field in the Philippines. The shift in cryptologic thinking began with Howard W. Brown, an obscure army second lieutenant and radio intelligence veteran. Until that devastating afternoon Brown, as a member of the Manila-based Second Signal Service Company, had been chasing Japanese diplomatic traffic. Wasting not a moment, Brown redirected his resources to the more pressing mission of attacking indecipherable Japanese air force communications. Until he was evacuated from Corregidor, Brown scrutinized as many Japanese circuits as he could find. Over time, he produced a clear picture of the size of Japanese naval forces in the Philippines and tactics they were employing. Burrowed deep inside the Malinta Tunnel, Brown kept MacArthur informed on the size and direction of Japanese Army Air Forces he was facing and movements of ground troops as they advanced across the Philippines. Based only on "inference from traffic analysis," he supplied his commanders with accurate "information as to where the Japanese might next be expected to move."[8]

What is "traffic analysis"? It is actually traffic "flow" analysis, a careful study of thousands of encrypted radio-transmitted messages by radio traffic analysts with no knowledge of the content. Its purpose was to supply commanders with warnings about enemy behavior or intentions. A first step in the process was the mapping of specific enemy circuit designations used by enemy headquarters staff and subordinate commands. Next, patterns of transmissions were examined. Sudden and unexpected spikes and a reduction in volumes of messages between field units and headquarters over time as well as unexplained silences were carefully recorded for hints of imminent enemy action. The lengths of messages were also revealing. From their analysis, RTAs could squeeze out hidden clues concerning enemy troop movements, identity of particular field units, personalities of unit commanders, and order of battle. Seasoned RTAs keeping a sharp eye out for sloppy communications practices by lazy operators could often cheat their way into unexpected backdoors to priceless enemy traffic.

Across all theaters of the war the time and patience devoted by RTAs to this arcane aspect of technical intelligence produced windfalls of important information. In the Pacific, for instance, every Japanese division south of Manchuria was pinpointed through examination of large volumes of messages sent between field unit and headquarters. In November 1942, Arlington Hall began issuing reports on Japanese troop movements, shipping traffic, aircraft redeployment, and other insights drawn only from the study of external features of Japanese radio transmissions. Actual penetration of encrypted Japanese Army messages didn't occur until November 1943. Until then, one NSA analyst later wrote, most of the intelligence derived from Japanese Army communications came from "analysis of the patterns of all other traffic phenomena." Looking back, he noted, that until the end of the war traffic analysis proved to be a "consistent source of intelligence about the locations and movements of Japanese units."[9]

In addition to studying volumes and patterns, they also attacked low-grade codes and ciphers on such things as weather and logistics. From the information amassed, statistical reports were produced on changing technical aspects of enemy communications. These proved valuable in identifying and analyzing traffic. Intercept logs and reports containing data on identified units, reported activities, current order of battle, and personalities were also updated daily. Situation maps were created and posted for easy reference.

Direction-finding experts, who constantly trolled the ether for communication sources, were also a vital part of the RTA's work. In the end RTA units published daily activity reports for higher and lateral headquarters that contained a complete record of radio technical intercept results.[10]

Weisband was not going to be an RTA from a long distance. A report issued in 1943 explained that traffic analysis when properly applied was "recognized as being able to not only provide strategic intelligence for the War Department but also to *support the local commanders directly*." [italics added] At the height of the debate over traffic analysis in February 1943, Colonel Carter Clarke, then chief of the Special Branch at Arlington Hall, prepared a study for Major General George V. Strong, head of the Military Intelligence Service. The always precise Clarke, a veteran military cryptanalyst, made it clear where RTAs should be assigned. Local commanders could obtain considerable benefit from traffic analysis regarding tactical and strategic intelligence because they were, as he wrote, based primarily on "enemy communications in close proximity to his sphere of activity." Continuing on, Clarke explained that while radio traffic analysis was not on a level with successful cryptanalytic study of high-grade cryptographic systems, the results could sometimes be available "instantaneously," and subject "only to proper interpretation on the part of the local staff."[11]

With training wrapped up on July 6, 1943, Weisband made last-minute preparations for his next assignment. Before embarkation from New York, however, he had a final personal obligation to perform. It was a dread-laden pilgrimage back to Brooklyn to see his brother Mark and his wife, Edith, and Edward, his only nephew, not yet age three, then living with his widowed mother, Sarah. The visit was not an easy one. William would soon board a ship that would carry him through treacherous Atlantic waters to war-torn Great Britain, where further assignment to somewhere unknown awaited him. Adding to the gloom, just a week or so earlier, Sarah experienced what every World War II mother feared. The yellow Western Union telegram was typed in laconic War Department prose. In three or so lines the Secretary of War expressed his "deep regret" that Sarah's eldest son, Harold, had been killed in Tunisia.

Harold was always viewed as the "black sheep" of the family, but he was very close to Bill. He had been instrumental in getting his youngest brother his first job when he arrived in America almost twenty years earlier. In 1938 he had embezzled funds from an employer, which he then gambled away at the casinos in Atlantic City, New Jersey. When Bill learned about Harold's possible arrest, he quickly replaced the money to get him off the hook.

In 1943, he was a private with the Fifth Army in North Africa assigned to the 214th Coast Artillery Battalion. On May 26, 1943, Harold Weisband was killed in a freak noncombat accident. Sarah later learned that his remains were temporarily buried at Carthage, Tunisia, in what later became known as the North Africa American Cemetery. It would be his permanent resting place.[12]

On July 17, 1943, nearly a year after his induction, training complete, Bill Weisband was ready to board a troopship that would carry him to England and from there to parts unknown.

## NOTES

1. John Pefero Lecture, Cold War History Museum, Undated.
2. David Alvarez, *Secret Messages* (Lawrence: University Press of Kansas, 2000), 113.
3. Liza Mundy, *Code Girls* (New York: Hachette Books, 2017), 13.
4. "Origination and Evolution of Radio Traffic Analysis," *Cryptologic Quarterly*, Winter 1989, Volume 7, No. 4.
5. Rick Atkinson, *The Day of Battle* (New York: Henry Holt & Company, 2007).
6. "Origination and Evolution of Radio Traffic Analysis," *Cryptologic Quarterly*, Winter 1989, Volume 7, No. 4.
7. Ibid.
8. Ibid.
9. Ibid.
10. Ibid.
11. Ibid.
12. Later he was awarded the American Campaign Medal, the Army Presidential Unit Citation, the Army Good Conduct Medal, and the European-African-Middle Eastern Campaign Medal. American Battle Monuments Commission, Clarendon, Virginia.

## Chapter 15

# European Theater of Operations

Second Lieutenant William Weisband was now ready for war, but there was one more important errand he had to complete before he shipped out. Following his army induction in September 1942, there was a brief assignment to Gardner Field followed by months of OCS Signal Corp training in New Jersey and advanced schooling as an RTA in Virginia. During that entire time, he had been out of touch with the KGB and off the payroll.

In the weeks before his departure, Weisband put down a signal for the KGB in New York requesting an emergency meeting. The mystery man who responded was Pavel Pastelnyak. To the few Americans who knew him, Pastelnyak posed as Pavel Klarin, a vice-consul at Russia's consulate in New York City. Weisband would have shuddered had he known the pedigree of the man who had risked all to meet him. Klarin had been in New York for four years starting as a supervisor of the security force guarding the Soviet Union's pavilion at the 1939 World's Fair. He had no espionage training, spoke little English, and had no experience in foreign operations. These shortcomings were brushed aside in 1940 when Moscow Center appointed him "acting resident" in the wake of the FBI's arrest of Gaik Ovakimian, a KGB officer assigned to Amtorg, for violating the Foreign Agents Registration Act. Following the arrival of Vasili Zarubin in January 1942, Klarin was reduced in rank to deputy resident.[1]

Weisband was a trusted KGB source, which made meeting with him an absolute Moscow imperative. As Klarin sat listening, Bill outlined his secret work in California, his induction into the army, months of officer training and advanced Signal Corp schooling, along with a crash course in Italian, all in preparation for an assignment to either Sicily or Italy. His next stop would be England for some last-minute training before moving on to North Africa. He didn't know where the war would take him, he explained, prompting his fear of losing his lucrative pipeline to Moscow.

Klarin had heard enough. Within hours he flashed a message to Moscow requesting instructions for Weisband before his leave ended on June 27,

1943. His departure was set for early July. Days later, Klarin instructed Weisband to stand at the front entrance of the Leicester Galleries, an art gallery next to Leicester Square in London's Mayfair district, starting on Sunday, July 24, and every Sunday thereafter. On Wednesdays he was to stand on the east corner of Orchard and Wigmore Street. Someone would approach him, Klarin explained, with a recognition signal in either Russian or English. The stranger would say "Hello Bill. Greetings from Gregorij."[2]

The 849th Signal Intelligence Service (SIS), with a strength of 16 officers and 102 enlisted men, was first activated at Fort Devens, Massachusetts, in December 1942, just weeks after the start of the North African campaign. Its mission was to provide US Signal Radio Intelligence (SRI) companies with a better field-processing capability. The team arrived in Algiers sixty days later on February 1, 1943. At full strength there were four SRI companies operating under the 849th. The commander was a Signal Corp veteran, Colonel Harold G. Hayes. It quickly began providing theater commanders with tactical intelligence intercepted from communications of German combat units operating in North Africa. One NSA historian wrote that with the arrival of the 849th in North Africa, "Army COMINT was very much in combat."[3]

Bill Weisband joined the 849th in Algeria in August 1943 around the time US and British troops were in the final phase of expelling Axis forces from Sicily. As the unit gained maturity and experience, Fifth Army leadership ordered a major restructuring in its organization. What was described as unwieldy, SRI companies from the 849th were broken into separate detachments. Small analytical elements were integrated into each detachment to handle processing and then assigned to combat units. Under normal circumstances Bill Weisband would have been sent to one of these new detachments as an RTA. But fate and Colonel Hayes had other plans in store for him.

For the next nine months he supported one of the greatest battle captains in French history. Alphonse Juin was born in the tiny Algerian town of Bone in 1888. He was the only child of a police officer in the local gendarmerie that included Constantine, an ancient city in northwest Algeria. Half a century later it would serve as General Eisenhower's advanced headquarters for the Sicilian campaign. Juin spoke French at home while acquiring fluency in an assortment of Arabic tongues, including Berber, a rare dialect spoken in Morocco. Strong mathematics talents led to his admission in 1910 to the prestigious Ecole Speciale Militaire d' Saint-Cyr, founded by Napoleon more than a century earlier. After two years of study, he graduated with honors. In a move that left his classmates baffled, Juin rejected high-profile service in France with its dull routine of garrison duty built around a tedious cycle of conscript training. Instead, he returned to his roots in North Africa by joining the 1st Regiment Tirailleurs Algeriens and opting for service in Morocco along the far-western fringes of France's African empire. He was at the time and would remain a soldier's soldier, eschewing crisp uniforms, in the words of Rick Atkinson, for "a Basque beret and mud-spattered cape."[4]

Juin emersed himself in a world that offered experiences and knowledge he could never acquire elsewhere. Working with highly skilled and experienced officers, he learned how to lead a colorful and exotic collection of North African troops who would make historic contributions to the successful mountain campaign in World War II Italy. They were a kaleidoscope of uniforms, tribal languages, cultures, and strange names. There was the Armee d'Afrique made up of Zouaves from Morocco, Legion Etrangere (Foreign Legion), Infanterie Coloniale, Maghrebs from across Tunisia, Libya, Mauritania, Goumiers from deep in the Atlas Mountains, and Tirailleurs Senegalese from Black Africa. Juin loved them all, his biographer said. But above all his greatest admiration was directed toward the Moroccans, whose skills "in the use of ground, toughness in mountain warfare, and aggressive spirit matched his own nature."[5]

Juin's military education in North Africa abruptly ended in August 1914 when he and his Moroccan troops landed in France at the outbreak of World War I. As the Sultan of Morocco was technically not at war with Germany, Juin's five units took on the new title of Brigade de Chasseurs Indigenes and were fitted out with the khaki uniforms of Chasseurs Alpins. They made a strange group both in appearance and in sound as they marched through the French towns and villages with Juin in front chanting their guttural expressions of themselves as mercenaries beyond the law fighting with a mixture of good humor and mysticism. "We come from (Sultan) Idriss, May God forgive our sins."[6]

For Juin the war was a relentless trial of hard fighting. Less than a month after his arrival at the front he suffered severe wounds to his left hand, forcing him to fight in considerable pain with his arm in a sling. For his heroism under fire, he was awarded the Legion of Honor. Six months later he was wounded again, this time in the right arm. So bad were his injuries that for the rest of his life he was authorized to salute with his left arm—"a distinctive characteristic of him."[7]

At the time of the Allied landings in 1942, Juin was commanding all Vichy government ground troops in North Africa. Not long after the invasion he joined the Allied cause in the fight against the Axis. When Weisband arrived in Algeria Juin was in the process of forming his collection of North African troops into the French Expeditionary Corps (FEC) in preparation for combat in Italy. On November 25, 1943, Juin, leading his FEC, arrived in Naples "to begin a nine-month command which would earn him a place of honour forever in the history of his country." In many respects Juin was immediately at ease with the terrain of Italy, which was not dissimilar to Morocco's rugged Atlas Mountains in the context of tactics—mobility on foot, infiltration, and junior leader initiative with supplies shipped in by tens of thousands of mules.[8]

An immediate problem for Juin and the FEC was the ability to securely communicate with Fifth Army forces. From the start of the campaign American and British commanders found themselves thrust into an environment that involved coordinating massive troop movements in which secrecy was paramount; a challenge that now included at least one hundred and twenty thousand soldiers who spoke not a word of English. Juin's forces had been supplied with US radio equipment and certain communications security procedures that were alien to FEC Signal Corp staff. To get a sense of the problem, Juin himself had to issue his special Orders of the Day in French, Arabic, and Berber.

To help remedy the problem Colonel Hayes, the head of the 849th, turned to Bill Weisband, a rare breed who was perfect for the assignment. He was an American military officer with nearly a year of training in Signal Corp procedures. In a Signal Corp in which language talents were at a premium, he spoke both French and Arabic and some newly acquired Italian. An added factor was his familiarity with the Muslim culture and ways of doing things, having spent the first sixteen years of his life among Arabs in Alexandria, Egypt.

Bill Weisband joined the FEC as a radio security officer (RSO) when it landed and would remain with it for the next nine months. In modern parlance, he would be described as being "embedded" with the FEC. Precise facts and figures describing Weisband's movements and whereabouts over those nine months remain elusive. The one thing that is certain is that he witnessed some hard and brutal winter fighting as the FEC battled its way north through the treacherous valleys and steep passes of Italy's Apennine Mountain Range. The record shows that the FEC was at the heart of some of most intense fighting of the war. Pushing steadily forward, Juin and his troops were at the point of attack starting with the battle of Garigliano and Monte Casino and moving on to help smash through first, the German Winter Line, then the Gustav Line and, finally, the Hitler Line—all at a cost of thousands of his men killed or wounded before Juin entered Rome in June 1944 seated proudly in a jeep next to General Mark Clark, the Fifth Army's commander. Throughout it all, Weisband's duties were to ensure the security of FEC communications both internally and with other Fifth Army elements. It was his job to teach FEC radio operators the use of codes and ciphers in communicating, proper coding and decoding procedures, avoiding casual chatter over the airwaves, and ensuring the strict maintenance of radio discipline.

Whether Bill Weisband ever made his London meeting with the KGB remains a question mark. A close look at his timeline while in England suggests that he was stationed at the Signal Intelligence Service (SIS), Signal Section, Headquarters, European Theater of Operations (ETOUSA). Over ten days or so, he underwent intense last-minute instruction about Allied procedures in intercepting German army field codes, German communications technique, and practical aspects of field intercept. Not long enough to make contact before departing again on August 3, 1943. A note in his KGB file in Moscow suggests that instructions were sent to either New York or London for delivery to Weisband. Whether he received them remains a mystery.

> Before severing the direct connection with [Link] it is essential to explain to him why it is necessary to suspend personal contact, and to instruct him about the need to observe caution and to keep an eye on himself. You should continue to pay him his wages. Warn him not to make any important decisions about his work in the future without our knowledge and consent. When addressing him at [present], we should make it clear to him that we are far from indifferent about his fate, that we value him as a worker, and that he absolutely can and should count on us for help.[9]

Over the next year the KGB remained keen to know his status, making repeated attempts to keep tabs on his whereabouts. In one instance in 1944, Lona Cohen was ordered to contact Bill Weisband's brother, Mark, for any news about him. Lona was a nanny for a wealthy Manhattan family and New York City schoolteacher and a low-level Russian agent. Her code name was "Leslie," and she was married to Morris Cohen, a KGB courier, code-named "Volunteer," who was then serving with the army in Europe.[10]

At some point during his service in Italy, Bill Weisband took matters into his own hands to reestablish contact. His language skills once again proved fortuitous when Colonel Hayes assigned him as a translator for a Russian military delegation visiting Italy to observe naval operations. Bill suddenly seized his chance to quietly inform someone in the delegation that he was a Russian agent. He asked that a message be delivered to his Moscow bosses that his stay in Italy would soon end, and he would be returning to the United States. The information was passed on to the KGB and he soon received instructions when he returned to the United States. The KGB was now ready and waiting for their trusted source to return home and resume his work as a courier. But oh, what a story he had for them.[11]

## NOTES

1. VN Concordance, 321–22.
2. Nigel West, *Venona* (New York: HarperCollins, 1999), 41.
3. Robert Louis Benson, *A History of U.S. Communications during World War II: Policy and Administration* (Washington, DC: Fort Meade, Maryland, Center for Cryptologic National Security Agency, Series IV, Volume 8, 1997).

4. Rick Atkinson, *An Army at Dawn* (New York: Henry Holt and Company, 2002), 94.

5. Anthony Clayton, *Three Marshals of France* (London: Brassey's UK, 1992), 15.

6. Ibid., 15.

7. Ibid., 16.

8. Ibid., 79.

9. VBN 133.

10. VWN 1, 112–13.

11. Robert Louis Benson provided the information regarding Weisband's approach to the Russian delegation. Benson learned about his role as an interpreter and translator from a former CIA officer who knew Weisband in the later 1940s. During a conversation he told this person that during his assignment in Italy he served as an interpreter/translator for Fifth Army leaders and the delegation. He served in this role for the duration of their stay in Italy. It is logical that he identified himself as a Russian agent who wanted to inform his KGB bosses that he would soon be returning to the United States. Someone, most likely a GRU officer in the delegation, relayed this information to Moscow for passage to the KGB. Robert Louis Benson, author interview, July 2, 2023. Benson memorandum entitled "Venona" to Deputy Director, NSA, May 16, 1996. NCM, NSA.

*Chapter 16*

# Rendezvous

A winter evening in New York City can be very unpleasant. Dampness and temperatures dipping into the twenties with stinging winds whipping around skyscrapers can produce a miserable experience.

It can be particularly onerous when you've worked all day at a "cover" job only to find yourself standing around nervously on a busy sidewalk trying to appear inconspicuous while searching a sea of faces for someone you've never laid eyes on.[1] A difficult enough task but for the dread that fills you at the thought of the FBI quietly watching and waiting to swoop in and arrest you.

This was the spot Alexander Feklisov found himself in February 1945. The schedule was fixed—it never varied. Every second Friday of the month at 8:45 p.m. for the previous five months he had stood waiting in front of the Astoria Theater in midtown Manhattan.

Feklisov had reason to fear the FBI. As a KGB officer assigned to the Soviet consulate in New York with no diplomatic immunity, he had no shield from federal espionage charges. Yet despite the danger, his mission that night, like all the others before, was to reestablish contact with Bill Weisband after more than eighteen months since his last meeting in New York with Pavel Klarin. The risks as well as the drudgery of standing on that sidewalk were all too clear to him. Waiting for endless hours was all part of an intelligence officer's life, but after so long with no results even the patient Feklisov was growing skeptical that his quarry would ever appear.

Moscow Center's instructions were clear and specific. The July 1944 message to the New York station ordered him to stand there and wait. After months of repeated reports that Bill was a no show, the Center simply instructed Feklisov again and again to "keep going."[2]

For an intelligence officer just getting to the rendezvous site is a complicated undertaking; one that took weeks and sometimes months of careful planning. The route, first laid out on paper, required practice on the street for any possible flaws before Moscow gave a final approval. Feklisov's movements had to appear innocuous and natural in order to lull any FBI surveillance into relaxing and concluding that nothing was amiss. Since the summer of 1943, security of such operations had only intensified following reports that Bureau surveillance of consulate officials had dramatically increased.

In Feklisov's case, every second Friday of the month became movie night with his wife, Nina. Like clockwork the couple casually strolled from their Manhattan apartment to a movie theater somewhere along Broadway where they purchased tickets, found their seats, and waited for the film to start. In the middle of the movie Feklisov stood up, alone, and slowly made his way to the lobby, carefully scanning his surroundings for strangers following him. His decision-making had to be quick—does he return to his seat or exit the theater and head down the street for a possible rendezvous. He had been repeating this same routine since August 1944.[3]

By 1945 Feklisov had developed into a skilled agent handler although he didn't start out that way. Born in 1914, the oldest of five children, he had set his sights on a life as a railway worker like his father. At fifteen he apprenticed at a repair shop with dreams of becoming a locomotive engineer. His mathematics talent, however, led him unexpectedly to workers college and from there to the Moscow School of Communications to become a "radio technician."[4] Good grades and a strong work ethic coupled with correct Communist Party discipline soon caught the eye of the KGB. In 1939, he started a one-year course in the basics of foreign espionage, which incorporated a two-month internship at the Ministry of Foreign Affairs. His performance was rewarded at graduation with the prestigious rank of captain and a coveted assignment to the elite American Section.

In 1940, the KGB's Moscow Center had a staff of about 120, including clerks and typists. Both the KGB along with GRU were suffering severe shortages, with most experienced officers having been murdered or imprisoned during Stalin's purges. So bad was the situation that Feklisov's processing for a New York assignment was accelerated when Foreign Minister Vyachislav Molotov, Stalin's closest advisor, took the unprecedented step of personally authorizing his departure to America without a spouse. As he later remembered, he had two missions to accomplish in New York: first, to construct a clandestine radio link between New York and Moscow Center, and then to "learn operational work as fast as possible."[5]

Departing Moscow on January 17, 1941, he traveled for a month, first crossing the broad expanse of Russia to Yokohama, Japan. There he boarded a ship that stopped briefly at Honolulu before sailing on to San Francisco, where an eastbound train carried him to the Soviet consulate in New York City. The name on his passport, "Alexander Fomin," described him as "an ordinary trainee," with no diplomatic status. It was, he later remembered, a "rather thin cover."[6]

As a bachelor ensconced at the Soviet school located on East 87th Street, he walked daily to the consulate on East 61st Street. Daytime cover work kept him confined to mundane chores of dealing with 120,000 American residents with "rights of a Soviet citizen," examining visa request forms, and handling problems of Russian sailors calling at East Coast ports.[7]

Feklisov's bachelor days soon took a sharp turn when Zina Osipova entered his life. Zina had been part of a group Moscow sent to Columbia University to study English, shorthand, and accounting as part of an effort to ease the paperwork strain stemming from the ever-increasing flow of American Lend-Lease supplies to the Soviet Union. Bright, pretty, and talented, she soon caught the eye of Amtorg's chairman, Mikhail Gusev, who picked her as his personal secretary. She and Feklisov were married in March 1944 in the basement of the consulate building.[8]

By the fall of 1944, the New York station knew that Weisband had returned home from North Africa in September. Yet a nagging question remained: If he had been back in New York for months why had he failed to make his contact earlier as ordered?

After months of the same routine, Feklisov finally got his break on February 9, 1945. As he once again took up his post in front of the Astoria Theater, he spotted a man in an army uniform nervously loitering around and examining movie posters as if waiting for someone. The height seemed right, but he looked thin, not "chubby" as the Center had described. After a few minutes of careful observation, Feklisov threw caution to the wind and approached him. What happened next made the many months of tedium pay off. "Excuse me, you're waiting for Helen, right?" Feklisov asked. Bill smilingly replied, "You must be her cousin, James?" The two men wasted no time getting off the busy sidewalk to a nearby bar where they could quietly talk.[9]

For Feklisov, such an operational recontact meeting had to be brief. Simply ensure they weren't followed, get some background information, provide Weisband with details for the next contact, and get away. But Weisband had other ideas. For him, it was a reunion. He was eager to describe his life in Italy and arrival back in the United States in September 1944. Then there were details about his brief assignment as a Signal Corp "special courier" and new duties at a place called Arlington Hall Station. What he didn't mention was a trip he had taken to the West Coast nor the confrontation he'd had with the military police in Salt Lake City for carrying two bottles of whiskey aboard an eastbound train. Such an admission would have loomed suspiciously large in the minds of his Kremlin bosses. He quickly briefed Feklisov on *Magic*, America's most important cryptologic secret. As Feklisov sat wide-eyed in the noisy restaurant, Weisband described how the Americans had broken the Japanese diplomatic and military attaché ciphers and were reading reports sent between Sato Naotake, the Japanese ambassador in

Moscow, and the foreign ministry in Tokyo. "We know" Bill blurted out "that Molotov often meets with [Sato] who is pressuring your foreign minister to sign a non-aggression pact."[10] Washington also knew every move that Japanese military and naval forces made. Japanese army codes had also been cracked; a feat that explained the success American forces were achieving throughout the Pacific Theater. As if this was not enough information for Feklisov to absorb, Bill then whispered that he was working at Arlington Hall Station as a Russian linguist. Since taking the assignment he had learned that cryptanalysts were expending considerable effort to break into enciphered Soviet messages sent between its American stations and Moscow and were experiencing some success. More than half a century later, Feklisov, an old man and retired from the KGB, still recalled how the beer he was drinking "suddenly tasted bitter" as the full impact of Bill's last intelligence nugget sunk in on him.[11]

Ever mindful of security and having heard enough, Feklisov was anxious to get away. He quickly cut Bill off with instructions—first to learn more about the *Magic* project and for Bill to wear civilian clothing for their next meeting to reduce suspicion. The two men parted. Decades later he still remembered leaving the bar that night in dread at the "enormity of the disaster that was looming over our heads." As he returned to Zina now waiting for him at a nearby subway station, his mind was a blur with what he had just learned. Catching his eye, Zina instinctively recognized her husband's anxiety despite his assurances that "everything was fine."[12]

A month later at their next meeting, Bill assured Feklisov he was not under suspicion. Carefully walking him through a list of memorized questions about Arlington Hall Station and the Russian program, Bill disgorged everything he knew. The rendezvous soon ended with Feklisov explaining that another officer, assigned to Washington, would appear within five minutes. He then walked away and never saw Bill again. But he had fulfilled his mission—contact was now reestablished. The KGB had hit the jackpot—their man was back in play as a trusted source at the heart of American code-breaking. And for Bill, the hope that he had expressed to Pat Grimes that final evening in Los Angeles before entering the army had been fulfilled. He was now back on the Kremlin payroll.[13]

## NOTES

1. Throughout the narrative description of his meetings with Weisband, Feklisov refers to him only as "Rupert." Alexander Feklisov, *The Man behind the Rosenbergs* (New York: Enigma Books, 2001), 92.

2. Ibid.

3. Ibid., 92–93.
4. Ibid., 5.
5. Ibid., 14.
6. Ibid., 25.
7. Ibid., 27–28.
8. Mikhail M. Gusev, KGB cryptonym, Matchmaker, was the head of Amtorg. Venona New York KGB, 1944, 438–39, 473, Venona Special Studies.
9. Feklisov, *The Man behind the Rosenbergs*, 93.
10. Ibid., 93.
11. Ibid., 94.
12. Feklisov, *The Man behind the Rosenbergs*, 94.
13. WFO Reports, April 24, 1950, and June 2, 1950, Weisband FBI file.

## Chapter 17

# Arlington Hall

Senora Blanca Renard did what she did most days by gazing across a collection of students sitting attentively in her salon awaiting instructions. In October 1934, the Chilean native had made her piano debut at New York City's Town Hall before a large and "markedly responsive" audience, playing a difficult repertoire that included Handel's Chaconne in G minor, Beethoven's Rondo in G major, and Brahms sonata in F minor.[1] Over the next seven or so years, she toured the world giving recitals and teaching workshops. She eventually ended her musical odyssey as director of the music department at Arlington Hall Junior College, a private Virginia boarding school about two miles from downtown Washington.

The school opened in 1927 catering to young women from wealthy families both local and as far away as Hawaii and Canada. Situated on a bucolic twenty-eight acres of verdant hills and grassland, the curriculum advertised a four-year high school academic program that prepared students for college entrance exams. There was also a two-year college certificate program blended with business courses in typing, filing, and basic accounting. Athletics included tennis on outdoor courts and horseback riding along miles of bridal paths and an indoor arena for poor weather. The centerpiece of the campus was a grand four-story L-shaped mansion filled with classrooms and staff offices. Visitors drove up a winding driveway that ended at a majestic porticoed entrance flanked by white columns reaching to the roof. Additional buildings serving as dormitories and offices, and even a large stable for horses dotted the campus.[2]

\* \* \*

For more than two decades the heart of American war-making was located at the west end of Constitution Avenue across from the Federal Reserve Building in Washington, DC. Employees worked in a collection of dilapidated "temporary" structures hastily assembled in 1918 to support "the country's entire military brain trust" during World War I. Technically, the two separate complexes sitting side by side were officially called the Main Navy and Munitions Building. Over the years nothing had been done to improve creature comforts. Thin and barely insulated walls forced workers to wear coats during the freezing winters and roast during sweltering summer months. Before the war, William Friedman and his handful of assistants worked there in a tiny warren of rooms outfitted with a few chairs, some large tables, and filing cabinets filled with coded cables. The space that had sufficed for peacetime code-breaking became hopelessly inadequate overnight when the Pearl Harbor attack launched cryptology on to the global stage.[3]

The national emergency forced Congress to pass legislation giving the armed forces sweeping authority to acquire private property for a military purpose anywhere in the country, often with little or no explanation to the owner. Seemingly overnight army camps and naval bases began springing up where just weeks earlier sat a family farm or boatyard. Cost was no object, and over the course of the war billions of dollars were spent that remained hidden from public view until well after the war. Washington, DC, was not spared. The military's craving for real estate in the capital seemed even more voracious. As the war heated up, buildings and vacant property were gobbled up around the city at an alarming rate.

War Department code breakers hungry for larger space soon cast an eye west a mile or so across the Potomac River to Arlington Hall Junior College. It was ideal for their purposes—sufficiently far away from the busy city, it was close to the newly opened five-sided Pentagon, a huge concrete monstrosity in suburban Virginia that now housed the nation's military leadership. It wasn't long before the school's director was handed a check for $650,000 with orders for all two hundred students and faculty members to find other accommodation.

What had once been a pristine campus quickly became—army. On June 14, 1942, soldiers suddenly appeared carrying miles of barbed wire that they quickly began stretching around everything in anticipation of the imminent arrival of armed military police who would start patrolling the perimeter. At the new front gate, stone-faced sentries began demanding proper badges before entry. Unauthorized visitors, even those with a legitimate reason to enter, were turned away. Discussing what went on at Arlington Hall was forbidden even with one's closest friend working in another section of the building.

Not to be outdone by the army, the US Navy, equally assiduous, began confiscating property to meet its own expanding cryptologic needs. It centered in on the northwest section of Washington at another girl's finishing school called Mount Vernon Seminary, situated on Nebraska Avenue near American University.[4] A government check for $800,000 was quickly issued with orders to vacate. The site became the headquarters for navy code-breaking operations masked by the name "Navy Annex." The steady disappearance of property to the military at such an alarming rate soon became the subject of wry humor for local wags. The joke soon went around the capital that if the military could capture enemy territory like they gobbled up real estate the war would be over in a week.

* * *

One of the leaders of the move to Arlington Hall was Frank Rowlett. Born in 1908, he was raised in Rose Hill in Lee County; a town with fewer than a thousand residents near the Tennessee–Kentucky border. After completing degrees in mathematics and chemistry at nearby Emory and Henry College, Frank briefly taught before being lured to Washington in April 1930 with the promise of a job as a "junior cryptanalyst" under William Friedman, the new head of the Signal Intelligence Service (SIS).[5]

The backgrounds of Rowlett's new colleagues, Solomon Kullback and Abraham Sinkov, could not have been more different. The two friends in their twenties came from Russian Jewish immigrant parents. Unlike Rowlett's small-town life, they grew up on the busy streets of Brooklyn, New York, attended Boys High School and City College of New York, graduating with mathematics degrees. Eschewing teaching and facing life in America still rife with anti-Semitism, they filled out a Civil Service application after reading a government advertisement for a "junior mathematician."[6] The two New Yorkers soon found themselves sitting next to Rowlett studying codes and ciphers under Friedman's watchful eye. None of them realized it at the time but this mismatched crew would become legendary in the world of cryptology and later serve as the nucleus of America's most secret cryptologic organization.

When Freidman and his young team began working together in 1930, their mandate was the strengthening of army codes and ciphers to prevent foreign interception. America's nascent code-breaking apparatus under relaxed censorship rules in force during World War I became problematic in peacetime when telegraph companies grew increasingly squeamish about turning encrypted messages over to Friedman. Compounding these issues was the passage of the Comprehensive Communications Act (CCA) in 1934; a law that made it a crime punishable by fine and imprisonment to "monitor and divulge to a third party the contents of any radio message." This thorny issue was sidestepped less than a year later when some legal legerdemain allowed the army's chief signal officer to produce a directive described by one observer as a "less than reassuring decision." "These penalties apply, of course, to the work done by the entire Signal Intelligence Service, but they may be ignored as this service operates in compliance with existing directions of the Secretary of War."[7]

In 1936, with the CCA question settled, the SIS inaugurated a program of intercepting communications with particular attention paid to Japanese diplomatic messages. During the 1930s, as Japan abandoned membership in the League of Nations and began aggressive military moves into China and Manchuria, it replaced its slow and inefficient book cipher system that had been the standard for centuries for a speedier and more mobile machine-generated system. It was this new coding device that Friedman's young team began attacking. To simplify their work, they gave the different machines a color designation, calling the first one "Red." Working in partnership, Rowlett and Sinkov, with only a few messages to work with and neither man knowing a word of Japanese, uncovered the machine's all-important "keying system" followed by the cryptographic patterns it generated. This led to their solution of Red, which offered policymakers behind the scenes access into the thinking and planning of Tokyo's leaders. Among the most important discoveries were details of secret negotiations then underway between Japan, Germany, and Italy that would lead to the signing of a Tri-Partite Pact. In 1936 a secret clause in the treaty was revealed committing each government to support their partners in war "regardless of the circumstances."[8] Over the next two years, SIS followed Japanese thinking until Tokyo slowly began a periodic upgrading of its communication security practices; a normal transition that strengthened its cipher systems, temporarily locking out the Americans from further information.

Adding to this headache, Friedman and his team now faced a new "Type-B" machine, nicknamed "Purple," introduced around the world in February 1939, replacing Red machines. Despite these setbacks Rowlett and Sinkov, gritting their teeth, set to work again confident that they could crack Purple one day with time and hard work.[9]

Hunching over hundreds of messages filled with gibberish, the two men soon discerned that in constructing both the Red and Purple machine-cipher systems, Japanese technicians had overlooked two basic flaws that left the system vulnerable to exploitation. Both were designed to split Japanese syllabary into vowels and consonants, which were separately enciphered. Exploiting this error both men began applying educated guesses or "cribs" as they worked their way into a readable message. A second stroke of luck had nothing to do with cryptanalysis. Rather than wait for the manufacture of a full complement of Purple machines, Japanese technicians began installing their limited supply at major world capitals, such as Washington, London, Paris, Berlin, and others. Since both Red and Purple were used at different sites, code clerks were forced to encode the same message in both Red and Purple codes, in effect, a double encoding that eventually offered Rowlett and Sinkov shortcuts into the Purple system. It took time, but in September 1940 Friedman's students solved the Purple mystery. For the rest of the war, SIS read *Magic*, the new code name given to the windfall of precious information. *Magic* would soon become "America's most closely guarded operational secret."[10]

Not satisfied with simply reading Purple messages, SIS undertook the construction of its own machine for more rapid solution of messages. Turning to Leo Rosen, a brilliant electrical engineer hired by Friedman, a so-called Purple Analog was completed with three copies produced; one each going to the army and navy and a third, originally earmarked for the Navy's Station HYPO in Hawaii, shipped instead to London when the two countries began cryptologic cooperation.[11]

* * *

What Rowlett and Sinkov discovered was Oshima Hiroshi, the "linchpin" in German–Japanese communications. Born in 1886 to a prominent family, his father was Japan's minister of war during World War I. After completing the Japanese version of West Point in 1905, Hiroshi rose steadily through the ranks, eventually landing a prestigious assignment to Berlin in 1934 as the military attaché. His nearly flawless German and almost maniacal belief in Adolf Hitler caught the eye of Nazi bigwigs, leading to meetings with Joachim Ribbentrop, a Hitler toady who served as ambassador to London before his appointment as foreign minister. Four years later, Oshima's performance as a keen military observer and warm relations with senior German military commanders was rewarded by Tokyo with a promotion to lieutenant general and ambassador to Germany. A year later, with his term at an end, he returned to Japan for a new assignment. Not wishing to lose such a valuable friend, German officials took the unusual step of lobbying Japanese leaders for his return to Berlin. In urging the move, they lauded the general's grasp of the "aims of our true policy" and the "complete confidence of the Fuhrer and the German army."[12] Oshima returned to Berlin in January 1941—just three months after Sinkov and Rowlett exposed the secrets of *Magic*.

In the spring of 1941, Oshima's reporting from Berlin began producing results. In December 1940 Hitler had made his decision to invade the Soviet Union. By April, German officers were filling in Oshima with details of the Reich's secret planning. As Arlington Hall code breakers listened, Oshima warned Tokyo of the top-secret military preparations then underway and the growing Wehrmacht readiness for an attack. Arlington Hall translators became transfixed as they read his steady stream of messages filled with fresh information. A message sent by the ambassador to the foreign ministry led one SIS translator to speak for everyone at Arlington Hall at the time.

Goring [Hermann Goring] was outlining Germany's plan to attack Russia . . . giving the numbers of planes and numbers and types of divisions to be used for this drive and that. *I was too excited to sleep that night. It was the liveliest news for many a day* . . . We and the British informed the Russians about . . . [Hitler's plan], but they were too dumbfounded to believe it as true.[13]

As the momentous day approached, Oshima began hinting about when the Germans would strike. "For the time being," he warned, "I think it would be a good idea for you in some inconspicuous manner, to postpone the departure of Japanese citizens for Europe via Siberia. You will understand why."[14] Days after the attack Tokyo received his summary of the general's five-hour conversation with Hitler at his East Prussia bunker where he was personally directing the battle. Each line was filled with the Fuhrer's assessment of Wehrmacht progress along with Oshima's careful observations made during an inspection of the expanding battlefield. Two months later in those early heady days of German success, following another visit with Hitler, Oshima assured Tokyo that "when the question of the United States came up in the course of the conversation, Hitler had said that if a clash occurs by any chance between Japan and the United States Germany will at once open war against the United States."[15]

Following the attack on Pearl Harbor, American code breakers witnessed a significant spike in Oshima's traffic. Over the course of the war the number jumped to one hundred in 1942, four hundred in 1943, six hundred in 1944, and another three hundred during the first five months of 1945, with Tokyo responding with equal numbers. The general's writings, always carefully crafted and brimming with insightful analyses, regularly ran from one page to as long as thirty single-spaced pages. From the outset of the war, it was clear to Allied strategists that Japan's ambassador was a priceless source of intelligence. One history later confirmed that "thanks to the knowledgeable and communicative Japanese ambassador in Berlin they would remain privy to German war plans."[16]

And so, they did. Decades later, historian Carl Boyd wrote that Oshima's reports were destined to become a "hallmark" in the planning of *Overlord*, code name for the Allied Cross-Channel invasion of Normandy, France, scheduled for May or June 1944. It came about through Hitler's offer to Oshima to inspect German coastal defenses in France starting in October 1943 and continuing until just weeks before the actual attack. The ambassador's insights into strengths and weaknesses of the Atlantic Wall accompanied by assessments from senior Wehrmacht officers proved invaluable. The Supreme Headquarters of the Allied Expeditionary Force (SHAEF) under General Dwight Eisenhower, commander of the surprise landings, larded his battle plan with important changes and adjustments based on Oshima's

## Chapter 17

assessments. With Arlington Hall's successful decipherment of Japan's diplomatic military attaché cipher system in November 1943 confirming Oshima's reporting, Eisenhower could breathe easier knowing he wasn't being deceived.[17]

On a par with Oshima, in the eyes of Arlington Hall, was his diplomatic colleague Sato Naotake, Japan's ambassador to the Soviet Union. The always secretive and paranoid strain that historically ran through the Russian psyche from the czars through Stalin made it essential to know what was going on behind the scenes in Moscow.[18]

Sato was an important figure in the Japanese diplomatic world. When he arrived at his Russian assignment, he was sixty years old with a distinguished record of service, having worked in Europe for thirty years. After joining the diplomatic service in 1905, he served in China and later as secretary for the Japanese delegation at negotiations that led to the London Naval Treaty in the early 1920s. Ambassadorships followed in Brussels, Paris, and Geneva as chief of the Japanese office of the League of Nations. The skill and talent that Sato had demonstrated in every major international conference during the 1920s and 1930s had earned him an informal honor as Japan's "greatest conference expert." In 1937, he was made foreign minister followed by a senior position as diplomatic advisor to the foreign ministry.[19]

Stalin and the Soviet Union were critically important to Japan's strategic thinking. In 1939 the two nations fought a brief border war. What followed was a nonaggression pact signed in April 1941, just two months before Germany invaded the Soviet Union. Throughout the war, Tokyo remained keenly sensitive to fragility of the pact, knowing full well that if Stalin suddenly turned on Japan, Tokyo would face a nightmare scenario of a two-front war while fighting American forces in the Pacific. Sato came to his new duties with a reputation as an astute observer, a professional who produced "remarkably sophisticated . . . wartime analysis" for his foreign ministry superiors.[20] From this Arlington Hall experts deduced that by carefully analyzing Sato's messages, it could surface important information for US and British policymakers.

But war and geography stymied them. To Arlington Hall's dismay Sato found himself leading an embassy staff marooned more than two thousand miles east of Moscow beyond the Ural Mountains in the far-off city of Kuybyshev. In the early days of the war as Hitler's forces moved ever closer to Moscow, Soviet officials evacuated all foreign diplomats to the city and out of harm's way.

Protocol demanded that Sato present his credentials to Josef Stalin. Instead, he was foisted off to a figurehead, Mikhail Kalinin, president of the Supreme Council of Soviet Ministers. Sato and his foreign colleagues, having little understanding of what was taking place in western Russia, produced few reports of any value. There were virtually no opportunities to meet with government or military officials of any consequence, witness for themselves what was happening on the streets of Moscow, nor monitor the fighting or develop sources with such access. Like his fellow ambassadors, Sato railed in vain against such treatment. As the war went on and the Russians took the offensive in the west, Tokyo continually pressed Sato for information. Avoiding awkward discussions with a representative of a government that was neither friend nor foe may have been Stalin's reason for continually rebuffing Sato. Franklin Roosevelt's secretary of state, Cordell Hull, later hinting in his memoirs to his own access to *Magic*, described his familiarity with Tokyo's repeated efforts to engage Moscow in conversations during the war.[21]

\* \* \*

1944 was a year of a once-in-a-lifetime event for General George Marshall, the army chief of staff and genius behind the creation of America's modern army. In November 1942 British and American forces began achieving victory after victory, starting with a sweep of Field Marshal Erwin Rommel, the legendary "Desert Fox," and his famed Afrika Corps off the African continent. Next came the island of Sicily and a rout of German and Italian forces that sent them reeling back to Italy, where the slog up the rugged Italian spine toward Rome was moving forward on an inch-by-inch basis. But it wasn't easy. The war had already cost tens of thousands of lives, producing heartache across America as families and sweethearts received word that a loved one had been killed on some far-off battlefield or distant ocean.[22]

Since the Japanese attack on Pearl Harbor, rumors had constantly swirled around Washington that Franklin Roosevelt had advanced knowledge of the tragedy but intentionally failed to warn his Hawaiian commanders. In January 1942, an investigation into the circumstances of the attack produced a largely redacted twenty-five-page report that laid the blame on Admiral Husband Kimmel and General Walter Short, the local commanders. There were no charges against higher-ups such as Marshall, Admiral Harold Stark, then the chief of naval operations, or the president. Two thousand pages of testimony and exhibits remained under wraps.

The flimsiness of the official judgment, however, did nothing to allay administration critics. As the war went on and accusations of a whitewash persisted, the issue gradually shifted from a military matter into the larger realm of national politics. In May 1944, the Republicans launched an election-year bid to embarrass the White House with Homer Ferguson, an obscure first-term Michigan senator. Ferguson introduced legislation that gave new life to the Pearl Harbor story by demanding court-martials for Kimmel and Short. The bill failed but did, however, force a congressional directive that the military reinvestigate the matter in camera. By August, as Allied forces were dashing toward Holland and Paris, a panel of officers, part of a joint board of inquiry, appeared at Marshall's Pentagon office to interview him regarding his role in the matter. Before questioning began, however, the general cleared the room of anyone not directly related to the investigation. When they were alone the chief of staff revealed the secrets of *Magic*. Indeed, American code breakers had broken Japan's most important diplomatic cipher a year before the Pearl Harbor attack, he told the assembled officers, and Japanese military planners steadfastly believing in the code's invincibility had never changed it. American use of the intelligence derived from this most important source since the war's start, he explained, had saved thousands of American lives.

Not to be outdone by his Senate colleague, Indiana congressman and ultra-conservative Forest Harness, a member of the House Military Affairs Committee, stood on the floor of the House the following month and in a few words nearly brought *Magic* to disaster. Harness announced to the world that he had ample evidence that Franklin Roosevelt knew about the planned attack on Pearl Harbor and intentionally delayed any warning to local commanders. The president had "inside information," he charged, and "did not want the truth of Pearl Harbor to become known." Switching tacks, he then turned his ire on the chief of staff, accusing him of having learned "very confidentially" about a Japanese "ultimatum" to the US government and instructions sent from Tokyo to its embassy in Washington to "destroy code machines" in the hours before the attack took place. The congressman accused Marshall of negligence for relying on a slower and unsafe commercial radio system to transmit a message rather than faster and more secure military communications channels; a failure that caused the warning to arrive in Hawaii hours after the attack. General Marshall's biographer summed up the War Department's deep concern over the breach, writing that "Harness didn't realize it at the time, but he came close to revealing America's most closely guarded operational secret."[23]

Around the time that Harness was making his accusations, James Forrestal, newly appointed secretary of the navy who replaced Frank Knox following his sudden death, drafted a confidential note to the White House with a grave concern requiring immediate action. Just a month or so earlier New York Republican governor Thomas Dewey had been nominated to run for the presidency against Franklin Roosevelt, then seeking a fourth term. The Dewey camp, Forrestal wrote, believing that the administration had advanced notice of the Pearl Harbor attack, planned to put the sensational news front and center as a campaign issue starting with an upcoming speech Dewey would soon deliver to a group in Tulsa, Oklahoma.

Forrestal's note quickly found its way to Marshall. After mulling the matter over he cautiously decided on a course of action that risked not only the loss of *Magic* but could doom the president's chances for a fourth term and ruin his own reputation forever. Marshall loathed politics and made it a practice of keeping politicians at arm's length. During his military career he never voted as a matter of principle and when asked once about his party affiliation, he wryly replied "Episcopalian."[24]

At the same time, however, Marshall believed that an army officer had a duty to act when politics threatened possible disclosure of an important military secret. Years later, long retired from public life, the general sat down for a series of recorded interviews. Even after all the time that had elapsed since the war ended, he remained crystal clear about that moment and what he had to do. "It was of tremendous importance to us to keep this code business quiet because if we lost it, we lost the most *valuable thing we could possibly have gotten regarding Japanese operations.*"[25] [italics added]

Over the coming days Marshall began secretly orchestrating an approach to Dewey. The plan called for an appeal to his sense of patriotism not to publicly reveal the secret of *Magic*. For an army chief of staff, much less anyone in the military, it was a bold and unprecedented move.[26]

He personally drafted a letter to Dewey in his name and in the name of Admiral Ernest King, the chief of naval operations. Before dispatching it, he shared the letter with King for his opinion and offered him a right of refusal in the unprecedented action. King fully agreed and joined Marshall in the action. Marshall had never confronted such a dilemma before and remained troubled about it throughout the episode. Later in a private memoir he wrote that after much thought and deliberation he concluded that he had no alternative other than providing a "frank statement of the situation and assurances that the President and the Cabinet were unaware of my action."[27]

The next hurdle was a tricky one. How should the message be delivered to Dewey? It was an explosive question and one that could put anyone in a very awkward position. Marshall couldn't deliver it himself. He was a nationally recognized figure. Meeting with a presidential candidate, even in private, risked sounding alarm bells that would draw hordes of reporters asking potentially dangerous questions.

To handle such a delicate mission, Marshall turned to a trusted forty-seven-year-old army officer and shadowy professional with a knack for keeping his mouth shut. Colonel Carter Clarke, a Kentuckian, had made the army his life. After briefly attending the University of Kentucky and the City College of New York, he joined the Kentucky National Guard in 1915. During the Mexican Border campaign against Poncho Villa, he worked as a cook. World War I saw him commissioned as an officer in the Signal Corps. After the war he rose slowly through the ranks, attending the Army Signal School at Fort Monmouth, the Army Command and Staff College at Fort Leavenworth, Kansas, and the prestigious Army War College in Washington, DC. Notwithstanding the stigma attached to intelligence work among army professionals during the interwar period, Clarke made signal intelligence and code-breaking the central focus of his entire army career.[28]

By the start of World War II, Clarke had emerged as a central figure in the world of codes and ciphers as the head of the branch responsible for safeguarding all military intelligence information. As the need for a vastly expanded cryptologic capability became vital, he took charge of a new group with the humdrum title of Special Services Branch, soon to be renamed "Special Branch." The new appointment, both a clear recognition of his skill and talent, suddenly thrust him into what a later NSA study called a "paramount position in Army COMINT management."[29] Special Branch was immediately charged with decrypting and analyzing all intercepted messages and distributing the top-secret *Magic* Diplomatic Summary daily to a select group of senior government and military leaders. Clarke's new assignment also made him the direct representative of the assistant chief of staff "for purposes of supervising all signal intelligence activities of the War Department."[30]

Five weeks before the November 1944 elections, as Bill Weisband was arriving at his new assignment at Arlington Hall, Clarke, clad in a business suit to deflect press attention, was ushered into Governor Dewey's hotel suite in Tulsa, Oklahoma, where he was campaigning. After introducing himself to Dewey, with the two men now alone, Clarke handed the governor a sealed envelope enclosing Marshall's letter. In the opening sentence Marshall asked Dewey not to read beyond the second sentence unless he was prepared not to communicate its contents to anyone because it contained top-secret information concerning the Pearl Harbor attack. A stunned Dewey quickly glanced down the page with his eyes falling on the word "cryptograph," at which point he looked up at Clarke. Clarke later recounted that moment for Marshall, noting Dewey saying that he "did not want his lips sealed on things that he already knew about Pearl Harbor, about facts already in his possession."[31]

Placing the letter back in the envelope, an increasingly angry Dewey handed it to Clarke while admonishing Marshall for approaching him in such a way in the midst of the presidential campaign. "Marshall does not do things like that," he told Clarke. "I'm confident that Franklin Roosevelt is behind this whole thing."[32] Conscious of Marshall's integrity, Dewey gradually cooled down. With his composure somewhat restored, the governor suggested to Colonel Clarke that he would be willing to meet again either with Marshall or his designee when he returned to his executive office in New York the next day or so.

Wasting no time, Marshall again dispatched Clarke, this time to Albany for a second meeting with Dewey. The letter he delivered was essentially the same as the first one. This time, however, Marshall's at the outset assured the governor that neither the "Secretary of War nor the President" had any knowledge of the letter's substance or its delivery to Dewey.[33] Before reading beyond the opening sentences, however, Dewey had some demands of his own. He insisted that a trusted campaign aide and speechwriter, Elliott Bell, be allowed to read the letter and, second, he wanted to keep a copy for his files. As Clarke had no authority to accede to these requests, Dewey telephoned a worried Marshall, who had no choice but to agree. What followed was some additional wrangling that forced Clarke to extend his writ by going into some detail about the wartime history of Japanese codes. He described the varieties of systems used by the Japanese while insisting that Japan had continued to rely on them as unlikely as that may seem. With that, a skeptical Dewey finally began digesting the letter.

In it, Marshall explained how Allied successes in the Pacific and Europe depended on continued access to intelligence produced from decoded Japanese diplomatic messages. In particular there was the Berlin to Tokyo circuit, which produced vast amounts of valuable information about Hitler's war plans and intentions. Ending on a cautionary note, Marshall warned Dewey about the "tragic consequences if the present political debates regarding Pearl Harbor [disclosed] to the enemy, German or Jap, any suspicion of the vital sources of information we possess." Nothing less than "American lives" and "early termination of the war" was at stake.[34] Over the next few months Dewey fought a hard campaign but, on November 9, Franklin Roosevelt won an unprecedented fourth presidential term. The secret of *Magic* held.

\* \* \*

Winston Churchill loved secret intelligence and used it whenever possible throughout his political career. Upon becoming prime minister in May 1940, he insisted on personally reading the most valuable raw communications intelligence produced by his code breakers over a previous twenty-four-hour period. Delivery to 10 Downing Street occurred every morning in what became known to generals, admirals, and aides alike simply as Winston's "small red box." Marked on it was the conspicuous warning "only to be opened by the Prime Minister in person." Opening the box required a key—there were only two—one kept by Churchill and another held by Stewart Menzies, head of MI6. By September 1940 the intelligence chiefs were including selected copies of intercepts gathered from *Ultra*, Britain's most valuable source, decrypts of messages from Germany's *Enigma* coding machine.[35]

Cooperation between US and British code breakers, authorized by the prime minister, secretly began as early as 1941 when America was still officially neutral. An American delegation that included Abraham Sinkov and

Leo Rosen visited London in January 1941, bringing with them a Purple analog machine that they gave to British code breakers while explaining how they read the secrets of *Magic*. The gift was reciprocated with top-secret details about their success in solving the mysteries of *Enigma*, the complex cipher machine used by Germany's military and civilian services. Sharing went dormant for more than a year until it revived in April 1942 when a British technical group visited Washington. The consultations that followed produced a top-secret agreement that opened the door to a vastly increased wartime intelligence-sharing arrangement with exchanges of liaison officers to Arlington Hall and Bletchley Park, Britain's code-breaking center, located forty miles north of London. Both sides also settled on a division of tasks, with Arlington Hall pursuing *Magic* and all other Japanese codes systems while the British concentrated on German ciphers. OP-20-G, the navy's code breakers, would do the same except for a small staff assigned to collaborate with the British on *Enigma* in the hunt for U-boats and protection of Atlantic convoys.

\* \* \*

The cultures that pervaded the work done at OP-20-G and Arlington Hall were radically different. Navy brass insisted that all workers be in one form or another "navy." Rank mattered as did indoctrination into the navy way of doing things. A requirement that personnel wear uniforms was de rigueur for assignment to the Naval Annex on Nebraska Avenue.

To an outsider, Arlington Hall, like the Navy Annex, screamed military with its drill fields, officer and enlisted barracks, and armed soldiers giving steely glances wherever one turned. Outward appearances were deceiving. Arlington Hall was a "flat line" arrangement; a bureaucracy that one employee, Cecil Phillips, called a "meritocracy" with military rank having little to do with breaking codes. Phillips was age eighteen when he arrived in Washington from North Carolina eager to do his bit for the war effort. Poor eyesight, even by wartime standards, ended his chances of wearing a uniform and soon led him to Arlington Hall as a cryptanalyst. Cryptanalysis was a special profession and finding a good cryptanalyst was like searching for a needle in a haystack. When you found one, regardless of gender, race, or creed, you held on to that person at all costs and got out of their way. Arlington Hall's mindset created a working environment where just as often as not a civilian would suddenly be in charge of a group of soldiers, both officers and enlisted men alike, directing their activities and issuing orders. Ignoring military rank occasionally landed people in a heap of trouble if they objected to this peculiar protocol. Liza Mundy, in her study of women code breakers in World War II, described how a lieutenant may report to a sergeant, or a civilian or even a private first class. If the officer objected, he was sent overseas. "You didn't go by rank," Solomon Kullback remembered, "you went by what people knew."[36]

Even efforts to turn civilians into instant officers failed. Frank Rowlett and Abraham Sinkov were commissioned as officers, Rowlett a major and Sinkov a captain; neither underwent a day of basic military training. The two Friedman protégés not knowing a cannon from a tank or regiment from a division continued to walk the floors throughout the war as "civilians in uniforms."[37]

So important were skilled employees to the mission that when someone received a draft notice or expressed interest in enlisting, certain wheels suddenly started turning behind the scenes. The candidate would be ordered to report to a certain recruiting officer in downtown Washington on a specific date and time. After giving his name, raising his right hand, and swearing allegiance to the country, he promptly became an army private with orders to report back to Arlington Hall for assignment. The "whole thing was rigged," one person later snickered.[38]

Many of these so-called soldiers were college students in their early twenties who left school to volunteer for military service. Others graduated from prestigious schools like Harvard or Yale or Stanford with degrees in code-breaking essentials like Japanese language studies, mathematics, or engineering. By 1943, the handful of Arlington Hall workers in 1941 had ballooned to more than seven thousand with a three to one ratio of civilian to military working in three shifts around the clock.[39]

The war brought a whole new lexicon of words to the code-breaking world. Arlington Hall was suddenly a huge and growing collection of men and women with strange titles such as "tabulators" working side by side with "keypunch operators" and "overlappers" assisted by "traffic analysts" and "bookbreakers."[40] Supporting them was an army of librarians, language teachers, file clerks, linguists, analysts, cryptanalysts, and scores of technicians either removing, installing, or maintaining hundreds of strange and complicated machines of all sizes and shapes that constantly whirred and hummed and buzzed twenty-four hours a day in a ceaseless battle against enemy codes.

At the start of the war Arlington Hall's hopes for victory rested on attacking any and all Japanese military codes and ciphers, but with few messages to work with they found themselves stymied. Having even the slightest chance of penetrating layers of protection that revealed intelligible sentences required as many messages as one could lay hands on; what in the parlance of the business was called "material in depth." The more messages one had to work with the better the chance of success. In December 1941, however, the Japanese army, with two million men primarily concentrated in Manchuria, communicated using low-powered transmitters that proved nearly impossible for widely scattered American and British intercept stations to pick up. The expansion of the empire, however, throughout Southeast Asia, the Dutch East Indies, and the Pacific Rim changed the equation. Japanese communicators were now forced to rely on more powerful equipment capable of reaching their far-off island strongholds. Massive antennas situated across the Pacific Ocean from Alaska to Hawaii to Australia started plucking Japanese messages out of the atmosphere in bulk and then streaming them electronically back to Arlington Hall, where technicians logged in, catalogued, and separated the messages before preparing them for analysis. As new circuits were identified they were assigned specific numerical designations. Messages sent in 1941 by airmail and standard commercial telegraph had arrived in Washington at an alarmingly low rate. At the time the army had only four high-speed teleprinters capable of speeding up the process. Two years later, forty-six printers were funneling nearly five thousand messages a month into Arlington Hall; a rate that skyrocketed to more than ten thousand a day by July 1945.[41]

Complicating this already mighty task, however, were Japanese code security practices. Nippon cryptographers used hidden tricks, ruses, and ploys in their already complex cipher systems designed to befuddle code-breaking efforts. To further lock down their communications, codes and ciphers were changed regularly to prevent a broken circuit from staying broken for long. The idea—keep the Americans blind, deaf, and always playing catch up.

A critical cog in the code-breaking process were RTAs. Traffic analysts were trained to map out western Pacific communications nodes and update new ones as they came online. When an identification was made, careful statistical records charting characteristics of the circuit were created. Anomalies, when discovered, were shared with librarians for any reference to a previous record and then with cryptanalysts for insights into whether the findings were meaningless or a more ominous sign that something was up. The information, once run to ground, was quickly shared with theater commanders for broader intelligence analysis.

In the spring of 1943, Arlington Hall began concentrating on "2468," a circuit that they had only archived for some time because of its seemingly unbreakable cipher system. As it turned out, what they were looking at was the all-important "Water Transport System" used by Japan's army to route supply ships called "marus." In an odd bureaucratic military twist, not all Japanese vessels fell under the command of the imperial navy. The army had its own fleet of transports and oil tankers controlled from Tokyo to ferry troops and supplies from island to island. A hint of the importance of 2468 first surfaced when a thin lead provided by British code breakers led to exchanges with cryptanalysts in Brisbane, Australia. The break into 2468, as one author recorded, was one of the most important discoveries of the war.[42]

The success of 2468 produced a cascade of new solutions of more and more enemy systems that just a short time earlier were unreadable. Now inside the thinking and next moves of Japanese strategists, American commanders began laying plans for the enemy's destruction by staunching its supply chain with traps set for increasingly isolated convoys slowly moving from one island to another. A typical success occurred in July 1943 when 2468 revealed the anticipated arrival date and times of four marus filled with troops and critical supplies destined for Wewak Harbor, a major Japanese air base in New Guinea. Sometime later Solomon Kullback learned with "satisfaction" that all four ships had been sunk. A similar debacle in the spring of 1944 involving a convoy carrying troop reinforcements occurred near a Japanese base at Palau in western New Guinea. Waiting American submarines struck with vengeance, drowning 3,900 sailors and soldiers.[43] Accompanying escort ships managed to recover 6,800 survivors, who arrived at Palau having lost all of their battle equipment to the sea.

The Japanese were no fools. They had to wonder how American submarines and aircraft knew precisely when and where to pounce. Luck could only account for these losses just so far. To reduce suspicions American commanders had with them by the middle of the war a little-known unit led by a signal liaison officer more commonly known as a "SLO." All intelligence produced from a broken message passed from Arlington Hall through top-secret channels to the SLO. The SLO then handed the information to the commander, who digested it in the presence of the SLO and then returned it to him for safekeeping.

Safeguarding the secret of code-breaking success meant sowing confusion in the minds of Japanese leaders by deflecting attention away from the real source behind these attacks. Army and navy rules required commanders to take no action based on code-breaking until an aircraft had been dispatched to spot the convoy. In doing so, the hope was that a crew member on a doomed ship would report the sighting to his headquarters, planting a belief that the convoy's destruction was due to a quick response to the sighting.

There was another stroke of luck that the Americans hadn't counted on. As losses mounted, Japanese commanders remained steadfast in the belief that their codes had not been compromised. In their search for answers, they chose to delude themselves by putting their faith in myths, such as treasonous dockworkers slipping reports to American spies or lucky traffic analysts. There were also the ubiquitous "coast watchers" lurking in jungles among indigenous island tribes, quietly observing the movements of Japanese shipping.[44]

As winter gradually gave way to spring in 1945, with Hitler's suicide just weeks away, the war in Europe was about to end. Along with the thousands of workers at Arlington Hall, the navy had also been hard at work breaking ciphers that led to the near total elimination of Japan's once mighty imperial fleet. Now only the *Yamato*, the largest and most powerful battleship, remained afloat along with her battle group, but navy code breakers already had their number as well. A five-week struggle for the tiny atoll of Iwo Jima was coming to a bloody end, which meant that an invasion of the island of Okinawa, only weeks away, would put the Allies a mere three hundred and fifty miles from Japan's home islands. To Allied strategists looking out toward the Pacific, the end game appeared with some kind of ghastly *Götterdämmerung* rapidly approaching.

Now was not the time for code breakers to let up. But changes were certainly in the wind.

## NOTES

1. "MUSIC; Debut of Blanca Renard," *New York Times*, October 25, 1934.
2. "Arlington Hall Enrollments Set All Time Record," *Washington Post*, September 9, 1939, F2; "Arlington Hall Prepares Girls for College Boards," *Washington Post*, September 8, 1935, X6.
3. Mundy, *Code Girls*, 85.
4. Budiansky, *Battle of Wits*, 223.
5. NSA.gov Hall of Fame Award, "Rose Hill Natives Honored for Decades of Codebreaking, Cryptographic Work," *Kingsport Times*, September 23, 2019.
6. Kahn, *The Codebreakers*, 386.
7. Budiansky, *Battle of Wits*, 35.
8. Ibid.
9. Ibid.
10. David Roll, *George Marshall: Defender of the Republic* (New York: Dutton/Caliber, 2019), 343.
11. Red and Purple, NSA.gov.
12. Carl Boyd, *Hitler's Japanese Confidant* (Lawrence: University Press of Kansas, 1991), 3–4.
13. Ibid., 21.
14. Ibid., 21.
15. Ibid., 31.
16. Ibid., 42–43.
17. One postwar study of the Normandy invasion concluded that the principal intelligence contributions reported in the *Magic* Summary from Oshima and his military attachés offered "detailed reports of Japanese officials in Europe who made inspection trips through German coastal defenses in France" and "accounts of German strategy before and after the June 1944 landings as outlined to Japanese officials by Hitler, Ribbentrop, and various Wehrmacht officials." Ibid., 115.
18. Ibid., 147.

19. "Naotake Sato, Diplomat, Dies; Was Envoy to Soviet 1942–45," *New York Times*, December 19, 1971.

20. Boyd, *Hitler's Japanese Confidant*, 148.

21. In a discussion with Vyacheslav Molotov, Stalin's foreign minister, Sato summed up his predicament. In an aside during a quiet moment, Sato mused that "This is a strange war. You are on one side and we are on the other. We see only the side of each other's faces." Still, after seventy-five years, most *Magic* intercepts between Moscow and Tokyo remain classified today. Ibid., 151.

22. Marshall himself was not spared. In the early 1930s, Colonel George Marshall, a widower with no children, married Katherine Brown, herself a widow with two boys. One of them, Allen, the younger, grew from teenager into manhood as the apple of George's eye. After commissioning as a second lieutenant, Allen Tupper Brown arrived in Naples, Italy, in November 1943 as a member of the 1st Armored Division. Not even a year later, on May 29, 1944, Allen was killed when he rose from his tank turret to get a clearer view of a German soldier waving "a white flag." A medic's report later cited cause of death as "hand grenade wounds in his head and neck." Roll, *George Marshall*, 325.

23. Ibid., 343.

24. He even once took a swipe at his commander in chief when Roosevelt overruled him regarding a 1942 cross-Channel attack on the continent, choosing instead an invasion of North Africa. "We failed to see," Marshall told some of his assembled generals, "that the leader in a democracy has to keep the people entertained." Atkinson, *Army at Dawn*, 17.

25. Roll, *George Marshall*, 344.

26. Ibid.

27. Leonard Mosely, *Marshall: Hero for Our Times* (New York: Hearst Books, 1982), 302.

28. "Retired Brigadier General Carter Clarke, 90, Dies," *Washington Post*, September 6, 1987.

29. "History of US Communications Intelligence during World War II: Policy and Administration," Robert Louis Benson, CCH, NSA, 1997, 135.

30. Budiansky, *Battle of Wits*, 233.

31. Roll, *George Marshall*, 344.

32. He then hinted that he knew the United States had broken Japan's codes and that FDR knew it too. Sensing a trap, the candidate again lashed out, charging that the president knew what was happening before the Pearl Harbor attack and "instead of being re-elected he ought to be impeached." Ibid.

33. Ibid.

34. Ibid., 345–46.

35. Keith Jeffery, *The Secret History of MI6* (New York: Penguin Press, 2010), 348.

36. Mundy, *Code Girls*, 210.

37. Budiansky, *Battle of Wits*, 227.

38. Ibid.

39. Ibid., 226.

40. Mundy, *Code Girls*, 210.

41. Boyd, *Hitler's Japanese Confidant*, 52.
42. Mundy, *Code Girls*, 227.
43. Ibid.
44. Cdr. E. A. Feldt, "Coast Watching in World War II," Annapolis, MD: Proceedings of the Naval Institute, September 1961.

*Chapter 18*

# Settling In

Just days after Feklisov's meeting with Bill Weisband, a bemused Andrei Gromyko found himself standing in front of the Russian embassy in Washington, DC, as a large State Department truck drove up carrying wooden crates filled with documents. As Russia's ambassador to Washington, he wasn't accustomed to receiving top-secret material in so open a manner, even from a wartime ally.

The diminutive thirty-five-year-old diplomat, who was destined to become the face of Soviet foreign policy during much of the Cold War, then in his second year in Russia's most important foreign assignment, had only joined the foreign service six years earlier. The decision to replace Ivan Maisky, a diplomat with far more expertise and wider contacts, and Maxim Litvinov in London with the relatively junior Fyodor Gusev emerged from Stalin's insistence on having representatives with no ties to Americans and British who could interfere with the "changing mood of Soviet policy." Both men, ice cold in personality and speaking not a word of English, marked them, in Stalin's view, as the "new Soviet man" in contrast to the worldlier ways of their predecessors.[1]

The strange odyssey of the boxes began on September 21, 1944, when Finland abandoned the Axis partnership. It was on that date that the entire Finnish military intelligence officer corps and their families, led by its chief, Colonel Reino Hallamaa, loaded two hundred wooden crates filled with secret files onto four small coastal steamers and set out for Stockholm, capital of neutral Sweden. Sensing an Axis defeat and fearful of Soviet retribution, Hallamaa was desperate for sanctuary and protection. The scheme he concocted called for an exchange of five years of Finnish cryptanalysis work to any country willing to give him and his group asylum. The mass defection, code-named Operation STELLA POLARIS, proved to be in the words of one historian, "one of the most remarkable events" in the intelligence history of World War II.[2]

Colonel Hallamaa made his first approach to the head of the station for the Office of Strategic Services (OSS), Wilho Tikander. As a further inducement he offered his staff's assistance to American code breakers once settled in the United States. On October 11, 1944, just days after receiving details of the offer, General William Donovan, head of OSS, wasted no time authorizing acceptance of the boxes along with his "complete approval and strongest support" for the entire deal. Donovan's enthusiasm for the project was not necessarily shared by State Department officials still livid over an earlier debacle when OSS agents conducted an unauthorized break-in of the Japanese legation in Lisbon. The botched burglary triggered monumental concern in Washington when *Magic* revealed urgent messages from Lisbon to Tokyo reporting the incident and prompting the very real threat of loss of *Magic* if the foreign ministry ordered a change of codes. These concerns only escalated when a second Tikander cable arrived in Washington, this time urging caution in the transaction based on growing Soviet criticism of the Finnish government for "insufficient compliance" with the terms of the armistice. Russian accusations that war criminals were escaping arrest and prosecution led to Tikander's fear that Colonel Hallamaa could be in this category. Adding to State Department worries was the fact that with the war in Europe nearing an end, the United States still needed Moscow's assistance against the Japanese in the Pacific; a fear that raised a real possibility that US-Russian relations could be ruined if Hallamaa's cooperation with the Americans should ever become known in Moscow. Finding himself caught in the middle of a bureaucratic dilemma yet fully appreciating the priceless value of the Finnish intelligence, Tikander came down squarely in the middle in his response to Washington. The trove of secrets, he wrote, would "undoubtedly be of great value if real differences arose between US and Moscow" but getting hold of it could wait for a more "propitious occasion."[3]

That was enough for Washington policymakers. Orders were issued to end all discussions with Hallamaa, noting that it would be "inadvisable and improper for the United States to have any connection with the Finnish files." At the same time Washington endorsed Tikander's view of acquiring them "when the present dangers of detection or exposure were no longer present."[4]

In December, a persistent Hallamaa renewed his offer to the OSS. Interpreting the State Department's guidance this time in the broadest sense possible and not wishing to lose out to other interested customers, Donovan issued orders to "accept delivery immediately of the materials previously rejected."[5] In return, Hallamaa would receive a onetime payment of a quarter of a million Swedish kroners. Probably sensing a bureaucratic row in Washington, he also insisted that copies of the documents be made before sending the entire collection to Washington.

At some point America's ambassador to Sweden, Herschel Johnson, having gotten wind of Donovan's plan, radioed his own objections to Washington, provoking an immediate impasse between the State Department and OSS. With neither side budging, the matter was bucked up to Edward Stettinius, now the acting secretary of state following the retirement of Cordell Hull. Both sides appealed to the White House with Donovan emphasizing that the material had already been delivered to the State Department and the War Department, which undoubtedly passed the cache to Arlington Hall.

In the end, a very ill Franklin Roosevelt, exhausted from his recent reelection victory and readying himself for a showdown with Stalin, sided with the State Department. Two hundred boxes of Finnish secrets were delivered to Gromyko, curiously on February 11, 1945, the final day of meetings between Roosevelt, Churchill, and Stalin at the Yalta Conference.

From the relentless horrors of mountain fighting in Italy, Bill Weisband transitioned nicely into a relaxed six-day workweek on the campus of Arlington Hall. Getting to the office required a brief stop at the main gate, guarded by sentries twenty-four hours a day. There a War Department photo badge was carefully checked to confirm Weisband's identity. Each worker, military or civilian, was required to carry one at all times, with it denoting levels of security clearance and authorization to enter Arlington Hall. Once cleared for entry, Bill casually strolled up the driveway to B Building and then up a flight of stairs and along a second-floor corridor to the back of the building. There he entered an uninspiring fifty-foot by fifty-foot open area workspace known as Woodgas—B-III-b9 (WDGS-93B), or "Special Problems Subsection." Insiders called it the "office." The staff worked six days a week (they were only paid for five and half days) in a cramped world of unmatched chairs placed astride a series of long tables. Blocking the space from its neighbors, the crew tackling Japanese weather ciphers, was a row of cheap plywood screens seven feet high and four feet wide abutting each other with a small gap between two of them serving as the only entrance and exit to the space. Weisband then took his assigned seat, where he began his day of attacking top-secret Russian cryptograms. The egalitarian nature of the environment was seen by the fact that the boss, Captain William B. S. Smith, sat at a table to the left of the tiny entrance with his back to the partitions. From there he could easily monitor staff movements as they squeezed by him when entering or leaving. By the end of the war the unit had grown to around a hundred employees—ninety-four civilians and six military officers. One person remembered everyone "packed in like sardines."[6]

Code-breaking drew a strange assortment of people. One new employee wondered what she was getting herself into when she walked to her assigned chair the first day. One person hunched over a table wearing a visor never looked up at her. Nearby, sat a woman holding an ice pack to her head as she struggled over pages of numbers while some guy casually strolled around unnoticed wearing only his underwear.[7]

Adding to the misery was Virginia's oppressive summertime heat and humidity—made only worse by a couple of spinning fans that did nothing but spread the agony around. So dreadful were the conditions that ASA leaders Rowlett and Friedman had little choice except to take some action. In typical government fashion they formulated a "hot weather policy," which allowed for worker release for the day when the air temperature drifted into the nineties. Consideration was also given to assigning a medical doctor to conduct workplace surveys on "particularly bad areas," "health of individuals," "humidity and temperature," and finally "dangerous areas." In the end, however, it appears that nothing really remedied the situation and workers just had to grin and bear it.[8]

After Weisband's reconnection with Feklisov in New York, he began meeting a KGB officer known today only by his code name, "Tikhon." He was working undercover at the Russian embassy during World War II. At the end of the decade, he returned to Moscow followed by a promotion to Paris as station chief. In 1951, he returned to Washington, this time as head of the KGB's most important Western post. That is where his trail runs cold.[9]

Despite his brief stay at Vint Hill Farms and some Italian language training two years earlier, Weisband had little understanding of what Arlington Hall had been doing while he was in Italy. It is highly unlikely that he was ever made aware of the Russian Program at the time as it was just starting when he shipped out for England. Like any new arrival, Weisband was briefed on his assignment, which included a history of the Russian Section and what it had accomplished thus far.

As Weisband sat quietly listening, he learned that glimmers of the Russian Program actually began before the army set one foot in Arlington Hall. At the outset of the war, Carter Clarke and his bosses understood that their primary task was to provide communications intelligence support for the war fighters. Clarke knew also that at some point in the future peace conferences would be convened and, when that day arrived, US negotiators would demand intelligence support. Clarke still retained vivid memories of the Washington Naval Conference of 1922 when Herbert Yardley, a government cryptologist, having broken Japan's diplomatic ciphers, kept the American delegation regularly informed about Tokyo's negotiating strategy as conferees met daily to hammer out an agreement to reduce the sizes of capital warships. It was Yardley's brilliant intelligence coup, Clarke knew, that gave the Americans such a lopsided victory in the settlement. Clarke gave voice to the value of intelligence for government leadership in making sound political decisions on May 6, 1942, writing that its end purpose was to enable "an American peace delegation to confront problems of the peace table with the fullest intimate knowledge possible to secure of the purposes and attitudes overt and covert, of those who will sit opposite them."[10] As such the army on its own initiative undertook a primitive program starting in 1942 of intercepting Russian military signals. They began with low-level codes and ciphers such as weather ciphers looking only for call signs and cryptographic procedures rather than actually trying to break into their actual systems.

The first concerted effort to penetrate the mysteries of Russian communications started during the week of February 6, 1943. While all the work performed at Arlington Hall was top secret, the attack on Russian ciphers was considered "eyes only," or deeper than top secret with knowledge strictly limited to only a tiny handful of top army brass. It was, as one author later described it, "secrets wrapped within that secret."[11] Part of the reasoning behind this extreme need for secrecy was that unlike the communications war underway against the Axis enemy, this effort was directed against a wartime ally whose track record for secrecy was legendary. So highly compartmentalized was the project that it was not shared with either White House officials nor with the British despite the unprecedented level of collaboration then underway with Bletchley Park. It was a nettlesome political problem, one fraught with danger for US policymakers to be seen spying on Josef Stalin, a gallant ally and popular figure among Americans; he had been *Time* magazine's Man of the Year in 1942, as leader of millions of mighty Russian forces bravely fighting the Axis enemy.

To say the program began modestly would be an understatement. It started with a young American named Leonard Martin Zubko, a native of Kearney, New Jersey, born the second son of an immigrant couple from the cities of Pinsk and Minsk in what today is Byelorussia. Zubko had completed a degree in mechanical engineering from Rutgers University in 1942, and after marrying his sweetheart he headed off for the advanced infantry course at Fort Benning, Georgia (he had been in ROTC at Rutgers). Trained and ready to lead troops, he was surprised when he received orders in November 1942 to report to Arlington Hall; a selection undoubtedly due to his high intelligence, technical training, and Russian fluency.[12]

Teamed with Zubko was a twenty-one-year-old woman fresh from a teaching job in Lynchburg, Virginia. Gene Grabeel, a Rose Hill, Virginia, native, had completed Mars Hill College and Farmville State Teachers College, now Longwood University, before taking a job teaching home economics at a local high school in Lynchburg, Virginia. Bored with teaching and wanting a challenge, she answered an advertisement for wartime work in Washington and soon found herself as one of thousands of young women flooding into Arlington Hall to do secret work about which she knew nothing. Her job may have been secured through Frank Rowlett, a Rose Hill neighbor, then in charge of Arlington Hall's cipher branch.[13]

Both Zubko and Grabeel, still in a daze and with no training, were thrown into a stifling world of utmost secrecy, even by Arlington Hall standards. They were relegated to a drab room with two chairs and a table surrounded by standard brown Metal Art file cabinets lining all four walls. The drawers, they soon discovered, were bursting with tens of thousands of unreadable messages sent between Moscow and its diplomatic missions in the United States; all collected by censorship authorities since the start of the European war in September 1939. Their job—decode them.

Even the army's possession of the original Russian cables was shrouded in mystery. When World War II erupted in September 1939 the War Department submitted a confidential proposal to David Sarnoff, then president of the RCA Corporation. RCA, in addition to being an electronics company, was also a cable company that sent and received international messages by undersea cables and radio for clients around the world. At the time they were handling Russian diplomatic messages sent between Moscow and its diplomatic posts in the United States. The War Department asked Sarnoff for copies of the Russian messages, and after getting Sarnoff's approval, they sent Colonel Earl Cooke to RCA's New York offices in January 1940 posing as a student "pursuing a course of study." Years later, Cooke laughed when asked about this strange a mission, telling an NSA interviewer that "All of this was nonsense—looking over the traffic was what I was there for." Cooke soon set up a special room with RCA-supplied cameras where he began photographing all messages, which he then sent to SIS in Washington. Another source of messages was an intercept site called Station Y at Fort Sam Houston, Texas, which gathered radio messages for SIS as well.[14]

By the time Zubko and Grabeel arrived, Arlington Hall had accumulated roughly one hundred and fifty thousand messages with more coming in every day. Two major problems were immediately evident as neither Zubko nor Grabeel had ever decoded a thing, nor had they any idea how or where to start.

They benefitted considerably, however, from support within the organization. Helping them make sense of the material were *Magic* analysts collecting data on Japanese Military Attaché (JMA) ciphers. The Helsinki, Berlin, Tokyo circuits had reported some Japanese cryptologic success with the discovery of five separate Russian systems, but none of them were solved. What they had found, however, were clues picked from the externals of the message. The Russians used the first and second digit of the first cipher group of the text in a message to signal the length of the message while the fourth and fifth digit identified the specific additive page used to encrypt the message.

Zubko and Grabeel spent much of their time sorting the mass of messages into separate piles designated by points of transmission and receipt used by the Russians. As they made their way through page after page of documents, evidence gradually emerged of five separate cryptographic systems used by different subscribers. One of them was the Soviet Trade Mission in Washington, which managed the complex system of Lend-Lease supplies to Russia. Under the guidance of the JMA section, Zubko and Grabeel determined that "Trade" messages constituted 75 percent of the volume of traffic, with "Diplomatic" making up the rest. What neither of them knew and analysts would not discover until years later was that KGB and GRU messages were buried in the Diplomatic traffic with the designators enciphered at the beginning of the messages.[15]

As the two sat daily hunched over mounds of paper, they faced the added headache of speaking to each other only in whispers and hushed tones. Prompting the near silent exchanges was a constant threat lurking just a few feet away. For some reason that has never been determined and was perhaps influenced by the low priority of the program, they were thrown together in a room already occupied by Geoffrey Stephens, a major in the British army serving as Bletchley Park's representative to Arlington Hall.

It is unimaginable today, to think that ASA leadership had allowed two Americans, both barely into their twenties, inexperienced, with virtually no security training, to struggle with a top-secret project while a seasoned military intelligence veteran sat just a few feet away carefully observing their every move. Just a few months after they started work, the program was abruptly shut down. No one was certain why, but later speculation was that Zubko and Stephens, both trained as infantrymen, became too friendly, producing fears that the British might pick up on Grabeel and Zubko's work.

A few months later the Russian Problem suddenly came to life again with the arrival of Ferdinand Wilmerding Coudert, a near perfect fit for the job. At age thirty-four, he was the well-bred son of Ferdinand Rene Coudert, a renowned international lawyer and good friend and Oyster Bay, New York, neighbor of President Theodore Roosevelt. The elder Coudert, a partner in the sparkling Manhattan practice Coudert Freres, had a glittering client list, one that included the British, French, and Russian governments and later the government of Alexander Kerensky before the Communist takeover.

After completing undergraduate and graduate degrees in Slavonic Studies at Harvard University, the younger Coudert earned a law degree at Columbia University, where he also took crash courses in Japanese to accompany his already excellent facility in Russian, French, German, Serbo-Croatian, and Bulgarian. Following a direct commission as an army first lieutenant came an assignment to Arlington Hall in November 1942 working for Major Solomon Kullback, who later placed him with Grabeel on the Russian Program after Zubko's departure. Coudert, according to a later interview he gave, arrived blind into the program. Kullback's only marching orders were that the program was "ultra secret" and not to be discussed with other workers at Arlington Hall or with the British. Coudert later recalled this as a "touchy issue." Kullback apparently left it to Grabeel to update him on Zubko's accomplishments.[16]

The two, sitting side by side, continued sorting the stacks of Soviet message traffic along with new material coming in. Like Grabeel's earlier experience with Zubko, she and Coudert remained isolated from other colleagues behind rows of file cabinets as they "whispered to each other or worked in silence." As the work got underway the challenge gradually became the identification of an unknown number of Russian words or "code," each with a corresponding four-digit number value collectively called a "code group," which was listed in a Russian codebook that they had never seen. Added to the code group was a series of random five-digit numbers called "key" or "cipher." When the sums of the code group and key were added together it produced the "cipher group." It was the cipher group that was used to hide the message. Finding the cipher or key, which was also referred to as "additive," meant stripping it from the cipher group and revealing the code group. After obtaining the code group, the next challenge was to "bookbreak," the term of art for finding the underlying word. The last step in the process could be accomplished only through tedious analysis or somehow locating the original Russian codebook(s). At the same time, Grabeel and Coudert along with far more experienced analysts were uncertain if the additive they were dealing with was, in fact, part of a one-time pad system. If it was and it worked as designed, then "it could not be solved."[17]

As the Russian diplomatic problem was so impenetrable, the team turned its attention to collaboration with its navy counterpart; they began breaking low-level police ciphers and Communist Party instructions, ship movements, and radio procedure changes largely because they were easily cracked while offering little of value. This effort was also influenced by the hope that these simpler codes and ciphers could offer clues that would help solve far more complex communications.

Coudert's team had made some progress. Through sheer drudgery and hard work, they had finally sorted out the various circuits into four separate systems, two of which were Diplomatic and Trade. By doing so they determined what circuits were carrying enough traffic to prioritize the section's resources on the most potentially profitable circuits.

Throughout the spring and summer, analysts on the Japanese side of the house had made their remarkable break into "2468," the complex Japanese army water code used to coordinate and direct convoys moving troops and supplies to far-flung outposts around the Pacific. The pace of work at Arlington Hall became transformed overnight. "New life had been given to the entire [Japanese] section" read one memo "and several problems seemingly heretofore are being attacked in the light of what has been proved in 2468." Almost overnight this success prompted major administrative changes throughout Arlington Hall that had important resonance for the Russian Section. Abraham Kullback, an original Friedman protégé and now a major and the head of B-II Branch, took over responsibility for everything Japanese while B-III's boss, Major Rowlett, handled everything else.[18]

Among Rowlett's changes was the installation of new section chiefs designed to speed production and make staff work more efficiently. In November 1943, Lieutenant Coudert was replaced as officer in charge by his close friend from their years at Harvard, Captain William B. S. Smith, while Coudert remained as Smith's deputy, turning his attention to language services and further education on code-breaking. Like his college classmate, Smith was fluent in French, especially the rare Breton dialect that had originally brought him to Arlington Hall two years earlier as an army private to work on "Jellyfish," code name for the French cipher problem. Before the war he had worked in the New York publishing business as an editor for the *Columbia Gazeteer* and Columbia University Press, producer of a popular one-volume encyclopedia. Smith was himself a contributor with entries on religion and linguistics. Coudert began by expanding his original training course. He now gave three thirty-minute lectures concentrating on code-breaking with twelve people taking a cryptanalysis course with six additional hours of individual study per week. Russian language courses were also given with Coudert as the instructor.[19]

Before handing over leadership to Smith, Coudert produced a morale survey that offered Smith a sort of road map for the future of the unit. "The efficiency of the unit is good. There is no idleness, and few complaints or grievances arise. Thus far, the work has been negative in results. *The aim is to break the systems and a staff of experts would be of value to the unit* [italics added]."[20] He went on to note "In the [Trade] system, work has been devoted mainly to finding further matches between series of initial digraphs. A considerable number have been found. Many of them were between . . . Washington–Moscow and Portland–Moscow. These matches give a basis for additional overlaps." Yet "nowhere, however, do we have a depth of more than two, and eventually some other means will have to be found to achieve adequate depth."[21]

Rowlett quickly seized on Coudert's report by ordering implementation of a series of recommendations from the B-III Executive Council, which included greater attention to military and diplomatic messages "as much as possible," increased use of IBM equipment to speed up the process, and assignment of experienced cryptanalysts to the problem.[22]

Access to the much in demand IBM tabulator machines, so much a part of the Japanese army work then underway, was achieved in September 1943. At the start of World War II, SIS had only fifteen machines operated by twenty-one technicians. By the spring of 1945 when Weisband arrived, Arlington

Hall was operating 407 keypunch machines handled by 1,275 technicians. At the beginning Arlington Hall used off-the-shelf equipment but also collaborated with IBM on new and revolutionary equipment custom built for code-breaking. They eventually produced one device costing millions of dollars that was called a Rapid Analytical Machine (RAM), the first computer without memory, employing vacuum tubes, relays, high-speed electrical circuits, and photo-electrical principles. By 1945 another new device was coming online that by the end of the year would have the capacity "equivalent to 5 million cryptanalysts."[23]

As the year of 1943 progressed, the unit began to grow with the addition of five young women with backgrounds similar to Grabeel. Arrangements were also made for the transfers of four experienced cryptanalysts. One of them was Lieutenant Richard Treadwell Hallock, a thirty-seven-year-old New Jersey native and a professor at the University of Chicago with a doctorate in Assyriology. In addition to speaking and reading the Assyrian language, he was also a Middle East archaeologist with a talent for deciphering ancient hieroglyphs.[24]

From the tabulated IBM runs of ten thousand Trade messages ordered by Coudert, Lieutenant Hallock made a surprising discovery that dramatically changed the future of the project. The machine had produced seven pairs of messages containing what appeared to suggest double encipherment. To Hallock's trained eye this meant that they were almost certainly in depth–enciphered using the same sequence of additive key. At least a few of the one-time pad pages had clearly been used a second time, "an astonishing and monumental security blunder."[25] Hallock's discovery galvanized the unit, leading it to jump-start efforts at stripping away the additives from the paired messages in depth revealing a few frequently used code groups in message openings, particularly stereotyped beginnings of multiple messages. This led to further startling realizations that the Russian's one-time encoding system was, in some cases, more like two-time pads. As Hallock dug deeper into the messages he confirmed that, in addition to additives starting in the upper left corner of the one-time cipher pad, it also consisted of sixty additive groups per page and every now and then an entire page had been reused. What he found was "unmistakable" depth of pairs of messages and groups in various portions of messages. "Thus, the core secret had been exposed" and "messages could be matched and depth of two found, meaning that the Russians were using the same additive key twice." One NSA history later recorded that the one-time pad or rather some of it was not "truly one time." And Russian code clerks were completely unaware that they were using it.[26]

Despite the growth over the past year, Smith still found himself leading, by Arlington Hall measurements, a bare-bones operation compared to the resources now pouring into Kulback's Japanese program. Looking around at his available equipment, he observed just two or three standard typewriters and one Cyrillic model. "Everything except paper and pencils were in short supply" an NSA history later recorded.[27]

The section had expanded from Zubko and Grabeel in February 1943 to a staff of thirty by November with Coudert projecting this figure to expand even further to one hundred by the start of the year. It acquired the new code name "Blue." In January 1944 the section, having outgrown its workspace, was moved to a much larger room where it was situated when Weisband arrived. Smith also discontinued work on all circuits except Trade messages, which was the only collection containing encryption in depth.

At Arlington Hall the Blue project was now referred to as "Special Problems Section" or by an organizational chart designation as "B-III-b9," which to outsiders meant only that it had something to do with Frank Rowlett's Cryptanalysis Branch. Security was especially tight. Smith maintained Coudert's practice of locking up all papers and notes along with language books and dictionaries at the end of each workday. Maps of Russia and Russian targets had to be taken down from walls in the evening and folded neatly for secure storage until the next morning when the process was reversed. At day's end with all work papers and notes returned to locked cabinets, classified waste was disposed of in special containers. Discussions among Blue team members was a necessity that often led to sounds rising at increasing decibel levels. Smith found himself constantly admonishing his team to lower their voices for fear of being overheard by colleagues sitting just a few feet away.[28] As one writer put it, "Even by the standards of the extremely tight security that surrounded everything having to do with codes and codebreaking, the secrecy of the Russian problem was exceptional."[29] At the same time a think piece summed up the outlook for the unit and its perceived need in the future.

> The alignment of powers in the next war cannot be predicted. A very few general considerations, which must suggest that it is imperative never to relax work on Russian and Chinese systems are all that can be seen with clarity by the contemporary eye.[30]

An important source for the Blue team appeared in June 1944 just around the time of the Normandy invasion. The US Army, seeking better coordination between British and American forces fighting in the west and the Russians in the east, made an agreement with the Soviet government to establish a direct radio teleprinter link between the Pentagon and Moscow with a relay located at an American radio station in Algiers. It was designed for efficiency and speed to replace a North Pole circuit that often proved temperamental and unpredictable. What the Russians did not know was that army officials had set up a separate teleprinter at Arlington Hall's A Building that copied the messages for intelligence purposes. "For several years it was the most important source of enciphered Russian traffic available to American codebreakers."[31]

Cecil Phillips joined Smith's team in May 1944 and quickly began laboring away on Trade messages, getting nowhere. In November 1944, just as Weisband arrived, he decided on a whim to turn his attention to a batch of New York to Moscow Diplomatic messages for any possible leads, momentarily setting the Trade messages aside. After considerable study certain anomalies began catching his attention. Phillips understood that under normal cryptographic principles an enciphered code produces a purely random distribution of digits. As he examined these messages closer, however, what he sensed in his mind's eye was not necessarily random. Something was different but he couldn't put his finger on it. So, getting down to the gritty work of cryptanalysis he began carefully hand-counting thousands of digits in hundreds of messages with a full expectation of finding them repeating about 10 percent of the time—indicative of randomness. What he found instead was simple yet profound in its implication. The digit "6" appeared 20 percent of the time. Uncertain about what to do next, he turned to Genevieve Grotjan for advice. Not yet thirty years old, Grotjan had already earned her hash marks as a veteran wartime code breaker. After graduating summa cum laude from the University of Buffalo with a degree in mathematics, she joined the Signal Intelligence Service when she was recruited by William Friedman. Before the war her role as a "junior cryptanalyst" with Rowlett and Sinkov proved pivotal in working out the mathematical complexities of the Purple machine that led to *Magic*.[32] After studying Phillips's findings, Grotjan concluded that he may have stumbled onto what she believed was "Clear Key." It meant that the same additive to Trade, which were the only messages then believed to have been enciphered in a depth of two, had also been used to encrypt Soviet Diplomatic messages as well. As if this discovery was not profound enough, Phillips and Grotjan also solved the "indicator" system that determined what page of the one-time pad had been used. The indicator, listed at the upper left-hand corner of the key page and transmitted as the first group of each message, signaled to the receiver the actual additive group that would encipher the following text. If she was right, it would have profound implications for future analytic approaches to Russian messages.[33]

To confirm these findings Phillips ran the messages through both Arlington Hall's IBM machines and OP-20-G's Copperhead, a revolutionary new rapid optical comparator that searched for double hits in several thousands of messages sent on other Soviet diplomatic systems. By February 1945, the original findings had been confirmed. Phillips then made an additional discovery. The Soviets were using the first key group of the one-time pad page as the indicator to tell the recipient of ZDT message (Soviet Diplomatic) which page had been used; a discovery that afforded a new shortcut to finding matching messages in depth. As William Weisband sat watching, B-III-b9 began to recognize that for the first time there was a "slim, but real chance that all [messages] could be cracked open."[34]

\* \* \*

Around June 1944, as last-minute preparations were in motion for the invasion of Europe, the leaders of Bletchley Park, Britain's code-breaking center, conceived a plan to collect German signal and cryptologic secrets. Unlike Operation STELLA POLARIS, which gifted Finland's cryptologic secrets to Moscow, this plan called for beating the Russians to the punch in a new cryptologic war that many saw coming. The idea was to gather as much communications intelligence as possible, which was sparse to begin with, about the best places to look for material in support of what became known as Target Intelligence Committee or TICOM teams. Small, mobile groups made up of American and British intelligence officers with cryptologic backgrounds assigned to Bletchley Park would follow the Allied advance hunting for German cryptographic equipment, documents, and technicians taken as prisoners of war. After approving the project in August 1944, General Marshall ordered General Eisenhower to render all assistance necessary to the teams. The four goals Marshall laid out for the TICOM teams included a complete assessment of the German cryptanalytic efforts against the United States and England, exploiting German cryptologic techniques and inventions before they were destroyed, uncovering items of communications intelligence that could be used in the continuing battle against Japan and, lastly, preventing German equipment, documents, and personnel from falling into "unauthorized hands."[35]

The program was slow to get off the ground. It didn't seem to start until April 1945, when six teams from the Army Security Agency, OP-20-G, and Bletchley Park ranging in size from as few as two to as many as twelve depending on the mission began fanning out across Europe.

Before any team was even dispatched, word was received from advanced units of a windfall of information found in the castle of Burgscheidungen, located near Leipzig in the German province of Saxony. TICOM teams wasted no time racing to the site knowing that it was within the Soviet zone of occupation and the Russians would soon arrive to claim it. What Allied troops found was the complete German foreign ministry Service Signals Archive, which included a number of Russian codes and ciphers. There were important records that Russian consulate officials in Helsinki hastily attempted to burn as they were fleeing when the Finnish government sided with the Axis in 1941. The collection, turned over to the Germans, also produced a KGB codebook called Kod Podeba, a one-time pad series scheduled for use between 1939 and 1943, replaced when a new system called JADE was introduced. POW interrogations reaped additional intriguing information about Russian transmission practices that TICOM found useful. Russian communicators were often "extremely careless" in preparing messages for transmission, which the Germans exploited to the fullest. Large quantities of valuable information were recovered by German collectors when transmitters gave away their starting indicator position of a message through preliminary unenciphered conversations called "Chat" with the receiving operator as they established a connection. When this occurred two or more messages would be sent from the same starting positions, offering eavesdroppers significant shortcuts in finding depth. A second vulnerability came from the sloppy use of standard preambles and addresses within enciphered messages rather than mixing them up in furtherance of good security. German listeners employing common sense and intuition could discern these highly predictable and stereotypical openings for use as shortcuts into encrypted messages. Another German reoccurring problem was poor synchronization of Russian communication equipment. Partially encrypted messages would frequently require retransmission, producing large amounts of duplicates, which proved to be a gold mine for German code breakers.

One of TICOM's greatest successes occurred in Bavaria when TICOM Team 1, made up of two drivers, five intelligence officers, and two radio operators, set off in the hunt for a very special item. They were looking for a T-52, or Geheimschreiber (Secret Writer), one of the Wehrmacht's most sophisticated on-line encrypted teletype machines assigned the code name *Fish* by the British. It was used only for generating German high-command ciphers. After traveling down a number of false trails, an intact T-52 with its all-important rotors still in place was found in the Alpine village of Pfunds, about forty miles from Hitler's famed mountain retreat at Berchtesgaden.

As the TICOM teams raced farther east, the hits kept on coming. In the small Bavarian village of Rosenheim, a group of POWs were found who had worked as radio operators for the German high command. Eager to avoid being turned over to the Russians, they were most cooperative in describing their work and pointing to a never-before-seen device buried nearby. It was specially designed to "intercept high level Soviet communications [system]" that split communications into nine separate channels, making interception difficult. The TICOM team, which nicknamed the device "Russian Fish," were directed to a field where seven tons of equipment were unearthed and reassembled by the Germans for demonstration. One writer later suggested that to have the "Russian Fish machine intercepting traffic as early as June 1945 along with all other German research and decrypts must have been instrumental in the immediate post-war Anglo-American effort against the Soviet Union."[36]

In many cases German code breakers never needed to know the key in order to get into the Russian message. Again, relying on intuition and guesswork based on a wealth of evidence from the operators' preliminary and often lengthy "Chat," they could produce fairly accurate reports on enemy troop levels and situations along with officer promotions and transfers, supply needs, results of POW interrogations, and adjustments and changes in Russian signal intelligence practices. Also able to be produced were reports on armed units of the KGB.[37]

Based on this accumulated material the Americans and the British immediately began a determined effort to recover long stretches of key. The hope was that ascertaining the wheel patterns of the Russian encipherment machines could lead to the eventual reconstruction of the device's key-generating algorithm. If the algorithm could be isolated, then powerful computational machines could brute-force every possible sequence of key against a received message text and test for statistical evidence of a likely match. "With such a complete system, any message—not just the small percentage that happened to be in depth—could be read consistently." The Germans called this system "Bandwurm," and the British called the Russian Baudot system "Russian Fish" after the attack on German *Enigma* and then "Caviar" and later "Longfellow."[38]

\* \* \*

On the morning of April 12, 1945, a Thursday, Bill Weisband walked past the security checkpoint at Arlington Hall and up the curved driveway as usual to B-III-b9 blissfully unaware that by day's end President Franklin Roosevelt would be dead from a cerebral hemorrhage. Over the previous six months, Roosevelt had lived a whirlwind existence. He had won an unprecedented fourth presidential term, celebrated his sixty-third birthday, traveled twelve thousand miles for a parlay with Josef Stalin and Winston Churchill in Crimean Russia and returned home to deliver his message to Congress on the results of the conference sitting in the well of the House chamber rather than standing at the podium as was customary. By April, exhausted and sick, he decided to take some time for a little peace and rest at his quiet retreat, "The Little White House," nestled in the white pine forest town of Warm Springs, Georgia. It was there while sitting for a portrait painter struggling to capture his likeness that the president suddenly complained of a terrible headache, slumped over, and died a short time later.

His successor was an obscure politician from Missouri who the country barely knew and probably couldn't recognize in those days before television.

Harry Truman was three weeks shy of his sixty-first birthday when Eleanor Roosevelt, the now former first lady, suddenly summoned him to the White House to deliver the news that he was now president of the United States. Looking at the man who now sat at the top of America's national security establishment, one would find little in his background that would have prepared him for the enormous task now facing him. He was born on a Missouri farm, was a high school graduate, and veteran of World War I with service in France as a captain of an artillery unit. He married Bess Wallace, his sweetheart, started a soon-to-fail haberdashery business in Kansas City and then won a seat as a Jackson County judge, similar to a county commissioner, in 1922. Twelve years later, he was elected to the US Senate, where he made a modest name for himself as the chairman of a Senate committee investigating fraud and abuse in the war industry.

President Roosevelt barely knew Truman when he chose him as his running mate for the 1944 election. The two rarely met during the campaign and only twice for lunch after the victory, with the conversation centering generally on politics. When he took the oath of office at the White House that April afternoon, he knew nothing about the war or Roosevelt's agreements and dealings with foreign leaders. Nor was he aware of the top-secret American-British intelligence partnership that was helping to forge victory against the Axis. He only learned of the existence of the atomic bomb project in a private conversation with his secretary of war four days after his swearing in.

Over the next few months, Truman spent much of his time cobbling together a staff while learning as much as he could in preparation for another summit with Churchill and Stalin (meeting both for the first time) scheduled for July in Potsdam, Germany. There was much to consider that summer. American forces were poised just hundreds of miles from Japan's southern coastline. The next stop would be a full-scale invasion of the Japanese home islands that military experts estimated would cost nearly a million American lives if the resistance of Japanese forces at Okinawa and Iwo Jima was any indicator. The Soviets had already declared war on Japan and were readying to send troops into Manchuria to block Japanese army forces from returning home to defend their country. In general, the focus of the Truman White House was ending the war in the Pacific and dealing with growing domestic pressure to bring the troops home. Truman's relations with Moscow, as one aide later recorded, "were low on our agenda."[39]

Behind the scenes, however, changes in the US communications intelligence approach to Russia were beginning to catch fire. In May 1945, a week after the German surrender, Admiral Ernest King, the chief of naval operations, ordered more emphasis on Russian code-breaking with more personnel devoted to it. At the same time, he suggested the removal of the project from the Navy Annex on Nebraska Avenue for greater security.

As the war drew to a close, memoranda passing between the navy and army began appearing with the notations "N.B.," which meant "No British."[40] The close wartime collaboration between America and Great Britain, unprecedented in the history of warfare, was now coming under reappraisal as US military leaders began questioning if the relationship should continue into peacetime. Everyone was aware that the cobbled-together sharing agreement was confined only to Axis communications and not neutral countries or the Grand Alliance's other partner, the Soviet Union. In fact, Great Britain, in contrast to the United States, discontinued all of its communications collection against Russia at the start of the war. American officials opposing further cooperation felt there was no need for such collaboration. America's intercept and analysis abilities using new and amazing computer-generated decoding techniques had outrun the need for partners. The belief in some quarters was that America could go it alone. American intelligence gathering was at a pivot point in its history and there were serious questions about where to go next in the new post-war world communications intelligence. "I do not think we should 'gang up' with one ally against another" wrote Admiral Richard E. Evans, the vice-chief of naval operations. "In the troubled time that lie ahead we shall have to side with one or another of our friends as differences of interest arise, but for the sake of the peace of the world we should do so openly and frankly. If we secretly join the British in this project, the secret is virtually certain to leak out in the course of time with results disastrous for our relations with USSR. The possible gain is not worth the probable loss."[41]

The War Department, in contrast to its navy colleagues, took a different view. Wartime collaboration with the British had been fruitful and would continue to be a value added for the future of American code-breaking. The structure had worked well over the past four years of war and there was no reason to suspect that it would weaken in the future. As a practical matter the British had assets not available to the United States. Britain still controlled trans-Atlantic undersea cables that they could tap for collection of messages at any time. It also had a vast array of listening posts across its empire, particularly in India and Pakistan along the southern rim of the Soviet Union that would prove useful for future collection. The Potsdam Conference would also assign them zones of occupation in Germany and in Berlin within the sector assigned to the Soviet government.

On June 2, 1945, British officials suggested working together on the Russian problem and three days later both General Marshall and Admiral King cautiously approved narrow exchanges of information on an informal basis. They insisted that a statement prepared by the Army-Navy Communications Intelligence Board outlining the agreed-upon terms "be shown but not given" to the British representative and that their own memorandum to the board be "burned immediately upon reading."[42]

Four months after the death of President Roosevelt his successor, Harry Truman, endorsed a letter sent to him by the joint chiefs of staff recommending a continuation of the wartime communications intelligence sharing with the same level of secrecy attached to the atomic bomb program. "All of the experts repeatedly emphasized the grave danger that might be done were any hint of the work to leak out; that secrecy meant that in turn there was simply no need to justify to the American public or Congress, or to risk the kind of newspaper debates in which the plans for a postwar OSS had to be embroiled." The president's one-line reply on August 28 approving the plan also ordered no public release of his decision "except with the special approval of the President in each case."[43] A watershed moment in America's history had been reached.

As for Bill Weisband, he sat quietly at his table in B-III-b9 watching it unfold and absorbing it all. He was now at the center of momentous changes in the nation's intelligence history while enjoying a money stream that would seemingly go on forever. But changes were in the wind.

## NOTES

1. Adam Ulam, *Stalin: The Man and His Era* (New York: Viking Press, 1973), 592.
2. Mathew Aid, "Stella Polaris and the Secret Code Battle in Post War Europe," *Journal of Intelligence and National Security* (September 2002): 17–86.
3. Ibid.
4. Ibid.
5. Juanita Moody Oral History June 21, 2001, NCM, NSA.
6. Ibid. The Russian diplomatic crypto materials did make their way to the West, through the now famous Stella Polaris project. *Benson Venona History*, 36.
7. D. Glen Starlin memorandum entitled "Minutes of Meeting Held 21 June 1946, Room 117, Headquarters," NCM, FOIPA.
8. VN Concordance 428.
9. Thomas R. Johnson, "The Sting—Enabling Codebreaking in the Twentieth Century." No Date DOCID 3860890 NCM, NSA.
10. Budiansky, *Code Warriors* (New York: Alfred A. Knopf, 2016), 28.
11. Ibid.
12. Tanya Cimminetti, author interview, April 19, 2018.
13. Grabeel remained at NSA for the rest of her career working in the Venona Project for nearly forty years until it was ended in 1980. "Grabeel, Gene," *Richmond Times Dispatch*, February 15, 2015.
14. Thomas R. Johnson, "The Sting—Enabling Codebreaking in the Twentieth Century," *Cryptologic Quarterly*, No Date DOCID 3860890 NCM, NSA. Venona Monograph.

15. Robert Louis Benson, *Venona* (Fort Meade, MD: National Security Agency) Document Number 2249509, 8.
16. Ibid., 26.
17. By VJ Day Arlington Hall was reading the diplomatic messages of forty-five countries, including Saudi Arabia, Finland, Liberia, Luxembourg, Ireland, Denmark, and Panama, but though it was now intercepting 5,500 Russian messages per month it had nothing yet to report for all of its efforts. Mundy, *Code Girls*, 226.
18. Robert Louis Benson, *Venona*, 28.
19. Ibid., 25.
20. Ibid., 28.
21. Ibid., 25.
22. Ibid., 27.
23. Robert Louis Benson, *Venona*, 26.
24. Budiansky, *Code Warriors*, 31.
25. Robert Louis Benson, *Venona*, 24.
26. Ibid., 36.
27. Ibid.
28. Budiansky, *Code Warriors*, 27.
29. Robert Louis Benson, *Venona*, 34.
30. Budiansky, *Code Warriors*, 23.
31. "Preliminary Historical Report on the Solution of the 'B' Machine," William Friedman, October 4, 1940, NCM.
32. Robert Louis Benson, *Venona*, 41.
33. Ibid., 49.
34. Ibid.
35. Budiansky, *Code Warriors*, 38.
36. Ibid.
37. Ibid.
38. Budiansky, *Battle of Wits*, 60.
39. Ibid., 308–9.
40. Clark Clifford, *Counsel to the President* (New York: Random House, 1991), 59.
41. Budiansky, *Code Warriors*, 33.
42. Ibid., 39.
43. Ibid.

*Chapter 19*

# Disaster

It took only days to make the decision. One that would forever change his life. Once made, he told no one except his young wife. Confiding a secret of such magnitude to friends or colleagues would mean a death sentence.

Now the moment had come. Three days after Japan formally surrendered, ending the World War II, Igor Gouzenko walked out of the Soviet embassy in Ottawa, Canada, for the last time on September 5, 1945. It was unusually warm and humid in the Canadian capital that evening, made even warmer by the hundreds of soggy documents and notebooks, large and small, crudely clamped to his sweaty body under a loose-fitting shirt. The feelings of terror that night still lingered with him later in life as he recalled his struggle to appear nonchalant walking down the stairs from the embassy's second-floor code room while controlling his nerves as he approached the guard in the lobby. "Sweat was standing out on my brow, and I felt my chest tightening," he recalled. "I didn't even dare reach into my pocket for a handkerchief lest the movement might disturb something." After signing the logbook for the last time, his "heart leapt with joy" as he stepped onto the sidewalk and freedom.[1]

Following a rocky start, Gouzenko along with his wife and two small children found themselves safely in the hands of the Royal Canadian Mounted Police ninety miles west of Ottawa while the KGB frantically hunted for them. His sanctuary was Special Training School Number Three, better known as "Camp X": a top-secret site on the banks of Lake Ontario set up at the start of the war to train OSS and British forces in guerilla tactics. Over the months to come Gouzenko, "Corby," as he was code-named (after a famed Canadian whiskey), sat for hours every day pouring out his life story to Canadian, British, and American investigators. At the same time, Canadian linguists busied themselves translating his stockpile of documents that for the first time revealed evidence of a vast Soviet espionage network spread across North America.

Gouzenko began his story by explaining that the papers filed about him to the Canadian Department of External Affairs by the Soviet foreign ministry were false. Yes, he was Igor Gouzenko, but he was not from the city of Gorky and had never attended Gorky Economic Technical Institute. Nor was he a mere "Employee of the Military Attaché" whose workdays were filled with reading newspapers and translating technical journals.[2]

In truth, he was a lieutenant in the Russian army working as a GRU cipher clerk—the most sensitive intelligence position in the embassy. Born in 1919 in Rogochov, a little village just a few miles from Moscow, he was the fourth and youngest child of a soldier who died of typhus during World War I. The loss forced his mother to return to her parents' village of Semeon, where extended family helped raise the children. Igor was by his own account an exceptional student receiving excellent test scores at school, particularly in math and science. As a teenager he took the all-important first step up the ladder to full membership in the Communist Party by joining the Young Komsomols, the party's youth organization. Later, he earned a seat at the Moscow Architectural School, where he met Anna, his future wife.

As war approached, his plans of becoming a builder took an abrupt turn when he was unexpectedly assigned to the Kubischev Military Engineering Academy of Moscow to study mathematics, structural materials, and military construction. Before long he abruptly moved again—this time to the Military Intelligence Administration. There he was thrust into a secret world that he later referred to as moving "behind the curtain."[3]

Here, for the first time, he learned about the seamier side of Soviet military intelligence work with lectures on "dry affairs" and "wet affairs." To broaden his understanding of operations, he spent long hours alone reading messages flowing in from GRU stations around the world; a practice that revealed names of both agents and officers. In addition to reading messages, he also spent considerable time absorbing "exhaustive files" holding case histories on each agent.[4] In a special Moscow laboratory, he studied microphotography, a task he would later handle in the embassy, using the latest equipment purchased from the United States.

Within a week of his defection Gouzenko became the teacher, giving daily tutorials to FBI agents sent from Washington and British officers from both MI5 and MI6. With the start of the war, he explained, the Chief Intelligence Headquarters of the Red Army took on a dual role of conducting espionage abroad and producing intelligence for frontline troops battling German forces. As intelligence requirements around the world accelerated, particularly regarding Japan and Canada and the United States, Soviet military intelligence leaders in March 1943 split the organization into two sections: one focusing on strategic and the other on rapidly changing battlefield conditions with tactical intelligence. Strategic intelligence was further expanded when

Stalin disbanded the Comintern under pressure from his Allied partners. The GRU began supporting and directing "Fifth Column" groups undermining democratic countries from within and fomenting crippling blows if the Russian leadership so ordered. These new responsibilities were an addition to providing the leadership with a clear and complete picture of happenings and trends around the world.[5] The best way to achieve these aims, he later wrote, was to "infiltrate unnoticed into vital organs of the democracies to plant agents in key positions of political, economic and military administration."[6]

\* \* \*

The carefully selected documents that Gouzenko filched opened the eyes of Western leaders to the incontrovertible fact of Russian spying in the United States, Canada, and Great Britain. They revealed Soviet awareness for years of US and British efforts to produce an atomic bomb as well as Stalin's aggressive pursuit of the secrets of the device. Among the names of Stalin's spies revealed by Gouzenko was Gordon Lunan, a Scotsman in his early thirties then living in Quebec. Gouzenko's records confirmed that Lunan worked as clandestine courier for four atomic espionage agents. There was also Raymond Boyer, a prominent professor of chemistry at McGill University, an engineer with the Canadian National Research Council, Edward Mazerall, along with Durnford Smith, an electrical engineer, and a young mathematics professor at Queen's University in Ontario named Israel Halperin. The biggest fish in the barrel, however, turned out to be British physicist Alan Nunn May. When the war began, he was recruited for the British atomic bomb project, called "Tube-Alloy" at the time.[7] The GRU received a steady supply of secrets from his work on uranium and later during his assignment to the Chalk River Nuclear Facility in western Canada, which was playing a role in the development of the atomic bomb.

Gouzenko's assignment to Canada came about as a result of the Canadian government ban on the Communist Party in 1940. Then in 1942, in a spirit of allied amity, it invited the Soviet Union to establish a legation in Ottawa. A year later Lieutenant Gouzenko along with Nikolai Zabotin, the GRU station chief, and his deputy Alexander Romanov arrived in Canada as part of the initial staffing. Only a year later the first major contretemps erupted when Romanov's repeated public drunkenness and boorish behavior forced his return to Moscow.[8]

One July afternoon in 1944 it was Gouzenko's turn to face his boss. At the time, Igor assumed that he was facing a reprimand after a charwoman cleaning the cipher room after hours discovered several drafts of cables carelessly left on his desk. Unfortunately, it wasn't his first lapse in judgment since arriving at the legation. Also chalked up against him were several errors including instances of tardiness. Worse still, was a report that made its way to Zabotin through KGB channels that his code clerk had been spotted chatting with an Ottawa police officer.

To Gouzenko's utter amazement he learned that his immediate recall to Moscow had been ordered by the deputy director of the GRU, Mikhail Milstein, following a recent inspection of Russian diplomatic establishments in North America. Milstein's irrevocable decree was supposedly issued in the interest of GRU security. No one wanted "to take a chance with an employee who had access to all their secret communications."[9]

Zabotin did manage, however, to persuade Milstein to delay Gouzenko's return with claims that a sudden loss of his indispensable skills as a cipher clerk would impose an immediate hardship on the station. Both men breathed a sigh of relief when a temporary reprieve was granted but only until a replacement could be found and trained. Still reeling from the news and knowing full well what awaited him in Moscow, he made his decision to defect to the West when the time came. "I felt a great load lifted from me. The die had finally been cast" he later wrote. "And best of all, Anna agreed on the course. There was no use pointing out the dangers—she knew them full well."[10]

Life slowly resumed an uncertain routine for the next nine months when word arrived that a replacement would soon be on his way to Canada. Another six more months went by as Gouzenko, recognizing the handwriting on the wall, quietly began gathering secrets that he knew would impress the Canadians and guarantee sanctuary. He started with the identities of all KGB personnel at the legation, along with their behavior, comings and goings, and anything else he could glean from captured snippets of conversations exposing their foibles, personal weaknesses, and vulnerabilities. Next, he selected, what he believed, were the choicest documents confirming the existence of active GRU espionage networks, agents' identities, along with the particulars of secret meetings, code names (his code name was "Clark"), and every important piece of intelligence making its way to Moscow. In his mind, anything priceless to the GRU and KGB would be priceless to the Canadians. Both the KGB and the GRU were helpless in staunching the intelligence disaster unfolding in front of them. They could not get to him as the Royal Canadian Mounted Police had Gouzenko and his family under secure guard, which meant a "wet affair" was out of the question.

But the KGB wasn't deaf to Gouzenko's revelations nor blind to where he was hiding. As a privileged member of the British upper class, Harold Adrian Russell Philby, called "Kim" by friends and colleagues, was born on New Year's Day in 1912 in Ambala in the Punjab Province of British-controlled India. His father, St. John Philby, then a minor official in the Indian civil service, later abandoned the family for a new life as an author, orientalist, and convert to Islam. He spent the rest of his life in the Middle East, taking up residence in Saudi Arabia as an advisor to King Ibn Saud. While he trapesed across the desert living the life of a pasha, his wife, Dora, returned to England, where she struggled to raise her children while desperately trying to keep up "old establishment" appearances. During his student years at Cambridge University Philby became drawn to Communism, which he and many of his classmates saw as a savior to a rot within a British establishment that had bankrupted the nation while continuing to govern it. Philby graduated in 1933 convinced that his life "must be devoted to Communism."[11]

From Cambridge he was off to Vienna, where he had a torrid affair with Litzi Friedman, a young divorcee, and secret courier for the Austrian Communist Party working for the International Workers Relief Organization. After marrying her in 1934, the couple returned to London, where Litzi introduced Kim to fellow communist Edith Suschitsky, now married to Alex Tudor Hart, another secret British communist. Friedman and the Tudor Harts had been recruited for Soviet espionage by Arnold Deutsch, an Austrian mathematician and one of the KGB's greatest illegal intelligence officers. At Edith's insistence, Deutsch met the twenty-two-year-old Philby on a bench one day in Regents Park. There he made the recruitment pitch that would propel Philby into the world of spying, making him one of the most reviled figures in the annals of twentieth-century espionage.[12]

Over the next three years Philby became a journalist, starting with articles for, what one critic called, the "uninfluential" *Review of Reviews*. To further burnish his right-wing credentials, he quietly divorced Litzi and joined the Anglo-German Fellowship, what Churchill called the "Heil Hitler Brigade." In 1937 he sailed for Spain to work as a freelance correspondent covering the Spanish Civil War. While there, Moscow ordered him to try to get close to Francisco Franco, head of Falangist forces, and murder him. After a brief return to London as a correspondent for *The Times* he went back to Spain to cover Franco's nationalist forces.[13]

While still with *The Times* in 1940, Philby was approached with a job offer from the British Secret Intelligence Service (SIS). Employment vetting in those days was a superficial affair having more to do with pedigree, the right school tie, and the relative strength of one's references. A "trace inquiry" was conducted, and the proper procedures carefully followed but, in the end, "it was not much of a vetting process" according to the SIS's authorized history.[14] In Philby's case he was on board in September 1941 after a couple of perfunctory interviews (one with fellow-spy Guy Burgess) and a simple name check with the British Security Service (MI5) revealing "Nothing Recorded Against."[15]

For the next three years as the war intensified, Philby steadily ascended the SIS's bureaucratic ladder until September 1944, two months before Gouzenko's fateful encounter with Zabotin, when a reorganization, which

Philby helped manipulate, positioned him where Moscow wanted him—Section IX, overseeing Russian counterespionage operations targeted against SIS. It was exactly what Philby intended, wrote Anthony Cave Brown, turning "the counterespionage of the SIS into the unwitting intelligence arm of the Soviet government." His new duties, which he personally laid out in a charter signed off by MI6 director Stewart Menzies, made him responsible for "collection and interpretation of information concerning Soviet and Communist espionage and subversion in all parts of the world outside British territory."[16]

The first report of the startling events unfolding in Ottawa landed on Philby's desk two days after Gouzenko's defection. As the counterintelligence and political implications of the Corby case continued to metastasize, Philby scrutinized every nugget of information, which he then synthesized into abstracts for Menzies to assist his briefing of newly elected British prime minister Clement Attlee. They were equally useful for updating Boris Krotenschield, Philby's KGB handler. So accurate were Philby's reports that two weeks after the defection Moscow signaled Krotenschield that "Stanley's" (Philby's code name) information about "events in Canada . . . does correspond to the facts."[17]

*  *  *

Eighteen days after Gouzenko's defection, Menzies wired an "immediate" message to the British representative at Arlington Hall. Most likely written by Philby on Menzies behalf, it informed the Americans about Gouzenko's defection, adding that he had already provided some "useful crypto information." The "Canadians have agreed at our request, that he should be interrogated at once by American officers, if Americans will consent." He added the British view that Gouzenko's information "will probably be of considerable assistance if he is interrogated on technical matters by an officer fully versed in crypto problem involved."[18]

The American officer dispatched to Camp X was Arlington Hall's Frank Rowlett. For the head of B-II Branch, this meeting must have been one of the great thrills of what had already been a momentous professional life. The code-breaking career that Rowlett embarked on as a junior cryptanalyst had now spanned fifteen years. A period of time during which his extraordinary achievement in solving the Japanese Purple Code, among other code-breaking successes, had saved the lives of tens of thousands of Allied sailors, soldiers, marines, and fliers who would never know his name. Throughout those years his work against foreign encryption machines was performed without his ever setting eyes on the devices or meeting the faceless operators who produced the messages. Over the last two and a half years he had watched as Zubko, Grabeel, Coudert, Hallock, and dozens of others struggled to make sense of the hundreds of thousands of Russian messages stored in Arlington Hall safes. Now a lieutenant colonel and eager to question a genuine Russian code clerk, Rowlett traveled to Camp X wearing a business suit to avoid attention. For the first time, he would be sitting across a table absorbing answers to countless questions from one of those previously faceless operators who actually performed the task.

Lengthy meetings over ten days proved to be a gold mine for "Bourbon" as the Russian program was now code-named. Gouzenko began by explaining that GRU code clerks were responsible to the KGB for security. Only the ambassador and chief of station had the authority to approve the dispatch of messages. In Ottawa, the process of sending a cable began when the GRU chief of station entered the cipher room, gathered his notes, and began drafting a message in the code clerk's presence. Next the code clerk enciphered it. When finished he gave it to the communications officer for assignment of a serial number before delivery to the commercial cable company for transmission to Moscow. KGB security rules prohibited the GRU station chief (in this case, Zabotin) from keeping copies of his drafted message for reference purposes. All notes, diaries, work papers, and any other materials could not leave the code room and had to be stored in a safe under the watchful eye of the code clerk. Next, he described encipherment/decipherment procedures beginning with the fact that all GRU code clerks had to be approved and trained over a nine-month course of study by the KGB. Using thirty-three coded GRU messages he removed from the embassy, Gouzenko described in "great and accurate detail" the GRU and KGB's exclusive reliance on codebooks and use of one-time pad systems for processing messages. Rowlett then learned of a second communications system. It used a substitution alphabet based on one- or two-digit equivalents from the Cyrillic alphabet that would then be enciphered using a one-time key generated from a standard book of fiction available in Moscow and used by agents in countries around the world. This system was only to be used for illicit or emergency communications. The KGB manufactured all one-time pads in 35- to 50-page packets. Each page contained ten lines of five-digit groups for a total of 50 groups or 250 digits per page.[19]

Gouzenko knew the identities of all KGB officers at the embassy in Ottawa as well as the GRU sources in Canada and some in the United States. He never knew any KGB sources, as the KGB had its own communications channels with Moscow. While such compartmentation ensured KGB operational security, there still remained a lingering uncertainty about the extent of the danger to their North American operations. After dithering for weeks, Moscow Center, relying on Philby's reporting, concluded that there was a threat sufficient enough to force a partial shutdown of certain sources in the wake of the crisis facing Stalin's relations with its former wartime allies.

Wasting no more time, Moscow signaled a brief but impactful warning on October 21, 1945, to Anatoliy Gorsky, then serving as both KGB station chief and ambassador in Washington. "The situation in [Canada] has become strained. Surveillance has been increased." Aware of FBI questioning of Gouzenko and growing surveillance pressure on embassy officials, Moscow reminded Gorsky of the paramount importance of local operations and the need to take steps to limit any chance of discovery. Gorsky's orders—immediately break contact with all "minor agents." And, above all "safeguard from failure" the station's five most important sources by limiting meetings with them to once or twice a month. Bill Weisband was near the top of Gorsky's short list.[20]

## NOTES

1. Igor Gouzenko, *Iron Curtain* (New York: E. P. Dutton & Co., Inc., 1948), 205–6.
2. Ibid.
3. Ibid., 61.
4. Ibid., 62–63, 67.
5. Ibid., 121.
6. Ibid., 121.
7. Haynes, Klehr, and Vassiliev, *Spies*, 68–69.
8. Romanov's behavior included inappropriate advances to the wife of a Canadian army general, which forced Zabotin to send him home in disgrace. Amy Knight, *How the Cold War Began* (New York: Carroll & Graf Publishers, 2005), 22.
9. Ibid., 23.
10. "There was no necessity of stressing absolute secrecy. She knew certain death lay ahead if the least hint of my intended desertion got about." Ibid., 23.
11. Andrew and Mitrokhin, *Mitrokhin Archive*, 58.
12. Ibid.
13. It was then that fate stepped in to make him a minor celebrity when a car that he and three other reporters had been driving was struck by an artillery shell, killing his colleagues but leaving him with only minor injuries. The seemingly always lucky Philby later recorded how his "wounding in Spain helped my work in journalism and intelligence—no end." His injury led General Franco on March 2, 1938 (Moscow had cancelled the assassination mission) to personally pin the Red Cross of Military Merit on Philby's chest. Ibid., 66–67.
14. Jeffery, *The Secret History of MI6*, 368.
15. Even Kim was shocked at how simple it all was. "The ease of my entry surprised me," he wrote decades later from exile in Russia. "Today, every new spy scandal in Britain produces a flurry of judicial statements on the subject of 'positive vetting.' But in that happier Eden positive vetting had never been heard of." Kim Philby, *My Silent War* (New York: Grove Press Inc., 1968), 30.

16. Anthony Cave Brown, *Treason in the Blood* (Boston: Houghton Mifflin Company, 1994), 333. It also called for the "closest liaison for the reciprocal exchange of intelligence on these subjects with MI5." Kim could now easily spot and then thwart any threat to his own safety while loyally feeding his KGB masters priceless British and American intelligence secrets. "I had easy access to the heart of SIS," he wrote, adding that "Now I was in the middle of it, in the best position to sniff the breezes of office politics and well placed to discover the personalities that passed me in the corridors." Philby, *My Silent War*, 126.

17. Jeffery, *The Secret History of MI6*, 657.

18. Robert Louis Benson, *History of Venona* (Washington, DC: National Security Agency, 1993), 62.

19. Benson, *History of Venona*, 62–63; Frank Rowlett, "Special Report on Bourbon Cryptography: Report on Interrogation of Corby, October 15, 1945." NCM.

20. VBN 57.

*Chapter 20*

# Disaster Times Two

It was Wednesday, November 7, 1945, around four-thirty in the afternoon. He should have been thinking about wrapping up his day and heading home. Instead, he found himself at a subway stop near Lower Manhattan scanning the faces of the growing rush-hour crowds hoping (and probably praying) to spot a woman he had never laid eyes on. Having no idea what she would be wearing, his only hope of recognizing her was the magazine she would be carrying under her arm.

For three weeks his repeated calls to her telephone number had gone unanswered. Finally, after the "unpteenth" time, she picked up the receiver. The voice at the end of the line was shaky. She was reluctant to talk to him. He urged her to do so, explaining the importance of providing any information "regarding un-American activities." When she finally appeared the next day, he gently took her by the arm and guided her down the street to a quiet room in the FBI's Foley Square office. For the next eight hours and twenty-three days thereafter, Elizabeth Terrill Bentley poured out her tale to Edward Buckley, a twenty-eight-year-old Special Agent of the FBI. In doing so she destroyed much of a US espionage network that the KGB had so carefully crafted over more than a decade.[1]

As Buckley sat listening, he could detect nothing in Elizabeth's early life that offered clues to why she had served for years as Moscow's most important wartime espionage courier. She was an only child born on New Year's Day in 1908 in the quaint Connecticut village of New Milford. Charles Bentley, a dry-goods salesman, appeared devoted to a wife whose ancestral roots extended deep into Connecticut's history. At age seven, Elizabeth began an itinerant existence moving from town to town as her father went from one failed job to another. In 1924, the family finances buoyed suddenly when Charles found permanent work as a store manager in Rochester, New York, and his wife got a teaching position. Elizabeth, then age sixteen, enrolled in East High School, where she excelled at academics with a particular flair for languages.

Her academic performance was strong enough to earn admission to Vassar College in Poughkeepsie, New York. A photo of Elizabeth taken at the time shows her sitting sedately under a tree staring into the camera. Her folded hands are resting on her lap, the right hand clutching her eyeglasses. She is neatly dressed in a sweater and skirt, wearing her hair in the fashionable "Bob" style, so popular with young women in the 1920s. Her visage, however, is unsmiling and a bit too intense. Looking at the photo one gets the sense of some sadness behind the serious face. Perhaps she is anxious over her parents' steadily declining health. Or maybe, it's because, unlike her wealthy, trust fund classmates, her presence on the Vassar campus was underwritten largely by financial aid. Whatever the case, Elizabeth Bentley did well, completing degrees in 1930 in English, Italian, and French.

Elizabeth Bentley's language talents led to a teaching job at the Foxcroft School, an exclusive girls' boarding academy nestled in the heart of Virginia horse country. The following summer she spent at the University of Perugia in Italy improving her Italian language skills. Two years later, she started a graduate program at Columbia University, where she won a fellowship to study at the University of Florence in Italy.[2]

By the time she left for Italy, she was alone as both her parents had died. Already approaching her mid-twenties, Elizabeth was sexually liberated with a string of lovers behind her and on the cusp of a drinking habit that would plague her for the rest of her life. In Florence she quickly began taking more pleasure in evenings at cafes with friends and classmates rather than in the classroom or study halls. Talk that year centered politics, particularly Benito Mussolini's fascism with its insistence on greater order and efficiency. As she learned more, Elizabeth found herself drawn to the politics of the right as a new member of a fascist student group, the Gruppo Universitate Fascisti.[3]

Elizabeth Bentley's lackluster academic performance only worsened when Mario Casella entered her life. A high-profile opponent of Mussolini, his newspaper and magazine articles critical of Il Duce had not gone unnoticed by the secret police, which put Casella on its political "watch list." In addition to authoring political screeds, he was also a literary critic and a professor of romance literature at the University of Florence. He soon became Bentley's academic advisor and lover. As the romance blossomed, Bentley's academic performance slipped further as the year went on: so much so that she risked a real possibility of being sent back to Columbia in disgrace for failing to complete the fellowship. In one of the grossest violations of the canons of educational ethics, Casella remedied the problem by ordering an assistant to ghostwrite Bentley's thesis. The young woman with so much promise, having risen so far on her own merits, eagerly embraced the lie by signing the bogus thesis as her own without a second thought or qualm. Perhaps it was the sudden loss of her parents coupled with a descent into alcohol but whatever the reason, it marked the moment when Bentley first "began taking risks . . . breaking the rules and deceiving the authorities," one biographer wrote. "Other people's regulations and laws didn't apply to her." With a year of Casella and Florence behind her, she stepped off a ship in New York City in the summer of 1934 with a chemical dependency, a fraudulent thesis, and a new "talent for deception."[4]

\* \* \*

What Elizabeth found was an America firmly in the grip of an economic calamity that showed no sign of abating. Unable to find steady employment herself, she opted for a return to Columbia University, this time to the business school for courses in shorthand and typing in the hope of landing a secretarial position. Her decision to rent an apartment in the Morningside Heights neighborhood near the campus led to a woman who played the opening role in Bentley's espionage journey.

Lee Morekirk Fuhr, three years older than Bentley and a widow with a four-year-old daughter, was a nurse pursuing a degree in public health at Columbia. The two women, living doors away from each other in the same building, struck up a friendship that soon led to long conversations. Bentley, with her Italian fluency and experiences in Florence with fascism, fascinated Fuhr, herself a vehement anti-fascist. The two women soon began attending meetings of the Columbia campus chapter of the American League against War and Fascism, which was established to expand and unify America's opposition fascism. Elizabeth, with her firsthand accounts of life in Italy, was soon cast as an "expert" on fascism and heroine for opposing it. It was as if she had suddenly found, what she later described, as a "new zest" for life along with a new "circle of friends." Eventually, after confessing to Bentley that the league was a front for the Communist Party and that she herself was a communist, Fuhr asked Bentley to commit herself to the cause. After some initial reluctance, Bentley slowly succumbed to her friend's persuasion.[5]

Elizabeth, Vassar graduate, talented linguist, and now a Communist Party member, still found herself struggling to make ends meet despite an assortment of part-time jobs. In her spare time, she devoted her energies to party activities like collecting dues, distributing propaganda literature, and regularly attending meetings. At some point, however, a decision was made by party leaders to remove her from the overt party with its very public profile. Bentley had all the credentials necessary for secret work. Her party loyalty was fanatical, she was unmarried with no family ties and no police record, spoke English with no accent, and was fluent in Italian.[6]

Her descent into the spy world began when she received instructions to meet a stranger. The date was October 15, 1938. She was to stand at the corner of Eighth Street and University Place in Manhattan, where a "Comrade Brown" would approach her. The less than glamorous Comrade Brown turned out to be a rather ordinary, short, stocky man in his mid-forties with bright red hair and "dazzling blue eyes," as Bentley later recalled. His well-spoken English was tinged with a slight European accent when he introduced himself to her only as "Timmy." Anthony Cave Brown, writing decades later, would place Timmy among "the cleverest, most mysterious, and powerful" Russian spies in America.[7]

Timmy swiftly moved Bentley off the street to a nearby restaurant and after some small talk turned to the purpose of their meeting. He began with compliments for the devotion she had shown to Marxism since joining the Communist Party. Her hard work was appreciated, and she was held in high esteem by fellow comrades. But her talents suggested that she could do more for the cause and that is what he wished to talk about. She had been selected for a new and even more important role, one that was offered to very few people. One that would require not only absolute secrecy, but abandonment of the open party along with old comrades and party associates. Following several such discussions, Bentley finally agreed, at which point Timmy shifted to educating her in the art of espionage tradecraft.

The strict rules of *konspiratsiia* were universal; it would be another three years before Bentley learned that the man she knew only as Timmy was Jacob Raisin. Like millions of other Russian Jews, the Raisin family supported Bolshevism as a counterweight to centuries of government-inspired pogroms and czarist oppression. At age eight, Jacob, already a Bolshevik agitator, could be found distributing propaganda leaflets and illegal Communist literature on Russian city streets, basic tasks that made him easy prey for the secret police. On one occasion he was rounded up and taken to a courtyard where he escaped execution by falling down on the cobblestone pavement and lying there for two days pretending to be dead. Later he was arrested again, this time for operating an illegal printing press, a serious charge that led to a two-year confinement at hard labor. Ever resourceful, he somehow escaped and then trekked east across Russia's vast expanse, making his way to Japan where the party helped him get passage to America. After settling in New York and acquiring his citizenship in 1915, he quickly resumed his radicalism and party organizing, which eventually led to his being ranked among the founders of the CPUSA. It was then that he dropped the name "Raisin," replacing it with "Golos," meaning "voice."[8]

In 1924, he returned to the Soviet Union for a time, joining millions of others now working to rebuild the Russian economy. His ideological pedigree, coupled with his fluency in English, familiarity with America, and US citizenship status, soon led to the start of his service with the Kremlin's intelligence organs. Back in New York his espionage career took off, starting with passport forgery and recruiting merchant seaman to act as couriers for documents crossing the Atlantic between America and Europe. Over time, he became skilled in practically all aspects of espionage, including liaison between the CPUSA and Russian intelligence and enforcer of ideological discipline.[9]

Loneliness and isolation became an accepted part of life for Golos. He had never married, at least not legally, but at the party's insistence he began living with an American woman and fellow communist named Celia through whom he acquired American passports. They stayed together for more than a decade, producing a son, Milton. When they finally separated in 1936, she and the child returned to the Soviet Union and were never seen nor contacted by him again.[10]

As the months passed, Golos and Bentley drew closer until one winter evening they crossed the line. The veil of professionalism dropped when the two made their way to her apartment and made love. What had been a professional association now became deeply personal, a clear violation of the rules of *konspiratsiia*, and one which would remain hidden from Moscow for years to come. Elizabeth called the relationship the "longest and most intense" of her life.[11]

This was a dangerous period for Golos. Growing government concerns about communism and fascism in America soon produced investigations into the political activities of extremist groups like the German American Bund and CPUSA. The House Un-American Activities Committee started asking questions and calling witnesses to Washington to testify. By now Golos was managing World Tourist, a Communist-controlled business on Broadway in Manhattan, established for the purposes of earning revenue for the party. On the surface the company was listed as an agent for Intourist, the Russian government's official travel agency. It prepared and received packages sent between America and Russia with Intourist handling the financial paperwork. Behind the scenes, however, it was busy producing false passports and moving agents between America and Europe.

Having picked up the scent of the real business of World Tourist, the Department of Justice ordered Golos to appear with all of his files at a special grand jury in Washington. Later when the FBI raided his office, they found documents that he failed to destroy showing that Earl Browder and other communists had traveled to Russia on false passports. Golos's costly mistake led to Browder's conviction for passport fraud and imprisonment. In the end he skirted jail, instead paying a fine, serving a period of probation, and being forced to register World Tourist with the Justice Department under the newly passed Foreign Agents Registration Act (FARA).[12]

Jacob Golos may have avoided jail but there was little question in his mind that he and World Tourists remained on the government's radar. Despite the pressure, forged American passports were still highly prized by the party and Moscow and a new company, out of government sight, would be required to produce them. Golos soon got work conjuring up US Services and Shipping Corporation, independent of World Tourist and Intourist, with offices in New York. The new venture was secretly underwritten with $15,000 from the Communist Party and another $5,000 from John Reynolds, the person Golos chose to run it. The choice of Reynolds was an interesting one. As a secret communist, born in 1886, he had rarely worked a day in his life. Nor did he know anything about operating a business, much less one that was required to make money while acting as a passport-forging factory and providing cover for spying. Reynolds was a trust fund baby who for years had a seat on the New York Stock Exchange and an association with the New York Guaranty Trust Company. While Golos often disparaged Reynolds, he still viewed him as a useful figurehead whose money and society connections served to deflect government attention, giving the business a patina of legitimacy. He was a figurehead with no official duties and no idea what was going on. "The type of person who likes to sit behind a desk and look important" Golos later quipped. To actually run the day-to-day business, he turned to Bentley as vice president and later as acting president of US Services and Shipping. She drew a decent salary along with a handsome expense account that amply compensated her for the espionage that would soon be underway.[13]

All went well for a few months until Golos once again reappeared on the government's screen. His headaches this time came from an obscure Russian agent he had never met. Armand Labis Feldman, born in Lithuania, had worked as an illegal in London during the 1930s, where he was connected to a spy ring stealing secrets from the Woolwich Arsenal. When he was unexpectedly called back to Moscow and believing he was targeted for liquidation, he fled to Canada with his family, where he contacted police officials. His information led the FBI to Gaik Ovakimian, a KGB intelligence officer, and Golos's boss under his cover role as an Amtorg official. In January 1941, FBI agents spotted Ovakimian meeting Golos on a street corner and exchanging packages. Over the next few months government investigators built a case against Ovakimian leading to his arrest in May 1941 for violating the FARA statute.[14]

Stunned by the arrest, Golos, once again feeling the heat of the government, was now forced into a fateful decision to expand Bentley's growing involvement in his secret work. Without her knowledge, he had been handling a major spy network in Washington. The members, all working in an assortment of federal agencies, had been supplying him with government secrets for years. To get the product to Moscow, Golos traveled to Washington to collect microfilm copies for delivery to Ovakimian in New York.

From vice president of US Services and Shipping, Bentley now became the courier for her lover's agents in Washington. Starting in the spring of 1941, she began a twice-monthly routine of train trips to the nation's capital that would span the next four years. There she was greeted by one of her agents at Union Station in a comradely fashion. The next day or so were taken up meeting in public with many of Moscow's most important American spies just a mile or two from the White House. Ignoring security Bentley stayed in their homes and received microfilm on street corners and in bars and restaurants in broad daylight, which she then carried in a knitting basket back to Golos in New York. Her businesslike regimen was always the same and continued with little interruption.

* * *

Josef Stalin's senseless purges in the 1930s decimated the ranks of Russian intelligence at a time when he most needed them. Reconstituted by 1943, Pavel Fitin, the thirty-year-old head of foreign intelligence, began sending officers to the United States to regain control of the KGB's North American operations. One of them, a Soviet Tatar and veteran illegal officer was Iskhak Akhmerov. During his first American assignment in 1934 he worked as the assistant for Boris Bazarov, the illegal resident. With Moscow's permission, he married Helen Lowry, a committed communist and sister-in-law of Earl Browder. One of his most important recruits at the time was Lawrence Duggan, Harvard graduate and later head of the State Department's Division of the American Republics as well as Political Adviser and Director of the Office of the American Republics. At the end of the 1930s he and Lowry returned to Russia. Having somehow survived the purges, Moscow again dispatched him to the United States in 1943, this time as an illegal resident, at the height of Russia's wartime espionage success, posing as an employee of a New York City fur and hat shop.[15]

At the time of Akhmerov's return, Bentley was delivering huge amounts of secrets, in fact, far more than Moscow could digest, but at a new and increasingly steep cost. In 1942, for instance, American sources produced fifty-nine microfilm cannisters. The following year that figure jumped to 211; many filled with documents supplied by Bentley's Washington sources.

What shocked Akhmerov immediately was Bentley's routine disregard for the cardinal principle of compartmentation of sources. Akhmerov saw Bentley's behavior as a formula for disaster. Not only did she know the identities of practically every member of the group, but they knew her as well as everyone else in the network. Under such circumstances, discovery or defection of just one agent could destroy KGB access to secret Washington information permanently. It was what Allen Weinstein referred to as an "older tradition of soviet espionage involving committed local Communist agents" colliding "directly with the increasingly professionalized imperatives of the USSR's wartime intelligence service."[16]

Akhmerov laid the blame for this dangerous situation squarely on Golos. Among the so-called deficiencies were questions concerning his involvement in espionage work in the first place. Golos had been too closely associated over the years with the CPUSA; a grave error because he was "known in the US as a prominent functionary of the [Communist Party] who had come from the USSR. This alone was enough to become a target of active investigation" by the FBI. Other warning signs included his close contact with Ovakimian.[17]

Golos, now working for Akhmerov, took offense, insisting that he wanted to keep control of his own agents while keeping Moscow at arm's length. In frustration, Akhmerov offered his analysis to Fitin.

> The fact that [Golos] turned out to be the main linchpin of our [intelligence]. work in the US is the result of an incorrect attitude toward the principles of our work. In turning over to recruiting and all kinds of other work to [Golos], we often blindly deferred to his authority, and were not informed about the substance of the actions he took. This subsequently led to the point where any attempt by us to check on [Golos's] activities to any extent or to study of any of his people in detail triggered vigorous resistance on his part.[18]

The moment of truth finally came on Thanksgiving Day 1943 as Bentley and Golos were sharing a quiet dinner in her New York apartment. Golos suddenly collapsed and died of a heart attack. For Elizabeth the blow became life altering. During their years together the man who she affectionately called "Yasha" (diminutive of Jacob) had shared practically everything—his inner feelings, his years of spying, his trust in her to assist him in getting secrets from Washington to the Russians and for the past year his growing sense that somehow Moscow was betraying him. The death did not end the strain or pent-up anger; instead, it was now Bentley who slowly began to seethe at Akhmerov, a man she had never met but who would soon be her direct supervisor—a man she knew only as "Bill Green." As they began working together, Akhmerov soon started noticing her behavior, causing him increasing concern. Like Golos, she was resistant to taking orders despite her ardent professions of loyalty and willingness to do so. When he asked to accompany her to an agent meeting, she became defensive, turning into "a completely different person," charging that she worked for Earl Browder, the Communist Party boss, and not him. Ignoring his repeated protestations, Bentley continued her risky practice of open meetings with agents, which no amount of hectoring, cajoling, or pleading could correct. Finally, in complete exasperation, Akhmerov sent an ominous warning to Moscow of things to come. Her failure to "follow the rules of konspiratsia" was unacceptable, making it imperative to "completely change the basis of the group's work." Everyone knew everyone else, he complained, placing the entire apparatus in danger. "If anyone begins so much as a cursory investigation, the whole group with their direct contacts will immediately be exposed." She was "precisely the type of person" he concluded, "who should not be involved with this group, let alone controlling it."[19]

Over the next year, Bentley's personal life also went into a free fall. Her growing sense of isolation and continued mourning over Golos's death led to feelings of loneliness and, at age thirty-six, a sense that she was rapidly aging. Life was consumed by espionage, leaving her no time for a personal life or a man in whom she could confide. Elizabeth Bentley was also changing, less concerned with spying, and more interested in the domestic life of family and children. Ovakimian, now back in Moscow, believing he had a possible remedy, posed to his bosses the "question of [Bentley] getting married." The KGB thought the idea reasonable but unfortunately, they had no "suitable candidate." So worried were they that they paid for a week at a health resort for her.[20]

As she grew ever more erratic, Moscow continued to demur, believing that all she needed was "a shoulder to cry on." She persisted in rejecting Soviet control of her agents while railing at her ever-diminishing espionage role. The growing disillusionment with communism that she felt was tied to her deepening mental depression and ever larger volumes of alcohol, which led to more frequent and violent outbursts filled with denunciations of the Soviet Union—a dangerous move. "Judging by her behavior she hasn't betrayed us yet," Akhmerov wrote, "but we can't rely on her. Unfortunately, she knows too much about us. Since she could damage us here very seriously only one remedy is left—the most drastic one—to get rid of her." The final nail in the KGB coffin came when they completely abandoned her. Browder and Akhmerov agreed that her role in espionage would end and her agents would be assigned to someone else. US Services and Shipping, the source of her income, and World Tourist would be divided between Moscow and Browder. Bentley would be removed from any involvement in both of them.[21]

So it was that on that fateful November evening in 1945, with Ed Buckley sitting at her side, she began telling a story. She opened with her biography, her attraction to communism in the 1930s, and her later descent into espionage. She poured out, in rich detail, the stories of the real work of World Tourist, US Services and Shipping, the fortnightly trips to Washington, ferrying government secrets destined for the KGB and, of course, her beloved Yasha. When she had exhausted those issues, she next started carefully running down her list of agents. As Buckley and his team sat frantically scribbling notes, she brought up the name Nathan Gregory Silvermaster and his wife, Helen—both committed communists. "Greg," as everyone called him, a mid-level economist with the Department of the Treasury, managed a large ring of spies that included four other economists also strategically situated in the Treasury Department. There was also William Remington, Harvard graduate and Communist Party member, working for the War Production Board. He supplied reports on aircraft production and other topics. Another, George Silverman, a former Treasury Department statistician, after moving to the Pentagon in 1942, had arranged for the transfer of another ring member, William Lud Ulmann. Together they removed bushels of military secrets, many dealing with aircraft and tank production along with troop deployment data and technological improvements on military hardware. There were Russian moles buried inside OSS, America's wartime espionage service. Chief among them was Duncan Chaplin Lee, son of missionaries to China, Rhodes scholar, Yale law school graduate, and an attorney with William Donovan's Manhattan law firm. As Donovan's executive assistant at OSS, he supplied troves of high-level intelligence that crossed the general's desk. Two others were the chief Latin American specialist, Maurice Halperin, and Helen Tenney, a New Yorker who moved to Washington on orders from Golos to work for OSS. On Capitol Hill there was Charles Kramer, an economist, who had changed his name from "Charles Krevitsky." Having come to Washington in the early 1930s as part of President Roosevelt's original Brain Trust, he remained in government working for many prominent members of Congress. Two other names that caught investigators' attention were Laughlin Currie and Harry Dexter White. Currie, a Canadian and naturalized citizen with a Harvard doctorate in economics, had been serving as a presidential counselor in the White House since 1939. White too, was an economist. A native of Massachusetts with a doctorate from Stanford, White joined the Treasury Department in 1934, climbing up the chain to an important liaison position with the State Department in 1941. By 1945 he was an assistant secretary. Another was Cedric Belfrage, a British journalist living in New York. Belfrage led a life of privilege having been born in 1905 in London to a wealthy physician and his wife. He attended Cambridge University and later moved to Hollywood, where he earned a living selling interviews with film stars to British magazines. Upon returning to England he became a film critic. When America entered the war, William Stephenson, MI6's man in New York, recruited him for a job with British Security Coordination. Before Bentley finished, her roster of spies exceeded more than forty names.[22]

The KGB would have remained unaware of Bentley's defection to the FBI had she not identified Belfrage. This information forced FBI director, J. Edgar Hoover, to alert William Stephenson to the accusations made against his man. Within days a wire sent to London reporting the Belfrage information was on Kim Philby's desk and soon on its way to Moscow. Yet, even though Philby had once again warned of a defection, unlike the Gouzenko debacle, Fitin had no clear picture of the unfolding disaster confronting him nor what the FBI was learning. In a panic, on November 22, two weeks after Bentley started talking, he issued a damage-control alert to his American stations. "[Bentley] has betrayed us. A directive has been issued to take the appropriate precautionary measures and not to meet with her anymore." Twenty-four hours later, he issued further orders to "break off" contact with all their sources. To prevent alarm, selected sources were to be told of Bentley's defection with others given a cover story. Instructions included steps to take if the FBI confronted them: aggressively challenge any accusations with assertions that her statements were lies and a provocation by the authorities; all documents and incriminating notes in the hands of agents must be immediately destroyed; any necessary meetings with agents in public must be minimized and agent-initiated contact prohibited. Finally, contacts with active agents would be suspended but not before arranging necessary passwords along with a time and place of a future recontact.[23]

Now that Fitin had given orders for protecting what remained of his tattered American operations, the next question was what to do about Bentley. Before acting he reached out to Anatoliy Gorsky, code name "Vadim," for his views. "We don't know yet which of our agents [Bentley] named. Let us know your opinion as to what measures must be taken with regard to [Bentley]." At age thirty-eight, Gorsky was an experienced intelligence officer with nearly twenty years of KGB service. Squat in appearance, blond hair swept back on his head and wearing thick eyeglasses, he was first posted to London in 1936 as an attaché in the Russian embassy. Over a four-year span, he ran eighteen agents, including Kim Philby and his Cambridge ring members. In early 1940 after a routine recall to Moscow as a new section chief, he was again back in London at the end of that year. Following another short stay in Moscow in January 1944, he was abruptly dispatched to Washington when an anonymous tell-all letter sent by a disgruntled KGB officer in New York to J. Edgar Hoover forced the abrupt departure of Gorsky's predecessor, Vasily Zarubin. Little is known about Gorsky except that he was thuggish, crude, and almost predatory. Bentley hated him. In his presence, she later remembered, "shivers run up and down [my] spine." Christopher Andrew described him as a "grimly efficient, humorless, orthodox Stalinist."[24]

The "only measure" that could be taken, in Gorsky's view, was to murder her. Shooting her would be "too noisy," a car accident or pushing her under a train, "unreliable." "Myrna [Bentley's KGB's code name] is a very strong, tall and healthy woman," which could make a staged suicide risky. The KGB knew a great deal about her, including her New York address, the names of people she knew, as well as, her habits, daily routine, and how to get to her without being discovered. After careful thought, however, Gorsky concluded that the best way of killing her would be poison. A potion that would take ten to twenty hours to take effect without leaving "any trace." An odorless solution could be soaked into her pillow or handkerchief or possibly into food delivered to her room. Or it could be administered at a restaurant by a friend over dinner. He could slip it into a glass of wine or offer her a lady's compact dabbed with poison in necessary spots. "Make it a gift" he thought, "a normal thing to do." Bentley can "open the compact and scratch her hand."[25]

Perhaps the political repercussions of failure given Stalin's growing tension with the Truman administration made such an operation too risky. Besides, Gorsky, the idea man behind the murder scheme, had no poison in stock at the embassy and it would take too long for a shipment to arrive from Moscow. Finally, after much back and forth, the plan was scrapped on orders from Lavrenti Beria, head of the KGB and Politburo member.

By December 1945, the Washington station, now in shambles, was frantically reviewing all documents with orders "to destroy anything that is unnecessary." Gorsky was soon on his way back to Moscow Center for "consultations." He would not return. In accordance with instructions, paid agents were to receive a four-month advance payment. All future agent meetings were cancelled until further notice.[26]

As 1945 blended into 1946 a now stunned Bill Weisband, Moscow's man seated at the heart of America's new Cold War code-breaking empire, was suddenly out of position again, on his own—now living a waiting game.

## NOTES

1. Kathryn S. Olmsted, *Red Spy Queen* (Chapel Hill: University of North Carolina Press, 2002).
2. Ibid., 5.
3. Ibid., 6.
4. Ibid., 7.
5. Ibid., 9.
6. Ibid.
7. Ibid., 18–19, 23.
8. Elizabeth Bentley, Hoover letter to New York, December 13, 1944, FBI File #61–6328, Ernie Lazar Collection.
9. Olmsted, *Red Spy Queen*, 21.
10. Elizabeth Bentley, Hoover letter to New York, December 13, 1944, FBI File #61–6328, Ernie Lazar Collection.
11. Olmsted, *Red Spy Queen*, 26.
12. Haynes, Klehr, and Vassiliev, *Spies*, 189.
13. Olmsted, *Red Spy Queen*, 76.
14. Ibid., 40.

15. Andrew and Mitrokhin, *Mitrokhin Archive*, 104.
16. Allen Weinstein and Alexander Vassiliev, *The Haunted Wood: Soviet Espionage in America—The Stalin Era* (New York: Random House, 1999), 166.
17. VWN1, 154.
18. Ibid.
19. VWN2, 18.
20. VWN2, 15.
21. Olmsted, *Red Spy Queen*, 94.
22. "Cedric Belfrage, 85, Target of Communist Inquiry," *New York Times*, June 22, 1990.
23. VWN2, 30.
24. Elizabeth Bentley, *Out of Bondage* (New York: The Devin-Adair Company, 1951), 333.
25. VWN2, 30.
26. VWN2, 30.

Admiral Earl Stone, USN. Stone was the director of the Armed Forces Security Agency. When asked to calculate the losses due to Weisband spying, he said, "I don't even want to think about it." *Courtesy of National Cryptologic Museum.*

Courtland Jones. Special Agent Jones led the FBI's investigation of Weisband. *Courtesy of Courtland Jones Jr.*

"B Building," center of the Russian Program on the grounds of Arlington Hall, where William Weisband worked as a linguist and research analyst from 1945 to 1950. *Courtesy of National Cryptologic Museum.*

Jones Orin York. An industrial spy recruited by the Russians in 1934. Sixteen years later, he identified Weisband as a courier he met with regularly in 1941 and 1942. *Courtesy of Jones Orin York FBI File.*

Jacob Gurin. Gurin joined Arlington Hall in 1946 and immediately launched a successful program to retrieve and analyze Russian plaintext messages, revealing rich details of Moscow's military/industrial complex. His small team of linguists included Weisband. Gurin was inducted into NSA's Cryptologic Hall of Honor in 2007. *Courtesy of National Cryptologic Museum.*

Meredith Gardner. A brilliant Russian linguist and cryptologist who broke the Russian one-time pad cipher system, revealing KGB espionage in the United States throughout World War II. Sitting nearby was Weisband, who would often stroll by, peering over Gardner's shoulder and offering help on complex language problems. *Courtesy of National Cryptologic Museum.*

Colonel Harold G. Hayes, USA. Director of the Army Security Agency and Weisband's close friend. *Courtesy of National Cryptologic Museum.*

William Weisband. Photo affixed to Weisband's US citizenship papers in 1938. *Courtesy of Federal Records Center, New York City, New York, NARA.*

S. Wesley Reynolds. Special Agent who served as the wartime liaison with army intelligence and later with the Army Security Agency. It was Reynolds who informed Admiral Stone that Weisband was a Russian spy. Reynolds would become the first head of security in 1952 for the new National Security Agency. *Courtesy of Society of Former Special Agents of the Federal Bureau of Investigation.*

Graduation photo of Signal Corp Officer Candidate School, Fort Monmouth, New Jersey, April 24, 1943. Weisband is in second row, sixth from the left. *Courtesy of Association of Signal Corp Officer Candidate School, Fort Monmouth, New Jersey.*

William Weisband. Army Security Agency identification photo taken when he joined Arlington Hall. It was this image of Weisband that Jones Orin York identified as his KGB handler in 1941 and 1942. *Courtesy of National Cryptologic Museum.*

Alexander Feklisov. Russian stamp depicting Feklisov's image as a Hero of the Russian Federation issued in 2002. It was Feklisov who secretly reestablished KGB contact with Weisband in February 1945 after his return from Italy. Posing as Alexander Fomin, he would later head the KGB station in Washington, DC. In 1962 he secretly met with journalist John Scali to signal Moscow's interest in a peaceful settlement of the Cuban Missile Crisis. *Courtesy of National Cryptologic Museum.*

Mabel Weisband. *Courtesy of Hot Springs, North Carolina, High School 1942 Yearbook.*

Stanislav Shumovsky. Russian foreign and MIT-educated aeronautical engineer who recruited Jones Orin York as an industrial spy. Shumovsky's photo hangs today on the wall of Russian Intelligence Service Hall of Honor. *Courtesy of Massachusetts Institute of Technology 1932 Yearbook.*

Brigadier General Carter Clarke. First briefed by S. Wesley Reynolds regarding Weisband's espionage. *Courtesy of National Cryptologic Museum.*

Hayes Group Photo. Front row (*seated from left to right*) are Solomon Kullback, William Friedman, Colonel Harold Hayes, Abraham Sinkov, and Frank Rowlett. *Courtesy of National Cryptologic Museum.*

William Weisband. War Department photo taken in April 1943 at Fort Monmouth, New Jersey, following his commission as a second lieutenant in the US Army Signal Corp. *Courtesy of War Department, Internet.*

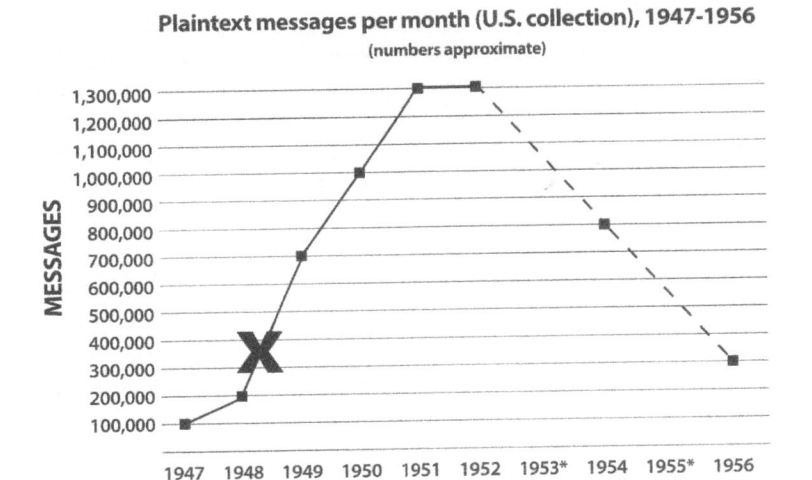

**Plaintext messages per month (U.S. collection), 1947-1956**
(numbers approximate)

*No number available

Weisband warned the KGB in 1948 (Marked by "X") about valuable intelligence collected by America from Russian plaintext messages. Within two years these messages leveled off followed by a steady decline as Moscow accelerated efforts to encrypt its radio transmissions.

## Chapter 21

# Top Secret—Cream

On August 15, 1945, thousands of cities, towns, and villages across America went wild and would stay that way for days to come. The sudden delirium came on the heels of stunning news crackling across the radio that the emperor of Japan had agreed to surrender. Nearly four years of bloody warfare had ended. What began at Pearl Harbor was now over. Millions of Americans across the country stopped what they were doing and surged into the streets laughing, crying, screaming, some simply jumping up and down, others joyously waving arms and hands while complete strangers aimlessly danced, walked arm in arm in no particular direction, others kissing anyone in sight. Americans remained wobbly for days as gleeful bartenders ignored bar tabs and gave away free booze to everyone. Typical of the scenes playing out across the country was one Greek immigrant and owner of a modest Long Island hot dog stand who threw open his sidewalk window counter and gave out free hot dogs and sodas to everyone until his stock was completely exhausted. The nation's capital was no different. Traffic came to a standstill as people abandoned buses and cars in the middle of the street to join the celebration. Washington was gridlocked. But nobody cared. Peace had arrived at last.[1]

Excitement along the corridors at Arlington Hall had been slowly building for days. Despite the rigid "need-to-know" rules, whispered rumors that something was up had been spreading like wildfire—the end was fast approaching. Hints started coming from as far away as Two Rocks Ranch, a tiny navy listening post nestled on farmland some miles north of San Francisco. An intercept operator monitoring circuits coming from the Japanese city of Hiroshima turned on her machine on August 7, 1945, as she had done daily for the last few years. When she put on her earphones, she heard only dead air. *Magic* was also pouring out its secrets. For days cryptanalysts raced to decipher every new message reporting Japan's desperate effort to find some sort of settlement with America. When the day finally came, thousands of Arlington Hall code breakers abandoned their posts and made their way across the Potomac River into downtown Washington to join in the celebration.

Overnight more than thirteen thousand code breakers, 70 percent of them women, went from three shifts a day running seven days a week to a complete stop. When the merriment finally died down, they returned to work only to discover they had nothing to do. Most, still woozy from the festivities, puttered around, many chatting aimlessly with co-workers, others busying themselves with crossword puzzles or writing long-overdue letters to friends and loved ones.

It did not take long for orders to come down from top brass directing everyone to assemble on the lawn of Arlington Hall for a special announcement. Three days after the surrender, Brigadier General Preston Corderman, head of the ASA, stepped up before the crowd. His original plan was to bring closure to the war with a sensitive speech recounting the remarkable contributions made by the staff to the final victory. What began as comments larded with platitudes quickly descended into a verbal pink slip. Corderman thanked everyone for their years of sacrifice and announced that it was now their patriotic duty "to get off the government payroll." Anne Caracristi, one of thousands of women standing there that day, called the general's remarks a "Here's your hat. What's your hurry" speech.[2]

Numbered among the departures were many of the intellectual and managerial firebrands behind Arlington Hall's success. One of the first to turn in his uniform was Lieutenant Richard Hallock. A key figure in the early successes against Russian diplomatic codes, he resumed a teaching career at the University of Chicago. As did Frederic Coudert, who headed back to his lucrative law practice in New York. Thousands of young women who had heeded their country's call began disappearing in droves, as well, with overdue plans of marriage to sweethearts, starting a family and just settling down. Among them was Genevieve Grotjan, one of the geniuses behind the *Magic* solution. She left to marry Hyman Feinstein, a chemist. As did Delia Taylor, a code breaker who led a number of important units. She married Abraham Sinkov. Still others were intent on picking up an interrupted education or looking forward to getting a long-overdue advanced degree. For those women lucky enough to have served in uniform, there were education funds available through the GI Bill. One Navy WAVE (Women Accepted for Volunteer Service) used the money to earn her doctorate at John Hopkins University, leading to a distinguished university professorship in classics.

A select few, however, decided to stay. Among them were veterans William Friedman, Frank Rowlett, Abe Sinkov, and Solly Kullback along with Leo Rosen, the geniuses behind *Magic*. There were many others, as well, such as Oliver Kirby, who spent his war in uniform in England working alongside

British code breakers. These were the men who would form the nucleus of the National Security Agency seven years later.

The gigantic wartime cryptologic enterprise assembled over three and a half years, now suddenly gone, would gradually be resurrected on a permanent footing. With it would come a new corporate philosophy as well. Back in March 1945, as the end of the European war was rapidly approaching, Frank Rowlett gave voice to the future when he was tasked by War Department leaders with examining what a peacetime American cryptologic service should look like. Calling on his fifteen years of experience, he prepared what turned out to be a visionary paper filled with ideas and suggestions that remain an integral part of how the NSA does business today. He began by discarding the divided Arlington Hall–Navy Annex wartime model as unacceptable for modern code-breaking. It was a necessity rapidly cobbled together in the face of an emergency that had no place in the future. Successfully completing simple aptitude tests and interest in games and puzzles would be insufficient for selecting a workforce facing the complexities and challenges of machine-encrypted communications. To achieve the level of technical competence that he envisioned, the government would have to find the best minds available and then carefully recruit them through a constant and never-ending process. Once on board, every effort would be needed to retain them for the long haul with the goal of producing a highly skilled workforce capable of anticipating and adjusting to the ever-changing realities of breaking encrypted communications. Rowlett called for casting a wide net for critical language skills, engineering, science, cryptanalysis, and other related subjects. Probably reflecting on his own career under Friedman, Rowlett believed that only time, institutional commitment, and careful cultivation of a candidate's career would produce an outstanding code breaker. A heavy investment in training was next on Rowlett's agenda. Unlike the simple ad hoc schooling during the war, the demands of future code-breaking would require employees to pursue a sophisticated and rigorous series of college-level courses coupled with intensive on-the-job instruction taught by subject matter experts with years of experience—much like he received from William Friedman during the 1930s.[3]

Some months after Rowlett produced his report, another equally far-reaching study began making the rounds of the cryptologic community. This time it was the navy that weighed in, with Captain Joseph Wenger the author. Like Rowlett, Wenger had emerged from the war as one of the giants in American cryptology. After completing the naval academy in 1923 and joining the Bureau of Naval Communications as a cryptanalyst, Wenger quickly earned respect for his mastery of the new science of traffic analysis. His innovative techniques soon became a critical facet of naval warfare doctrine. When the war broke out it fell to Wenger to convert the navy's largely fragmented code-breaking structure into a more efficient centralized organization, which he completed by February 1942. As an engineer he also pressed hard for replacing traditional paper-and-pencil decryption methods with machine-based systems starting with IBM tabulators and later "bombes"—high-speed forerunner of the modern computer. By war's end he was the head of the navy code-breaking center in Washington. The National Security Agency later honored him as "one of the most influential figures in American cryptologic history."[4]

For Wenger, the atomic bomb had irrevocably changed the nature of war. No longer could communications intelligence be used mainly as a tool for monitoring the behavior of real and potential enemies. It was insufficient to simply watch political and military developments unfold in order to prepare a response. America, Wenger argued, now faced a terrifying new prospect—nuclear annihilation from an attack that could occur without warning. National leaders, he concluded, had to secure the nation's safety through "effective intelligence," which meant "in large measure communications intelligence."[5]

The lessons offered by Rowlett and Wenger were not lost on James Byrnes, President Truman's new secretary of state. The sixty-seven-year-old South Carolinian had amassed decades of public service in all three branches of the federal government. For nearly twenty-five years, he had served in Congress, followed by a year as a Supreme Court justice before President Roosevelt appointed him head of the wartime Office of Economic Stabilization and then Office of War Mobilization. Byrnes was no stranger to the value of good intelligence. His wartime assignments had routinely kept him on a short list of government officials receiving intelligence summaries, including large supplies of Arlington Hall and Navy Annex products. Upon taking on his new cabinet post, he quickly began demanding daily *Magic* Summaries as a critical source of information on Tokyo's thinking and intentions in the run-up to the dropping of the atomic bombs.

As with many government leaders, Byrnes too was concerned about the future of such a valuable asset after the war. So worried was he, in fact, that he penned a note to his fellow cabinet officer, Henry Stimson, the secretary of war, expressing his fears. Harboring no illusions about what America faced in peacetime, Byrnes sought assurances that the military's communications intelligence apparatus built up over the war would not disappear but rather would continue to supply the State Department with high-grade secrets gathered from electronic eavesdropping. What he insisted upon was the "product of [Arlington Hall] cryptanalytic work in the diplomatic field." Not yet satisfied, Byrnes continued his plea with another note of worry stressing that the need for such vital information will be equally great "as we face postwar problems."[6]

Clearly the biggest booster for a peacetime communications surveillance capability was President Truman himself. Even after the passage of seventy-five years, the mystery of when Truman first learned about Allied wartime code-breaking successes remains. It most likely occurred on April 19, 1945, a Monday, exactly one week after President Roosevelt's death. Around eleven-thirty that morning, General George Marshall was ushered into the Oval Office for his first private meeting with the new president. The two men knew each other slightly. They had met during Truman's Senate days and formally the day after FDR's death, when other senior military officials visited the White House to brief Truman on the imminent collapse of the Third Reich. As with most of official Washington, Truman revered Marshall.

Now alone with the president, Marshall, in his crisp, no-nonsense manner, disclosed the crown jewels of Allied intelligence successes. First to be revealed was the full range of Ultra, Britain's spectacular break into Germany's *Enigma* cipher system. Next came the work of army and navy code breakers in gaining a monopoly over Japan's most important military ciphers. What followed was a review of *Magic* and the revelations it was producing as American forces moved ever closer to the Japanese home islands. What was also unique about *Magic*'s secrets were the insights it was producing about Kremlin thinking—an issue of particular importance for Truman, who was scheduled to meet the next week with Russia's foreign minister, Vyacheslav Molotov.[7] Marshall introduced the president to Sato Naotake, Japan's ambassador to the Soviet Union, whose activities Arlington Hall Station had been cataloguing for the past five years.

Not long after his meeting with Marshall, Harry Truman got his first chance to see COMINT in action. It involved the international conference hosted by the American government that would produce the United Nations. Even before the war started it had been FDR's dream for a new United Nations; one that would replace the failed League of Nations. His hope was that it would serve as a valuable tool for peacefully settling conflicts and, if necessary, interceding in local wars with an international military force before they became global in size. Thirteen days after assuming office, Truman was in San Francisco hosting the opening ceremonies of the United Nations Conference on International Organization more commonly known as the San Francisco Conference. He was there to kick off two months of intense negotiations and diplomatic jockeying preparatory to signing a final charter. Like President Warren Harding nearly a quarter of a century earlier, who relied on code-breaking to control the outcome of the Washington Naval Conference, Truman got what he wanted thanks in large part to Arlington Hall keeping his negotiators informed about the strategies of nearly all fifty-one participating delegations. Armed with this information, the United States easily outmaneuvered other member nations; in particular French government efforts to thwart the US position concerning the delicate question of veto authority by the major powers in the Security Council.

\* \* \*

As the summer dragged on Arlington Hall continued to draw back the curtain on Japanese thinking for Truman as he wrestled with the idea of dropping the atomic bomb. As he approached the decision, he continued to follow developments mainly through top-secret COMINT reports prepared for him by Colonel Carter Clarke in the form of a compendium entitled "MAGIC—Diplomatic Summary." The tight restrictions on its distribution can be seen as follows in the cover-page warning that accompanied each summary:

> No one without express permission from the proper authorities, may disseminate the information in this summary or communicate it to any other person. Those authorized to disseminate such information must employ only the most secure means, must take every precaution to avoid compromising the source, and must limit dissemination to the minimum number of secure and responsible persons who need the information in order to discharge their duties. No action is to be taken on information herein reported, regardless of temporary advantage, if such action might have the effect of revealing the existence of the source to the enemy. The enemy knows that we attempt to exploit these sources. He does not know, and must not be permitted to learn, either the degree of our success or the particular sources with which we have been successful.[8]

A week after Japan's surrender, the Joint Chiefs of Staff met to prepare a top-secret memorandum for the president's consideration. They unanimously recommended the peacetime retention of a communications intelligence system. They based their thinking on the value of wartime communications intelligence to victory and the growing consensus, as outlined by Captain Wenger, that new political realities across the globe demanded the continuation of a large-scale COMINT apparatus.

In a terse response issued on August 28, 1945, approving the chiefs' request, President Truman issued one additional order that would have far-reaching consequences for the United States in the decades to come. The president's men had warned him of the grave dangers to the country if such a fragile technique was lost. First, there were the operational costs, which could drastically reduce America's ability to control the behavior of adversaries and help shape events. There were also political consequences not only from targeted countries, but domestic backlash should word ever leak out. Truman understood the realities facing him. What he was authorizing was top secret with neither Congress nor the American public informed nor asked for comment. As a result, there would be no public announcement of his instructions except, as he wrote, "with the special approval of the President in each case." To further conceal the existence of COMINT, he ordered stringent government classification on any "information regarding the past and present status of techniques or procedures, degree of success attained, or any specific results of any cryptanalytic unit acting under the authority of the U.S. Government or any Department thereof."[9]

In March 1946, the critical importance of communications intelligence was demonstrated in a different way. The Army Security Agency became an independent agency that now took directions from army intelligence requirements. That same month Colonel Harold Gray Hayes, West Point graduate, seasoned Signal Corp officer, and Bill Weisband's old friend, took over as head of the new organization.

Cooperation among America's military services had always been fraught with difficulty. Since the founding of the Republic both the army and navy had treated the other with a stovepipe mentality that saw collaboration as alien and something that neither side felt any reason to pursue. The service cryptologic units were no different. World War II had forced a grudging shift in this attitude. The pressing need for closer inter-service cooperation came about with the advent of a new style of warfare involving amphibious invasions of Japanese-held atolls in the Pacific and major landings in North Africa and Europe. In early 1944, Arlington Hall broke the all-important Japanese Army Water Code, which provided times, dates of departure and arrival, along with destinations of troop and equipment convoys moving throughout the western Pacific. Such intelligence was crucial for the navy, but the army, in its bureaucratic tug of war, held it back until an agreement to cooperate could be achieved. Navy leaders quickly came around and the situation improved when a wartime memorandum initialed by General Marshall and Admiral King ordered a total exchange of COMINT materials.

This modest first step led to the formation in April 1944 of what became known as the Army–Navy Communications Intelligence Coordinating Committee (ANCICC). What emerged next was the Army–Navy Intelligence Communications Board (ANCIB) with the ANCICC reduced to a working committee answerable to ANCIB. Later the name was changed again to STANCIB with the addition of the Department of State. It became official in March 1945. It was "purely voluntary" in nature, but it was a start.[10]

The Corderman-Wenger Agreement of February 15, 1946, marked another change by creating, for the first time, a new position of coordinator of joint operations (CJO). The idea behind the CJO was a step toward centralization of COMINT through development of policies and procedures that would improve communications collection and processing among the different cryptologic organizations. The CJO became the designated authority to implement and allocate joint collection with approval of STANCIB. With it came three new groups under the CJO's command: Joint Intercept Control Group (JICG), Joint Processing Allocation Group (JPAG), and Joint Liaison Group (JIG). To ensure equity each service would appoint a CJO for a one-year term on a rotating basis.

* * *

As the war drew to a finish, debate began to grow in American ranks over continued collaboration with the British. Memoranda soon began passing between the navy and army with the notations "N.B."—"No British." The unprecedented wartime collaboration between America and Great Britain that had done so much to winning the war now came under a reappraisal as some US military leaders began questioning its necessity in peacetime. Some felt no need for such collaboration. They were convinced that America's ability to intercept and analyze signals using new and amazing computer-generated decoding techniques had outrun the need for partners. We could go it alone was the thinking in certain quarters. Some took a more moralistic view. "I do not think we should 'gang up' with one ally against another" wrote Admiral Richard E. Evans, the vice-chief of naval operations. He went on to note:

> In the troubled time that lie ahead we shall have to side with one or another of our friends as differences of interest arise, but for the sake of the peace of the world we should do so openly and frankly. If we secretly join the British in this project, the secret is virtually certain to leak out in the course of time with results disastrous for our relations with USSR. The possible gain is not worth the probable loss.[11]

Others saw it differently. The British had a great deal to offer. They still retained many of the finest code breakers in the world and important listening posts in strategic locations inaccessible to the Americans. Following a series of joint meetings held in the greatest secrecy in London and Washington, cryptologic leaders on both sides of the Atlantic agreed to continue working together against new targets in the emerging post-war world. These discussions produced a series of recommendations from the Joint Chiefs of Staff to the president urging his approval of continued cooperation due to the "disturbed conditions of the world and the necessity of keeping informed of the technical developments and possible hostile intentions of foreign nations." Again, wasting no time, Truman penned a crisp reply to his military commanders.

The Secretary of War and the Secretary of the Navy are hereby authorized to direct the Chief of Staff, US Army, Commander-in-Chief, US Fleet, and Chief of Naval Operations to continue collaboration in the field of communications intelligence between the United States Army and Navy and the British, and to extend, modify, discontinue this collaboration as determined to be in the best interests of the United States.[12]

Following five months of discussions, the British and Americans hammered out the "British–US Communications Intelligence Agreement." It was signed on March 16, 1946, for the British by Colonel Patrick Marr-Johnson and Lieutenant General Hoyt Vandenberg, senior member of STANCIB. The top-secret accord was unlike any document ever agreed to both for its historical significance and the scope in sharing communications intelligence of every kind. It would cover the whole swath of the "signal intelligence process from collection of traffic, documents and equipment to cryptanalysis and translations." Nothing would be off the table. Any questions arising about restrictions would be kept, in the words of the agreement, to an "absolute minimum."[13]

By the spring of 1946, as Weisband watched and took it all in, so secret had code-breaking become that any reference to the term or its resulting product was erased from official records or correspondence. Replacing it was a new closely guarded term called "special intelligence." To most it would be known only as "CREAM"—top-secret code word for "All information which results from decryption of the texts or substance of encrypted communications." The goal was to restrict top-secret CREAM material as narrowly as possible based on an absolute need to know; sealed off from the American public, the Congress, and the prying eyes of foreign adversaries. The distribution of "eyes only" Arlington Hall and navy communications intelligence starting with the president would be confined to only a tiny handful of senior military and civilian government officials.[14]

## NOTES

1. Barbara Henry, author interview, August 12, 2010.
2. Mundy, *Code Girls*, 330–31.
3. Frank Rowlett, "Staff Study on Personnel Needs," March 17, 1945, NCM, NSA.
4. Cryptologic Almanac 50th Anniversary Series, Joseph N. Wenger; "Rear Admiral Joseph N. Wenger, USN 2005 Hall of Honor Inductee," NSA/CSS.
5. Budiansky, *Code Warriors*, 38–39.
6. Ibid.
7. General George C. Marshall Papers, Pentagon Office Collection, George C. Marshall Library, Lexington, Virginia.

8. Boyd, *Hitler's Japanese Confidant*, 148. Still after seventy-five years, most *Magic* intercepts between Moscow and Tokyo remain classified.

9. MAGIC—Diplomatic Summary, No. 974, 11/24/1944, Internet Archives.

10. Budiansky, *Code Warriors*, 38.

11. Budiansky, *Code Warriors*, 41–42.

12. Budiansky, *Code Warriors*, 32.

13. Johnson, "The Sting—Enabling Codebreaking in the Twentieth Century," *Cryptologic Quarterly*, Undated, DOCID 3860890 NCM, NSA. Venona Monograph, 16.

14. Budiansky, *Code Warriors*, 65.

*Chapter 22*

# Charter Member

"I telephoned your office yesterday about a condition which has been going on for several months in Apartment B-2, 3046 South Abingdon Street."[1]

B-2 was occupied by Bill Weisband. It was situated in a sprawling housing development known as the "Fairlington Projects." First conceived by President Roosevelt as a garden apartment complex, it was built to house defense workers and their families during World War II on land purchased in Arlington County, Virginia, by the Defense Homes Corporation, part of the Federal Housing Administration. Construction started in 1942 and by May 1943 the first families began moving in. When finally completed at the end of 1943, more than 2,400 apartments were available for occupancy at a total construction cost of thirty-five million dollars.

Around June 1945, Weisband moved in flush with cash. His promotion to first lieutenant finally came through a month earlier with a salary bump to $2,040 ($29,646 in February 2021) plus the regular cash infusions from Tikhon. Now living just a few miles from Arlington Hall Station and the Pentagon with the Russians just across the Potomac River, Bill was a happy man.

The December 26, 1945, letter from an angry neighbor to Fairlington's management was filled with furious complaints. Weisband held huge gatherings at his place "several times per week." There were "wild parties" often lasting to the wee hours of the morning with "women guests" frequently staying over "all night." Frequent calls were made to Bill complaining about noise so loud "the whole building seemed to shake." When the police arrived, Bill profoundly apologized with assurances that his soiree was breaking up, but on it went until ending in choruses of "loud goodbyes."[2]

When Weisband learned of the complaints he countered with threats of a lawsuit for "infringing" on his rights. What began as a simple neighborly dispute soon landed Bill in an Arlington County courtroom. For six months he had been rooming with the apartment's leaseholder until he moved out, selling the furniture to Bill and quietly subletting the place to him in violation of the rental agreement. Management sued him for eviction until Weisband finally gave up and vacated in July 1946.³

As the Special Division's "language advisor," Weisband's native Russian fluency was in high demand. The end of the war brought with it a mass exodus of GIs anxious to shed their uniforms and resume a normal way of life. The word of the day was demobilization, or "demob," with troops mustering out at an alarming rate of ten thousand a month. Even though the Bourbon Program was steadily growing, it too was losing crucial skill sets provided by wartime cryptanalysts and linguists. Arlington Hall, which had grown to a wartime high of more than seven thousand employees, would shrink to a level of just more than two thousand by the summer of 1946. One NSA history called peace "devastating" in an era of "damaging retrenchment." The shortage meant that talented prospects like Weisband would be essential if ASA was going to meet the new demands of the post-war world. Credentials as a combat veteran, a Signal Corp officer trained at Fort Monmouth and Vint Hill Farms, fluency in five languages, particularly Russian, put him high on the retention list. "ASA needed all the help it could get in 1945," a later history recorded, "and getting a linguist like Weisband was a good day's work."⁴

Cryptanalysts and other specialists, struggling to tease Russian words and meanings from masses of scrambled numbers, found him critical to the process. As did twenty officers, making up almost half of the staff. Having recently graduated from a top-secret Russian-language training course set up by the navy in Boulder, Colorado, they still required careful guidance in their ongoing struggle to grasp the complexities of translation. The Russian people took great pride in their "very rich language" with all sorts of words having a multitude of meanings. It used an entirely different alphabet from the Romance language called Cyrillic. It required students to learn both the letter and the sound of the letter. To find the context of a sentence a translator had to find the verb, which was not consistent with Romance language sentence structure. To figure out the English word, a translator first had to find the Russian word in Cyrillic and then transliterate it into English—not an easy process. Words were often unrecognizable with many different meanings depending on where it was located in the sentence or how it was used. Subtle nuances were often produced by heavy use of idioms, which often made no sense, slowing the translation process for inexperienced newcomers. Just as frustrating were nicknames such as "Vanya" for "Ivan," or strange code names, regionalisms, quirks in language, colloquialisms, and the occasional misspelling, all of which could easily distort the meaning of a sentence beyond comprehension. Problems such as these and others regularly sent the rookies to Weisband, who carefully examined the message in an attempt to work out the meaning and its context in the sentence. This process often led him to examine other messages or engage in technical discussions with nearby colleagues. Sometimes further study was necessary of the many Russian synonym and antonym dictionaries kept nearby for reference or archived documents filed in cabinets under lock and key. All would prove valuable for Weisband's increasing understanding of the range of Russian targets under investigation by his section, the success or difficulty they were experiencing, and his steady hunt for human vulnerabilities among the young translators who could prove useful for later KGB recruitment.[5]

Having taken ill in 1946, Captain Smith resigned his commission and returned to New York. Replacing him was a civilian named Waldo H. Dubberstein. Born in 1907 in Bellefont, Kansas, he completed St. Johns College before entering a seminary in St. Louis, Missouri, with plans of becoming a Lutheran minister. Eschewing the ministry, he turned instead to the study of ancient civilizations, earning a doctorate in 1934 at the University of Chicago's Institute of Oriental Studies. For the next eight years he taught there until the war brought him to ASA doing code work against Japanese ciphers. "Dubbie," as friends called him, was garrulous and personable, if sometimes abrasive and indiscreet. "He was always telling me inside stories of the type I didn't need," one colleague remembered. In 1945 having joined the Bourbon Program, he quickly rose into the supervisory ranks. For the next two years he led the unit until moving over to the newly created CIA in 1947. He worked there as a Middle East analyst until his retirement in 1970.[6]

Weisband had been assigned to Bourbon from its earliest days. Along with Frank Rowlett and Dubberstein, he worked closely with many of ASA's finest linguists and cryptanalysts, including some true superstars. One of them was Mary Jo Dunning, a natural cryptanalyst from the moment she arrived at Arlington Hall near the start of the war. As she gained experience her services were frequently called upon to tackle problems that often defied the efforts of veteran code breakers. In April 1943, for instance, Dunning took on the mission of solving the Japanese Army Water Transportation cipher system. Since the start of the war many of ASA's best minds had already struggled and failed to solve it. Some even came to believe that it defied solution.

Hunkered down in a small room that she placed off-limits to visitors, Dunning got down to business. Working around the clock for several days taking time only for quick meals and naps, the solution finally appeared before the eyes of stunned onlookers. It was a eureka moment for Arlington Hall. "New life had been given to the entire section," read one memo. Someone later wrote that "several problems heretofore seeming impregnable are being attacked in the light of what had been proved in 2468."[7] David Kahn called Dunning's success one of the most important of the war.[8] Several months later William Friedman nominated Dunning for the Legion of Merit for her success and dedication to maintaining the Purple Analog System, which was producing *Magic*.[9]

Another new arrival destined for fame was Juanita Moody. Born Juanita Morris, she was the first of nine children, born on May 29, 1924, in a tiny house with no running water or electricity. Her father was a railroad worker turned cotton and soybean farmer and her mother was a homemaker. While in high school she entertained ideas of further education after the school superintendent recommended her for college.

After graduating she attended Western Carolina Teachers College in Cullowhee, North Carolina, with some borrowed funds until the war changed her life. Decades later, she still recalled her feelings as the young men on the campus started disappearing. "I felt that it was wrong to be spending my time in this beautiful place—clear blue skies, going around campus and studying and going to classes at leisure when my country was at war." After completing a few tests at the local army recruiting office, Moody abandoned college at age nineteen and headed for Arlington Hall to take up what turned out to be a career in code-breaking.[10]

Starting as a clerk she quickly advanced into the ranks of cryptanalysis as a supervisor working on the German problem. At the end of the war in Europe, she turned her talents to Japanese ciphers while continuing work after hours on German one-time pad systems that were still producing valuable intelligence on the Japanese. "Actually, from the time I started working before the war ended, I worked every waking moment. I did not require very much sleep, and I didn't want to be anywhere else. And there was so much to do, and so much to learn that that's the only thing I wanted to do, and that's what I did."[11]

Like thousands of other young women at the end of the war, she too suddenly faced the question of what to do next in life. Finishing college and marrying a certain young man still overseas were her highest priorities. Her decision came about by accident with a casual conversation one day with her boss, Dr. Karl Krensky. After explaining her plans, Krensky told her that since arriving at Arlington Hall, she had earned the equivalent of two doctorates in cryptology and the government still desperately needed her skills to help tackle problems yet to come. With her experience dealing with German one-time pads, Russian ciphers would be the next great challenge of her life. Days later, the decision made, she found herself sitting next to Dunning and Weisband.[12]

* * *

At the same time that Weisband's landlord was hauling him into court, his bosses at Arlington Hall were facing serious problems of their own. In the years before the war, the Signal Corp relied on a small handful of talented code breakers, some having nearly a decade of experience, toiling away with paper and pencils. In just one morning, the Japanese attack on Pearl Harbor changed everything. The sudden thrust of America into a global conflict forced an expansion of cryptanalysis that over a span of just four years would produce breathtaking success. The peace that came in August 1945 ended it all. Now the strange machines that had incessantly buzzed and whizzed around the clock seven days a week sat eerily silent next to hundreds of empty tables and thousands of chairs slowly gathering dust in empty rooms and hallways producing an almost ghostlike atmosphere. "Overnight" one veteran remembered, "the targets that occupied most of the wartime cryptologic resources—Germany and Japan—had become non-entities."[13]

The start of 1946 emerged as a moment of great uncertainty for America's code-breaking future. Looking forward many intelligence leaders saw no new enemies. Certainly, Russia was raising concerns, but her real motives had yet to be fully discerned. To millions of Americans still basking in the afterglow of a long-sought victory, Josef Stalin remained a faithful ally leading a nation that had suffered so much for the sake of defeating the Axis. Code breakers now found themselves suspended in a twilight world wondering if breaking foreign ciphers had any future. One ASA official summed it up perfectly. "We had no targets . . . no markets" and "no big distribution list" and "we didn't know what else might be of interest."[14]

A helpful reprieve that would have significant long-term implications for Arlington Hall occurred without warning around Christmas 1945. General George Catlett Marshall Jr. had submitted his resignation as chief of staff in September 1945, just weeks before General Douglas MacArthur took Japan's formal surrender in Tokyo. His departure would not become official until General Eisenhower returned from Europe in November to assume his duties.

After forty-four years of public service Marshall had had enough. His only plan, except for some fishing in the Gulf of Mexico, was to settle into a long-overdue retirement with his wife, Katherine, at Dodona, their new home in Leesburg, Virginia. All of that changed on November 26 as the general stood in the Pentagon courtyard attending his formal retirement ceremony. That same day Patrick Hurley had quietly arrived in Washington for consultations with the new president. An oil man from Oklahoma and a former secretary of war, Hurley had been America's ambassador to China since President Roosevelt appointed him to the post in 1944. Since then, his efforts had been concentrated on producing a settlement between the government of Chiang Kai-shek and his Nationalist Peoples Party, the Kuomintang (KMT), and the Chinese Communist Party (CCP) under Mao Zedong.

The ambassador brought with him a personal assurance to Truman that following a brief rest he would return to his post in Chungking. Just days later, however, without warning, he unleashed a very public denunciation of the Truman administration while announcing his resignation in a manner designed to embarrass the president. Standing before a packed audience at the National Press Club, Hurley accused Truman of undermining his efforts to achieve peace in the region. Turning to the State Department, he charged unnamed "career men" who were soft on Communism with undercutting his work and in doing so aiding the CCP and Mao. Caught off guard by accusations of Communist sympathizers in the government, the White House quickly sought recovery with an appeal to Marshall to travel to China as America's new special envoy. Marshall was a momentous choice for the assignment. Dean Acheson, a prominent Washington lawyer who would later serve as Marshall's undersecretary of state, expressed the feelings of most people who came in contact with him. "From the moment [Marshall] entered a room everyone in it felt his presence. It was a striking and communicated force."[15]

President Truman's choice of Marshall had a twofold objective. First, there was the hope that his global stature as the forger of victory in World War II would signal to both Chiang and Mao the president's seriousness of purpose in securing a cease-fire; one that could hopefully produce a permanent political settlement. On the domestic political front, Marshall's appointment would blunt mounting criticism from Republicans anxious to reclaim the White House after sixteen years in the wilderness.

Chiang Kai-shek was six years younger than Marshall. Born in the eastern coastal province of Chekiang Chiang, he, like Marshall, had dedicated his life to military service starting first at Paotang Academy and later completing his formal military schooling at Tokyo Military Academy. In 1924, he became director of Whampoa Academy, where he began his political career. In personal style, he was laconic with an inscrutable gaze that revealed not a hint of his feelings or thinking. Famed historian Barbara Tuchman had spent time in China as a young researcher during the 1920s developing some understanding of the Asian mind. Decades later, she would publish her Pulitzer Prize–winning biography of Joseph Stillwell, the American general, whose World War II struggles with Chiang cost him his job. Tuchman wrote that for all of his years of army experience, Chiang's talents were not military but rather political, which he exercised "through mastery of balance among factions and plots." For his deftness and skills, he came to be called "Billiken" after the weighted dolls that cannot be knocked over.[16]

Before the war, Mao Zedong and Chiang had been locked in a bitter struggle for control of China. In 1937, both sides temporarily ceased fighting, turning instead to ridding China of invading Japanese forces. Official US wartime policy called for recognition of Chiang and the KMT as the legitimate government of China. Promoted as one of the "Big Four" leaders in the struggle against the Axis, President Roosevelt placed him on the world stage at Cairo in November 1943 as a photo of FDR and Churchill seated next to a beaming Generalissimo Chiang flashed around the world. During the war,

Chiang had been the beneficiary of billions of US dollars in Lend-Lease military equipment. From the Allied strategic perspective such massive aid was vital for keeping KMT forces in the field fighting as a blocking force to prevent Japanese troops from sweeping across Asia and overrunning American air bases. With peace came an end to the uneasy eight-year CCP-KMT truce and increased American pressure on Chiang to end the conflict and form a coalition government with Mao as the junior partner.

Mao was the son of a prosperous peasant farmer from Shaoshan, Hunan Province. Born in 1893, he emerged early as a Chinese nationalist and anti-imperialist. As a teenager he was particularly influenced by the Xinhau Revolution and the May Fourth Movement of 1919. Later, while working at Peking University, he was swept up in Marxism-Leninism and soon became a founder of the CCP. During the Chinese civil war, Mao helped found the Chinese Workers and Peasants Red Army and rose to the top of the CCP following the Long March. CCP forces were tough and disciplined with a reputation as vicious fighters willing to take on Japan's finest military units. After nearly a decade of constant warfare and sacrifice, Mao and the CCP were not going to be denied their share of the spoils of victory. By contrast, the KMT government controlled a collection of undisciplined political and military cadres far larger than Mao's forces but riddled with corruption and incompetence. As a masterful political strategist, Chiang believed he could remain obdurate and ignore a serious parlay with Mao—his implacable enemy. Tensions ran high between Chiang and his American and British partners throughout the war over his refusal to bring his finest military divisions into action against Japan, instead keeping them fresh and on the sidelines for the day the struggle against the communists would again resume.

As Marshall prepared for his mission, he was also conscious of the nearby Russians closely monitoring events. Nine months earlier when Stalin, Churchill, and Roosevelt gathered together at Yalta in February 1945 for their second wartime parley, the Russian leader promised the American president that within ninety days of Hitler's defeat he would turn his forces loose against Japan. That commitment was fulfilled on August 9, the day after an American atomic bomb struck the Japanese city of Nagasaki. Ten Soviet armies surprised the Japanese Kwantung Army in Manchuria, "shattering" its defenses in record time. A week later, on August 16, the attack code-named "Operation August Storm" ended with the Russians occupying all of Manchuria and as far east as the Sakhalin and Kurile Islands and Korea down to the thirty-eighth parallel. In the end, more than a million Soviet troops killed one hundred thousand Japanese soldiers while taking another six hundred thousand as prisoners. With the triumph came a massive horde of captured equipment. There were six hundred tanks, nine hundred aircraft, thirty-seven hundred heavy guns and mortars, and more than twenty-three hundred vehicles of all kinds as well as hundreds of thousands of small arms and tons of ammunition.[17]

When Marshall's C-54 aircraft lifted off for China from Washington's National Airport on the morning of December 15, he had no illusions about the nearly impossible task ahead of him. He took with him valuable lessons about the complexities of life on the Asian continent. As a young officer he had served in China. Two decades later, as chief of staff, his commanders in China routinely streamed reports into his Pentagon office filled with frustrations about Chiang. Criticisms centered on the hoarding of Lend-Lease equipment and refusal to commit the KMT's best troops divisions against a Japanese army that remained a very powerful force. During the summer of 1944 as it began sweeping across unoccupied China, the mounting crisis became so dire that President Roosevelt was forced to intercede. In a personal note, he cautioned Chiang, that "desperate" situations required "desperate remedies." The president's stinging message brought with it a stark warning coupled with an ultimatum. "The future of all Asia is at stake along with the tremendous effort which America had expended in that part of the world." FDR then instructed his wartime partner to turn over command of the KMT army to Joseph Stillwell, one of Marshall's closest friends. As a "get it done" leader with a wartime track record of success that was the envy of the world, Marshall now faced a Gordian knot that neither side had any interest in untangling.[18]

A negotiator needs accurate and timely information if he has any hope of bringing about a cease-fire between two determined opponents. It was no different with Marshall. If he was to successfully accomplish the mission laid out for him by the president, he needed to know the thinking and intentions of both parties. His dilemma, however, was the absence of a robust American intelligence collection system in China. Human spy networks set up by OSS during the war had disappeared. Created in 1942 by General William Donovan, the OSS was now out of business having been shut down by President Truman in October 1945. Left behind were a few Army G2 units along with remnants of Donovan's outfit composed of a disorganized hodgepodge of local businessmen, missionaries, mercenaries, and some local State Department contacts.

As the president's special envoy to China, Marshall was accredited to the legitimate Chinese government. As such he met regularly with President Chiang Kai-shek and his government ministers from his headquarters in Chunking. Through these encounters Marshall explained and reexplained the US position while cajoling and threatening Chiang to end the war. The same could not be said for his relationship with the CCP holed up hundreds of miles away in Yenan. Representing Mao in Chunking was his inscrutable advisor and Communist Party veteran Chou En-lai. Three months after arriving in

China, a deeply frustrated Marshall briefly returned to Washington with a warning to his State Department bosses that he needed adequate intelligence about the true intentions of both sides if he was going to make any headway. Under the circumstances communications intelligence was the only asset that could "shape American policy in China for years to come."[19]

Arlington Hall faced a similar predicament. Since the surrender of Japan, its Far East collection stations could offer little help in acquiring encrypted KMT and CCP messages. Having no mission and nothing to collect, field sites had been steadily dismantling equipment and crating up tons of boxes for shipment home along with thousands of experienced technicians. Especially hard hit were the War Department and Theater monitoring stations. One station in Hawaii was typical of the problem. In July 1945, it had a strength of 9 officers and 261 enlisted men. Over the next six months that figure shrank to just 5 officers and 12 enlisted men, all engaged in maintenance.[20] At Arlington Hall the situation, while less serious, was still critically short of experienced personnel at all levels, "especially officers." So bad had the situation become that officers routinely found themselves taking on double and triple duty just to keep the base running. One case in point involved the post adjutant. In addition to his own responsibilities, he also acted as the personal affairs officer, legal assistance officer, civilian personnel officer, army emergency relief officer, and post signal officer.[21]

Having no instructions or directives from army brass, Arlington Hall quickly went to work on its own initiative in an attempt to supply Marshall with necessary communications intelligence. Today, very little is known about ASA's top-secret project dubbed "Operation Taber." It was assigned to Oliver Kirby, then the deputy to Dubberstein, head of the Bourbon Program. Kirby later said that as no one was expecting anything from Arlington Hall, "we put our own priority" on this project. In short order, the Bletchley Park and TICOM veteran pulled together an experienced team of traffic analysts and Russian linguists that undoubtedly included Weisband. Their job—prepare a crash program of translating Russian messages. At the same time emergency orders were issued to the twelve functioning Far East listening stations in Japan, Korea, and the Philippines as well as two sites in Hawaii along with new stations hastily put together in Chunking and Nanking, Marshall's new operating bases. Nearly half of these stations were barely operable. One had a total staff complement of nine and another eight while others functioned with two operators. Shanghai, at the heart of the action, coped with only an officer and a Women's Auxiliary Corp enlistee. By the end of June 1946, nearly three hundred military personnel (half were in the Philippines) in the Pacific and Far East were committed to Operation Taber. The instructions—point their antennas toward the Asian mainland as far as the Soviet Far East, and north toward Manchuria, and start hunting for Chinese and Russian military communications.²²

Arlington Hall was still in the early stages of coming to grips with Soviet high-frequency encrypted communications. As a consequence, it had "no ability" at the time to read communications sent between Moscow leaders and CCP headquarters in the northern China region of Yenan. To accomplish this new mission, ASA deployed a special detachment to Marshall's headquarters at Chungking. Interception from Chungking was carried on from February 17 through May 1, 1946, when following the transfer of the Chinese government, the unit moved to Nanking. While higher-level codes used one-time encipherment, some progress was made in reading a system called "CQA" interchangeably with the "Ming Code" while others that remain classified today were completely solved.

Intelligence derived from Communist traffic was "a priority objective." The problem, however, was difficulty picking up CCP messages. Mao's radio communications were small and primitive. Most messages didn't travel across the airwaves but instead were carried by courier on foot or bicycles. With these sources blacked out, Arlington Hall began searching for message centers that were transmitting "plain language" messages. Plain language was a term of art used by ASA to describe unencrypted communications sent from station to station. These messages, transmitted with great frequency and in huge volumes, proved incapable of encryption even for the security-conscious Russians. In making their security calculations, Russian military leaders appreciated a probability of interception but surmised that the value of the messages was so low that any risk of interception by foreign eavesdroppers was worth taking.

From the few American collection sites still functioning, raw messages were sent for processing through a radio-teleprinter system back to Arlington Hall. Kirby's small team of analysts and linguists then began sorting out thousands of readable messages looking for the most valuable. After some effort they discovered that the most fruitful sources of intelligence came from networks transmitting in areas where Russians troops were in close contact with CCP forces. Company- and regimental-level units together with other subordinate cadres assigned to railway nodes, shipping depots, warehouses, and various types of storage and transportation facilities were particularly choice targets for exploitation. Working seven days a week, the Operation Taber team, while producing no finished intelligence reports, translated voice conversations and reports for passage to higher echelons. They generally contained important details on shipment of commercial equipment, bills of lading, manifests, train routes and schedules, and other rolling stock data. Equally important were messages filled with summaries of meetings and exchanges between Russian and Chinese Communist troops. The intelligence was "strictly operational stuff" yet very valuable, Kirby later recalled. Once translated the product was then placed on cards and catalogued before being turned over to the State Department for analysis. Despite the low-level nature of the intelligence collected, State Department analysts still gobbled it up. As ASA handed over "even scraps or partial translations," State officials pleaded for more.[23]

Over the thirteen-month life of Operation Taber, ASA regularly supplied top-secret information to US policymakers that could only have disheartened them about chances of successfully bringing the two sides together. Before the end of the war, Stalin had given his pledge to Roosevelt and Churchill that Chiang and the KMT represented the legitimate government of China, and he would provide it with his full support. Over the course of the Marshall mission, Kirby and his team proved otherwise. The translations they were producing revealed clear collaboration between Russian forces and the CCP with Mao well supplied with both Russian and captured Japanese equipment. In some cases, it was simply given to them while in others Mao paid hard cash for the product. Equally troubling evidence came from messages exposing shocking levels of corruption by KMT officials. As Marshall struggled mightily to find a settlement, Chiang's own military and civilian officials were cutting financial deals with the CCP and other guerrilla elements. Woodgas 93-IIIB determined that all across China, American Lend-Lease supplies such as trucks and weapons were being pilfered from KMT warehouses and storage lots and then sold for cash to Chinese Communist forces. In the end, Kirby surmised, "they were selling it because they had given up on the idea of a Chiang victory," choosing instead "to be on the winning side."[24]

* * *

As winter turned to spring in 1946, both Arlington Hall and OP-20-G also began turning their attention to Russian military, naval, and air communications systems. A prohibition against collecting high-frequency transmissions of a wartime ally meant that America had no storehouse of material that they could now mine for clues. What was known was that the Russian military relied on a five-digit cipher system—what it did not know was whether it was a one-time pad, or some other type of machine-generated system. These facts about Soviet teleprinter transmissions would emerge slowly through TICOM and STELLA POLARIS, but that was yet to come.

What Dubberstein's team did have in abundance were Russian diplomatic messages sent between Moscow and its stations in the United States. With war now over, a top-secret and controversial decision was made to continue what was known in the closed world of government code-breaking as the "Shamrock" Program. Under censorship laws during both world wars, cable companies were required to furnish the US government with copies of all telegrams transmitted overseas, even by private individuals. The practice, started in World War I, continued until the late 1920s when a vague piece of legislation, the Radio Act of 1927, made this practice illegal. Collection resumed at the beginning of World War II with a succession of attorneys general repeatedly assuring nervous cable company executives that the practice was perfectly legal and would not result in prosecution for undertaking a patriotic duty. ASA and its successor, NSA, calling the material "drop copies," continued the Shamrock Program until the early 1970s when it finally ended.[25]

The veteran code breaker of *Magic* fame, Frank Rowlett, was the impetus behind continuing the program in the post-war years, believing that it was a "valuable" tool for cryptology. It was a "real cheap" way of intercepting messages, he later said. Furthermore, it was secure. Government leaders could breathe a lot easier not having to worry about the "waves you generated" by an intercept station with weird antennas raising awkward questions from a curious public. Possessing an actual message was also crucial. The "technical plums" produced from pouring over unreadable message were critically important. Although indecipherable, just examining a message offered a host of "wonderful clues" into the nature of a message. From Rowlett's interviews of Gouzenko a year earlier, ASA knew that the KGB and the GRU relied on a key-based one-time pad system; a major revelation that made it easier for a skilled cryptanalyst to explore the unseen code clerk's methods of preparation. By examining the "external characteristics," a trained eye could discern clues such as intentional scratching out of an indicator and replacing it with something else. Careful attention to columns of numbers and letters for even tiny alterations could signal important leads into the actual length of the column or more critically the length of the key, both of which could have significant implications for a code breaker's chances of success. It would pay off handsomely, not at the time, but in the not-too-distant future.[26]

\* \* \*

In addition to his participation in Operation Taber and Operation Shamrock, new and exciting possibilities appeared for a smiling Weisband. Harold George Hayes was less than a year older than William Weisband. Called "Dink" by his friends, he was born in Pittsburgh, Pennsylvania, on September 23, 1907. After high school came Carnegie Institute of Technology for a year before accepting an appointment in 1925 to West Point.

The less than auspicious start of his military career offered no hint of the heights he would one day attain. As a first-year man he managed to sink near the academic basement of his class while spending hours outdoors with a shouldered rifle "walking the yard" as punishment for violations of various infractions.[27] Small in stature, but good with his fists, he joined the boxing team in the lightweight division as a 117-pounder. Over the four years at West Point he recovered his grade point average sufficiently enough to earn an army commission, a Bachelor of Science degree, and an assignment to flight school at San Antonio, Texas. Two years later, a poor solo performance ended his aviation career, but not before his picking up a Bachelor of Arts degree from nearby St. Mary's College.

In 1931, still only twenty-four years old, Lieutenant Hayes made the decision that would set the course of his military career by joining the Signal Corps at Fort Sam Houston. Years later a scribe for the academy alumni journal offered an insight into Hayes's choice of branch. "He went into the cryptographic field because he thought he could learn about this complex field and be on a higher level than most in at least one field." The next decade saw Hayes make strong progress in developing his expertise with an assortment of technical assignments as he steadily rose through the ranks. When America entered the war, he was already a major serving as executive officer of the Signal Corp. One of his first wartime duties was helping to select and set up Arlington Hall Station as the army's new code-breaking nerve center.[28]

Weisband and Hayes first met in Algiers in August 1943. Despite their disparity in rank, Bill's bonhomie, along with his catalogue of languages and eagerness to please, made him a godsend for Hayes and his circle of officers. First was his detachment to Colonel Juin and his FEC forces, where his French fluency proved essential as a communication security officer. Then came Bill's usefulness as a Fifth Army spy. Before leaving Italy in September 1944, he had successfully snatched and copied Juin's codes, which Hayes later put to good use in monitoring French military communications. Weisband also won his commander's favor in another important way. While in Italy, his Russian language fluency came in handy again as an interpreter for a delegation of Russian naval officers sent from Moscow to observe Fifth Army's Mediterranean operations. So impressed was Hayes with Weisband's talents that after returning stateside in the spring of 1944, he ordered him transferred to Arlington Hall. The war that brought these two very different men together had produced a close friendship that would later have sinister implications. Weisband became a "favorite" of Hayes according to one historian.[29]

Nearly four years had passed since Bill Weisband was drafted into the army. After a brief stint in the enlisted ranks, followed by officer training at Fort Monmouth's Signal Corp, he had been commissioned a second lieutenant. Next came advanced schooling in Radio Traffic Analysis at Vint Hill Farms Station and a stop in London before shipping out to Algiers for Fifth Army duties with the 849th Signal Service. Months later in Italy with the

FEC, he struggled to stay alive in the face of brutal mountain warfare against a determined Wehrmacht enemy. Having made it out alive, he returned home to new and safer environs at Arlington Hall. Through luck and Russian language fluency, he found himself much in demand as a linguist embedded with select group of code breakers, segregated from the rest of Arlington Hall, attacking the codes of America's wartime ally, the Soviet Union. Lieutenant Weisband became a "charter member" of the "Bourbon Program," a colleague later recalled.[30]

Forty-seven months in uniform was enough for Weisband. He had his fill of soldiering. May 1946 saw him begin the process of mustering out of the army by requesting the seemingly endless series of forms that needed signing before once again resuming civilian life.

Ever cunning, in planning his new life he made a very careful calculation. Bill had no intention of leaving Arlington Hall. His job was secure and certainly important. And one day, it would once again prove lucrative. In fact, dwarfing his weekly government salary once Tikhon recontacted him. Which he undoubtedly would.

Applicants seeking civilian employment with the National Security Agency in the twenty-first century face a long and grueling process before receiving a job offer. First, and foremost, is the security clearance. Assuming a person meets the technical qualifications for a position, NSA's Office of Personnel and Clearances (OPC) first requires the completion of a Standard Form 86—all 133 pages. OPC is responsible for the issuance and denial of new security clearances, as well as upgrading existing ones following a reinvestigation or, if necessary, revoking them.[31]

Every detail of a person's life has to be listed on the form. There can be no unexplained gaps. Once the form is completed, the applicant undergoes a polygraph examination. The test is designed to chart physiological reactions to key lifestyle and counterintelligence questions that would indicate truthfulness or attempts to deceive. Failure of the test means immediate rejection.[32]

After successfully passing this hurdle, the applicant's past undergoes a rigorous screening. Using the form, the date and place of birth, along with schooling, past employment, military service, arrests, and convictions must be confirmed through careful record reviews. Foreign travel is also important. Considerable attention is paid to the length, purpose, places visited, and persons accompanying the applicant on foreign trips along with identities of individuals they met along the way. Investigators also bore deeply for details concerning people from foreign countries living or visiting the United States who the applicant may know. Interviews are conducted with as many current and former neighbors, teachers, employers, co-workers, supervisors, fellow GIs, commanding officers, and personal references as can be located. Candid comments and observations from such individuals can often flesh out revealing insights into past behavior, producing a portrait of the candidate's character, loyalty, and overall suitability for security clearance. As one observer of the process wryly noted, the applicant should be prepared "to have [his or her] life splayed out on the table and fully dissected by those who are processing and ultimately adjudicating [his or her] security clearance."

Weisband, however, was not some new civilian applying for a job or a security clearance. He was already onboard at Arlington Hall. A study conducted in 1955 by the Security Division of the National Security Agency suggested the ideal three-stage process that Bill Weisband should have faced in applying for his new position. First, the candidate filled out a much-abbreviated version of the Standard Form 86 in what was termed the pre-employment or pre-access screening phase. After a thorough review of the form everything was verified to confirm what the candidate did, who he knew, and where he was every day of his life. Once hired, the security process would continue. Supervisors and co-workers were to be on alert for any indications of questionable behavior such as heavy drinking, gambling, spousal abuse, and excessive and unexplained funds or spending—what was later referred to as "conspicuous consumption." Chronic tardiness and excessive and unexplained absences from work were also recorded. Security infractions, such as failure to properly handle and secure paperwork and workspace at the end of the day, were recorded. A separate security file would be opened containing issues relating to security questions, complaints, and anomalies and kept with the personnel file for each employee. Looking back today from the perspective of three-quarters of a century, we recognize that none of these procedures were in place at that time. Before the war, when Signal Corp code-breaking was a small operation, the rules governing security clearances were often arbitrary and confusing. "They weren't very well thought out," Frank Rowlett recalled.[33]

When hiring linguists and other professionals before World War II, the military's fear centered on immigrants and the pressure they may be subjected to by intelligence services of their country of origin. Under no circumstances could they be hired or receive a clearance under the rules then in place. The children of these immigrants, however, could be granted clearances in the belief that they were sufficiently removed by a generation from such foreign influences. Geographical factors also played a role in the decision process. Candidates from a "bigger center" like New York City and Philadelphia often populated by large immigrant groups were looked at more closely than someone coming from small rural areas of the country. It was generally accepted that anyone born in a foreign country was prohibited from receiving a security clearance. This rule was routinely ignored, and if enforced William Friedman would have been denied one having been born in Russia.[34]

The war only added pressure on the system. The sudden need for large numbers of warm bodies to fill the thousands of slots required for cryptology on an industrial scale temporarily curtailed thorough personnel screening. Replacing it was an informal recruitment system and a few perfunctory checks. "If somebody knew someone who was possibly a good candidate for our kind of work contact was immediately made with them." Once inside ASA's walls, the problem only worsened. Not wishing to lose an employee who could not be replaced, the agency regularly experienced "a terrible time screening these people," one person recalled. At the same time, the war also produced a strange "loyalty" hierarchy. ASA civilians were forced to sign a formal loyalty oath of secrecy while military personnel, for some unknown reason, had no such obligation. Frank Rowlett had been a government code breaker for nearly a decade and a half before donning an army uniform with a major's oak leaves on his shoulders. Years later looking back on those days, he still questioned the reasons behind this strange anomaly. "People in uniform [were] a cut above people who [were] not in uniform in the military establishment. I don't know, they are born of a different womb or something. Something happens to them." The end of the war brought no respite. When Bill Weisband applied for his civilian security clearance, the situation had not changed. Frank Rowlett called it "chaotic."[35]

As Weisband began filling out his forms, he faced a far easier process than modern-day NSA applicants. He knew from the start that he had a job and security clearance. ASA had no Security Division, no polygraph program, nor any dedicated counterintelligence specialists with experience working hand in hand with the FBI and the yet to be created CIA. Nor were there any pre-employment screenings or interviews for military officers with Signal Corp and Arlington Hall backgrounds. Weisband had skills that were vital to ASA's new mission. And rather than being considered a "new hire," he was instead undergoing, what was popularly called at the time, "reconversion"—a simple and seamless transition from military to civilian status.[36]

The Army Security Agency now faced a point of "no return" with Weisband. Had there been adequate systems in place, perhaps the future would have developed differently. Careful scrutiny of his past life would certainly have raised troubling questions. There was his enrollment a decade earlier at the RCA Institutes, while unemployed, paying tuition costs he clearly could not afford or explain. Then there were the numerous traffic citations that led to a judge's rejection of Bill's citizenship application. An arrest record for trying to skip out on his rent and threatening a landlady would have surfaced. A bit of snooping would have revealed his role in smuggling John Francis Pollock across the Canadian border into New York. Then there was Pollock's release from Ellis Island, his bail funds put up by a mystery woman claiming to be his wife, his subsequent disappearance, and a lawyer with ties to the Communist Party. The eyebrows of a serious-minded investigator would have been raised, as well, at Weisband's freewheeling, well-heeled lifestyle in the late 1930s despite only spotty employment. Perhaps his old girlfriend, Patricia Grimes, could have shed some light on his secret and very lucrative job for a mysterious old man; work that required meetings with strangers on street corners for exchanges of packages and envelopes at odd hours of the day and night. Grimes may have even recounted their conversation that final evening together before Bill entered the army when he expressed the hope that his secret work would continue after the war. Even a simple local check would have revealed the dispute with his neighbor that landed him in court and his eviction just months earlier.

But none of this happened. As spring became summer, backed by Colonel Hayes's clout, and a personal reference from Colonel Robert Schukraft, another influential Signal Corp officer, a gleeful Weisband inched ever closer toward his goal—a permanent job with ASA. In July he traveled briefly to Camp Beale, California, where he formally separated from the army on July 11, 1946. Finally, with army discharge in hand, he gladly signed the required loyalty oath on August 26, 1946, before taking an "Excepted Appointment," as an "analytical specialist." With a yearly salary of $4,149.60 ($54,035.00 in February 2021) and marked by everyone in the Woodgas Unit with the official stamp of trustworthiness, he was now a key Bourbon Program asset with unlimited access to everything at the heart of American code-breaking. Exactly where he wanted to be.[37]

## NOTES

1. WFO Report, July 20, 1950, Weisband FBI file.
2. Ibid.
3. Ibid.
4. "L'Affaire Weisband," American Cryptology during the Cold War, 1945–1989, The Struggle for Centralization, 1945–1946, NSA FOIPA.
5. "L'Affaire Weisband," American Cryptology during the Cold War, 1945–1989, The Struggle for Centralization, 1945–1946, NSA FOIPA.
6. In 1983 Dubberstein was indicted for helping convicted arms dealer and ex-CIA officer Edwin P. Wilson trade classified military information through Wilson to Libyan ruler Muammar Qaddafi for money. He committed suicide in 1983, the day before he was to appear in a court in Washington, D.C. "The Last Battle of an Old War Horse," *Washington Post*, May 8, 1983. D. Glen Starlin memorandum entitled "Minutes of Meeting Held 21 June 1946, Room 117, Headquarters," NCM, FOIPA.
7. Kahn, *Codebreakers*, 594.
8. Ibid.
9. Friedman memorandum to Cordeman, September 27, 1943, NCM.

10. NSA Oral History Interview of Juanita Moody, June 21, 2001, NCM, OH-2001–28; Benson, *Venona History*, 36.
11. Ibid.
12. Ibid.
13. David Wolman, "Cuba Confidential," *Smithsonian*, March 2021, 64.
14. Kirby Oral History.
15. Roll, *Marshall*, 113.
16. Barbara Tuchman, *Stillwell and the American Experience in China, 1911–1945* (New York: The MacMillen Company, 1971), 93.
17. David M. Glantz, "Soviet Operational and Tactical Combat in Manchuria, 1945," "Operation August Storm" (London: Frank Cass Publishers, 2003).
18. Roll, *Marshall*, 113.
19. Annual Report 1946, 3.
20. Ibid.
21. Ibid.
22. Ibid.
23. Kirby Oral History.
24. Ibid., Annual Report, 1946, 20.
25. Director Lew Allen decided the practice, although probably legal, did not pass the "smell test" and terminated it. Cryptologic Almanac 50th Anniversary Series. The Time of Investigation Part 1 of 2, NCM.
26. Rowlett Oral History.
27. Norman H. Evans, Cullum No. 8548, List of U.S. Military Academy Graduates.
28. Ibid., Rowlett Oral History, 360–61.
29. Benson, author interview, October 10, 2020, "L'Affaire Weisband."
30. Rough Draft Notes, Undated, NSA FOIPA.
31. William Hird, author interview, April 3, 2023.
32. Ibid.
33. Rowlett Oral History.
34. Ibid.
35. Ibid. "NSA Security Clearances—Work for the Intel Community's Sigint Experts," NCM, NSA.
36. Rowlett Oral History.
37. NSA FOIPA, Rough Notes of Timeline, Undated, WFO Report, June 2, 1950, Weisband FBI file.

*Chapter 23*

# Mabel

By all accounts, she was a real "stunner." "Knock-out" had been a similar refrain, particularly by men who could not help but glance at her as she ambled along the hallways of Arlington Hall Station. Many decades later, the FBI agents who interviewed her and Bill Weisband for hours had only dim recollections of him. But her image instantly appeared from the deep recesses of two men already in their eighties.

She and Bill Weisband were as different as night and day. In many respects a true odd couple. Only the chaos and confusion of a global war could have thrown two more unlikely people together. At the age of thirty-seven, Weisband was stocky, but after returning from Europe and resuming a more regular routine he began putting on weight. He was a rapidly balding middle-ager, with a fully formed personality and years of life experience under his belt. There was also his smooth, fast-talking hustler style, heavy drinking, and never-ending yen for the good life. He was an immigrant from Egypt, a Russian Jew from the streets of New York City, fluent in several languages with only a hint of an accent. As an army officer and combat veteran of North Africa and Italy, he was now stateside flush with large rolls of unexplained pocket cash. Enhancing his mystique even further were whispered rumors floating around the already secretive world of Arlington Hall that he was emersed in some type of special hush-hush project.

She, on the other hand, was still an innocent. A tall willowy teenager from a tiny speck on the map that no one ever heard of. Barely out of high school, she spoke English with an easy drawl common to her region of the country. She had never gone anywhere beyond ten miles of the family home. Her only travel occurred in 1943 when she boarded the train that carried her a couple hundred miles north to wartime Washington, DC, for her first job at Arlington Hall.

\* \* \*

Her name was Mabel Elizabeth Woody and she hailed from Del Rio, Tennessee. Del Rio, the Spanish word meaning "from the river," was tucked away in rural Cocke County, founded just a decade after the establishment of America's Constitution. The town, bordering North Carolina in the heart of Appalachia, sits at the confluence of the French Broad River and Big Creek, surrounded on all sides by ancient deep-forested mountains, some reaching a height of three thousand feet. Evidence suggests a Native American presence centuries before the arrival of Europeans on American shores.[1]

Increasing western settlement and expansion over the Appalachian Mountains during the nineteenth century created a growing need for wood products like shingles and roofing materials for new homes. This led to the start of logging in the area on an industrial scale, which in turn brought railroads to Del Rio, making it an important shipping hub. The trains hauling these new goods to distant markets needing fuel to power them spawned a new coal mining industry in the region. While some folks benefitted from the economic boom most residents found themselves shut out of the rewards of progress. What we call "infrastructure" today never caught up. Roads were few, and those that were built were of poor quality. So also, was health care, antiquated at best, nonexistent at worst, with malnourishment a common thing.

Del Rio's heydays abruptly ended at the start of the twentieth century when the federal government stepped in to address massive logging operations that were leveling old-growth forests at a staggering rate. In 1911, Congress passed legislation ending the industry in Southern Appalachia; a move that marked the start of a decline into poverty from which Del Rio never recovered. The 2000 US Census figures, for example, revealed a Del Rio population of two thousand with more than 20 percent living below the poverty line.[2]

Over the years, Del Rio gained a reputation as a center for "moonshining." Known by such nicknames as "fire water," "white lightning," and "pass around," this "clear unaged whiskey" carrying a whopping 40 percent alcohol content could easily be brewed in homemade stills behind a barn while garnering little attention from local authorities. Producing illegal spirits was common in rural Appalachia communities. Poor soil for growing marketable crops and depressed corn prices in the 1920s and '30s forced farmers to moonshine both for personal use and to supplement the family income. When not farming or making home brew, the favorite pastime was "cockfighting." Throughout the mountain villages, whispered word would spread signaling when and where a cockfight would take place. Dozens of cars and pickup trucks would suddenly start arriving at a predetermined spot with men and women eager to watch and wager on two gamecocks, fitted with sharp metal spurs, battling, and flailing in a ring called a cockpit.[3]

\* \* \*

Mabel's father, James Woody, a native of the region, worked as a junction foreman for the railroad that ran between Ashville, North Carolina, and Newport, Tennessee. Over his lifetime, he married three times. After producing two children, his first wife died in childbirth along with the third child. Next, James married Pearl Rickett, a local woman who gave him seven more children, including Mabel, born on June 6, 1925. Following Pearl's death, James married again, this time to Maggie Sweeten. She birthed five more children. By the time Maggie finished producing, Mabel had six brothers and sisters and another seven half siblings.[4]

The Woody children grew up poor in a tiny, crudely furnished wooden house with no frills. As for living arrangements, James and his wives had their own bedroom while the kids doubled up wherever they could find space. No central heating or indoor plumbing made chopping wood and hauling water from a nearby well a daily family ritual. The evidence suggests a claustrophobic world, one in which privacy was out of the question for a young girl like Mabel, wanting to be alone with her thoughts and dreams. She was constantly surrounded by incessant commotion from children ranging from teenagers to newborns—all with different needs and wants.

Del Rio was too small to support a high school. It had only a grammar school, which took local children to the eighth grade. Mary Bell Smith, an elementary school teacher in the region during the early twentieth century, described the poverty she witnessed. "Many students in large families brought their lunches in tin pails which had been emptied of the pure pork lard which was originally brought in them. These lunch pails contained either blackberry pie or dried beans and cornbread. Sharing equally, sisters and brothers dipped harmoniously from the same lunch bucket."[5]

The absence of a high school in Del Rio was a blessing for Mabel; one that allowed her a chance to replace crushing family life with some type of normal existence. It came around the age of thirteen when she moved to nearby Hot Springs, North Carolina, to live for the next four years with the parents of Dorothy Jewel Runion. The two girls were the "closest of friends" Dorothy later recalled while acknowledging that Mabel "came from a large family who lived in a small house in the country."[6]

Every day, Mabel and Dorothy walked to the simple one-story clapboard wood-framed school that made up Hot Springs High School. Leading the eighty-member student body and sixteen faculty members was the principal, Mr. Grover L. Angel. Mabel had eighteen students in her class.

Mable made the most of her high school experience. In addition to her studies, she joined the glee club and was a regular on the girls' basketball team. Sadly, the team lost all thirteen games played in her junior year. As a member of the theater group, she was cast in *Hobgoblin House*, a play written in 1933 by Bugbee Beacon. For her performance she received a credit from her Dramatics class for playing the niece of one of the leading characters.[7]

After graduating in 1942, Mabel and Dorothy suddenly had life decisions to make. With the war on, they traveled to nearby Asheville, North Carolina, for an interview with an army recruiter who was looking for young women interested in performing secret war work in the nation's capital. A few cursory background checks later, the two teenagers found themselves in the spring of 1943 on a northbound train heading for a new adventure at Arlington Hall Station.

A first order of business for them in Washington was finding a place to live. With wartime housing tight and getting tighter, ASA had arranged with owners of carefully selected boardinghouses around the city to take in the flood of women arriving every day. Within days, Mabel and Dorothy found themselves ensconced in a large house on Kalorama Road in northwest Washington, DC, crammed in with dozens of women from all over America.

This sudden loss of privacy may have been too much for them. Particularly for Mabel, for they stayed there only a few weeks before hunting for new lodgings of their own. After a first false start, the two friends finally moved across town, settling into a cozy row house on R Street Northeast, where they lived for the next six years.

Mabel had been working at Arlington Hall for two years before she first met Lieutenant William Weisband. It was in late summer of 1945 at a party she and Dorothy held at their home. The two began dating soon after and from the start they seemed inseparable. Friends and co-workers regularly saw them together during the day chatting away while eating lunch at the post cafeteria. Over time the general consensus was that they were "going steady."[8]

## NOTES

1. Mary Ruble, *Del Rio* (Newport, TN: Clifton Club, 1970), 82.
2. US Census website, United States Census Bureau.
3. "Cockfighting Pit at Center of Federal Investigation for Sale," *Newport Plain Talk*, April 7, 2008.
4. Author interview of Vonda Blackwell, October 20, 2020.

5. Mary Bell Smith, *In the Shadow of the White Rock* (Boone, NC: Minor's Publishing Company, 1979), 74.

6. Robert Murray interview of Dorothy Runion, October 21 and 24, 1960. NSA FOIPA.

7. *The Spa*, Hot Springs High School Yearbook, Hot Springs, North Carolina, 1940–1941.

8. Robert Murray interview of Dorothy Jewel Runion, October 21 and 24, 1960. NSA FOIPA.

## Chapter 24

# Jimmy's Place

When not romancing Mabel, Bill had other pleasures to fill his time. Bill was a heavy drinker whose love of quality booze was always displayed in the fully stocked bar he kept in his apartment. On most nights after work, he could be spotted at the Arlington Hall Officers' Club leaning against the bar, drink in hand, chatting with co-workers, mainly gossip about work matters. Chief among them was his close friend, ASA's boss, Colonel Harold Hayes. Weisband was probably an alcoholic who, while still in his thirties, could function well despite swilling large quantities of liquor and spirits. He "drinks heavily," a co-worker recalled, but at no time was he "not in complete possession of his faculties."[1]

But Bill's fatal weakness was neither women nor alcohol. He was a serial gambler who laid down bets on just about any type of wagering scheme. It was a compulsion that kept him in constant debt and in need of fresh cash. Gambling seemed to be in the Weisband family blood. In the 1930s when millions of Americans had no money and were struggling to keep food on the table and a roof overhead, any type of investing was treacherous at best. Perhaps the worst offender (next to Bill) was Harold, Bill's older brother. He too was a compulsive gambler always scrambling for cash. So serious was his addiction that during the mid-1930s, he stole funds from an employer to cover a debt incurred one night at a casino at Atlantic City, New Jersey. He only escaped prosecution when Bill replaced the cash, most likely using KGB funds.

Bill had been gambling since his teenage years when he first arrived in America. In those early days it was strictly penny-ante with co-workers from various New York City hotels. Weisband was always in the action. After his return from Italy, he resumed the habit by regularly hosting poker games at his apartment with Arlington Hall colleagues, including the compound's security chief.

Bill Weisband lived just a short drive through Washington to Maryland, the heart of the nation's Thoroughbred horse racing industry. On any day of

205

the year, he would drive his Buick Roadster twenty-five miles or so to bet on horses rounding tracks at Laurel, Bowie, or Upper Marlboro where the trotters ran. If he was really adventurous, he drove to Pimlico Racecourse in Baltimore, home of the Preakness, famed second leg of Thoroughbred horse racing's "Triple Crown." When visiting New York, he could be found along the rails at Belmont Park on Long Island shouting home a winner together with thousands of other hopefuls.

It wasn't long after returning from Europe that Weisband began making regular visits to a large house situated on an even larger piece of property in nearby Maryland. It was officially known as the "Maryland Athletic Club." But to Bill and everyone else in the know, it was simply called "Jimmy's Place." One reporter would later describe it as the "best known gambling casino between Saratoga and Palm Beach."[2]

Jimmy was James A. La Fontaine, born on March 8, 1868, just three years after the end of the Civil War. He was the oldest child of a prosperous owner of a chicken and vegetable stand located at the Old Central Market on the corner of 9th Street and Pennsylvania Avenue Northwest, site today of the FBI headquarters building. The family were devout Catholics and well regarded in the community.

Mr. La Fontaine always wanted his son to take over the business, but after a few half-hearted attempts the boy quickly realized that a life of poultry and vegetable sales was not for him. Jimmy's taste ran in a much riskier direction. Gambling was prodigious around the market. It was common for farmers bringing their products to market for sale to gamble after unloading their carts and awaiting payment from the vendors. Legend has it that Jimmy found his calling in those early days when he began running a number of low-level businesses matching odd-man pennies and betting on the popular sport of chicken fighting. Some said he ran numbers for local bookmakers and once won something called the St. Louis Lottery.

From the small time Jimmy graduated to the big leagues around 1890 as a professional blackjack dealer working across the Potomac River in Virginia at a place called Heaths. Before long, Jimmy, along with some backers, bought a table and then a casino at Jackson City, situated on what is now known as Potomac Park. It did not take long before Virginia law enforcement authorities got wind of the operation, ordering them to close down and vacate the state.

Jimmy may have been forced out of Virginia but not out of the gambling business. For years he managed boxers and operated a local boxing club. He enjoyed the fight game and often boasted that he had seen every heavyweight bout from the time John L. Sullivan battled Jim Corbett for the world heavyweight championship. In 1897, he was twice at ringside in Rochester, New York, as one his stable of fighters, Washington's Patsy Raedy, lost the world's middleweight title to Tommy Ryan. From 1914 to 1921 he ran the

Armode Club, a nearby Maryland boxing center. Later he got in to boxing promotion. One time he tried to lure the Jack Dempsey–Georges Carpentier fight to Washington, but the plan fell through. It is said that he later posted a $100,000 guarantee for the Joe Louis–Jim Braddock fight. In the years to come he continued to pursue his favorite pastime of cockfighting. He kept dozens of chickens, which he fought up and down the East Coast and as far south as Florida. Cockfighting was a lucrative business that he kept up until the end of his life.

La Fontaine finally found permanence in 1922 when he opened the Maryland Athletic Club. Jimmy took great care to strategically locate his joint in Prince George's County, Maryland, as close as he could get to the District of Columbia but just far enough away to avoid pestering from a big-city racket-busting police department. His club sat along Bladensburg Road on the Maryland side of Eastern Avenue, the border of Washington. The site was perfect for other reasons as well. A municipal bus ran along Eastern Avenue, making it convenient for passengers to access the club. For those high rollers located in the city center, he kept a fleet of seven Packard limos idling on nearby street corners to chauffeur guests to and from the club.

As the owner of a gambling casino raking in tens of thousands of dollars a week, Jimmy was not physically intimidating. Club members remembered him standing just five foot six inches tall at 150 pounds with an ever-present cigar clenched between his teeth. One newspaper reporter likened him to a "gnome like character."[3] He didn't have to personally keep everyone in line. He hired force to watch his customers. While Jimmy had found his stronghold, he had been busy on other matters as well. His shrewd eye was cast for the proper crowd—and he found it in Prince George's County where politics, at the time, went a long way and in many directions. Under the careful tutelage of influential friends both new and old, he soon began contributing to both political parties, trying to ensure the success of his chosen candidates. He soon found himself making regular payoffs to local politicians and cops, calling them his "blackbirds." They were critical if he was to stay in business and avoid periodic grand juries and spasms of anti-corruption attacks.[4]

Jimmy steered clear of female gamblers. He found them to be sore losers. So, they were routinely barred. They also impacted on certain of his male customers. The one thing that Jimmy hated was publicity. When you are running a gambling casino operating on the thin side of the law, the last thing you needed was your name or the name of your place in the newspapers. It was understood by all that if word got back to him that the wife of a customer was complaining about her husband's losses that client was shown the door with a warning never to return.

Operating outside the law with big money rolling in made Jimmy easy prey for criminal elements. One story has it that he was kidnapped and paid $40,000 for his own release. Another legend was he was shot in the back with a shotgun while somehow remaining untouched with $1,000 still in his pocket. Just before World War II, Montgomery County, Maryland, made Jimmy pay $30,000 to a guy who sustained gambling losses despite his claims that he embezzled the funds from his boss. The verdict was later upheld by the Court of Appeals.

In the world of illegal betting the less one knew the better. Nobody ever talked if they knew what was good for them. Yet one rumor floating around for years hinted that Jimmy was not his own boss but rather a front man for powerful organized crime syndicates farther up the East Coast. La Fontaine's payoffs to the top were said to be made through Nig Rosen, a Philadelphia gangster, who passed the cash to Meyer Lansky in New York. Lansky was the famed money man for Frank Costello and a gambling partner of crime boss Joe Adonis. When Jimmy died in 1949 at the age of eighty-one, he left behind $2,245,430, of which $1,818,763 was in cash. Years later it was still a running joke that Jimmy's death brought massive confusion as to what was his and what belonged to the mob.

\* \* \*

Jimmy opened his doors at eleven in the morning and closed at six the next morning seven days a week (except Christmas or when the grand jury was in session). A Prince George's County history described it as the "preeminent gambling establishment in the Washington area."[5]

The casino was fortress like, sitting on thirty acres of land surrounded by a large metal fence topped with barbed wire. For years Jimmy kept what one reporter called a pack of "ferocious" dogs patrolling the property for unwanted visitors. Parking was never a problem except on Saturdays and holidays.[6]

When Bill Weisband arrived, he first drove through a gate on to a large estate. After parking his car, he approached the main entrance—an ominous-looking steel door with a strategically placed peephole at eye level. Assuming the visitor was "OK," the doorman, with an encyclopedic memory for faces, allowed Bill to pass through without challenge. But getting past the first door did not guarantee entry. Bill would walk up a flight of stairs to another steel door. There a second doorman would give him the once over and only after frisking him for a gun would he allow him in. (Weapons were confiscated and returned to the customer when he left.) The joint's second floor had several black doors and a lunchroom serving customers any time of the day or night. What it did not have was a bar where Weisband could buy a drink. Jimmy had a no-drinking rule that was almost an obsession. Drunks, especially those losing money, were bad for business. One of those black doors opened onto another flight of stairs that led to a spacious third-floor gambling layout. On the walls hung the usual horse-room blackboard filled with chalk entries, rundowns, and so forth on several tracks. Bill placed his bets at one of six betting windows next to a giant tote board where odds and results were recorded. Amid the swirling odor (the place wasn't air-conditioned) of sweat mingled with cigar and cigarette smoke, Weisband often stood for hours listening to races announced from wire to wire over a loudspeaker by a La Fontaine man reading from the Western Union ticker tape. Jimmy, ever wise to the ways of gamblers, kept no telephones in his place. Telephones enticed cheating. It was called "past posting," a scheme that allowed a confederate at the track to call the gambler who would then place his bet before the Western Union results came in. Bookmakers at the time capped their payoffs at 20 to 1 but La Fontaine always paid track odds. One story goes that a guy struck gold when he hit a $100 three-horse parlay; Jimmy paid him $13,000 in cash—no questions asked. For dice players there were four tables—others were set up if business warranted. Rounding out the room were two blackjack tables, sometimes more, a roulette wheel, and a "birdcage" for three dice chuck-a-luck.[7]

Some insight into the vast extent of Bill's gambling, however, can be gleaned from an Arlington Hall co-worker and friend. Together with Weisband he visited the club on "four or five occasions" and each time he watched as Bill "gambled heavily," the friend remembered. One time he stood there wild-eyed as Bill lost $3,600 ($46,638.13 in December 2021) in four hours. He based this figure on the large number of chips Bill bought when they arrived and the few he cashed in when they left. Years later he told the FBI that he found such staggering losses "unusual." Yet he never reported his concerns to Arlington Hall authorities, dismissing the losses as money Bill earned on sales of jewelry from his mother's estate. The one time he did question him, Weisband merely smiled and quickly waived it off claiming he always kept a "cupful of diamonds" in his car.[8]

After nearly eighty years, little is known about the frequency of Weisband's visits to Jimmy's Place. But as later events would make clear, he was a regular at the club, losing huge chunks of cash.

## NOTES

1. WFO Report, July 20, 1950, Weisband FBI file.
2. "Gamblers Found Action at Jimmy's," *Washington Times Herald*, January 17, 1955, 3.
3. "Jimmy Gets Chummy at Rummy," *Washington Times Herald*, January 18, 1955, P3.

4. "Jimmy's Choice of Site a 'Natural,'" *Washington Times Herald*, January 19, 1955, P3.

5. Lieutenant Dennis Campbell, "The Way We Were," Open Mike, Prince George's County Government, Undated.

6. "Jimmy's Place Big County Industry," *Washington Times Herald*, January 23, 1955, A3.

7. Ibid.

8. WFO Report, July 20, 1950, Weisband FBI file.

*Chapter 25*

# Top-Secret Glint

It was 1946, as Weisband was planning his discharge from the army, that an unprecedented project got underway at ASA. One that Oliver Kirby, a future NSA deputy director for Operations, would describe as the "greatest continuous thing that [ASA] ever invented."[1] It began with a decision to collect and analyze Russian "plaintext." Plaintext was generally understood to consist of "all Soviet plain language communications passed on all Soviet internal links and all plain language and commercial codes passed on international commercial circuits (ICR)."[2]

This windfall of intelligence had its roots in Adolf Hitler's decision to invade the Soviet Union in June 1941. As Wehrmacht forces sped eastward toward Moscow, Josef Stalin faced the prospect that his arms factories and research centers would quickly fall into enemy hands. Within weeks of the attack the Russian leader made the fateful decision to disassemble his industrial facilities and move them all east behind the Ural Mountains into the vast wilderness of far-off Siberia and central Eurasia.

For wartime purposes, this move worked well. Soviet manufacturing continued without interruption as the war in the western part of the country raged on. After the war, however, what had been a deft move quickly became a serious handicap for Russian communications security. Throughout the war and afterwards most armed forces and police circuits remained secure behind hardened encryption. The same could not be said for messages moving between Moscow and Russia's massive industrial centers spread out over a thousand miles.

Unlike military and KGB networks, the civilian system was controlled by the USSR Ministry of Communications. Looking back today, it appears like a hodgepodge of largely unencrypted networks crudely spliced together in the wake of an emergency. Used by ordinary citizens and government officials, it included landline links between major cities that did not stretch across the entire country. To fill in the large gaps, high-frequency radio was required to reach industrial plants in remote regions. As ASA began studying them, they found circuits filled with a mixture of plaintext telegrams, Morse code, and enciphered traffic as well as clear speech. Analysts watched as nearly 2.5 million monthly messages and voice conversations traveled across the nearly twelve Russian time zones—a situation that made encryption impossible and ripe for ASA exploitation. It may also have been due to Russian leadership failure to grasp the potential for serious loss of valuable intelligence to savvy collectors and analysts. As one study later put it, the Soviet civil communications network was "highly vulnerable"[3] to exploitation in the 1940s.

ASA and Bletchley Park had no culture for collecting plaintext messages. Both organizations were led by code breakers who helped win the war by successfully cracking German and Japanese ciphers. Plaintext messages in the United States had been the wartime responsibility of the Office of Censorship set up in the wake of Pearl Harbor. It would become, as one study later recorded, "a main source of information" on Russian activities and a "major departure from what had been established practice by the US and [United Kingdom] cryptologic services."[4]

Starting in April 1945 with the war winding down, the US and UK cryptologic services started intercepting Soviet messages to assess them for intelligence value. The project was soon abandoned in the face of unpromising results with only insignificant bits and pieces of short messages.

This second initiative in 1946 was the brainchild of one of Arlington Hall's new arrivals. Born into a Russian Jewish family in the city of Odessa, Jacob Gurin emigrated to America with his parents as a child, settling in New York City, where he completed a degree at New York University before joining the army during World War II. Rising to the rank of captain, he spent most of the war in the Pacific translating and interpreting Japanese. After the war he joined ASA as a Russian linguist and speech researcher, eventually becoming chief of language research for NSA. He immediately recognized that merely translating isolated messages was worthless. Gurin saw the vast potential of assembling these individual tidbits of data into a mosaic that could provide policymakers with a clear picture of the Soviet Union's industrial activities.[5]

In pushing his ideas, Gurin faced considerable opposition from his cryptologic colleagues. If Soviet authorities considered the information of any significance, they charged, it would be enciphered. Gurin disagreed and held his ground. He saw what the others did not. He conceded that the Russians would impose strict regulations on what subjects and information were to be protected, but due to relentless pressure from Moscow officials for information and updates these prohibitions were often ignored. He argued further that despite Russian insistence on absolute communications security, the sheer volume of communications between these distant sites made this impossible. ASA had stumbled upon a window, he argued, into the work underway on

Moscow's top-priority programs as well as other defense initiatives that were part of Stalin's fourth Five-Year Plan started in 1946.[6]

Soon a tiny group from the WDGAS-93-B language staff led by Gurin set about in absolute secrecy to prove what could be achieved through exploitation of plaintext material. A team of four experienced Russian linguists were assembled to work on the project. They included Olin Adams, who was also knowledgeable about economic matters, Juliana Mickwitz, Constantin Oustinoff, and Bill Weisband.[7]

Like Gurin, Mickwitz would one day become a star at NSA. Juliana Charlotte von Mickwitz was born into wealth and status in 1889 at "Halila," her grandfather's estate at Vyborg, Grand Duchy of Finland, then part of the Russian Empire. As a child she was tutored at home, where she learned Russian, English, and German. Later she attended school at St. Petersburg, earning a gold medal for academic work and staying on as a tutor until 1909. That same year she took a job as a secretary to the president of a Russian oil company and following his death continued working for his wife. In 1919 with the start of the Russian Civil War, Mickwitz courageously hid the woman's assets from confiscation. She in turn arranged for them both to flee to Poland under the guise of Juliana's engagement to a Polish doctor. For the next five years, she worked as a translator for various companies as well as the American and British consulates before briefly taking a position as a foreign correspondent. By 1926 she found permanence living in Warsaw and working as a translator and analyst for the US military attaché. Thirteen years later, she was again on the run, this time with her embassy colleagues to the Hague as Hitler began his campaign to gobble up Europe starting with Poland. Within a year she moved again—first to Berlin, then Athens, and finally to the American legation in Lisbon. Through the efforts of American military authorities, she secured passage in 1942 to the United States, where she found herself at the War Department in Washington translating Russian, German, and Polish documents for military intelligence. In October 1946, the same year she joined ASA, Mickwitz was awarded a Meritorious Civilian Service Medal.[8]

Initial processing of plaintext information began under Gurin's direction in late 1946 or early 1947 in the strictest secrecy. The millions of intercepted messages and voice conversations required a slow and laborious process of manual scanning and selecting the most worthwhile messages for inclusion in the top-secret *ASA Bulletin* that was distributed to select government officials.

The team soon set their sights on producing a system of winnowing them down to messages of intelligence value with thousands more discarded. By the end of 1947 Gurin and his team had reduced interception to one hundred thousand of the most fruitful communications. As they moved forward the group began organizing their work into categories such as Ministry of

Aviation, Navy, Air Force, atomic research, and so on. As they collected messages, they would compare them with other messages looking for linkages and patterns to produce a clear picture of the Soviet economy and war-making capability. The finished analysis was then incorporated into ministerial studies, which they continually updated as new information became available. Success soon followed with positive feedback from senior government officials who were on the short list of customers for Gurin's reports. One report on the USSR Ministry of Nonferrous Metallurgy even produced a letter of appreciation from the State Department.

Talented and experienced Russian linguists like Weisband were the keys to ASA's plaintext triumph. They had to first translate the message, or the voice recording, and then try to tease out missing words or phrases. Weisband and the others often had to make educated guesses at elements of the text in order to determine the correct word, term, name, or phrase. A daily headache for Weisband and his team was the nature of high-frequency voice communications. Trying to listen to a conversation stretching over thousands of miles was often exasperating due to atmospheric interference that corrupted volume, causing it to suddenly cut out or rise and then fall to almost inaudible levels. Further compounding the problem were speakers who mumbled and garbled, making listening for accuracy almost impossible. Interference was so bad many times that the two people talking could not understand each other. "Linguists had to cope frequently with corrupt, sometimes very corrupt text and voice" one NSA study recorded. "This might involve the occasional missing or incorrect letter(s) or, worst case, the corruption of significant portions of the text making recovery difficult or impossible."[9]

As the program grew, Weisband became intimately familiar with a specific collection target or targets ASA was studying. And like Gurin and his three colleagues, he became fully aware of the success they were achieving. There was an average of 2.5 million messages passing across the civil network of which through analysis approximately 15 percent were singled out for analysis and of these about 6 or 7 percent were found to contain major intelligence topics and assigned "top priority for immediate processing."[10] By November 1947 ASA was capturing roughly 100,000 messages a month. Five years later that number would jump to 1,300,000 a month.[11] This figure then began a steep decline with a reduction by 1954 to around 800,000 a month followed just two years later to 300,000 a month.[12]

By the end of 1947, plaintext was suddenly placed on a backburner with linguists moved on to something bigger and potentially more explosive. ASA was moving back into the heydays of wartime glory.

## NOTES

1. Kirby Oral History.
2. Carol B. Davis, *Candle in Dark: COMINT and Soviet Industrial Secrets, 1946–1956* (Fort Meade, MD: Center for Cryptologic History, National Security Agency, 2017), 9.
3. Ibid.
4. Ibid.
5. "Jacob Gurin, 2007 Hall of Honor Induction," NSA Historical Figures, NSA.org.
6. Davis, *Candle in Dark*, 18, 24.
7. Ibid., 24.
8. In 1952, she joined NSA and later founded a linguistic unit to translate plaintext voice. She remained with the NSA until her retirement in 1963 but not before receiving a second Meritorious Civilian Service Award. She was inducted into the NSA cryptologic Hall of Honor in 2012. NSA.org.
9. Davis, *Candle in Dark*, 17–18.
10. Ibid., 18.
11. Ibid., 10.
12. Ibid., 13.

## Chapter 26

# The Big Stuff

During World War II, Oliver Kirby served as a US Army officer at Bletchley Park, the United Kingdom's code-breaking center located about forty miles north of London. At the end of the war, he became part of the joint US-UK Target Intelligence Committee as a member of one of the many small teams scouring newly liberated Germany for German communications equipment and personnel. Upon returning to the United States, he left the military and joined ASA, rising over the next twenty-five years to the position of deputy director of production for the NSA.

In June 1999, Kirby recounted many events and changes that occurred, knowing that most of them were still classified. So secret were the projects underway during 1947 and 1948, he could only refer to this period as the era of the "Big Stuff."[1]

With the war now over and the Soviet Union beginning to stir, both US and British code breakers began turning their attention to the idea of breaking Russian military and police communications. For some time, Russian messages had been streaming into Washington and London in ever-increasing numbers. By 1946 Arlington Hall was receiving what Stephen Budiansky called a "vast mountain" of unprocessed material on a daily basis.[2] They measured more than twenty thousand a month of mainly Russian military Morse code traffic. As cryptanalysts examined the dozens of code systems used by the Russian military, they found some of them readable albeit producing only intelligence of marginal value.

Among their discoveries were the use of Russian hand ciphers with additive keys drawn from reused codebooks, which posed little difficulty for Anglo and American code breakers. They also determined that Russia was hiding its most sensitive communications behind hard-to-crack machine-generated cipher systems. As this reality sank in, Allied cryptologic leaders now faced the crucial question, as Budiansky writes, "whether the still tedious and manpower intensive drudgery required in each case was worth it."[3]

What the Americans and British did not understand was how the Russian machines worked or what they looked like. Americans had originally pinned their hopes for success against high-level ciphers on the remarkable British wartime achievements against German reliance on a radio-enciphered teleprinter system for communicating its important information. The British called the German machines "Tunny" and "Sturgeon" (collectively "Fish"). As the war went on, they were able to build the strings of additive ciphers generated by these devices and then break into them using a specially built computer. Known as "Colossus," the revolutionary device successfully brute-forced matches of intercepted messages with strings of additive keys. Buoyed by the British success, Arlington Hall officials hoped to duplicate the accomplishment in the belief that the Russians may be using a similar system to the Germans. The idea was to build a supercomputer that would draw the curtain back on Russian troop dispositions, plans, and intentions.

For the Americans the first major hurdle was making sense of the internal process used by the Russians to transmit and receive messages. Russian communicators relied on a system called "multiplexing" that was designed to pack two and as many as nine messages on a single-channel radio. Research revealed that two-channel radios contained enciphered military and police material while several channels were made up of plaintext messages. Enciphered Russian two-channel systems used a form of Morse code called the Baudot system named after its inventor, the nineteenth century French cryptographer Emile Baudot. It permitted the interlacing of all the messages sent in a single stream. Author Stephen Budiansky compared it to a card dealer perfectly shuffling two decks of cards together. Adding to the dilemma was the extra wrinkle that the Russian version of the Baudot code had been converted into the Cyrillic alphabet.

The Russian system required a "multiplexor" at the origin to scramble the message and a "demultiplexer" at the receiving end that automatically separated out the signals using a rotating distributor. This ingenious device shunted each successive incoming message or bit onto a separate wire attached to its own printer. Amazingly, the Russians had perfected the system to such a degree that it was capable of simultaneously carrying as many as nine encrypted and plain-language messages simultaneously.

To further stymie enemies, the Russians added another ingenious feature. The operator shifted his keyboard carriage up for punctuation marks and numbers, then back down to letters, and then returned the type carriage back to the left side of the paper up a line and idle. Through an electrical arrangement involving rotating commutators, the proper sequence of pulses were transmitted when a character's key was struck on the keyboard. David Kahn offers the following example. The letter *a* is mark mark space space space. The figure shift *i* is space mark mark space space. At the receiving end, a demultiplexer with energized electromagnets converts the combination of pulses into the proper characters and prints them out. In punched paper, which was frequently used in teleprinters, marks were expressed by holes and spaces leaving the tape intact. To read the tape, metal fingers pushed through the holes making contact with the pulses. Where there was a space, the paper kept the finger from completing the circuit.[4]

Once the originator prepared the message by punching it on to a tape, the entire process was fully automatic. At the receiving end the paper tape filled with dots and dashes were fed into a reader with a printer spitting out the complete text. Anyone listening to the transmission over the airwaves heard only rapid continuous signals consisting of marks and spaces with marks represented by a small shift in frequency of the transmitter signal.

Relying initially on a handful of off-the-shelf "demultiplexers," the Americans set to work trying to break out the messages. As Stephen Budiansky writes, "keeping the demultiplexer's distributor turning in exact synchronization with incoming communications proved to be a maddeningly touchy business." So much so that frustrated navy and Arlington Hall leaders growing discouraged in the face of increasing personnel shortages began viewing the cryptanalytic challenges as a "colossal" waste of time. One young army officer pressing for more attention to the effort was told that it was pointless throwing more money and time on a project that only added to the "growing stack of unprocessed intercepts."[5]

But there were weaknesses in the Russian system that the Americans had overlooked. And once again the code breakers of Arlington Hall and Nebraska Avenue turned to the past for answers. This time it was TICOM material that came to the rescue. During a foray across Germany after the war, one American TICOM team learned that Wehrmacht soldiers were observed dropping a strange collection of crates and boxes into Lake Schliersee in Bavaria. Orders were issued to search the bottom and after several futile days, divers spotted what they were looking for. Salvage experts were soon pulling up crate after wooden crate, a total of four tons of documents. What they had discovered was the complete German high-command Cipher Bureau archives in excellent condition. The cache was quickly flown to an airfield outside London where they were taken to waiting analysts at Bletchley Park.

Around that same time another TICOM team had arrived in Rosenheim, Germany, where they unearthed eight tons of radio-intercept equipment. Among the haul was a Hartmehrfachternschreiber (HMFS). It was a demultiplexer that worked by inserting different distributors that could separate out from two to nine multiplexed channels. Budiansky called it an "extremely sophisticated piece of equipment."[6]

Seventh Army intelligence officers soon added to the treasure trove after learning that an obscure officer with some special talents was among tens of thousands of German prisoners of war cooling their heels behind barbed-wire fences. Unteroffizier Erich Kartenberg was born into a wealthy family of German merchants. Before the war he had spent many childhood years living in the Soviet Union, where he learned to speak Russian. Growing up he developed an interest in music, leading him to a career as both a concert pianist and lecturer on art history at the University of Berlin. Kartenberg also possessed a highly refined gift for mathematics; a talent that made him ideal for code-breaking. Like the four tons of documents and radio-intercept equipment, he too was hustled off to England where a team of Bletchley Park questioners awaited him. For weeks he poured out everything he knew to interrogators about German success at reading Russian encrypted communications.

Kartenberg described Red Army radio networks, call-sign and contact routines, and encipherment systems used in radio teleprinter traffic. German research had deduced that there was a considerable amount of text on two-channel circuits enciphered by a sophisticated online device using a bank of cipher wheels that generated a stream of continually changing key that was automatically added to the Baudot code of each character as it was transmitted to produce the outgoing cipher text. The wheels advanced automatically in step with the outgoing or incoming text. Once the wheels at each end were properly aligned, the entire encryption and decryption process was "invisible and seamless."[7]

These debriefings went a long way toward Allied understanding of the weaknesses in "Bandwurm," the German code word for Russian communications. There was frequent Russian operator "chat" and careless handling of message setup procedures. Another "gaping insecurity" was the inclusion of standard preambles and addresses within enciphered portions of messages, causing highly predictable stereotyped openings that were often identical from one message to another. Kartenberg described how Russian transmitters and receivers were often out of sync; a mechanical flaw that often required retransmission of messages, resulting in large chunks of duplicated plain-text being enciphered. Even without cracking the key-generating algorithm, Kartenberg explained, German code breakers, using informed guesswork, often surfaced a message content. Eventually they were able to read Russian front headquarters messages to Moscow revealing troop positions and situations, transfer orders and promotion of officers along with signal intelligence data, intelligence the Russians had learned from POW interrogations, and other information of intelligence value.

The British referring to Bandwurm as "Caviar" and the Americans calling it "Longfellow" ("Longfellow" was soon settled on as the code word on both sides of the Atlantic) began a concerted effort to recover long stretches of Russian key as had been done against the German *Enigma* cipher machine during the war. The main problem besides a shortage of manpower was insufficient intercepted traffic to work from. The navy gave voice to this frustration in a war diary entry the following spring noting that work was going slowly—"The greatest need is longer key which is only available for reading in-depth." The HMFS demultiplexers had saved six to nine months' work that would have otherwise been spent designing and building equally advanced devices. But their numbers, amounting to ten to fifteen in Europe and three or four in the Far East, were insufficient to provide complete coverage of Soviet teleprinter networks. At best they could only do spot checks.[8]

War Department funding for new projects was scarce after the war in the face of fiscal retrenchment. So, it took the better part of a year before the pleas of cryptanalysts for adequate machinery to fully cover teleprinter traffic was finally heard. Facing mounting pressure, the army and navy finally agreed to budget $200,000 ($2,500,000 in February 2023) for the manufacture of new demultiplexers to attack Russian communications.[9]

The goal was to deduce Longfellow's key-generation algorithm using powerful computational machinery that could slide every possible sequence of key against a received message text and test for statistical evidence of a likely match. With such a complete system any message, not just a small percentage that happened to be in-depth, could be read consistently.

The British were able to report a "rapid advance" in early 1947 on Longfellow, but it was still not possible to break all the traffic. Doing so hinged on the construction of a planned "suprebombe" that would be able to statistically match each message with its encipherment key, allowing continuous reading of the Longfellow messages. But building a supercomputer, especially in the pre-computer age of the 1940s, at a cost of $1,000,000 ($13,900,000 in January 2023) was an "ambitious gamble." It would require calculating and logic circuits built around forty thousand vacuum tubes; more than twice the number contained in any pioneering digital computers then under development in the United States and Britain.[10]

The leader of the new multiplexers and "Hiawatha," code name for the supercomputer project, was Mitford M. Mathews—"Mit" to his friends and colleagues. Born in Alabama in 1922, Mathews graduated with a degree in mathematics from the University of Illinois with honors at age twenty-one. After receiving a US Army commission, he was assigned to the Research & Development Division at Arlington Hall, where he worked from 1944 to 1946. For his scientific and engineering accomplishments, he was awarded the Legion of Merit. Following his military discharge in 1946, he joined ASA as a civilian engineer. Mathews was quickly tagged as a leader who transitioned World War II rotor-based equipment to high-tech electronic devices and ciphony hardware. In later years his efforts transformed NSA's fundamental processing of radar signals from analog to digital.[11]

Mathews soon found himself in charge of a small army of "In House" specialists crammed along the halls of the basement under Arlington Hall's cafeteria to prevent leaks to outside vendors and exposing what was underway. This setup made it easy for Weisband to casually walk along and observe the progress without arousing any suspicion while chatting with the technicians building the devices.

The new machines were designed to replace the limited number of German systems then in use. As these devices became more available in larger numbers, they were distributed to twenty-six collection stations in the United States and overseas. As the program advanced, both British and American officials agreed to balance collection responsibilities with British focusing on European Russia and the Americans pointing their antennas toward the Soviet Far East. Bletchley Park, which came into its own in 1947 as Government Communications Headquarters, had major listening sites at Cheadle and Scarborough in England as well as in Germany, Cyprus, Malta, and Jerusalem and as far away as Masirah Island in the Indian Ocean.[12]

Mr. Herbert Conley, who had served on the Special US Liaison Office (SUSLO) staff in London in 1947, and by late 1948 was an ASA supervisor involved in analysis and reporting of Soviet targets, assessed the Anglo-American strides made in collection and forwarding. He spoke about advances in collection, analysis, and reporting. First, improvements on recent intercept capability and the continued buildup of intercept strength made it possible by the summer of 1948 to begin to capture Russian operational or low-level military and military air circuits in certain areas. "The intercept and analysis of such links has been increased during the past few months, with emphasis being accelerated as the Russians have reduced transmission! Operational air links employing radio-telephone transmissions have not been intercepted regularly but the cover of Morse links is extensive." Then Conley pointed out how forwarding to ASA of selected intercept had been made timely by December 1948. "At the present rate, Army Security Agency, Washington, is receiving daily by teletype all air defense and operational air traffic at U.S. Station (Blank) Information on flights of Russian planes in few hours after the flight has been scheduled."[13]

After more than seventy-five years, all the details of this project remain classified. Yet what we can discern is that by the end of 1947 the United States and Britain were making significant progress in reading enciphered Russian military, police, leadership, and gulag communications on real-time basis with Weisband at the center of it all.[14]

## NOTES

1. Kirby Oral History.
2. Budiansky, *Code Warriors*, 58–59. Ibid., 60.
3. Ibid., 51.
4. Kahn, *The Codebreakers*, 395.
5. Budiansky, *Code Warriors*, 94.
6. Ibid., 56.
7. Ibid.
8. Ibid., 60.
9. Ibid.
10. Ibid., 61.
11. Mitford Mathews was a 2002 NSA Hall of Honor Inductee. From 1962 until his death in 1971, he was the assistant director for Research and Development. NSA Historical Figures, NSA.gov.
12. Budiansky, *Code Warriors*, 61.
13. Michael L. Peterson, *Bourbon to Black Friday, The Allied Collaborative COMINT Effort against the Soviet Union, 1945–1948* (Fort Meade, MD: Center for Cryptologic History, Vol. 2, Series V, National Security Agency, 1995), 88. NSA Doc #4314635.
14. Benson, author interview, June 25, 2023.

*Chapter 27*

# The Jewels in the Amber

Every day, Bill Weisband sat at his table closely watching a very strange figure quietly going about his work just a few feet away. His tall, lanky six-foot-plus frame stood out noticeably in the bullpen-like space that made up the ultra-secret Bourbon Program. The mystery man buried deep in a desk full of papers and books spoke to hardly anyone, and when he did it was brief and only out of absolutely necessity. For those sitting around him his manner suggested an aloofness or a haughtiness. A closer look, however, revealed a rare creature living in a self-made world. "He wasn't interested in what anyone had to say," one biographer wrote. "What was going on [in] his mind was good enough for him."[1]

\* \* \*

Meredith Knox Gardner began life in 1912 in the tiny town of Okolona, Mississippi. His childhood was spent in a Texas boardinghouse managed by his widowed mother. As a kid, he earned his keep by delivering mail and newspapers to tenants' rooms. Legend has it that one day he handled a newspaper with writing he had never seen. Before long, he was immersing himself in the study of the Yiddish language. That epiphany moment launched young Meredith on a lifelong love affair with foreign tongues. By the time he died at age ninety, he had mastered twelve languages.

Gardner's journey to Arlington Hall began at the University of Texas, where he spent six years earning undergraduate and graduate degrees in German studies. Next came the University of Wisconsin in pursuit of a doctorate. Cutting short his studies, he took a job in Ohio at the University of Akron teaching Spanish and German. One day at the start of the war, a dean approached him with a proposal. The army, now desperate for linguists with Gardner's skills, believed he could make an important contribution to the war effort. With no hesitation, he abandoned Akron for a new mission at Arlington Hall. Just a year later he was thrown into the Japanese Section to attack the complexities of Military Attaché ciphers. Under the tutelage of senior linguist Edwin O. Reischauer and much self-study, Gardner mastered the mysteries of the Japanese language and digraphs in a matter of months.[2]

After three years at Arlington Hall, Gardner had emerged from the pack as a man with rare qualities. Cryptanalysis and linguistics are two very different skill sets, both essential for successful code-breaking. It is difficult enough for a cryptanalyst to spend hours, days, and even months picking apart ciphers made up of seemingly endless lines of unintelligible numbers. Equally frustrating for a nearby linguist is trying to discern the meaning of a foreign word, or partial word, that appeared from behind these numbers. Gardner uniquely possessed both skills. Adding further to his already impressive resume was a mastery of the Russian language, which he had picked up through private lessons from the grandmother of a fellow student at the University of Texas.[3] He joined the Bourbon Program in October 1945, just two months after the war ended. His membership came at the suggestion of Dr. Waldo Dubberstein and Bill Smith, an original head of the unit.

Gardner became a Bourbon team member in January 1946 on a full-time basis. For the first few months, he concentrated on Trade Ministry messages until one day he overheard some analysts talking about a system called JADE. When he inquired about it, he learned that it referred to "Russian secret police" messages. JADE was considered too tough to crack and, as such, was largely ignored in favor of Trade and Consular traffic, which were deemed more exploitable.[4]

Turning fresh attention to JADE, Gardner began hunting for code names. Every four-digit code number hidden behind a cipher number had a specific meaning. What he was trying to do, in effect, was to construct a Russian dictionary of numbers and corresponding words that he had never seen. He knew from Frank Rowlett's interviews of Igor Gouzenko a year earlier that GRU and KGB code clerks used such a dictionary to encode and decode messages. By gradually building his own, Gardner believed that he could more easily make headway into KGB messages and expose their secrets.

As he later told an interviewer, he started with "easy to identify common words such as prepositions and conjunctions." From there he fanned out and, relying on his knowledge of linguistics combined with basic instincts and informed guesses, he tried to determine what word would logically follow a certain word. In this way he slowly began building a vocabulary of Russian nouns and verbs. Typical among them was the Russian word "dubok" (meaning "hiding place") and American words like "roof" (meaning a "front to conceal an espionage operation"), "shoemaker" ("passport forger"), "nash" ("he works for us"), and so forth.

As he delved further into the structure of the messages, he made an important discovery. The Cyrillic language used a subcode to form English letters.

*The Jewels in the Amber*

This allowed him to spell out certain proper names. It was a huge leap forward that eventually led to the discovery of "code names." Gardner found, for instance, that President Roosevelt's code name was KAPITAN, New York City was TYRE, San Francisco was BABYLON, and ISLAND meant Great Britain. The work was a tedious trial-and-error process dealing not only with the frustration of words and meanings, but the complexities of Russian punctuation as well. Despite Gardner's confidence in the growing number of nouns and verbs and code names he was producing, they often remained, as one study put it, a "best guess" until they could be confirmed through testing against other messages.[5]

It took a year of painstaking effort examining thousands of catalogued diplomatic messages until finally on December 20, 1946, a break was made that suddenly caught everyone's attention. It was a KGB message sent from New York to Moscow nearly two years earlier. It read:

> [someone]enumerates [the following] scientists who are working on the problem—Hans Bethe, Niels Bohr, Enrico Fermi, John Newman, Bruno Rossi, George Kistiakowski, Emilio Segre, G. I. Taylor, William Penny, Arthur Compton, Ernest Lawrence, Harold Urey, Hans Stanarm, Edward Teller, Percy Bridgeman, Werner Eisenberg, Strassenman.[6]

The "problem" mentioned in the message was the top-secret development of the atomic bomb and these were the names of the key physicists and mathematicians working on it.

Months later, in the spring of 1947, two more breaks occurred in rapid succession that sent further shivers through War Department ranks. One was a December 1944 New York KGB message to VIKTOR (VIKTOR was code name for Pavel Fitin, head of foreign intelligence for KGB) in Moscow mentioning receipt of a report from ROBERT prepared for the Army General Staff. The message carrying the title "Postwar Troop Basis of The War Department" was identified as a top-secret list of troop strength facts and figures. The author of the message was an unknown KGB officer, code name "MAJ." Adding to army jitters was a second message sent that same month quoting a second top-secret document entitled "War Department Troop Deployment 1 October 1944." It originated in the Operations Division of the General Staff and was handed over to the KGB by a second source, code-named PILOT.[7] The discovery of the code names was no surprise. Gardner expected to find them based on Gouzenko's information. But who were VIKTOR, MAJ, PILOT, ROBERT?

As May turned into June 1947, Weisband and the Russian Unit directed their full attention to KGB diplomatic traffic. By then Gardner had accumulated a list of twenty-two code names with twenty of them coming from the New York to Moscow link. Along with these new finds, he also started a second list of true names from messages much like the scientists listed in the December 20, 1944, atomic bomb message. Gardner's frustration over G2 handling of his discoveries soon began to bubble over. In a memo to his now panicked bosses, Gardner cautioned against making false assumptions based on the code names, due in large measure to the "inherent cryptanalysis difficulties" resulting in "fragmentary and incomplete" findings.[8]

For the Russian Unit and Weisband, the summer of 1947 was a busy period. Gardner's hard work was beginning to produce evidence of widespread KGB espionage penetration of the War Department and other government agencies. In an outline of the code names prepared in July 1947, Gardner wrote that the entire Russian Unit was then "currently undertaking a careful search for [code names] and the names of possible agents." The full enormity of what he was producing was becoming crystal clear "as it probably had been since the atomic scientists message translation of 20 December 1946."[9]

As Gardner made greater inroads, a worried Weisband began taking a keen interest in his work. Meredith remembered him as he frequently strolled by looking "over my shoulder as I was [breaking out] a message," trying to engage him in conversation with generous offers of translation assistance on particularly difficult words. The sudden attention he showed was due to a growing terror at the thought that his name may suddenly appear in one of the messages.[10]

As Gardner's successes grew, the looming question for ASA leadership was what to do with them. The frustration was that in almost every case there was no way of determining the true identities behind the code names. At the end of July, Frank Rowlett warned Waldo Dubberstein that Gardner's discoveries, while shocking, were too sensitive to share with anyone. Instead, they should be held tightly by Gardner and remain within the strict confines of the Russian Unit. If any distribution was necessary, he recommended that only Army G2 should receive it with a proviso that "no action will be taken on it or the information contained therein."[11]

"The sensational nature of the material was now apparent." Dubberstein and his boss, Oliver Kirby, not knowing what to do and having no experience with such matters, ordered Gardner to "carefully control internal access" while Colonel Hayes, head of ASA, and Weisband's friend, did the same concerning dissemination outside of ASA. Until a proper system of distribution could be developed, Hayes opted to retain all information in his office.

*  *  *

It was then that Colonel Carter Clarke stepped in to set things on a correct course. As head of Army G2, he was steeped in the intelligence business and fully grasped the need for secrecy. At the same time, however, he also understood that collecting more and more code names without trying to determine true identities was worthless. This was particularly so due to the distinct possibility that many of these spies might still be in position to do continuing harm. Clarke soon put things on a "right course" by ordering ASA to create some type of sharing arrangement. Backing Clarke was General Omar Bradley, the army chief of staff, who instructed Hayes to confine distribution only to G2 and FBI.[12] Clarke's next move was to reach out to the FBI in July or August 1947. His call went to an old friend, Special Agent S. Wesley Reynolds, the FBI's liaison man with G2.

Reynolds was born in 1914 in Calabash, a sleepy fishing village dating from 1691, nestled along the Outer Banks of North Carolina. After high school he headed north to Colgate University in the equally tiny town of Hamilton, New York. For a time, he practiced law in Calabash after completing St. Johns Law School in New York. Many years later he would earn an MBA from Harvard University. In 1941, he joined the FBI as a Special Agent and, after a brief tour in New Orleans, he returned to Washington to assume liaison duties with Army G2.[13]

Reynolds knew Clarke well. The two men were on friendly terms having closely worked together since the start of the war. Most importantly, they trusted each other's judgment and discretion. During the war Reynold met frequently with Clarke as well as assistant chiefs of staff for intelligence George V. Strong and Clayton Bissell. Their relationship allowed Reynolds regular entry to the situation room of the Army General Staff and for J. Edgar Hoover's access to daily "eyes only" military situation reports.

Clarke briefed Reynolds on Gardner's work, now called "BRIDE," and the success he was having with KGB messages. Then he explained the futility of producing them with no way to determine the true identities. Clarke appealed for any help the FBI could offer through its own investigations. Reynolds quickly briefed Mickey Ladd, head of the Bureau's National Defense Division, who, in turn, got a go-ahead from J. Edgar Hoover for the start of a new and unique cooperative venture. A thorough search was ordered of FBI records for anything that could in any way assist ASA in its work. Hoping for a few scraps, Reynolds delivered more than two hundred "cover names" to Clarke over the weeks that followed. The list was an amalgam that originated from interrogations of former KGB and GRU agents including Elizabeth Bentley, Igor Gouzenko, Whittaker Chambers, as well as British sources and

Walter Krivitsky, a KGB colonel who made his way to the United States after his defection in Europe in the late 1930s.

\* \* \*

The conundrum facing the new ASA/FBI partnership was a simple one; code names and cover names were completely different. Both the KGB and the GRU, in strict adherence to the rules of *konspiratsiia*, used a complicated security system requiring layers of false names to protect their officers and agents from exposure. For example, one agent using the cover name "Tom" handles another agent known to him only by the cover name "John." Tom receives secret documents from John for delivery to a KGB officer who he knows only as "Jim." From there Jim forwards the package of documents to Moscow through the diplomatic courier system. Jim then sends an encrypted message to Moscow Center referring to himself as "Fred" or "Joe" for Tom, "cryptonyms" that his KGB bosses had assigned to them for transmittal of top-secret radio messages. When properly used the system is foolproof. In essence, the FBI had produced the street cover names Jim, John, and Tom while ASA uncovered "Fred," "Joe," "Tyre," "Kapitan," and dozens of other code names used only in radio communications. It quickly became apparent that the information Reynolds had produced was of no value to Gardner and his growing team of assistants. What it did demonstrate, however, was FBI seriousness for a closer working relationship with ASA.

The situation remained static for several months with Reynolds ferrying ever-growing lists of cover names to Arlington Hall and returning with new code names to Bureau headquarters. As the FBI-ASA relationship dragged on during the summer of 1947, a frustrated Rowlett took the bold step of asking Reynolds for copies of Elizabeth Bentley's secret testimony before a special grand jury established to investigate her charges. He also requested transcripts of House Committee on Un-American Activities hearings on subversion and espionage during the Roosevelt years. Rowlett emphasized to Colonel Hayes the importance of such information in helping to uncover clues to Russian intelligence activities, noting that "any external material on the same subject is of potential value in recovering code text and codebook values in this system." Ignoring Federal rules prohibiting release of grand jury testimony, Reynolds secretly delivered the material to Clarke.[14]

After a time, Reynolds concluded that the exchange arrangement between cryptanalysts and investigators who neither knew nor spoke with each other was unacceptable for the growing task at hand. Together with Clarke, Hayes, and Rowlett, Reynolds agreed that what was needed was a full-time project with an experienced FBI agent working side by side with Gardner. Approval was quickly secured from Ladd and the candidate chosen for the assignment was Robert L. Lamphere, a new agent classmate of Reynolds. As history later recorded—this decision would spark "one of the most remarkable partnerships in intelligence history."[15]

\* \* \*

Lamphere's family roots ran deep in America's history, going back to original seventeenth-century settlers of Westerly, Rhode Island. One of Bob's grandfathers lost his arm fighting with Union forces in the Civil War. After the war he became chief administrator for the Treasury Department and later moved to Minnesota for a career in the newspaper business.

Born the second of three children in Coeur d'Alene, Idaho, Bob grew up in the small mining town of Mullen, Idaho, where his father scraped out a living hiring miners to dig silver, zinc, and lead ore from mines he leased. As a kid, Bob learned firsthand the value of brutally hard work in deep underground darkness and the need for quick reliance on his fists in scrapes with rowdy miners.

Following his mother's death in 1940 and with his father's health declining, he made a choice to ease the family's financial strain by striking out on his own. He was soon in Washington, DC, working as a government auditor while studying law at George Washington University. Just months before America entered the war, Bob passed the bar exam and joined fifty other recruits in a new agent class for the FBI.

Next came a year in Huntsville, Alabama, for some experience investigating general criminal matters. From there he moved again, this time to New York City, the FBI's largest office. For a time, he chased draft dodgers and military deserters through streets and alleys of New York City while taking full advantage of the nightlife afforded by the city. Eventually, he was reassigned to the Soviet espionage squad, where he spent the next four years studying GRU and KGB tactics through long and often tedious hours surveilling Russian officials.

The fall of 1945 became a busy time for the Soviet squad in New York. In September it was inundated with fresh intelligence pouring in from Igor Gouzenko in Canada about widespread GRU espionage across North America. Two months later the squad faced even more work from Elizabeth Bentley's daily identification of spies she had been handling since before the war.

For Bob, it was a particularly hectic period. After the war he was assigned a case that would consume him for the next two years. To look at Gerhart Eisler one saw only a short, round, balding little man rapidly approaching fifty years old. He was an inconspicuous figure who lived quietly with his wife in a modest walk-up apartment in Long Island City. Lamphere thought he looked like a "bookkeeper." In fact, he was the "Number One Communist in the U.S."[16]

Eisler landed in New York in 1941 and was now planning his return to Europe. To do so, he was required to fill out an application for an exit visa. Upon close examination, Lamphere found that Eisler had made a number of false entries. In the heightened anti-communist atmosphere that was spreading across the nation, the investigation continued until March 1947 when Eisler was compelled to appear before an Alien Review Board. Under intense questioning more lies came out, which soon led to his indictment. After a brief trial in Washington, Eisler was found guilty of making false statements. Bob later called the Eisler conviction "the first major case in the United States to involve an International Communist figure."[17]

During the trial, Bob gave daily briefings to Bill Harvey, an FBI agent at headquarters monitoring the proceedings. It was from these discussions with Harvey and others that Lamphere decided to leave New York for a promotion to Washington.

\* \* \*

During the early fall of 1947 as Weisband continued to monitor Gardner's growing list of code names, Lamphere arrived in Washington to take up new duties in the Espionage Section at FBI headquarters. His first assignment was a disappointment. With Russia's new satellite states setting up embassies and consulates around the country, Bob's job was the management of new FBI counterintelligence coverage. Unhappy and anxious to return to Russian work, he prevailed upon Pat Coyne, his section chief, to allow him to explore the fragmentary and largely ignored messages that were starting to dribble in from Arlington Hall.[18]

Around this same time Reynolds approached Ladd with the new ASA partnership proposal. After a quick approval, Lamphere received the assignment. Over the next few months Reynolds and Lamphere made several visits to Arlington Hall conferring with senior staff and working out the details of this new and unprecedented working arrangement. After careful consideration an operating agreement was reached. First, the project was top-secret, which meant that it would remain tightly held within ASA and the FBI. It could not be spoken about, nor even hinted at in any way. It could be shared only with FBI officials holding top-secret clearances regardless of their rank. All communications within the FBI system would be subject to strict document control and had to be sent to field offices by teletype. Internal correspondence could include no quotes from deciphered cables nor any mention of code-breaking or Arlington Hall. Instead, they would contain only the preamble "a confidential source who has provided reliable information in the past has advised" with no quotes from the messages included.[19]

As final arrangements got underway, Lamphere sensed that he was on the brink of something momentous. Years later, reflecting back on that time, he summed up his feelings on what he was about to embark on.

> I stood in the vestibule of the enemy's house, having entered by stealth. I held in my hand a set of keys. Each would fit one of the doors of the place and lead us, I hoped, to matters of importance to our country. I had no idea where the corridors to the KGB's edifice would take us, or what we would find when we reached the end of our search—but the keys were ours, and we were determined to use them.[20]

Lamphere was a thirty-year-old street guy most comfortable chasing hoods and thugs up and down stairways and through seedy bars. He had never dealt with a cryptanalyst. As such, before meeting Meredith Gardner, Frank Rowlett thought it best to warn the already uneasy FBI man about what to expect. "He's unusual and brilliant. He speaks six or seven languages" and was one of the "few western scholars who reads Sanskrit." As if that wasn't intimidating enough, Rowlett described Bob's new partner as a "shy, introverted loner." His final warning to the FBI man—"you'll have a hard time getting to know him."[21]

As expected, progress began at a crawl. One was outgoing, gregarious, not afraid to use his fists, and eager to find some way to exploit this new and historic partnership. The other, guarded, seemingly indifferent, and reluctant to discuss anything about his work. It was an awkward start.

Until one day when Gardner grudgingly posed a question that would change everything. As Lamphere sat quietly listening, Meredith explained how he worked. Every day for a year and a half since joining the Bourbon Program, he sat before a string of unintelligible numbers struggling to find an actual message. In all that time, however, he had never seen an actual KGB message. In passing, he asked his FBI partner if he could locate a plaintext message that had not yet been enciphered. A discouraged Lamphere explained that he "didn't hold out much hope" but would do what he could. Without explaining why, he asked the New York office for help. To his amazement, a package appeared on his desk a week later. When he opened it, he found stacks of plaintext messages that had been secretly photographed by FBI agents in 1944 during a break-in of Amtorg. Two weeks after delivering the material to Arlington Hall, Lamphere was greeted by a completely changed man. "I found Gardner in the most excited mood I'd ever seen him display." In his shy way, he beamed, saying simply—we had "hit the jackpot."[22]

It was a "bonanza." One that now permitted Gardner to compare enciphered traffic against unenciphered plaintext messages.[23] Lamphere later called it an "important new phase in the breakthrough." Within weeks Gardner, using his new supply of FBI-produced messages as cribs, gradually began deciphering complete messages and fragments of others at a more rapid pace. KGB and GRU plaintext messages soon began arriving weekly at the FBI. "As the messages became more readable," Lamphere later wrote, "I could set in motion investigations based on what they said."[24]

The Gardner-Lamphere team would produce spectacular results over the next three years. For the FBI, it would turn out to be the most important counterintelligence investigation in its forty-year existence. Code names such as "Liberal," "Osa," and "Wasp" would produce the arrests and convictions of Julius Rosenberg, his wife Ethel, and David Greenglass, Ethel's brother. "Ales" was found to be the GRU agent Alger Hiss, a former State Department official and later head of the Carnegie Endowment for International Peace. The "BRIDE" project, later renamed "Venona," over time produced the names of nearly one hundred and fifty Americans spies, many positioned at the highest levels across the government.[25] Among them were Laughlin Currie, White House economic advisor to President Roosevelt, and assistant treasury secretary and director of the International Monetary Fund, Harry Dexter White. It would take Gardner another two decades before deciphering KGB messages reporting on, "Zveno (Link)," "Zhora," and "Vasin"—three KGB code names for Weisband, his Russian Unit colleague.[26] For the KGB and GRU it was the jewel trapped in the amber and, had they known about it, there was still nothing they could do to salvage the disaster.

The implications of the shattering breakthrough were not lost on Weisband. It was the fall of 1947 and Gardner was just starting to make inroads in his relentless quest for Russia's American spies. To make matters worse the FBI was now involved. He was in danger, and he knew it. But there was nothing he could do to stop it. All Weisband could do was to sit at his desk nervously watching Gardner silently working a few feet away from him—wondering if at any moment his name would suddenly appear from behind those jumbles of numbers.

But he had to do something—he somehow had to warn his KGB bosses.

## NOTES

1. Howard Blum, *In the Enemies House* (New York: HarperCollins Publishers, 2018), 28.
2. Year later Reischauer served as US ambassador to Japan. Robert Louis Benson, Venona Monograph, 69, NCM.
3. Ibid.
4. Benson, Venona Monograph, 82.

5. Benson, Venona Monograph, 41; Tug Youngren, *Secret Lies and Atomic Spies*, NOVA, Public Broadcasting, 2002.
6. Benson, Venona Monograph, 74.
7. Ibid.
8. Ibid. Waldo Dubberstein left the Army Security Agency for the newly formed Central Intelligence Agency. In 1983, while working for the Defense Intelligence Agency, he was indicted for passing classified documents to the Libyan government. On April 30, 1983, the date of his scheduled arraignment, he committed suicide in his Arlington, Virginia, apartment building. He was seventy-five years old. "Indicted Expert on Mideast Is Found Dead in Virginia," *New York Times*, April 30, 1983, 6.
9. Benson, *History of Venona*, 74.
10. Youngren, *Secret Lies and Atomic Spies*.
11. Benson, *History of Venona*, 75.
12. DOCID 3034869, 91, NCM, Fort Meade, Maryland.
13. Wesley Reynolds Obituary, *The Grapevine*, March 1997.
14. Benson, *Venona*, 82.
15. DOCID 3188691, NCM.
16. Robert J. Lamphere, *The FBI-KGB War* (New York: Random House, 1986), 42.
17. Ibid., 59.
18. Ibid., 31.
19. Ibid., 82.
20. Blum, *In the Enemy's House*, 114–15; Lamphere, *FBI-KGB War*, 86.
21. Blum, *In the Enemy's House*, 114.
22. Lamphere, *FBI-KGB Wars*, 85.
23. *The Soviet Problem*, 162, NSA, DOCID 3188619, *FBI-KGB War*, 85.
24. Lamphere, *FBI-KGB War*, 86.
25. Robert Louis Benson and Michael Warner, Ed., *Venona: Soviet Espionage and the American Response 1939–1957* (Washington, DC: National Security Agency and Central Intelligence Agency, 1996), vii–xiv.
26. VBN 17, 57, 84.

*Chapter 28*

# Strange Odyssey

Bill Weisband's mother, Sarah, had passed away in 1944, leaving behind the family's Brooklyn, New York, jewelry business, which she had operated alone since her husband's death in 1936. After Bill returned from Italy, it became common knowledge around Arlington Hall that he made periodic trips to New York for what he told everyone was settlement of his mother's estate, including her store inventory. Gradually, taking the jewelry from the now-defunct shop, Bill started his own side business as a jewelry salesman. Every day, Arlington Hall workers watched him as he roamed the hallways, getting to know everyone and displaying his products with offers of significant discount. How much he earned from his sales was never recorded nor questioned by his superiors. Yet, it certainly proved to be a useful tool for deflecting unwanted attention away from someone with so much cash engaged in sensitive intelligence work.

Bill never sought to hide his spending. In 1946, he bought a new Buick Roadster. A lot of his money was spent entertaining Mabel. Both of them enjoyed dancing and frequented dance halls in the area. On one occasion the couple won a rhumba competition. They were also regulars on the Washington nightclub scene. One in particular was the Neptune Room in the city center, where they drank and dined and made a point of catching the latest act passing through town. One evening they sat back and watched a performance by Edward Liberace, a young pianist who would later drop his first name and go on to a star-studded entertainment career.

Bill stopped at nothing to display his sophistication and wealth. He always sported a pinky ring centered with a large diamond. He and Mabel made frequent visits to New York City for weekend getaways staying at Manhattan hotels, dining at fine restaurants, then on to some swanky nightclub or a Broadway production.

Dot Runion was an occasional guest on some of these excursions. Bill hosted her once, along with Mabel and another friend for a "sightseeing" trip to New York City. The ladies were thrilled with their midtown hotel rooms, while he presumably stayed with his brother in Brooklyn. Runion remembered marveling at the fashions, the sights, dining at fancy restaurants, watching a Broadway play—all on Bill's nickel. Before returning home, they all went to Brooklyn for a visit with Mark, his brother, and Mark's wife, Edith. On another occasion the two women returned to New York again to watch the Easter Parade marching down Fifth Avenue. Many years later, Vonda Blackwell, Mabel's half sister, described one of Mabel's first visits back to Tennessee. She was more sophisticated, Blackwell remembered, donned in fine clothes and expensive jewelry. It was a world away from the Del Rio life she had left behind years earlier.[1]

Life was not all bliss for the couple. Both Mabel and Bill had hot tempers that could explode with only the slightest spark. Friends remembered frequent shouting matches infused with painful exchanges. For her part, Mabel often shot barbs at him laced with demeaning remarks, mainly about his lack of education. She went so far, on at least one occasion, to call him a "dumb Jew."[2]

Bill grimly took it until one day he hit his boiling point. One observer remembered the couple returning to his apartment one day in Arlington in a furious state. Mabel continued to mercilessly needle him until he finally lashed out. Without warning, he suddenly disappeared into his bedroom, emerging moments later brandishing a loaded 45-caliber pistol. For the next few minutes, he wildly waived the weapon at her until she finally calmed down. When later asked about his behavior, Weisband merely replied that he only wanted to "scare the hell out of her."[3]

* * *

Much of what we know about the Woody-Weisband relationship comes from Runion, who spent much time with both of them. Mabel lived with her family for four years while attending high school and they shared an apartment in Washington for another six before Mabel and Bill married. She saw him regularly when he visited Mabel and often double-dated with the couple.

Perhaps Runion's most intense experience with them occurred suddenly in August 1947. One day Mabel asked her to accompany Mabel and Bill on a cross-country road trip to the West Coast. Dorothy was surprised at the unexpected offer and approached it with concern. It would mean taking precious vacation time away from her job at Arlington Hall. Then there were the huge travel costs on her modest government salary and, most importantly, the uneasiness she felt traveling with them as a third wheel over such a long period of time. Despite voicing her concerns, Mabel kept up the pressure until Runion finally relented and agreed to go.

When she asked the purpose of such a lengthy trip, Bill gave Runion a strange response. He had recently bought the new Buick Roadster and now he suddenly wished to sell it. He had heard that cars on the West Coast were in short supply, he explained, kicking up resale prices and convincing him that he could easily sell the car "at a profit."[4] Weisband further touted the trip as a leisurely nationwide travel experience for Mabel and Dorothy, who had never been anywhere except North Carolina and Washington, DC. Within days, the three of them packed up and headed west.

Runion later recounted to investigators that from the start the westbound leg was nothing close to Bill's description. As they raced across the country, they stopped only for fuel, meals, and overnight rest at motels along the way and then were on the road again early the next morning. She found it strange that they never visited anyone from their wartime Arlington Hall days nor stopped even briefly at tourist sites along the way. Rather than a relaxed excursion, Bill drove with the intensity of a man in a hurry that surprised her. He seemed "extremely anxious" she recalled, "to get to the West Coast as soon as possible."[5]

Once across the California border, they headed straight for Los Angeles, where another surprise awaited Runion. Their first stop was the home of Vivian and Victor Cubarkin, old friends of both Weisband and Stanislav Shumovsky, aviation expert, KGB officer, and pre-war recruiter of Jones Orin York. The couple greeted the travelers warmly and invited them to stay in their home during the California visit. Runion quietly expressed her discomfort to Mabel at the thought of staying with strangers for such a long time period. Once again Bill quickly stepped in to assuage her concerns, encouraging the stay as a way of saving funds that would otherwise be spent on lodging and meals.

Another odd thought for Runion was Weisband's original rationale for the trip. Bill had insisted that the California trip was to find a buyer for his car. It never dawned on her at the time, but years later after Bill and Mabel fell under government suspicion of espionage it struck her. The morning after they arrived in Los Angeles and began their stay with the Cubarkins, Weisband left the house alone. "Two hours" later he returned, blithely announcing to everyone that he had failed to receive a price he wanted for the car.[6] Over the remainder of their stay not another word was mentioned about a car sale, nor did Weisband make any attempt to sell it.

Another strange moment occurred one day during an excursion south to Tijuana, Mexico. While en route back to Los Angeles through the outskirts of San Diego, Weisband stopped the car on the side of the road. He then got out alone, leaving the two women behind and claiming he wished to visit a friend. As suddenly as he had disappeared, twenty minutes later he reappeared and resumed the trip without explanation.

After a week with the Cubarkins, the trio headed home, but this time with Victor Cubarkin in tow. Vivian had begged off because she had to work. As for Victor, he told everyone that he was an old friend of Mark Weisband and Bill's deceased brother, Harold. He wanted to visit the East Coast and stay a few days in New York City catching up with Mark. In retrospect it seemed "unusual" to Runion that he joined them, particularly without his wife.[7]

The return leg of the journey was a polar opposite from the westbound trip. Weisband was relaxed and interested in stopping along the way. The four travelers left Los Angeles taking their leisurely time heading north along the California coast for a few days in San Francisco. Then it was back on the road again—this time following a northern route through Colorado and Utah, across the Great Plains, across the Missouri River, passing the route used by Meriwether Lewis and William Clark and their Corps of Discovery Expedition in 1803. On they went at an easy pace through Kansas and Nebraska to Illinois, stopping at Chicago for another few days of casual layover and more sightseeing. Then back on the road again, this time swinging north across the Canadian border and then turning east toward Niagara Falls and reentering the United States at Jamestown, New York, before returning to Washington.

While in Washington, Cubarkin stayed with Weisband. Bill never tried to hide their relationship. In fact, one evening Bill hosted an elaborate party at his apartment to, as Runion put it, "introduce Cubarkin to his friends at ASA."[8] Among the thirty or so guests in attendance were a number of "high officials" from Arlington Hall, including Maurice Klein, Waldo Dubberstein, and a large collection of colleagues from the Russia Section.

* * *

Runion was interviewed by the FBI when the case broke. Seven years after that fateful trip to California she spoke with NSA investigators as part of a reexamination of Bill and Mabel's time with ASA. In 1960, she gave another interview to NSA officials. By the time the third interview had been completed, thirteen years had elapsed since she took that fateful journey to California. Over that time, she continued working for NSA all the while pondering the full impact of the trip. In the end she concluded that Bill had lied to her. Even more devastating was the thought that Mabel, her closest friend in the world, may have lied to her as well. Weisband made the journey for some secret illegal purpose, and she had been used as a cover to hide his mission. As she conceded to investigators—in the end the car sale "had never been Weisband's intention."[9]

Within months of the trip the reason would reveal itself—but only to Weisband.

## NOTES

1. Author interview of Vonda Blackwell, October 20, 2020. NSA interview of Dorothy Runion, September 16, 1954. Robert Murray interview of Dorothy Runion, October 21 and 24, 1960. NSA FOIPA.
2. WFO Report, July 7, 1950, Weisband FBI file.
3. Cleveland teletype, July 23, 1950, Weisband FBI file.
4. Runion Interviews. NSA FOIPA.
5. Ibid.
6. Ibid.
7. Ibid.
8. Ibid.
9. Ibid.

*Chapter 29*

# Vladimir Arrives

Two weeks before Christmas in 1947, Americans across the country were busying themselves getting ready for the holidays. So, it was no surprise that the RMS *Mauretania* went unnoticed as she steamed up New York's Lower Bay through the Narrows and then with the aid of a small fleet of tugboats quietly slipped into a Manhattan berth along the Hudson River.

The great ship was a workhorse of the Cunard White Star Line, which had made numerous Atlantic crossings to America since first sailing from Liverpool in June 1939. At the start of World War II, she was redesignated HMT *Mauretania*. For the next six years, she saw constant military service carrying troops along with vital supplies destined for far-flung battle fronts. With the end of the war came a return to civilian service after a two-year refitting.[1]

On this voyage the ship carried a very special passenger. Stepping on to American shores for the first time was the man known in KGB circles as "Vladimir." It was a secret cryptonym, assigned a decade earlier to one of Moscow's most talented, experienced, and resourceful intelligence officers.[2] At age forty-two, he had arrived to take up new duties as Josef Stalin's ambassador to Washington.

\* \* \*

He was Alexander Semyonovich Panyushkin. Born into a working-class family on August 2, 1905, in Samara, a city located in European Russia, Panyushkin joined the Red Army at age fifteen and for the next year fought on several fronts during the Russian civil war.

What followed next came in rapid succession. He was assigned to a Border Guard detachment along the Soviet-Chinese frontier after completing cavalry school. At age twenty-two came advancement to director of a border patrol post followed by a second promotion; this time as a district patrol commander with the KGB's 99th Maritime Cavalry Detachment.

In May 1935, he was picked for a three-year course of study as a military officer at the prestigious Mikhail Frunze Military Academy in Moscow. Four years later, with extended service already in the Far East and a mastery of the Chinese language, he was appointed a brigadier commander and membership in the KGB as a foreign intelligence officer. Soon came a new appointment as a deputy director of a section and later as a department head.

Panyushkin came of age during a perilous time for Russia's intelligence services. Starting in the middle of the 1930s, Stalin's paranoia burst full force with the opening round of purges that would last for the rest of the decade. Through a series of show trials, he eliminated his chief political rivals by forcing them to publicly incriminate colleagues and falsely admit treason against the state followed by almost daily executions. Next came the extermination of the cream of Russia's military establishment as one general and colonel after another faced a similar fate. The instrument of Stalin's terror was the KGB, which, after their bloody work was done, saw its officers steadily disappear.

Panyushkin was part of the next generation of intelligence officers rapidly brought up to fill the void left behind by Stalin's terror. Others like Pavel Fitin, educated in agriculture, who joined the KGB in 1939, found himself a lieutenant general two years later heading the foreign espionage directorate. Others included twenty-seven-year-old Anatoli Yatzkov, who was dispatched to the Russian consulate in New York, where he helped steal the secrets of the atomic bomb. And of course, there was Alexander Feklisov, Bill Weisband's initial contact after his return from North Africa.

By 1939, Panyushkin, just thirty-four years old, had a military education, training in the art of espionage, nearly a decade of experience dealing with Chinese matters, and command of the language. Equipped with such impressive credentials, Panyushkin was transferred to the diplomatic service and promptly dispatched to Chuntsin, China, where he took over duties as plenipotentiary of the Soviet Peoples Committee on the Implementation of the Soviet-Chinese Trade Agreement. And in another rare move, certainly related to Stalin's purge of the KGB, he was named chief resident for foreign intelligence.

\* \* \*

Panyushkin delivered his credentials to the president of China, Lin Senu, on September 1, 1939, the same day Hitler's forces invaded Poland. He would spend much of the next five years in Chuntsin, an important Russian eavesdropping center against Japan and a base for extensive operations against the West. The city also sat in the middle of an active war zone facing Japanese air attacks on a regular basis. His orders were to do everything possible to keep the Chinese government fighting in order to pin down Japanese forces as a way of reducing the chances of a surprise attack against the Soviet Union.

Rising so high and so rapidly in Stalin's Orwellian world certainly suggests that Panyushkin had developed a powerful ego. Yet images of him left behind point to something altogether different. Peter Deriabin was a KGB officer who knew him well. He remembered a tall man, lean, and unpretentious who walked in a stooped-over manner. Deriabin surmised that this was probably due to the weight of responsibility that he had carried from such young age. He exhibited a rather bland appearance with a gray, almost unhealthy, pallor that blended with the gray suits that he always wore. There was always an affable and disarming charm about him suggesting easy approachability. Yet this sense of openness masked a certain ruthlessness that required fellow officers and subordinates to maintain a constant vigilance.[3]

Not everyone shared Deriabin's assessment of Panyushkin. Pavel Sudoplatov was a long-time senior intelligence officer with considerable operational experience. During World War II, he was put in charge of a very secret unit designated only as "Special Tasks" within the already secret KGB. It was charged with eliminating Stalin's enemies, with the word "Special" referring, in his words, to "blood, poison and terrorism." Chief among his successes was the assassination of Stalin's bitter rival, Leon Trotsky. To eliminate Trotsky, Sudoplatov used a young Spanish Marxist, Ramon Mercader, to murder him with an ice axe to his head. Sudoplatov later took a very critical view of Panyushkin, dismissively describing him as "an overconfident bureaucrat who had not acquired any competence in intelligence operations."[4]

Years later a Russian history of the KGB described Panyushkin's own bewilderment at his meteoric rise. In an interview for the history, he still marveled at the arc of his career, explaining how "border service is so far from diplomacy and intelligence." Despite the views of his colleagues, Russian historians later looked back favorably on him. He possessed a "brilliant memory," and an uncanny ability, one of them wrote, which made him capable of distinguishing through the dark, murky waters of spying a "fish-eye from a gem."[5]

In the end, however, only Stalin's opinion mattered. Five years after arriving in China, Panyushkin returned to Moscow, where the prestigious Order of Lenin medal awaited him. Over the next three years he stayed focused on China until Stalin ordered him to return to Moscow to begin a concentrated course of study of the English language.

*　*　*

Closely watching from the Kremlin was Vyacheslav Molotov, Stalin's long-time foreign minister and advisor. The new ambassador, he knew, faced a monumental challenge whose success would be crucial for Soviet foreign policy for years to come.

By the end of 1947, the Big Three wartime alliance that defeated fascism had collapsed. The new enemy was Stalin, who had revealed his true colors over the two years since the end of World War II. First was the Russian leader's violations of his wartime promises guaranteeing free elections in European countries controlled by the Red Army. KGB operatives backed by Soviet troops ensured that Moscow lackies eager to do Stalin's bidding were installed in sham elections. Already weakened from the war, Greece was collapsing amidst a communist-backed civil war. Great Britain, long a backer of Greece, had informed a shocked Washington that the nation was broke and would have to end further financial help for Greece. Following an emergency appeal to Congress, the Truman administration began rushing military aid to the Greek government.

January saw General George Marshall, fresh off his failed diplomatic mission to China, confirmed by the Senate as President Truman's new secretary of state, replacing James Byrnes. Five months later, the Harvard University president, James Conant, invited Marshall to visit the school and deliver the 265th commencement speech.

What had been expected to be some standard remarks from a revered American hero became one of the most monumental speeches in the nation's history. General Marshall used the moment to address the crisis facing Europe. In his clipped, staccato style he opened by outlining the "visible destruction" of cities, railroads, mines, and factories across Europe, which had led to what he called dislocation of "the entire fabric of the European economy." European governments were being forced to pay for essentials like food and fuel, particularly to the United States, using loans that were contributing to a condition of economic, social, and political deterioration of a "very grave character." It was only logical, he went on to say, that the United States should do whatever it is able to do "to assist in the return of economic health in the world, without which there can be no political stability nor assured peace. Our policy is not directed against any country or doctrine but against hunger, poverty, desperation and chaos," he charged. The audience listened closely as Marshall pledged the US government's "full cooperation" to any country willing to assist in the task. Then in a direct challenge to Soviet leaders, he offered a veiled warning that governments choosing to block recovery of other countries "cannot expect help from the United States."[6]

French and British leaders, eagerly embracing Marshall's offer, called for a foreign ministers' conference in Paris the next month to discuss the matter. The United States, Great Britain, and France all recognized that the key to a healthy European community was the recovery of the German economy. For his part, Stalin rejected this notion, fearing that a German resurgence could lead to another war, posing a renewed military threat to the Soviet Union. After days of contentious wrangling, Molotov, to everyone's surprise, stormed out of the meetings on Stalin's orders in a deliberate attempt to sabotage the process. The Soviet premier would accept no US interference in solving Europe's economic calamity nor any assistance for the Soviet zone of occupation in Germany and its new satellite states. "Stalin considered the Soviet zone of influence" wrote Russian historian Mikhail Narinsky, "to be the most important legacy of World War II."[7]

It fell to General Marshall years later to sum up the acceleration of the historic aid package—what became known as the Marshall Plan. It was, he said, "an outgrowth of the disillusionment . . . , which proved conclusively that the Soviet Union was not negotiating in good faith and could not be induced to cooperate in achieving European recovery."[8]

\* \* \*

For Molotov's new man the challenge facing him on the American home front was equally grim. Cries of "better dead than red," a popular refrain, could be heard everywhere.

George Gallup was an American pioneer in the science of surveys and sampling techniques. Over the years, he developed statistical methods for measuring public opinion on a wide range of issues. In the fall of 1947, Gallup polled the American electorate on their attitudes toward the Soviet Union asking if Stalin was seeking protection against attack in another war or was he pushing for dominance in the world. More than 75 percent responded that Russia wanted to be the "ruling power." Seventy percent, when asked, believed that Communism would "destroy the Christian religion if they could." Writing decades later, one observer noted that for most Americans "the thought of being made subject to the 'ghoulish' rule of the Kremlin had become *the* American nightmare."[9]

One leading contributor to these attitudes was President Truman's so-called "Loyalty Program." In the 1946 off-year elections, the Republican Party soundly defeated the Democrats, taking control of both Houses of Congress with an eye on a return to the White House in 1948. Throughout the campaign, Republican candidates continually bashed Truman and the Democrats for not standing up to the Soviet Union and being soft on Communism at home. Fearing that a new Republican-controlled House Committee on Un-American Activities would go on the hunt for communist penetration of the government, Truman sought to blunt his opponents. On March 21, 1947, Executive Order No. 9835 was announced to the public with great fanfare. Officially referred to as the Federal Employees Loyalty and Security Program, it authorized the FBI to investigate any federal employee suspected of disloyalty to the United States *whatever their job* (italics added).[10] Three months later more fuel was added to the fire. In June, federal prosecutors in New York announced the empaneling of a grand jury to hear evidence that the Communist Party of the United States was a conspiratorial organization whose purpose was the overthrow of the US government.

\* \* \*

In Molotov's view, Panyushkin was a perfect fit for the Washington, DC, post. Just months before his arrival, Congress passed the National Security Act, which created the Central Intelligence Agency. With it came a charter requiring the new CIA to coordinate the activities of US intelligence agencies and produce finished analytical assessments for the White House.

Reacting to this move, Molotov approached Stalin with a similar idea. The two principal spy services since the start of the Bolshevik regime in 1917, the KGB and GRU, had always operated independently with an uneasy competitive relationship. Over the past two years, both were still experiencing fallout from the disasters of 1945. In the case of the GRU, the Canadian government had released a blistering royal commission report laying out Igor Gouzenko's revelations about the vast extent of espionage across North America. The KGB fared no better. Elizabeth Bentley, the courier who defected in 1945 with dozens of names on her list, was still talking and working as an FBI informant.

The Russian foreign minister proposed a reorganization of the two spy services in a single agency. It was a radical step based largely on Molotov's fear that a single American intelligence system would give the United States a permanent advantage over a fragmented Soviet structure. From Stalin's viewpoint the change made sense with an additional advantage having to do with internal politics. He saw an opportunity to weaken the power of Lavrenti Beria, a Politburo member and potential rival, whose protégé, Victor Abakumov, headed the KGB.

Following Stalin's approval, the merge occurred on September 30, 1947. A new organization called the Committee of Information (Komitet Informatsii), known as "KI," and headed by Molotov was born, giving the foreign ministry greater influence over foreign intelligence operations. To strengthen his control, Molotov anointed a loyal deputy, Pyotr Fedetov, to lead foreign operations. Fedetov had no intelligence background nor any familiarity with the West.[11]

In the weeks that followed, steps were taken to organize the new service in conformance with Molotov's vision. KI made all decisions including approval of low-level tactical matters like planning agent meetings, reliability investigations, and other tactical necessities. Experienced intelligence officers were fired or shuffled around while others were promoted. In one case, Roland Abbiate, the legal resident in New York, probably the only person with extensive knowledge of the West, was dismissed. In another sharp departure from past practices, the duties of diplomacy and chief legal resident intelligence officer were now assigned to the ambassador. Suddenly and with little warning, seasoned Russian diplomats around the world with no training or experience found themselves assuming new duties as spy masters. It was in this atmosphere of crisis and change that Panyushkin arrived in Washington to take personal charge of the Russian embassy.

The stage was now set for the next act in the Weisband saga.

## NOTES

1. SS Maritime.com, RMS *Mauretania*, Cunard/White Star Line, MyHeritage.com.
2. VN Concordance 455.
3. Panyushkin supervised "Operation Rhine" personally. It dealt with the attempted assassination of a Ukrainian émigré living in West Germany who was the head of the Ukrainian NTS. Panyushkin closely managed all aspects of the training of the assassin, Nikolai Khoklov, to ensure that nothing was missed. Khoklov defected to the West in 1954 before the assassination could be carried out. Christopher Andrew and Oleg Gordievsky, *KGB: The Inside Story* (New York: HarperCollins Publishers, 1990), 425–26.
4. Pavel Sudoplatov and Anatoli Sudoplatov, *Special Tasks* (Boston: Little Brown and Company, 1994), xiii, 380.
5. No author, *Great Concerns of the Resident A. S. Panyushkin. Essay from the History of Russian Intelligence, Volume 4, 1941–1945* (Moscow: Federal Book Publishing Program of Russia, 1999), 323–29.
6. George C. Marshall Commencement Speech, June 7, 1947, George C. Marshall Center, Lexington, Virginia.
7. Roll, *George Marshall*, 448.
8. Ibid.
9. David A. Smith, "American Nightmare: Images of Brainwashing Thought and Control and Terror in Soviet Union," *Journal of American Culture*, Vol. 23, No. 3 (September 2010): 217–29, Introduction (Source: "Gallup Vault: 70 Years Ago, Five Grievances Against Russia," Lydia Saad, August 3, 2017).
10. David McCullough, *Truman* (New York: Simon & Schuster, 1991) 551–52.
11. KI would later disappear and the KGB and GRU would once again become separate services. During the 1950s, Panyushkin would become the head of the KGB's First Chief Directorate, its foreign intelligence service. Andrew and Gordievsky, *KGB: The Inside Story*, 381–83.

## Chapter 30

# Catastrophe

As Russia's new ambassador to Washington and KGB and GRU chief, Alexander Panyushkin wasted no time getting his mission underway. He began in February 1948 in the face of withering Truman administration criticism over the Kremlin's menacing threats in East Germany and Central Europe. Chief among them was the Russian-inspired coup that brought Czechoslovakia into the Soviet Union's growing collection of satellite partners on its western borders. For months, Secretary of State Marshall's predictions of such a move had provoked growing American outrage at Russian treachery. From Prague, America's ambassador, Laurence Steinhart, had been sounding the alarm and now it had come. Stalin and local Communists "have wiped out every vestige of representative government" he warned.[1]

Panyushkin was just as busy on the espionage side of the house. A local KGB officer named Boris Mikhailovich Krotov was struggling with "Homer," Moscow's most important spy in the United States. Krotov had handled Homer in London during the war. After arriving in New York in October 1947 as part of a Russian diplomatic delegation to the UN General Assembly, he became Panyushkin's assistant resident intelligence officer posing as a first secretary covering political matters. By the winter of 1948, Krotov was pressuring Homer to use dead drops for passage of documents or his wife as a courier. All to no avail as Homer remained adamant, insisting on personal meetings with Krotov in New York.[2]

Homer was the code name for Donald Maclean, an Englishman and career diplomat working at the British embassy in Washington. The son of a liberal member of Parliament, Maclean was born in 1913 and completed a degree in contemporary languages in 1934 from Cambridge University's Trinity Hall. While attending Trinity he took up the cause of Communism. By his final year of college, he had been recruited as a Russian agent. Maclean would go on to infamy as one of the "Magnificent Five," a Moscow-run spy ring that operated at the highest levels of the British government for years along with fellow Cambridge graduates Kim Philby, Anthony Blunt, Guy Burgess, and John Cairncross.³

\* \* \*

Another key figure in the Weisband story was Yuri Mikhailovich Bruslov: a KGB officer, code-named PAVEL, he had already been working at the embassy as a second secretary for cultural affairs when Panyushkin arrived in December 1947. Little is known about him other than a previous assignment in London. Married to Yevgenia Alekseyevna, the couple shared an apartment in Washington on R Street Northwest. Bruslov would later return to London (perhaps as a consequence of Weisband's discovery) as "cultural attaché" with a new rank of first secretary. Years later back in Moscow Centre, Bruslov trained KGB recruits in the art of assessing and recruiting Americans and with other officers authored a textbook on the topic.⁴

One of Bruslov's first assignments under Panyushkin was recontacting an old source code-named IDE. He was Samuel Krafsur, a thirty-five-year-old American from Boston, Massachusetts. He had spent a year studying at Northeastern University and in his twenties, he joined CPUSA. As a member of the Abraham Lincoln Brigades, he returned to the United States after being wounded in Spain during the Spanish Civil War. In 1938 he turned to journalism with *Liberty Volunteers*, an organ of the Veterans of the Abraham Lincoln Brigade headquartered in New York City. Krafsur was recruited for service with TASS, the Russian news agency, by Vladimir Pravdin, a KGB officer and assassin, who later served in New York under the alias Roland Abbiate.⁵

Panyushkin took the month of January 1948 to assess his situation before ordering Bruslov to renew contact with Krafsur. After a twenty-seven-month break following Elizabeth Bentley's defection in November 1945, the journalist was excited by Bruslov's appearance and was more than willing to assist the Russians in any way. In his assessment, Bruslov assured Moscow Center that Krafsur remained "absolutely loyal to the USSR" and was eager to assist Moscow through his wide range of contacts as a correspondent and journalist in Washington. Among his twenty or so important contacts, Bruslov learned, was Joseph Berger, a personal aide to the chairman of the Democratic National Committee. Panyushkin soon signaled his Moscow bosses that their meeting went well, so well in fact, that Bruslov urged IDE "to think of ways to step up his work."⁶

At the same time Bruslov was reactivating Krafsur, he also contacted Weisband. How they met is unknown. Most likely he called Weisband, now code-named ZHORA, at his home using a coded exchange identifying himself and suggesting a personal meeting at a prearranged spot. Security of agent meetings being paramount, Bruslov chose a restaurant outside of

Washington where they could talk and exchange packages (envelopes of cash going one way and secret documents going the other), all the time minimizing chances of being seen. They spoke Russian to reduce the chances of eavesdropping from other diners. Personal meetings were always risky but essential for the KGB assessment of an agent's mental and emotional stability. Bruslov focused on details of Weisband's life in the wilderness over the past two years. Along with additional questions about possible discovery of Weisband's spying, Bruslov probed for insights about his work situation, along with any unexplained changes or upgrades in security at Arlington Hall. He also looked for clues that Weisband may have been "doubled" by the FBI. What Weisband had to say at this first encounter left Bruslov breathless.[7]

Throughout his years at ASA, Bill Weisband skillfully concealed his treachery by scoring high marks from his superiors. When he came on board as a civilian in 1946, he was assigned to Norman Dillinger working plain language in the Cryptanalytic Branch. Dillinger supervised his work for a year to September 6, 1947, around the time Weisband took his sudden trip to California and Lamphere arrival in Washington, DC. Dillinger rated him "excellent" with an "outstanding" mark for security. James K. Lively, the reviewing officer, approved the rating. His next supervisor was Marie Meyer, another cryptologic war veteran. During the summer of 1946 she undertook a Russian correspondence course at the University of Chicago before joining the Venona program under Meredith Gardner. Gardner later credited her with making a number of recoveries for the Venona codebook that he was creating.[8]

As a senior linguist from April 1, 1947, until March 21, 1948, she supervised Weisband's performance in the Woodgas 97F section responsible for the Linguistic Control. Like Dillinger she too found his work "excellent" and his attention to security "outstanding." It was Lively again who endorsed her rating. Next came Paul G. Young, Weisband's rating officer from April 1, 1948, to March 31, 1949. Young, an ASA war veteran, as well as a Russian linguist and traffic analyst, also scored his work as "excellent" with no record concerning security. The reviewing officer was John J. Connelley. It was during this period that Bill was reassigned to the Special Processing Branch with duties as a traffic control specialist with the Russian program from June 27, 1948, through October 31, 1948, under Theodore Squier Jr. and his deputy John J. Connelley. For a few months there is a blank before he shows up again: this time under the supervision of Herbert Connelly, whose specialties included Japanese traffic analysis, Russian traffic analysis, liaison with British officials, and traffic analyst consultant. No rating was available. Finally, from August 21, 1949, until February 28, 1950, less than three months before his suspension, Herbert Conley rated him and Oliver Kirby reviewed him as "excellent." It was also during this period that he received his first promotion as a "research analyst (Foreign Affairs)" in the Operations Division of ASA.⁹

Around January 1949, Bill found himself working for someone on her way to becoming a cryptologic legend. Julia Ward was born in December 1900. After earning a degree in history from Bryn Mawr College, she stayed on first as a residence hall warden, earning a doctorate in history and advancing up the academic ladder to a variety of deanships. After twenty years in academia, she joined Arlington Hall in 1942 as a librarian working in the reference section. What she found surprised her. For such a massive and sophisticated code-breaking operation, Arlington Hall had a primitive library system. It was a poorly organized reactive organization that was fragmented and focused only on supplying information to existing customers performing analysis against established targets. Ward, ever the visionary, believed that much could be done to anticipate the needs of cryptanalysts by collaborating with them in a more proactive fashion. Her idea was to gather and organize data that would save time and prove useful for code breakers. By the end of the war, she had been promoted to the head of the reference section.

Over the next four years she set her sights on creating a world-class central reference organization known as "C-Ref" where code breakers could study archived classified product, analytical reports, internal unclassified material, and open sources including newspaper clippings, published articles, and books. Her growing collection included captured documents, source reports from other agencies, defector reports, and analytical records supplied by foreign allied services. As Ward moved along, she steadily built up what one NSA study called a "highly respected organization to which other federal agencies CIA and FBI came for collateral information." Using Ward's skills, ASA began to develop a system capable of multiplying the code breakers' talents and supporting them by reducing the time for skills having to be taught and having to recover the text by "brute force." It was a "valuable" thing for speeding up production and saving cryptanalysts "a lot of effort" Frank Rowlett later said. This is where Ward was so well suited for code-breaking because she "came to age by compiling and organizing and cataloguing collateral information." For her work, she was named the first female head of the Collateral Branch in 1949 in the Office of Operations.[10]

Bill Weisband's job was to assist Ward by pulling together and identifying "traffic": the most important intercepted, deciphered, and translated Russian messages in Arlington Hall's top-secret arsenal. It was a position that gave him complete access to ASA's cryptologic successes, weaknesses, and vulnerabilities against Russian communications on both a deep and broad scale. He now knew the complete details of exact circuits producing the most valuable intelligence needed for Ward's expanding operation as well as Arlington Hall chiefs and national policymakers.

\* \* \*

Bruslov quickly recognized Weisband's extraordinary value and his eagerness to resume working for the KGB. It did not take long before he set a contact schedule that called for personal meetings every six weeks. To further ensure security, Bruslov informed Weisband at each meeting of the date, time, and location of their next meeting together with a follow-up date, time, and location if one or the other failed to appear. Between February and July 1948, they rendezvoused at least four times, each lasting about an hour.[11]

The system worked well until Kremlin behavior abruptly ended their routine in July 1948. Hoping to deny the West access to its designated sectors in Berlin, Stalin suddenly ratcheted up international tensions by stopping all international traffic in and out of Berlin with plans to take control of the entire city. It began one day in June when Russian troops halted all eastbound traffic for a day claiming the need for repairing a bridge. It was a direct violation of the accords signed with Allied leaders at Potsdam allowing all parties unfettered access to their designated sectors in Berlin.

Tensions had been building for almost a year. Secretary of State Marshall had been growing increasingly truculent in his public remarks about Stalin. In one national broadcast, he accused the Russian leader of trying to exploit the economic and political crisis in Europe for his own purposes. He called out the Soviet Union and the Communist Party for the first time as enemies of the United States. "The Soviet Union and their Communist allies," he charged "have been seeking to exploit the crisis in Europe so as to gain a controlling influence all over Europe."[12]

With whispers of war growing ever louder, President Truman signed on April 3, 1948, the European Cooperation Act into law. The historic document authorized a total of $6.2 billion—$5.3 billion for European recovery (Marshall Plan) and the rest for aid to China, Greece, and Turkey and international child relief.

In Washington, Panyushkin's headaches were intensifying as well. On July 20, 1948, thirteen months after it was empaneled, a New York grand jury returned indictments against twelve national board members of the Communist Party of the United States. All were charged with violations of the Smith Act for having conspired to advocate the overthrow of the US government.

The charges prompted sensational headlines around the country hinting at testimony given by Elizabeth Bentley, described in the press as a "beautiful blond" ex-Communist who revealed the names of dozens of Russian spies in government during the war. Eight days after the indictments, Bentley testified before a Senate committee and on July 31, 1948, she was pouring out her story to the House Committee on Un-American Activities (HUAC).

Next came Whittaker Chambers, the *Time* magazine editor and former GRU espionage courier. Chambers walked into a HUAC hearing room on August 3, 1948, and for the next several hours gave testimony that would lead to accusations of espionage against Alger Hiss.

Daily newspaper headlines revealing widespread Russian espionage forced Panyushkin's newly developing espionage apparatus to change tactics. In addition, FBI surveillance of Russian embassy staff was growing at an alarming rate. So concerned had he become over the oppressive atmosphere that he cabled Moscow recommending the transfer of key agents to an illegal network given that "all our legal workers in the USA are being closely shadowed."[13]

Normally, such an uproar would dictate another shutdown of KGB North American operations until the political climate had cooled down. In this case, however, Panyushkin took a different course. Intelligence on future US actions was vital for Russia's leaders, which meant that any interruption of operations, even a temporary one, was out of the question. Instead, he instituted a more rigorous tactic for meeting agents: one that further ensured security while keeping operations going at this critical moment in Soviet history. The ambassador ordered Bruslov to alter meetings with Weisband by continuing personal contact every six to eight weeks, in parks and rural areas outside the Washington area where they could safely talk. Bruslov used these opportunities to give Weisband verbal instructions and directions. Many of their personal meetings after July 1948 dealt with "terms of contact," which incorporated identification, passwords, and two-way signals for summons to an emergency meeting, Panyushkin later wrote.[14] If caught, there would be no incriminating evidence. As for passage of cash and documents, this procedure would now be handled by dead drops, impersonal contacts. This change required Weisband to place his documents in a concealment device such as a bag of trash, a piece of car radiator hose, or a dirty milk carton. He would then place the package at some predetermined spot like the base of a telephone pole or a street sign for later pickup by Bruslov. Bruslov would take money and instructions and hide them in a similar concealment device, for placement at a different predetermined site for later pickup by Weisband.

While army and navy code breakers were reading many of Russia's secret messages in real time, concern was growing over signs of Moscow's tightening its communications security. Around September 1947, when Weisband made his mysterious trip to California, ASA began noticing a drop in the number of messages transmitted over Russian internal radio telegraph networks. In December of that same year, code breakers reported a worrying message from Soviet telegraph authorities ordering an end to transmission of coded messages over unencrypted radio teleprinter channels. Instead, they were to be confined to landlines only. At the same time American analysts recorded noticeable upticks in enciphered radio teleprinter traffic. British and US chiefs saw none of these changes as significant and comforted themselves in the belief that they were part of routine Russian upgrades in communications security.

Over the many decades that have passed, NSA still remembers the moment simply as "Black Friday." Unbeknownst to Western intelligence, these earlier changes were merely a prelude to Monday morning, November 1, 1948, when something occurred that the "US and British had never seen before." The next day panic roared through the halls of the Pentagon over sweeping changes that had occurred in virtually every communications system used by the Soviet military and the KGB. "Beginning 1 November," the navy warned, "extensive changes, which overshadow all previously recorded changes in type and areas affected, were effected in Russian Naval, Military, and Police Communications Networks."[15]

Army and navy officials sat speechless at the "efficiency" of these changes, the seamlessness of the coordination, and the extensive area of coverage that included "European and Far Eastern Police and European and Far Eastern Military area." Not only were they stunned by the rapidity of the changes, they had no explanation for the reasons behind them other than readiness of all services to do so. As Stephen Budiansky writes, the Soviets "pulled the plug" on its military, naval, and police radio links replacing them with dummy and practice messages. The much more disciplined systems that replaced them in effect "slammed the cryptanalytic door shut."[16]

Days later the US Communications Intelligence Board convened an emergency meeting to review the losses and figure out what happened. Some anxiety was eased partially when British officials offered assurances that the Russian actions were not a prelude to war. As the panel sat speculating, questions arose about possible root causes for the sudden and dramatic loss. Seeking advice, the board turned to the chiefs of ASA and the navy's codebreaking service known as "Communications Supplementary Activities Washington" (CSAW) to weigh in with their thoughts. Captain Wenger for the navy saw it as a "methodical improvement" in overall Russian cryptographic practice. Ironically, it was Weisband's close friend, Colonel Harold Hayes, who dismissed the upgrade theory, warning the board that "leakage of information had been the primary cause."[17]

Over the course of 1947 and 1948, more than a thousand of the 3,100 workers at ASA and CSAW, along with another 400 in Great Britain, had been dedicated to monitoring these Russian circuits. Hundreds more were scattered around the United States and the globe manning 524 radio-intercept sites. In just twenty-four hours it became questionable if any of them had a job.

In his end-of-year report for 1948, Panyushkin proudly touted Weisband's accomplishments to his Moscow bosses.

> In a single year, we received from "Zhora" large quantities of highly valuable [documentary] material on the efforts of America to decipher Soviet ciphers on the interception and analysis of the open radio correspondence of [Soviet] agencies. From the material received from Zhora we learned that as a result of this work [American] intelligence was able to obtain important information about the disposition of Soviet armed forces, the production capacity of various branches of industry, and the work being done in the USSR in the field of atomic energy.[18]

He then went on to note that,

> on the basis of the material received from Zhora our state security agencies implemented a set of defensive measures, which resulted in significant decreases in the effectiveness of the efforts of the American decryption service. As a result, at [present] the volume of the American decryption and analysis service's work has decreased significantly.[19]

Since February 1948, Weisband had revealed Operation Taber, Operation Shamrock, the Venona Project, the success of plain-language, full details of progress against Russian enciphered communications, and dozens of other Anglo-American initiatives that still remain classified today. Aside from long-term consequences of Weisband's treachery to NSA, within eighteen months it would produce a catastrophe for US policymakers who had no strategic warning when North Korean forces suddenly invaded South Korea on June 25, 1950. His spying cost untold numbers of American lives by offering the Soviet Union, in the words of one writer, a "significant strategic advantage" by denying America any meaningful warning of the outbreak of the Korean War.[20]

As the calendar turned to the new year of 1949 there was nothing that American code breakers were doing that Moscow didn't know. Panyushkin lavishly compensated Bill for his contributions. Over the course of the year, Weisband received cash payments of nearly $9,500. Adjusted for inflation this figure amounted to nearly $122,000 in 2023.[21]

## NOTES

1. Roll, *George Marshall*, 470.

2. VYN#1–82, VBN 70.
3. Andrew and Mitrokhin, *Mitrokhin Archive*, 56–57.
4. VBN 74, 80.
5. VBN 75, Klehr, Haynes, Vassiliev, *Spies*, 148–49.
6. VBN 72.
7. VBN 74–75.
8. "Marie Meyer, Historical Figures," NSA.gov.
9. Miscellaneous Papers, Undated. NSA FOIPA.
10. Rowlett Oral History. NCM.
11. VBN 75.
12. Roll, *George Marshall*, 467.
13. VBN 71, 81.
14. VBN 75.
15. Budiansky, *Code Warriors*, 112.
16. Ibid.
17. Ibid.
18. VBN 75.
19. Ibid.
20. Naiomi Gonzalez, "William Weisband," *The Intelligencer*, Vol. 26, No. 1, 2020, 51.
21. NSA Special Research Report, Undated, NSA FOIPA.

## Chapter 31

# Reckoning

The accident occurred on December 10, 1948, around seven-thirty in the morning. Mabel and Bill were driving to work when a fender bender occurred as Bill was rounding the Lincoln Memorial Circle in Washington, DC. A driver in front of him stopped suddenly to avoid striking a stalled car, causing Weisband to rear-end him. Mabel received scratches requiring a brief hospital visit. Bill was furious as he jumped out of his damaged car and started screaming at the driver. It was months before the person Bill struck received $185 in damages. The delay was due to a lawsuit Bill filed against his insurance company and his arrears of many months on his insurance premiums.[1]

With no car, Weisband quickly set a signal for an emergency meeting with Bruslov. Weeks later he rendezvoused with Nikolay Statskevich, who paid him $1,000 ($12,842 in February 2023) for a new car and some "big expenses."[2]

Statskevich was one of nine intelligence officers assigned to the Russian embassy's KGB station. Code-named "Larry," his cover title was "employee," probably without diplomatic immunity; much like Alexander Feklisov, who reconnected with Bill in New York three years earlier. Statskevich began sharing responsibility for Weisband with Bruslov around November 1948 when Arlington Hall suddenly lost access to Russian ciphers.

Despite his low level in the station hierarchy, he was no novice at spying. In 1945, the KGB recruited an unknown American group that quickly became inactive in the wake of the Gouzenko and Bentley crises. Today we know them only as "Relative," "Intermediary," "Godfather," and "Godsend," their KGB code names. Their original recruitment was based on what Moscow Center called "ideological affinity . . . and blood ties." As part of Panyushkin's agent reactivation plan, Statkevich took over control of Relative with orders to break ties with his three associates who Moscow Center suspected were being watched by the FBI. He also handled two sources at the Romanian embassy known only as "Sotsul" and "Zhana," a code clerk code-named "Jose" at the Yugoslav embassy, and Jan Pitak, code-named "Plucky," a counselor at the

Czech embassy who had been recruited by Boris Krotov, the deputy chief of station.[3]

For Bill Weisband the new year of 1949 was shaping up as something special. For nearly a year he had been in contact with the Russians. Secret meetings around Washington with Yuri Bruslov and dead drops filled with documents cataloging US code-breaking successes against Russian ciphers had become a routine part of Bill's life. Moscow payments for this treasure trove of information could only be described as beyond imagination. A content William Weisband had every reason to believe that the gravy train would continue to roll along for the foreseeable future.

As Panyushkin reported to Moscow, Bill did have big expenses coming up. When he and Mabel decided to marry, he threw a bachelor party for himself, going all out with a major soiree with friends and co-workers. For large parties most of Washington's uber rich usually gravitated to the Willard Hotel, a block from the White House, or the Mayflower on Connecticut Avenue. Perhaps as a nod to his secret life, Bill instead chose a venue that was once called the "Plaza of Washington." It was the Cairo Hotel, tucked away in an old residential neighborhood on P Street Northwest. Built before the Civil War, the Cairo was a strange-looking place. One reporter described it as filled with lavish ornamentation, over-the-top style, and dramatic curves: the "perfect ritzy, glitzy magnet for early 20th century's rich and famous." Over the years socialites from around the world congregated there, preferring its "more shadowy kind of glamour." A place where "Casablanca meets Cleopatra and guests who appreciated a little dark poetry with their stay," one observer recalled. Numbered among the hotel's more famous guests were such luminaries as the novelist F. Scott Fitzgerald and famed inventor Thomas Edison.[4]

As for the marriage, it took place on January 19, 1949, and cost Bill nearly twenty-five hundred dollars ($31,000 in October 2022). The guest list has been lost to history, but legend still has it that most of America's intelligence glitterati were in attendance. For years afterward, it would still be remembered as a "who's who of America's cryptologic weddings." After the nuptials, the couple took a few weeks for themselves with a honeymoon driving trip throughout the American Southwest.

Over the ensuing months Bill's contact routine with the Russians continued as usual. On days when he was scheduled to meet with Pavel or Larry, he orchestrated a two-stage process. As the noon lunch hour approached, he began stuffing carefully selected documents under his shirt. He then casually walked out of the building to the parking lot and hid them in the trunk of his car. At the end of the workday, he repeated the process. His two handlers repeatedly warned him against taking unnecessary risks. Placing documents in his car trunk was a poor security practice. "Careless storage or use could lead to failure," they told him. His new instructions from Bruslov called for him to deliver only the "most valuable" documents. To increase his production, Bill asked for a camera to photograph material at home—a suggestion Moscow rejected.[5]

Bill and Mabel had been married for five months when Wayne Woody moved in with them in June 1949. Wayne was Mabel's brother and a year younger than her. He grew up in Del Rio, completed high school, joined the army in 1945, and had been recently discharged. Following in his big sister's footsteps, he too took a job at ASA. His stay would be temporary until he found a place of his own.

In July Bill started a running battle with the Internal Revenue Service over his filing for the 1948 tax year. Bill had listed his sister-in-law, Edith, and her son, Edward, then living in New York, as dependents since the sudden death of his brother, Mark, in December 1947. He claimed to have supported them in the amount of $1,500 ($19,040 in February 2023) for the year and another gift of $500. When the skeptical IRS rejected his claim, he again challenged them. In a reply dated July 21, 1950, the IRS wasted no time questioning his claims with demands for Weisband to supply an itemized list of expenses. Two days later, a chastened Bill responded with a new claim that he gifted $500 to Edith upon Mark's death in December 1947 and thereafter monthly support payments of $125 ($1,587 in February 2023).

By the summer of 1949, the full impact of ASA's catastrophic losses was fully setting in. Questions continued to fly among the leadership as to how it happened so quickly and so thoroughly. As time went on there was a growing sense that someone on the inside was passing secrets. ASA leadership was worried, Panyushkin told Moscow, and it "was suggested that there is an agent at work." A worried Weisband suspected that at any moment a mole hunt could start; one that could point directly to him. Now it was Weisband's turn to urge caution to his KGB bosses. He began by warning them to take their time making security changes and not be "overly hasty" in introducing reforms "based on his reports."[6] Probably because of Weisbard's disquieting news, Larry and Moscow Center began seeing ghosts. Larry reported intensified counterintelligence behavior, which provoked fears in Moscow that the FBI had recorded his meeting with Bill. He was the "most valuable" agent in the KGB's Washington station, they warned Panyushkin. Careful attention had to be paid to the preparation for all meetings with him.

> It is completely obvious that before his last meeting with Zhora, Larry had not been properly instructed by you. This is the only way one can explain why Larry went to meet Zhora despite having noticed that he was under surveillance. Such an attitude towards meetings with Zhora is completely at odds with our repeated instructions about the need to observe all precautions during work with this valuable agent.[7]

## Chapter 31

As July merged into August, Panyushkin's security anxieties over his "most valuable" source gradually eased. It was now safe to feel that a crisis had passed following a Bruslov report that Weisband had been promoted. His new position, effective on August 21, 1949, would be "research analyst (Foreign Affairs)." With the new title came new responsibilities and deeper access to more secrets along with an increase in grade to GS-11. Four months later his title changed again, this time to "research analyst–linguistic cryptographer," with an annual salary of $5,400 ($68,836 in February 2023).[8]

The feeling of relief at the Russian embassy, however, was short lived when Weisband reported that he had become the subject of President Truman's Loyalty Program. The inquiry began in late September when Wes Reynolds, the FBI liaison man with ASA, delivered some disturbing news. For some time, the FBI's Los Angeles Office had been investigating Vivian and Victor Cubarkin, Bill Weisband's old friends from 1941. Victor had been considered to be heavily involved in radical activities on the West Coast and was suspected of holding a high-level position in the Communist Party. It had been recently learned either through a wiretap on Victor's phone or mail monitoring that he had contacted Weisband. Further checks revealed that Weisband had corresponded with Cubarkin from Italy in 1944. On October 18, 1949, Lieutenant Colonel Charles Hiser, deputy chief of ASA, asked the FBI to conduct a full field loyalty investigation of Weisband.[9]

The purpose of the FBI investigation was to determine the relationship between Cubarkin and Weisband. How were they connected? Were they friends or was he a family member? If not related, then how and when did they first meet? Particularly concerning was Bill's mysterious trip to California in August 1947. Why did he travel to California and meet Cubarkin? What did he do while in Los Angeles and why did Cubarkin return with Bill to Washington?[10]

Over the course of the next three months, FBI agents interviewed co-workers and did extensive record checks. It appeared that everyone in the Bourbon Program was aware of his trip to California to sell his new Buick sedan in the hope of making a "great profit." He made the trip, according to one person, because he was experiencing financial problems and hoped to "secure funds which he was in need of at the time." Another person confirmed that Bill wished to "aid his financial situation." Others remembered Weisband holding a party at his home after returning from California and introducing his friend Victor as the "guest of honor." Over the course of the investigation, FBI agents in New York uncovered his 1938 arrest with Pollock and the rejection of his citizenship application in 1937 for lying about his extensive traffic violations. When Cubarkin was interviewed by the FBI he offered only vague responses. He had known Weisband since 1941 and had no reason to believe that he was disloyal. He was aware of Bill's confidential employment for the government but didn't know the nature of the work.[11]

Panyushkin and Bruslov closely followed the FBI's investigation through monthly meetings with Weisband. It appeared to be going smoothly but to be careful Panyushkin ordered changes in their meeting schedule for security's sake. Until October 1949, Bill had been met on a monthly basis. Now he would be met at restaurants outside the city of Washington every three months with new dates set at January 16, 1950, and again on April 16, 1950.[12]

On October 19, 1949, Weisband suddenly began attending the Georgetown University School of Languages as an evening student. His decision was based on his new duties with the Training Branch teaching Russian to new linguists destined for the Bourbon Program. These were one-on-one tutorial courses consisting of conversations with a professor. The course was designed to improve conversational ability for students with strong language skills. He took lessons ten hours a week broken down into tutorial Russian for three hours, French for three hours, and Arabic for four hours. There was no classroom study but there was a laboratory, which required the student to cut a record of their conversations and listen to it to improve their skill.

On November 12, 1949, a seemingly unfazed Weisband decided to get out of town for the weekend. He and Mabel flew to New York to witness the University of North Carolina play undefeated Notre Dame at Yankee Stadium.

By the end of 1949, Mabel and Bill had a combined income of $8,189 ($104,400 in February 2023). They also had unexplained cash deposits totaling $9,000 ($109,000 in February 2023) into their account. As for Panyushkin, his plan for 1950 was to continue working with Weisband, who was regularly providing volumes of information. As the new year approached Panyushkin proudly touted Bill's brilliant performance to Moscow. Over the past year he supplied unimaginable priceless information from the "[Arlington Hall station] regarding work on our codes, as well as materials from American intelligence, compiled through agents and analysis, regarding our industry and disposition of armed forces."[13]

While no finding of disloyalty was uncovered against Weisband, what the FBI did unearth should have sent off alarm bells for ASA leadership. His association with a suspected Communist Party member and his hosting him as a "guest of honor" at his home with ASA colleagues was ignored. He had been denied his citizenship in 1937 for failure to pay traffic charges. Then there was his arrest in 1938 with an illegal alien with no explanation as to the charges. He had been in serious financial straits just months before ASA lost all access to Russian communications. Yet no one thought to question the details. And in the end the investigation was closed on January 29, 1950, with neither the FBI or army security officials questioning William Weisband for details. As 1949 became 1950, a bemused Panyushkin could only sit on the sidelines just miles away from Arlington Hall and watch in wonder as Zhora, his "most valuable source," once again dodged a crisis.

In the spring of 1950, the walls once again began closing in on Bill—this time for good. It began when the FBI caught up with "Nik," the KGB code name for Amadeo Sabatini. Born in Italy in 1909, Sabatini came to America with his family and settled in Pennsylvania. As a child he quit school to work in the coal mines. He joined the Communist Party and the National Miners Union and became active in the labor movement. In 1933, he traveled to Moscow to study at the International Lenin School before being assigned to courier duties for the Comintern in Europe. Later he saw service in Spain during the Spanish Civil War as a member of the Communist Party's "Control Commission," which exercised political discipline over Americans fighting with the Abraham Lincoln Brigades. In 1938, the KGB sent him to France to hunt for KGB defector Walter Krivitsky. After returning to the United States in November 1938, he came under the control of veteran KGB operative Joseph Katz. In late 1942 or early 1943, he moved to California, where he began running a string of agents including Jones Orin York. For the next year the two men met approximately thirteen times with York delivering film cannisters filled with images of documents York stole from the Lockheed Company in Santa Monica. Fearing that he was under surveillance, Sabatini broke off contact with York at the same time Moscow Center had become disillusioned with York's poor production and discontinued his use. Like Weisband, the KGB broke contact with Sabatini in the fall of 1945 following the Bentley defection.[14] Following three dormant years, Statskevich reconnected with Sabatini issuing new orders for Nik to create a group that could provide intelligence on America's atomic weapons program.[15]

The FBI was already looking at Sabatini before his reactivation. In 1947 when agents interviewed him, he denied everything. Months later a KGB message deciphered by Meredith Garner with the name "Nick" contained enough identifying information to lead Robert Lamphere to Sabatini's door in the spring of 1950. Once again, he struggled to deny all but in doing so admitted that he had handled York in the early 1940s while he was working at Lockheed.[16]

By then York had been under FBI investigation since February 2, 1948, following Meredith Gardner's new success in revealing him under his KGB code name, "Needle," and employment in the West Coast aircraft industry. Coverage of him included placing a false mirror in his home to observe his movements along with a microphone and tap on his telephone. All of which produced nothing of value. Finally in March 1950 the Los Angeles FBI office requested authority to interview York with the objective of identifying his current Soviet espionage handler, the names of other possible espionage agents, and current information on Soviet activities.[17]

On April 10, 1950, Jones Orin York sat down with FBI agents for five hours. Unlike his interview a decade earlier, this time he admitted everything. He gave details of his recruitment by Stanislav Shumovsky in 1936 and his subsequent business arrangement, which quickly led to spying on his employers for cash. Next came his meetings with two strangers he knew only as "Brooks" and "Werner" with descriptions of how, when, and where he met them. He then gave the real story behind his yearlong disappearance at the end of 1939 in New Hampshire when Werner failed to make a scheduled meeting. He outlined the circumstances of their reconnection and after a year of contact, Werner's sudden announcement in May 1941 that he was leaving and would be replaced by someone else. He even described the torn halves of the Shirley Temple photo agreed upon as the recognition signal with his new courier.

York met his contact man a month or so later. After the passage of almost a decade he still recalled this person introducing himself as "Bill" or "William." He described him as about thirty-six or thirty-eight years old, five feet six inches tall, and weighing around a hundred and sixty pounds. York learned that he was born in North Africa, possibly "Algeria," and was unmarried. He remembered him once mentioning that he was Russian or French and spoke Arabic. Perhaps to impress York with his intelligence, he prattled on one time about tribal activities among the indigenous people of Mongolia. After more thought York suddenly had a new recollection. It was his name. After the passage of a decade, he recalled it as something like "Bill Villesbend." Following the interview, Weisband's ASA badge photo was shown to York. Without hesitating he "positively identified" him as the person he knew years earlier as "Bill."[18]

## NOTES

1. WFO Report, July 20, 1950, Weisband FBI file.
2. VBN 91.
3. VBN 74, 130.
4. High Times, Will Dory, January 9, 2003.
5. VBN 91.
6. VBN 81.
7. Ibid.
8. Ibid.
9. Handwritten Notes Undated, NSA FOIPA.
10. Hoover Letter to WFO, December 1, 1949, Weisband FBI file.
11. Memorandum, Undated, Weisband FBI file.
12. VBN 74–75.
13. VBN 80.

14. Haynes, Klehr, Vassiliev, *Spies*, 401.

15. While still in Los Angeles in 1943 Sabatini began suspecting that he was under surveillance. He even thought that York had been recruited as a double agent for the FBI. What he had spotted was indeed surveillance of Gregory Kheiffets, the senior KGB officer assigned to the Russian consulate in San Francisco, and Sabatini's boss. This FBI coverage emerged from an anonymous letter to FBI director received by J. Edgar Hoover in August 1943 from a disgruntled KGB officer working in Moscow's consulate in New York City. Sabatini was placed on ice and remained so through his call up to army duty in February 1945 and discharge in September 1946. Once again, he was reactivated and returned to the East Coast to perform courier and other assignments for Katz. In 1948 when Moscow ordered the reactivation of its agents, Sabatini was again ordered to return to the West Coast to reestablish "a group on Enormous—atomic intelligence." VBN 130.

16. Haynes, Klehr, Vassiliev, *Spies*, 416–18.

17. A. H. Belmont memorandum to D. M. Ladd, 3/30/1950, Weisband FBI file.

18. Los Angeles Letter to Hoover, 4/11/1950, Weisband FBI file.

*Chapter 32*

# Face-Off

On Thursday, April 13, 1950, Jones York's identification of Bill Weisband as his pre-war Russian contact landed on the desk of Alan H. Belmont. Belmont was a forty-three-year-old Californian with a degree from Stanford and a fourteen-year veteran of the FBI. Following stints in Birmingham and Chicago, he moved to New York as a supervisor before returning to Chicago as assistant special agent in charge. In January 1943, he took charge of the Cincinnati office until his transfer back to New York in 1944 as assistant agent in charge. He was later promoted to head criminal and counterintelligence matters. In 1946, he transferred to headquarters in Washington as the new head of all espionage matters nationwide.[1]

Within twenty-four hours the wheels were in motion, starting with the authorization of a full espionage investigation of Weisband. Belmont's next move was to brief Guy Hottel, head of the local Washington office. He ordered Hottel to contact Arlington Hall officials to arrange coverage of Weisband while he was at work. Next on his list was round-the-clock surveillance of the Weisbands starting that evening at their Arlington, Virginia. apartment. His mission statement to Hottel was crisp and clear—surveillance should be as "complete as possible but yet discreet and every effort should be made to identify his contacts and ascertain his associates." Next came a warning that Weisband not learn of the investigation. All information produced had to be immediately furnished to Belmont for passage to Arlington Hall officials through Wesley Reynolds with full reports every thirty days. What came next was crucial. The investigator selected to manage the case must rank among the FBI's most "well qualified and thoroughly experienced Agents." Due to the intensity of the case, Belmont contemplated that the investigation "will be limited to a period of approximately six months."[2]

* * *

The task of selecting the agents to investigate the case fell to Special Agent Ludwig Rudolf Oberndorf. "Obie," as everyone called him, was a "legendary" figure who acted as Hottel's "coordinating supervisor." He oversaw day-to-day management of the various counterespionage programs including the Communist Party and Nationalities, as well as the new KGB, GRU, satellite squads, and surveillance personnel. Oberndorf grew up in a German family from New Jersey where his father operated a German-language newspaper. For a year he attended Harvard University before dropping out for financial reasons. Before the war he joined the Bureau as a German linguist in Philadelphia. In an age when tall, rugged looks mattered for advancement in the FBI, Oberndorf was shortchanged. His physical features, someone later remembered, "were not in his favor." He was short with a pockmarked face possibly from tuberculosis in early life and he cared little about his appearance. Nor was he eager for advancement considering the personal sacrifices one had to make to reach the top. One of his closest friends in the Bureau believed that if he was "six feet he could have been an assistant director."[3]

The case agent Oberndorf chose to confront Weisband was Courtland Jones, known as "Court," a ten-year FBI veteran. He was tall and lean with a style and manner befitting his upbringing in Lynchburg, Virginia. When he got to the Washington Field Office in November 1945, he ranked among twenty-five agents newly assigned to handle leads growing out of the Elizabeth Bentley and Gouzenko defections.

Oberndorf next chose Donald Walter as Jones's partner. Walter was a South Dakota native with a Phi Beta Kappa key from the University of Minnesota. He was taciturn and quiet and took a thoughtful approach to everything he did. Jones viewed him as an unassuming type who "looks like a schoolteacher and acts like a schoolteacher."[4]

* * *

Conducting an espionage interrogation is no easy matter. It is a complicated dance in which interrogators try to get someone already nervous and highly alert to relax, with the goal of lulling the person into offering a full confession of his crimes. To ease the person's anxiety, questioners first focus on easy questions starting with his personal history, early years to the present, all the while looking for clues as to what makes him tick, how he'll respond to more sensitive topics, and what approaches would most likely elicit the best responses. To be most effective, FBI agents should know everything about him including details of his family background, arrest record, if any, military, and work record and so on before sitting down with him. Even more beneficial would be advanced knowledge of the details concerning his spying career.

An excellent example of this point occurred in January 1980 when the FBI intercepted a telephone call to the Russian embassy in Washington, DC, from someone wishing to sell information that could prove useful to Russian security interests. The mystery man remained unidentified until July 1985 when Vitaliy Yurchenko, a colonel in the KGB's foreign espionage directorate, defected to the United States. The information that he brought with him about that January caller soon led to the identification of Ronald William Pelton.

As a longtime employee of the NSA, Pelton's work concentrated on breaking enciphered Russian communications. In the late 1970s he resigned from NSA fearing that a routine polygraph examination would reveal his excessive spending and bankruptcy. Following a series of disastrous business decisions, he sought to remedy his financial woes in January 1980 by walking into the Soviet embassy in Washington and selling top-secret NSA programs targeting Russian military communications.

The FBI placed Pelton under a microscope for three months. His background was carefully scrutinized as were his daily routine, personal habits, friends, girlfriend, behavioral characteristics, personality traits, and so forth. Constant surveillance supported by microphones and phone taps captured his conversations. From this huge cache of data, FBI profilers constructed a psychological road map for the proper way to approach him. Adding to this collection were his recorded calls to the Russian embassy plus Yurchenko's description of his conversations with Pelton, how the Russians handled their meetings with him over the next five years, and what NSA secrets he gave up. This helped produce an interview strategy that was continually refined through practice sessions with someone posing as Pelton. When finally interviewed, the agents knew their man very well. Pelton knew nothing of the investigation until November 24, 1985, when an FBI agent invited him to a local hotel room to discuss the matter. Over the course of that afternoon and evening, Pelton confessed to his crimes. The damaging statements he made led to his conviction and a life term in prison. When later challenged to the Supreme Court the confession was upheld, and the conviction was sustained.

Court Jones was not so lucky. From the opening moments of the case, he had lost any element of surprise. It began when Brigadier General Carter Clarke, head of army intelligence, first learned of York's identification of Weisband. Uncertain about what to do with him and worried about his continued access to the "most sensitive material at Arlington Hall," Clarke turned to Reynolds for advice. Reynolds urged him to keep Weisband in place so as not to alert him—a circumstance that could jeopardize the FBI investigation. Clarke agreed that he should be "left where he is" while cautioning that a final decision would be up to Admiral Earl Stone, the new head of the Armed Forces Security Agency (AFSA).⁵

On April 14, 1950, the same day the FBI opened its case on Weisband, Clarke telephoned Reynolds around five-thirty in the evening with some stunning news. The conversation was as brief as it was worrisome. Someone at ASA suddenly and without warning had reassigned Weisband. Clarke had just learned of the move and had no details other then he remained in the Russian Section. His access to the "most sensitive" material had been reduced but he was still positioned to "jeopardize the security of Arlington Hall." After seventeen profitable years operating anonymously for Moscow, Weisband suddenly faced the reality that his spying may have been blown, and he now stood in the bull's-eye of a new and far more serious government investigation.⁶

Two days later a now frantic Bill met Statskevich as scheduled. His work situation had changed, he told him. He had little idea why he had been suddenly denied access to certain information, but the implications were ominous. At that point he pressed the idea of fleeing the country and asked for asylum. The Russians acted quickly and on April 25, 1950, Moscow assured Panyushkin that Weisband had been granted naturalization as a "secret Soviet citizen."⁷

Over the next two weeks. ASA and FBI investigators watched as a now-rattled Weisband began showing signs of desperation. It started with a sudden appearance in his supervisor's office asking if he was under investigation. Then in the next breath he announced that he planned to leave for France on June 5, 1950. He had signed up for a French language refresher course sponsored by the Yale–Reid Language Training School, a subsidiary of Yale University. It would be a six-week summer program held in Paris, he explained. When the request was denied due to his shortage of leave, Weisband became angry, insisting that "he be allowed to go." The supervisor later told Jones that he sensed that Weisband planned to depart anyway and handle the "leave problem later."⁸

Just days later on April 25, he again visited his boss's office with new concerns. This time he feared that he was being followed. Pushed for details, he could only describe his pursuers as looking like "detectives." Later that same day during a second meeting with his boss, he noted that his first observation of vehicles occurred in Baltimore while driving to the Havre de Grace racetrack. Days later he saw another suspicious car, which he could not describe. At this point he again asked if he was under investigation. Once again, he was assured that it was all part of a routine Counterintelligence Corp (CIC) probe necessitated by his planned transfer to the newly created AFSA. Before his boss could respond, Weisband asked what he should do and then offered the possibility of going to the FBI.[9]

Weisband did not give his interlocutors the full story. He was not casually going about his business while occasionally spotting what he thought were vehicles following him. He was, in fact, very surveillance conscious. Agents reported to Jones that he often behaved erratically, driving at normal speeds then suddenly accelerating and just as quickly slowing to a crawl. There were frequent and sudden turns before stopping his car in the middle of the road to study traffic passing him. Effective surveillance soon became so difficult that orders were issued to back off the coverage to an "extreme loose type and spot checks of his residence."[10]

For someone now fearing he was being watched, he nevertheless appeared to continue life as usual. In early May the Weisbands flew to New York City for another weekend getaway. After checking into a Manhattan hotel, the couple played the role of tourists starting with an afternoon at a racetrack in Jamaica followed by dinner at a Manhattan restaurant and then two seats at the Morosco Theater for a showing of Arthur Miller's new play, *Death of a Salesman*. When the play first debuted on Broadway it was a box office smash starring actor Lee J. Cobb in the role of Willy Loman, a sixty-three-year-old down-on-his-luck salesman. Advanced ticket sales reached an astronomical quarter of million dollars for an evening at "one of the finest tragedies written by an American" according to *Life* magazine.[11] A year after its debut, when Bill and Mabel attended, it was still one of the hottest tickets in town and would remain so for another year.

\* \* \*

Weisband's strange behavior immediately raised warning flags. What did his actions signal? Why did he suggest contacting the FBI? Was he trying to determine if his spying had been uncovered? Was he struggling with thoughts of fleeing the country? What did Mabel, his young wife of fifteen months, know about his crimes and would she run with him?

This sudden turn of events forced ASA officials to devise a way to throw him off of the scent. In a matter of days, they concocted a plan to have him interviewed by army intelligence personnel under a guise of getting details of his observations while making every effort to "throw off any suspicion which Weisband may have concerning the FBI." At the time, Weisband was a reserve officer in military intelligence with an application pending for transfer to AFSA. The objective of the interview was to convince him that the Counterintelligence Corp was conducting surveillance as part of the background investigation for the transfer. Weisband's supervisor informed Jones that it was common knowledge around ASA that he was "somewhat of a gambler," a fact that would give CIC a logical excuse for investigating him.[12]

Three days later on the morning of April 28, Bill approached his supervisor again with questions about the investigation. During the course of this conversation, Weisband blurted out the name of someone he knew in New York in the 1930s. He said nothing more other than "he did not see him anymore." The boss later described the remark as coming from "out of the clear sky."[13]

Based on these reports of Weisband's increasingly erratic behavior, Belmont saw an opening for Jones to approach him. The idea was to gently sound him out on the New York contact while gauging his reaction to the presence of an FBI agent interested in what he had been experiencing over the previous few weeks.

Belmont ordered Jones to meet Weisband at Arlington Hall. Later that day following introductions, the boss explained to Bill the nature of the FBI man's visit and then gave Jones the name of the person Weisband knew in New York. Weisband immediately corrected him, denying that was the name he had mentioned earlier. He then gave him another name, a person later determined to be a character reference Weisband listed on his August 5, 1949, application to AFSA. This individual worked in Washington at the Statler Hotel, where Bill had a credit card and often cashed checks. When asked about the first person mentioned, he denied any knowledge of him. Jones then expressed regret for having inconvenienced him and closed by explaining that the FBI had an interest in speaking to anyone concerning that person. Later the supervisor insisted that Weisband had lied and had, in fact, named the person in New York. In a commentary on the encounter, Jones noted that Weisband "made a point of closely observing him" and was clearly "very nervous" during their conversation.[14]

* * *

During the course of these cat-and-mouse games between Jones and Bill, another looming issue arose. Weisband was now the target of a criminal probe with FBI efforts concentrated on uncovering evidence against him that could be presented in an open federal courtroom. Like any espionage trial, the most important items for the jury in considering guilt or innocence would be the actual top-secret material that he passed to the Russians. Each juror would have to examine the evidence and make their own determination if the disclosures were gravely damaging to security of the United States as asserted by the government. Arlington Hall's well-kept secrets would also have to emerge about its function, how long it had been in business, and how it worked, together with details of Weisband's daily routine along with his past and present duties and assignments. Telling this story to a jury would require public testimony from ASA leadership, co-workers, and friends who would then be subjected to withering questions from Weisband's defense attorney about the inner workings of America's code-breaking system—none of which government prosecutors could control.

Knowing how loathe ASA felt about revealing anything concerning its activities, Wes Reynolds nonetheless felt it essential to take the matter up with them. Admiral Earl Everett Stone was the head of the new AFSA, created in May 1949 to bring the cryptologic activities of the army, navy and the new US Air Force under one roof. Stone was a naval academy graduate and career officer from Milwaukee, Wisconsin, with an advanced degree in communications engineering from Harvard University. While not a cryptologist, he spent most of his career on land and sea specializing in communications.[15]

The fifty-four-year-old navy veteran reacted as expected. From his point of view no information about AFSA's work must ever be revealed. In Reynolds memo of the conversation, he laid out Stone's position directly. "Operations of AFSA are highly classified, and success of their operations depends upon such activities being cloaked in a veil of secrecy." Any prosecution of Weisband, Stone warned, would reveal key details of American code-breaking to the world that would "jeopardize the success" of this work. To Stone's plea if Weisband could be tried without revealing sensitive material, Reynolds replied that he could "make no promises."[16]

Admiral Stone's position on the question of balancing security of Arlington Hall's work with the danger of prosecuting Weisband in open court soon made it to the top tier of the FBI. Mickey Ladd, head of the Bureau's Domestic Intelligence Division, and Belmont's boss, clearly recognized the conundrum for his investigators. They were faced with a probability of further leaks that could occur during an extended investigation and the need to staunch the hemorrhage by the immediate removal of Weisband from access to all information. In a warning to J. Edgar Hoover, Ladd called the prosecution of Weisband a "very delicate matter," explaining that a lengthy investigation brought with it the risk of prolonging "any current espionage acts of [Weisband] and place the Bureau in the position of permitting an unfavorable situation to occur." Ladd then set strict parameters on the length of the inquiry by ordering Jones and Walter to pursue a "concentrated investigation" in order to "determine Weisband's contacts and associates." Hoover quickly agreed.[17]

\* \* \*

While all this was going on, Jones continued to learn more about Weisband's past. Near the top was his in-house jewelry business. AFSA estimated that he had inherited $15,000 worth of jewelry from his mother's estate, which he had been peddling to fellow employees ever since. Within days a request was made to the Treasury Department for his tax returns from 1938 to 1949. His ASA personnel file was pulled for review along with the files of his wife, Mabel, and her brother, Wayne Woody.

Among the standard paperwork that normally filled a personnel file was a form that had been overlooked by ASA officials for years. As part of his application for a civilian employment position was a signed loyalty questionnaire dated May 20, 1946. A year later on May 7, 1947, as an ASA employee, he executed and signed a second one. On both he answered "Yes" to the question "Do you advocate, or have you ever advocated or are you now or have you ever been a member of any organization that advocates the overthrow of the Government of the United States by force or violence." Nowhere in the file was there evidence that anyone ever questioned this discrepancy.[18]

At the same time, agents in New York were trying to piece together Weisband's life in New York during the 1930s. His 1938 arrest with John Pollock was noted but with few details. Those few co-workers who could be located from his hotel days offered no useful insights. Internal investigation at ASA resurrected his sudden trip in 1947 to California to sell his car but with no details except that a sale never occurred. His Virginia income taxes surfaced nothing unusual. Then there was Victor and Vivian Cubarkin. Both had been under FBI investigation for some time, but little information was available regarding Bill's relationship with them. And finally, there was the matter of what Jones knew about his espionage, which was nothing. All the FBI had was Jones York's claim that Weisband was his handler a decade earlier and nothing else.

During this covert phase of the investigation, inquiries were restricted to the most senior Arlington Hall officials. Yet the person who knew Bill the best was several thousands of miles away from Washington with no plans for an immediate return.

As later interviews of his co-workers would reveal, Weisband was clearly a favorite of Colonel Harold Hayes. The two men had grown very friendly since their wartime service together in North Africa and Italy seven years earlier. It was Hayes who brought Weisband back from Italy to the Russian Section of Arlington Hall in the fall of 1944. It was Hayes who had pressed for Bill's military discharge and immediate reemployment as a civilian Russian translator. Among the staff of the Russian Section, it was common knowledge that the two of them were frequently seen standing together laughing, drinking, and talking at the officers' club bar. One person with knowledge of Hayes's official routine as head of ASA described the ease that Weisband displayed as he walked in and out of Hayes's office at all hours of the day to chat with the boss. And despite Bill's lowly position in ASA's hierarchy, Hayes nonetheless authorized him to read the top-secret *Daily Intelligence Digest* containing the best intelligence collected by ASA every twenty-four hours.

It was a few months after the wedding of Mabel and Bill in January 1949 that Hayes was promoted to the top job at the army's Alaska Command at Fort Richardson, Alaska. It was there that a local FBI agent appeared one day seeking information about Weisband. Given the gravity of circumstances, Hayes seemed remarkably indifferent to the fact that he was being questioned about a close friend accused of espionage. He offered little to an FBI agent who knew nothing about the case. The two men first met in North Africa, he claimed, when Hayes was commanding the 849th Signal Intelligence Service. He found him to be a "well qualified" translator in French, German, Russian, and Italian. After returning to Arlington Hall, he made a "routine" request for Weisband's services, finding him "capable of performing the work to which he was assigned." Hayes assured his interviewer that while overseas he had no access to top-secret material. At Arlington Hall, however, "all kinds of classified matters" passed across his desk.[19]

Despite a year earlier being convinced that America's catastrophic cryptologic losses against Russian communications were due to a leak, Hayes saw no reason to question Weisband's loyalty yet cautioned that he was "not intimately acquainted with him." Their relationship had always been "entirely official" with little social interaction other than one occasion when he visited the subject's home to attend a party and "possibly" a few other events. As for Bill's family background he knew nothing except that he may have been born in "one of the Balkan countries." Hayes thought that before the war he was a traveling jewelry salesman in Europe. In 1949, he recalled, Weisband had married a co-worker whose name he could not recall.[20]

* * *

As for Jones and the FBI—two weeks after the start of the case, a crossroads had been reached. Weisband had been removed from access to certain top-secret information just days after the start of the investigation, and pressure was mounting from ASA officials to completely close the door to all secrets. For a brief moment Belmont considered installing a wiretap on his home telephone; a step that was rejected in light of Bill's knowledge of surveillance and an ongoing government investigation. In the end the decision was made for Jones to confront him with the facts as he knew them in the hope of eliciting a confession or at least damaging admissions that could aid further investigation.

The interview with William Weisband began around 3:00 p.m. on May 9, 1950, when Jones and Walter arrived at Arlington Hall to meet with him. For the next hour and a half, they waited at his desk as no one knew where he was.

Weisband was surprised and became "extremely nervous" when he found the FBI men waiting for him. His anxiety, however, "visibly subsided" when told that they wished to interview him, and it would be strictly voluntary. Weisband agreed, Jones later recorded, because his "curiosity was aroused."[21]

After driving Mabel home, he joined Jones for the ride to the Washington Field Office located on the first floor of the Department of Justice Building along Pennsylvania Avenue. The interview began at 5:20 that evening.

Jones opened the discussion by getting to the heart of the matter. The FBI had recently interviewed Jones Orin York, who had worked in the California aircraft industry before the war. During that period, he had been a source for Russian intelligence, providing them with blueprints and documents on military aircraft. He delivered these items through a series of handlers and when shown a photo of Weisband, York recognized him as one of them. When Jones asked for an explanation, Weisband was incredulous. He had no idea why York picked him out as a spy. Perhaps he had been misidentified or confused with someone else. He insisted that he did not know York, nor had he ever met him. Along with his denials came assurances that he had never committed espionage, nor did he know any Russian spies, all the while insisting that he was 100 percent loyal to the United States.

Jones then shifted the questioning to the coincidence of Bill's sudden departure from New York to California in June 1941. Over the next hour or so Bill offered a variety of interesting answers. War was on the horizon and military service was not far off. As an East Coast guy who had never been out of New York, he wanted to head west to "see the country" before being drafted. After arriving in Los Angeles, he found he liked the lifestyle the city offered and decided to stay. His second tale dealt with getting away from a personal headache. She was his old girlfriend, Patricia Grimes, a woman he met at the Roseland Ballroom. She was separated from her husband when they first met. He explained that while the two of them were lovers he still tried to help her reconcile with her husband. As for any comments he may have made to her about "secret work," clearly, she misconstrued them as something sinister or it may have been his simple attempt to impress her. (Note: He failed to mention that shortly after his arrival in California she joined him in Los Angeles and picked up the relationship.) Finally, he volunteered a third reason—he wanted to put his New York years behind him because of his late brother, Harold, the "black sheep" of the family. Weisband recounted Harold's embezzlement of funds from the Lexington Hotel and theft of jewelry from the family business to help finance his gambling habit. As for his own employment in California, the conversation turned to the Miramar Hotel, where he got a job through Joe Gray, an old friend from the New York hotel business. That job soon ended when he became dissatisfied with the position and "unable to get along" with his bosses. He closed by joking that "management was undoubtedly pleased to learn that he was leaving as their relationship had been unsatisfactory."[22]

Jones then began delving deeper into Bill's past. Why did he suddenly leave his job at the Waldorf-Astoria in 1936 for full-time enrolment at the RCA Institute? In a blithe response, Bill explained that the radio field offered a pathway to a prosperous career and better income. After taking a series of courses, he found that this brief foray into academia did not offer the big money he had hoped for.

The conversation then switched to his arrest with John Pollock. It was all a misunderstanding, Bill charged, starting innocently enough when he traveled to Philadelphia for an "unexpected" visit with relatives. When they weren't at home, he began "wandering aimlessly about," eventually making his way to a local pool hall. It was there that he fell into a brief conversation with Pollock, who spoke English with a heavy Russian accent. He soon left the pool hall to meet his relatives, claiming that he never gave Pollock his Brooklyn address nor made any arrangements to meet him again. Then one day while standing in front of the family's jewelry store, Pollock walked by him "purely by chance." He was in New York looking for work and a place to live. Bill also remembered him carrying "several thousand dollars."[23] Weisband shared his own difficulties with Pollock, telling him that he was experiencing problems living with his mother and that his brother, Mark, had very little room for him in his apartment. With that the two men decided to room together at the Haven Avenue address. After a month or so they became dissatisfied with the apartment and decided to leave. Bill conveniently slid over the fact that the rent was due and the landlady called the police. Both men were arrested with Weisband released a day or so later and Pollock taken to Ellis Island as an illegal alien. He had neither seen nor heard from him since the day they were arrested. The best he could remember was that Pollock was of average height and weight, in his early thirties, drank liquor, spoke with a heavy Russian accent, and had been an auto mechanic in the Detroit, Michigan, area.

Next, Bill outlined his overseas military service. He was assigned to the Fifth Army in North Africa and Italy, where he was detailed to the French Expeditionary Corp as a radio security specialist teaching coding to communicators and ensuring the security of radio transmissions. He then deviated from his own script revealing a request from his commanders to steal codes used by the FEC to communicate within their higher echelons. Somehow, he accomplished this feat by approaching a French general and passing them to Fifth Army leaders. Colonel Hayes was "highly delighted" with his success.[24] From this coup came an opportunity from Hayes to leave Italy and return to a new assignment at Arlington Hall.

By this stage of the interview, Weisband knew that Jones had nothing on him except York's word. As his confidence grew, he became increasingly relaxed. The more he was questioned the more long-winded and "extremely nebulous" he became, answering Jones's questions in a casual and "offhand manner." At the same time, the agents began to sense that he was trying to take control by prolonging the interview. It became apparent that he was asking his own questions, Jones reported, in what he saw as an "effort to determine whether Bureau sources could be divulged." Perhaps with thoughts of Meredith Gardner and Venona, he challenged Jones on whether the FBI's sources in this case were "indisputable."[25]

Moving on, Jones turned to Vivian and Victor Cubarkin. Without missing a beat, Weisband conjured up another convenient lie. Like his encounter with Pollock, he met Victor by accident one day when he approached the bar at the Miramar Hotel where Bill was working. Again, Weisband picked up on his Russian accent and the two men fell into conversation. From this chance meeting a friendship developed that had lasted to the present time. He was then confronted with the name Stanislav Shumovsky, the KGB officer who recruited York in 1936. Weisband denied knowing him but just as quickly offered that the name did "sound familiar." He believed that Shumovsky was a friend of the Cubarkins, and that Victor Cubarkin once showed him a photo of someone named "Stan." He thought "by chance" he might be the person Jones was referring to. As for Cubarkin, he knew him well and believed that he was a loyal citizen of the United States.[26]

Bill was then asked why in 1946 and again in 1947 he marked "Yes" on official loyalty forms when asked if he supports the overthrow of the United State government by force or violence. Once again, he breezily brushed Jones aside. It was a simple mistake, he claimed, made in haste while rushing to complete the form.

As the interview continued Jones turned to the topic of finances. After some prodding, the first critical break occurred in Weisband's armor. At first he shied away from discussing the sources of his income. Eventually he admitted that he had been a "heavy gambler in the past."[27] After returning from overseas he began betting large sums at Jimmy La Fontaine's gambling casino. When Fontaine's closed he moved on to a gambling den in Laurel, Maryland, which he refused to identify. As for wins and losses he estimated that, over the five years he had worked at Arlington Hall, his gambling losses had totaled a jaw-dropping $25,000 ($274,000 in January 2020). When asked how he could afford such staggering losses he dismissed the question by pointing to sales of jewelry to Arlington Hall employees as well as occasional winnings and finally his government salary. When asked, he could not estimate the number of sales he had made. Pressed further he said that upon his mother's death in 1944, jewelry from the store was left to him and Mark, who would send him pieces as well as items from his job with the Harry Winston firm in New York. He remembered his largest sale in 1948 to a dentist in New York City totaling three thousand dollars. Yet, when asked, he refused to identify the buyer. Another big purchaser was a woman co-worker at Arlington Hall.

When asked about his spending habits he told Jones that he and Mabel often traveled to New York City because of their "boredom" with life in Washington.[28] How often they visited was determined by how "dissatisfied" they became "with the lack of activity in metropolitan Washington." He never owned a camera, had little interest in them, and the only camera he ever purchased was in January 1949 for his honeymoon.[29]

These startling revelations logically moved the conversation in the direction of his borrowing habits. He had taken a loan, he conceded, from Edith Weisband, his sister-in-law, for $1,000 ($11,671 in January 2020), which he was still in the process of repaying. He also felt personally "indebted" to her for having furnished him with the proceeds of Mark's share of the jewelry inventory from their mother's estate. When asked about his current relationship with Edith, he described it as "friendly," but he never saw her when he went to New York. Then in another startling admission he revealed that he claimed Edith and her son as dependents on his federal income tax forms. When asked if he contributes to their livelihood, he replied "occasionally." She lived modestly on Social Security, he noted, earning some additional income through the sale of stockings to tenants in her apartment building.[30]

At 11:30 p.m., six hours after first sitting down with Jones, the interview finally ended. One of the last agenda items was a request for a voluntary search of his home. At first, he agreed but as they drove closer to his home, he wavered. He would still sign the consent form with "reservations" but was opposed to the search due to the lateness of the hour and the fact that his wife was most likely asleep. She had to wake up early for work. There was also his concern that Jones would probably find a 45-caliber handgun, which was not registered in Virginia.

Jones met Weisband the next morning at the Arlington Trust Company in Arlington, Virginia, where he agreed to a voluntary search for safe-deposit box number 1053. With Weisband looking on, Jones removed three one-hundred-dollar bills and two fifty-dollar bills (September 2020 value of $4,400). Stored with the cash was a pawn ticket from the Provident Loan Society located at Times Square in New York City. A close examination revealed that it had been renewed on February 17, 1950, for $209 ($2,300 in September 2020) and collateralized by eighteen pieces of jewelry ranging from pins and bracelets to chains, necklaces, and a knife. When asked, Weisband estimated their value at $1,000 (September 2023 value of $11,000). Also found were the marriage license to Mabel before Judge George D. Nielson in Washington, DC, on January 15, 1949, and Bill's certificate of naturalization.[31]

Two days later it was a distraught Mabel's turn to face Jones. After Bill's May 9 interview, he had lied to her by describing it as a mix-up due to an "immigration matter he was involved in at one time." She expressed "shock" to learn that the FBI believed that her husband had committed espionage, calling the charges "incredible." Mabel couldn't believe her husband capable of such treachery, she told Jones, yet she remained troubled at the "seriousness of the matter and accuracy of the allegations" against him. If he was a spy, it occurred before they met as she had seen no hint of such behavior since they had been together. She then pondered the consequences with concerns about possible loss of their employment, as well as his denaturalization and the resultant publicity. She knew nothing about such matters and believed that some misidentification or mistake had been made. If the charges were true, however, than he must confess to Jones. In the end she assured the FBI man that in view of the seriousness of the charges she would make every effort to convince Bill to sit down once again with the FBI and tell the full story.[32]

While Mabel sat pouring out her concerns to Jones, Los Angeles office agents were busy interviewing Victor Cubarkin. He only added to Weisband's woes by denying that he first met him at the bar of the Hotel Miramar. They met in 1941 when Bill appeared unannounced at the front door of his home. After warmly greeting Victor, he explained that he was a friend of Stanislav Shumovsky, who urged him to look up the Cubarkins when he arrived in California.

What Bill and Mabel did not know was that overnight word had been received from Los Angeles that Bill's old girlfriend, Patricia Grimes, had been reinterviewed. As before, she once again insisted that she had misconstrued nothing as Weisband claimed. She repeated her charges that while they were together in New York he would suddenly stop the car, get out, and meet people on a street corner who were engaged with him in "secret work." After envelopes and package were exchanged, he would return to the car elated. Grimes was also certain that on a number of occasions, he warned her not to be surprised if one day he could suddenly "disappear." She also insisted that she and Bill visited a couple in New Jersey and brought a gift of painted glasses with them.[33]

A day later, an angry Weisband telephoned Jones telling him that he and Mabel wished to sit down once again with him to discuss the matter. He explained that since the last interview on May 9, 1950, he and his wife had both been suspended without pay from ASA. When they arrived, Bill warned Jones that he had little to say and was only there at the insistence of his wife, who was pressuring him to clear up the matter. A hardened Jones minced no words with Weisband. The FBI suspected him of spying for the Russians and he once again was being afforded the opportunity to tell the truth. For Jones the next three hours were a repeat of the first interview with Bill claiming once again that he had done nothing wrong while "steadfastly" denying any involvement in espionage.

When confronted with Grimes's statements to the FBI just hours earlier, he parried her claims with flat-out denials. It had been years since they were together, which may account for her confusion and poor recollection. He never visited anyone in New Jersey as she claimed. Then suddenly he changed his story. He now recalled visits to the home of a couple named George and Frances Goldman who lived with their child in Brooklyn. George was an engineer and Frances was a homemaker. He first met them in 1934 at Mark and Edith's wedding and they had remained friends ever since. As for gifts of painted glasses—this never happened but may be confused with his "usual practice to take a small gift to the host and hostess when invited to dinner."[34]

As for her charges about his secret work and odd behavior while driving along the street—he called them ridiculous. Turning to his comments about disappearing, he again changed his story. It is possible that he did make such remarks. But then just as quickly, he bizarrely excused his behavior saying that he often said such things to Mabel when they quarreled. When questioned further, he could not recall any of his contacts in California. Jones prompted him with a couple of names, including Gregori Heiffets, the Soviet consul in San Francisco, but he denied knowing any of them. His attitude never changed when faced with Cubarkin's recent contradiction of how and where they met in June 1941. Boxed in with nowhere to turn he stood his ground, asserting that York, Grimes, and Cubarkin were all mistaken.

Mabel was interviewed separately from Bill. She repeated her amazement at the charges, telling Jones that she would provide him with anything that she learned from her husband. She explained that she opens the mail at home but has found nothing unusual. All telephone calls are from people that she and Bill know with the one infrequent exception from a mystery man who never leaves a name or call-back number. When asked, Bill described him as a "bookie" pestering him for fifty dollars he owes him (January 2020 equivalent of $550).

After more futile questioning, Weisband's nine-hour face-off with Jones finally ended with a second request to search his home. Mabel agreed but Bill refused. The ordeal of the past few days was overwhelming, he said. He was just "too tired" and "overwrought."[35]

## NOTES

1. Unknown to Belmont at the time were the fragments of information Meredith Gardner and Bob Lamphere were extracting from Russian messages that would lead

to the arrest and conviction of atomic spies Julius Rosenberg and his wife, Ethel. Three years later Belmont would be anxiously sitting in a room at Sing Sing Prison in New York, just feet away from the death house, waiting and hoping that one of them would confess to their crimes, sparing Ethel's execution. Weisband FBI file, Alan H. Belmont, FBI Personnel File, 67–94639, Internet Archives.

2. A. H. Belmont memorandum to Ladd, April 14, 1950, Weisband FBI file.

3. Author interview of Courtland Jones, November 28, 2004. Hereafter referred to as "Jones Interview."

4. Jones Interview. Author interview of Donald Walter, December 2, 2004.

5. DM Ladd memorandum to Hoover, April 14, 1950. Hoover initialed "I agree" on the memorandum. Weisband FBI file.

6. Ibid.

7. It seems that Panyushkin's concerns for overall security of the Weisband operation had been building for some months. At some point he had asked Moscow to switch contact with him from a Washington station officer to an illegal. On March 28, 1950, two weeks before York's identification of him as his handler, Panyushkin received the news that there were "no opportunities to give the connection with Zhora to an illegal." VBN 95.

8. DM Ladd memorandum to Hoover, April 21, 1950, Weisband FBI file.

9. AH Belmont to DM Ladd, April 25, 1950, Weisband FBI file.

10. Ibid.

11. *Life*, February 21, 1949. New York Report, May 8, 1950, Weisband FBI file.

12. AH Belmont Memorandum to DM Ladd, April 25, 1950, Weisband FBI file.

13. WFO letter to Hoover, April 26, 1950, Weisband FBI file.

14. Belmont memorandum to Ladd, April 30, /1950, Weisband FBI file.

15. Remembering RADM Earl Stone, 14th Commander to lead our Community, Station HYPO, Celebrating the Past, Present, and Future of Navy Cryptology, Cryptology Information Warfare, Undated, Author interview of Ellen Haring, 5/7/2002.

16. DM Ladd memorandum to Hoover, April 21, 1950, Weisband FBI file.

17. Ibid.

18. AH Belmont Memorandum to DM Ladd, April 30, 1950, Weisband FBI file.

19. FBI Alaska Report, May 5, 1950, Weisband FBI file.

20. Ibid.

21. Jones interview of Weisband, May 9, 1950, Weisband FBI file.

22. Ibid.

23. Ibid.

24. Ibid.

25. Ibid.

26. Ibid.

27. Ibid.

28. Ibid.

29. Ibid.

30. Ibid.

31. WFO Report, June 2, 1950, Weisband FBI file.

32. CA Hennrich memorandum to Belmont, May 11, 1950, WFO teletype, May 11, 1950, Weisband FBI file.
33. Los Angeles Report, June 1, 1950, Weisband FBI file.
34. Jones interview of Weisband, May 9, 1950, Weisband FBI file.
35. Ibid.

## Chapter 33

# Flight

Days after Jones's interviews of Bill and Mabel, agents were sitting in Edith Weisband's Brooklyn apartment. From the start of the conversation, she was defensive with little interest in providing any meaningful information. As Bill and Mabel lived in Virginia, she hardly saw them except during their rare visits to New York. He had been in the army during the war and was now working in a secret government job. As for any financial relationship with her brother-in-law, she assured the agents she had none. When asked, she confirmed Bill's statement to Jones that he had been contributing one thousand dollars a year to her for support since the death of her husband, Mark.

A week later, FBI agents were again at Edith's door after receiving a phone call from her. Her tone and behavior this time were vastly different. Following the first interview with the FBI, she called Bill to alert him. A day or so later he and Mabel unexpectedly appeared at her door. She remembered Bill, seeming nervous and distracted, offering no reason for a sudden visit with his widowed sister-in-law after such a long time.

During the stay Edith brought up FBI questions about George and Francis Goldman, a couple Bill claimed to have met in 1934 at Edith's wedding. When she asked him who they were he expressed surprise. He reminded her that they met at the wedding and have since remained friends. He even took Patricia Grimes to their "New Jersey" home on one occasion for a visit. Edith assured the agents that she knew no one by that name.

Building up a head of steam, Edith then got to the real reason for calling the FBI. She had not been truthful during her first interview because she wanted to protect Bill and herself. For nearly two years Weisband had been claiming Edith and her son, Edward, as dependents on his income tax filings. After some thought she now realized that going along with Bill's scheme "could falsely reflect on her and her son," causing them legal troubles. She wanted it known that Weisband had never contributed anything toward her support.

With the truth now out in the open, Edith suddenly felt free to lower the boom on Bill. As the agents sat listening, she explained that for six months following her husband's death in December 1947 she loaned Bill large sums of money. The purpose of the loans, she explained, was to cover "gambling losses and bills due." To prove her point she produced six canceled checks drawn on the Colonial Trust Company of New York from December 15, 1947, through May 18, 1948, payable to Bill totaling $2,151 ($25,300 in April 2022). Bill also knew that Edith had cashed in a $1,500 life insurance policy.[1]

The embittered woman now went further. On the death of Sarah Weisband in 1944, Bill and Mark each received $800 ($12,000 in September 2020) from her insurance policy plus jewelry she kept at her home, some which had since been sold. When Mark died, Bill seized the entire collection with a promise to sell it and split the proceeds with Edith. The loan remained outstanding, and she had never seen a dime from the jewelry sale.

* * *

William Weisband had every reason to be nervous during his visit with Edith. Within hours of the conclusion of the FBI interviews, the new head of AFSA, Admiral Earl Stone, abruptly placed both Weisband and his wife on "administrative leave" without pay for ninety days. Since then, Stone had made several inquiries with the Department of the Army concerning his decision and had come away with some disturbing findings. As for Mabel, she had joined ASA as a civilian and could be fired without administrative worry. Bill, on the other hand, was far more problematic. His status as a military veteran with wartime service overseas created serious obstacles that could make it "difficult to take action against him." During one discussion, Jones made it clear to Stone that Weisband's admissions of massive gambling losses and espionage in 1943 for the Fifth Army while serving in Italy "certainly appeared sufficient" to warrant the admiral's actions. Stone remained concerned, however, that despite Jones's points, he was wading in uncharted waters as this was the first such case of its kind at AFSA. Furthermore, he was unsure if he actually had the authority to suspend him in light of recently passed legislation governing employee rights of veterans. Stone, in fact, hoped that both Weisbands would resign in light of the serious charges facing them. Such a move would solve the government's problem by avoiding any embarrassment and security implications of Weisband filing a complaint that could publicize the case and expose the work underway at AFSA. Jones cautioned Stone that the Bureau could make no recommendations yet urged him to consider all "ramifications" before making any further decisions. Weisband might still confess to his espionage activities, Jones suggested, and could "express a willingness to operate against the Russians." There was also a concern that Stone might later be the target of criticism for "merely requesting the resignation of a serious security risk." Stone then acknowledged not thinking about this so instead issued the order to "suspend" both pending the outcome of the investigation.²

Armed with Edith's admissions, investigators began combing through Bill Weisband's finances. His income tax records for 1946 showed a salary of $1,260.84, for 1947 it was $4,183.34, and for 1948 it was $4,472.64. There were three loans with General Motors Acceptance Corporation between 1947 and 1949. The first was on August 26, 1947 (two months before Weisband's sudden trip to California) for $1,852.65 on the purchase of a new 1947 Buick and another on December 15, 1948, for the repairs of the car in the amount of $321.48. A third was a follow-up loan on August 9, 1949, for $57.30 for additional auto repairs. The account was paid off on February 17, 1950. There were also signature loans starting on November 26, 1946, for $200; October 2, 1948, for $300; January 13, 1949, for $300; and later that year on September 22, 1949, for $575 collateralized with the 1947 Buick (total $17,740 in 2023). At the time of the FBI inquiry, he had paid off most of it with $193.40 still outstanding. On December 16, 1948, he opened an account with Garfinkel's Department Store in Washington on purchases of $399.24 ($5,083 in 2023). On August 3, 1949, he and Mabel, now married, spent $675 ($7,280 in September 2020) for a Stromberg-Carlson television set with an outstanding balance of $420.45.³

A closer look at Weisband's banking history produced some equally disturbing results. In 1948, for instance, he made large unexplained cash deposits totaling $9,447 ($103,000 in January 2020) into his account. For the tax year 1949, Bill and Mabel filed a joint income tax return claiming an adjusted income of $8,259 ($93,384 in January 2020) while still listing Edith, her son, Edward, and Wayne Woody as dependents. That same year there were further unexplained cash deposits amounting to $9,336 ($102,428 in January 2020).⁴

Over the ensuing months, Jones's suspicions of Weisband's treachery only deepened as investigators dug further. While assigned to Vint Hill Farm in 1943 for military training, he had opened a bank account at Arlington Trust Company in Arlington, Virginia. Over nearly seven years from the date of its opening to May 19, 1950 (a week after his FBI interviews), he had deposited a staggering sum of $43,567.30 ($519,738.04 in April 2022). Equally startling for Jones and the FBI was discovering that during that time he had steadily wiped out these huge savings with withdrawals totaling $42,854.99.⁵

\* \* \*

While Stone grappled with the bureaucratic tangles of Weisband's suspension, the FBI's discreet investigation now burst out into the open. Interviews of anyone who could shed light on Bill's past promptly got underway. Leads were set out around the country to display Weisband's photo to important sources, including Harry Gold, doing jail time for his role in the Julius and Ethel Rosenberg case, as well as Elizabeth Bentley, Louis Budenz, a Communist Party defector in New York, and Jay David Whittaker Chamber in Baltimore, Maryland—none of whom knew him. With the authority of headquarters and the assistance of AFSA, a list of current and former employees was developed of those who knew him and they too began to be interviewed for insights into his activities at Arlington Hall.

Chief among them were friends and co-workers from his past five years at ASA. Most of them recounted how Colonel Hayes had placed Weisband in the Russian Section. One person recalled that Hayes "thought most highly of him," echoing the observations of many, that the two men were often seen together at the office and in social settings. Hayes made it a practice of "frequently" inviting junior officers to his home for a drink with Weisband among them. He was also known for his close association with the other "top officials at Arlington Hall." One resentful co-worker acidly described how Bill often "threw his weight around" in the section based on his high-powered connections.[6]

Bill Weisband's spending habits were also a matter of gossip. He was a "playboy," someone said, living "beyond his means"; a "continental" type who liked to drink and entertain women. One female colleague told agents she had as little to do with him as possible. He was slick—always coming off as "too suave." Investigators also kept hearing repeated stories about his gambling activities. Another oddly described him as a "lone wolf" who was "not friendly with anyone." He was a heavy gambler and made no effort to hide it. So brazen was he that on one occasion he approached someone with a scheme to create a partnership by "making book." They could make money, Bill suggested, placing bets on horses for Arlington Hall co-workers. The source declined the offer and never knew if Bill ever followed through with his plan.[7]

It was through these relationships at all levels plus his many and varied assignments in the Russian program over five years that gave him both broad and deep access to everything going on at Arlington Hall. There was a "shrewdness" about him one person noted that gave him a "coherent knowledge of what went on at AFSA."[8]

Agents also probed his politics and attitude toward the Soviet Union. The few times he did discuss such matters, he would make a big point of "declaring himself an American." To one person he expressed his resentment of discrimination in the United States against Negroes and Jews. When the source agreed, Weisband went on to claim that such attitudes could not occur in the Soviet Union because the communists were, in his words, "progressive." Still another person recalled group conversations at the officers' club about the nature of communism and the Soviet Union. When asked for his thoughts, he would smile and reply simply "let's have a drink."[9]

Bill had been assigned to the Russian program since returning from Italy in 1945. Since his conversion to civilian status in 1946 he had received only one promotion, which rankled him terribly. One person calling him "goldbrick" noted that he worked hard trying to get out of work. Many described his habit of walking around chatting with people outside his workspace when he should have been at his station doing his work. He was always visiting people, one critic remembered, "ostensibly for the purpose of friendship" but "really to avoid work in his section." Efforts to assist him in advancement often failed. One person outlined his shortcomings best by describing how he would be assigned to lead a project and then work diligently only to be pressed by management to complete it. He moved around a lot to various assignments and at one time ran a school for new employees. After three years with no advancement, he finally took his complaints to higher management. When he groused about his salary, he went silent when a supervisor suggested he consider a transfer to the new CIA. Another urged him to leave ASA and return to the hotel business for which he seemed well qualified and had numerous contacts. This suggestion was quickly rejected. "It was more important," Weisband said, "to be employed on an intelligence level and to do work important to the country." What followed were more moves, which eventually led to his promotion in 1949.[10]

Among Weisband's biggest workplace frustrations was the growing quality of linguists being recruited by ASA. When he started in 1945 his colloquial language skills were highly coveted in a cryptologic world where Russian linguists were at a premium. Over the next five years as America and Great Britain turned increasing attention to Moscow, the code-breaking communities began actively recruiting college and university graduates with critical language skills and knowledge of the culture and politics. Bill felt threatened by these new hires, calling them "effeminate" because they were talented, many with graduate degrees, who were suddenly competing with him for jobs and promotions that he felt rightfully belonged to him. Weisband felt the sting and made no effort to conceal his feelings, telling one supervisor that "they generally didn't like him."[11]

Bill Weisband's enrollment in 1949 as a language student at the Georgetown University Institute of Foreign Languages came under scrutiny. Even there he faced criticism. His professors described him as "poorly regarded" among his classmates and instructors alike due to his colloquial command of the language. He also expressed little interest in learning the more formal aspects of the language as evidenced by his attitude in class and frequent absences. There were also comments on Weisband's "egotism," as evidenced by his claims of superior knowledge of the language and interest in pursuing a formal degree for "appearances sake." More than once he bragged that he had "Ph.Ds" working for him. One professor went so far as to suggest that his boasting was a way of masking his "inadequacy" in the language and in doing so made him appear "stupid."[12]

Investigation at Georgetown also produced a particularly intriguing observation from a faculty member who got to know him. The two men had a series of conversations about the Soviet Union with the professor describing his puzzlement over whether Bill was taking an "anti-czarist" stand or merely questioning him out of general curiosity. As they talked more, he came to believe that Weisband was "whitewashing" the Russians and was "prone to forgive" their tyranny by rationalizing the need of the Russian people for strong leadership and stringent discipline because they had only known despotism throughout their history. When asked, the professor concluded that Weisband did not have "enough intelligence to be a good operative."[13]

A source familiar with the investigation reported Weisband's claim that he was being "shadowed" by the FBI and when interviewed had been treated "rather rough" and then just as quickly reversed himself saying that he was treated "nicely." As for his suspension he called Stone's action a "raw deal," accusing the FBI of holding something over his head from 1938 and pressuring him to admit it. They learned that he had applied for and began receiving a $78.75 a month allowance from Veterans Administration under the GI Bill of Rights.[14]

Investigators soon found themselves in downtown Washington at the Statler Hotel interviewing a friend from Bill's New York hotel days. When he applied for a credit card a few weeks earlier the two men fell into talking. It was then that he learned that Weisband was under investigation by the FBI and had been interviewed without going into details. Bill told him that the investigation would end "should he officially resign his position" at AFSA. He was "so certain" that he would be cleared that he planned to return to his job with no intention of resigning. Weisband hinted that in the meantime he needed a job to "tide him over financially" until this matter was settled. His friend introduced him to the employment office but was doubtful of his getting the job. In his experience he found it "unsatisfactory" when experienced people are assigned to a "menial job" as it often led the person to throw his "weight around."[15]

\* \* \*

At the same time FBI agents continued to follow him. Just days after his interviews alarm bells sounded when he was seen peering at directories in the lobbies housing the offices of the *Washington Post* and the *Washington Evening Standard*. FBI and army officials shuddered at the thought that he was considering retaliation by telling his story to the press. He also purchased tickets to the circus for Mabel and himself and continued to attend language classes at Georgetown University.

But despite the business-as-usual demeanor, Weisband was beginning to feel the pressure of losing his livelihood and standing in the bull's-eye of a major FBI espionage investigation. On June 23, 1950, while returning the Bureau car to the garage, an agent noticed Weisband following him. When stopped at a traffic light, Bill came alongside the agent's vehicle. He said simply that he "wasn't feeling well" because he had no money and then drove off. A few nights later, it was an intoxicated Weisband who telephoned Jones for more than an hour berating him for putting him in this terrible position. His family life had been "disturbed," he thundered, saying that he had been "degraded . . . in the eyes of his wife." Cursing and swearing, he demanded to be arrested and face his "accusers" or be cleared of all charges. Next, he began ranting about FBI questioning of his teachers and classmates at Georgetown University and then pivoted to criticizing the FBI for his "grillings" and just as quickly describing Jones and other agents in "favorable terms." He knew his rights he claimed and planned to charge the FBI with "defamation of character and defied agents to arrest him." But in the next breath he admitted an unfamiliarity with the law and asked Jones for legal advice. In the end he called Jones a "liar" and an abuser of the Constitution, saying that he would appear at his office on June 26, 1950, for more interviews.[16]

Days later he again telephoned Jones, this time apologizing for his behavior. He regretted his actions, citing the fact he had been "drinking and his wife had threatened to leave him." When asked why he did not appear as promised for further interview, he denied ever making this statement as he had already provided all he knew. He then told Jones that he intended to travel to Los Angeles "in the immediate future" in order to confront Grimes about the "malicious information" she provided to the FBI and then curiously asked Jones if he would be interested in the results of his conversations with her. When Jones expressed interest, Weisband asked if the FBI could provide travel funds for the trip.[17]

Weisband and Mabel departed their home at noon by car on June 28, 1950, with the FBI hot on his heels. Before long agents pulled him over to the side of the road with offers of another chance to explain his side of the story. He had done his talking, he screamed, and then taunted the agents, hinting that he was traveling either to Los Angeles or possibly Massachusetts. Next came a warning that he would attempt to embarrass the agents if he detected surveillance.[18]

Agents next spotted him two weeks later on the morning of July 9 crossing into California near the town of San Bernadino. To their surprise he was now driving a new Buick with the original Virginia license plates. Bill was soon overheard telling a gas station attendant that his car broke down, forcing him to buy a new one in Laramie, Wyoming. Agents later learned that he paid a $45 ($486 in 2020) towing charge and purchased a new Buick with a $318 ($3,434 in 2020) cash down payment while financing the rest through GMAC Finance Corporation.

Later that day, having arrived in Santa Monica, California, the couple's first stop was the home of Vivian and Victor Cubarkin. Seeing that the couple were not at home, they checked into a local hotel. The following day Bill and Mabel returned to the Cubarkin home, spending eight hours with the couple and another hour that evening at Weisband's hotel room. Unbeknownst to Weisband, the FBI was eavesdropping on his conversations through a microphone installed in his hotel room. During one conversation he remarked that he felt that regarding the government's investigation he was psychologically in a favorable position. He told Cubarkin that "if they get rough, I'll go to another country. Of course, they wouldn't let me out legally." As for his appearance before a grand jury he wobbled, saying "I'm not sure whether to perjure myself if need be. I'm willing to go to jail for a while rather than talk."[19]

The following day, July 12, the FBI turned up the heat with the delivery of a subpoena demanding his appearance at a grand jury that same day. Having spoken to a local attorney, Weisband met with US attorney Ernest A. Tolin at his office. When Tolin explained that his appearance had been postponed for a week until July 19, 1950, Weisband became "very angry" and "very much put out." He had traveled cross-country to California for a much-needed vacation, to visit friends, and to show his wife the sights. Having to wait around for such a length of time, he charged, would place an onerous hardship on him and to prove it he opened his wallet, displaying $200 ($2,160 in September 2020). The shortage of funds, he conceded, was due to a stop in Las Vegas, where he "lost heavily gambling." Unmoved, Tolin told him to appear on July 19, 1950, as ordered or face arrest. Weisband explained that he would leave for Washington that same day and return for his appearance on July 19, 1950, but then asked what would happen if he was late in arriving. A bench warrant for his arrest would be issued, Tolin reminded him. In the end, Weisband made no promise but agreed to "try to return to Los Angeles on time." Just five days after arriving in Los Angeles, Weisband departed for home, arriving in Arlington, Virginia, on July 19, 1950, the date set for his grand jury appearance. The FBI confirmed that Bill was "visibly upset" at having to drive back to Virginia and was threatening not to return "unless the government brings him back."[20]

\* \* \*

Behind the scenes, Weisband's erratic behavior was becoming a source of serious concern within the FBI leadership. What would be his next move? "He has no binding ties" to the area, Belmont wrote, and serious consideration must be given to the possibility that he will "sever all connections and attempt to disappear." Belmont's observations, most likely based on the FBI's recorded conversations, characterized him as desperate based on his suggestion that he may flee to Mexico "if the heat gets on." A feverish debate quickly ensued within the FBI regarding possible criminal charges. Denaturalization proceedings were off the table while perjury charges were possible especially in regard to his false statements to Jones concerning meetings with principals, accepting packages and envelopes, and having extra funds. This was supported by Grimes's statements and his denials with FBI agents reporting that she would make a "strong witness."[21]

On July 13, 1950, the day after Weisband's testy meeting with Tolin, Assistant attorney general James McInerney weighed in on the matter with Belmont. He informed him how "very fresh" Bill was with Tolin the day before. He had put up "considerable objection" at returning to Los Angeles for the grand jury appearance, citing how such a long stay in California would impose a "great hardship" on him. McInerney told Tolin to "stand firm" on the July 19 appearance date as "venue for any violation involved as a result of Weisband's activities lies in Los Angeles." McInerney then asked about Weisband's money situation. Belmont noted that the FBI had little understanding about his finances. What was known was that he seemed to have sufficient funds to travel cross country on his own volition for a vacation, gamble for a day or so at Las Vegas, and still have enough for a cash down payment on a new Buick automobile. That was enough for McInerney.[22]

\* \* \*

While Bill and Mabel headed east, FBI agents once again interviewed Grimes. After nearly a decade of no contact, Bill had suddenly appeared at her door. He was "frantic," she told agents, claiming that he was in "a lot of trouble." He and Mabel had been suspended from their employment and he feared they would be unable to get a job. He raged at the subpoena to testify at a grand jury and being "persecuted" by the FBI. The FBI was trying to "get him" for contempt of court or perjury, telling Grimes that he and his wife were now taking it for granted that he would be going to jail. He then started pressuring Grimes, ranting that his former friends were abandoning him when he was in trouble and then telling her that she was not compelled to make any statements to the FBI.

Grimes then recalled another incident while they were together in New York. One day while driving in New York City the subject pulled over to the curb and got out. Before doing so he told Grimes not to look back nor to watch him in the rearview mirror while he made his contact. He warned her that if he did not return, she was to take the car and not to return to the area. Asking about him would come to the "attention of the people he was working for," signaling that he had taken her into his confidence about his "secret work" and prompting them to "take action against him." Weisband was "definitely afraid" that these unknowns would "take action" against him. Bill feared that he could become the victim of a cleverly handled "accident" so that even his family and friends could not know what happened.[23]

Next on the FBI lists of interviews was Victor Cubarkin. Over the course of a few hours, he railed at Weisband for "putting he and Vivian in a bad position" with lies about the two men first meeting at the Miramar Hotel bar. Cubarkin clearly recalled their first encounter at his front door in 1941 when Bill introduced himself as a friend of "Stan." Cubarkin freely acknowledged having known Stanislaw Shumovsky but had never seen the two men together. But taking Bill's claim on face value, Victor accepted him as a friend.[24]

\* \* \*

Within hours of arriving home, Bill began maneuvering to cover himself. In a telegram he defiantly threw the matter back into Tolin's lap. "Arrived home last night," Bill wrote. "Address 2503 South Adams Street Arlington, Virginia. Please advise further instructions."[25] A day later came a visit to the US Marshal's office, where he explained his missed appearance as due to a shortage of funds and Mabel's new mystery illness. If need be, he could be reached at his Arlington home.

Despite his bravado, panic still gripped him. On July 21, while walking down a street in Washington he ran into a CIA employee he had known for some time. After explaining his dilemma, he suddenly told him, "You know what I have in my head is worth a million dollars." The person quickly reported the encounter, telling officials that he interpreted the remark as a "feeler" through him to AFSA pressuring the agency for a return to his job under threat of "relaying his knowledge of AFSA operations to an enemy agent."[26]

With Bill now back in Virginia and clearly defying the subpoena, uncertainty as to how to proceed once again overtook McInerney. His original instructions to Tolin to stand firm on the July 19 date suddenly began evaporating in a cloud of doubt. What had been an order now became a "matter . . . under consideration . . . but a decision had not yet been reached." Belmont told McInerney that Weisband had returned home on the scheduled date of his appearance. When asked if he could still make it to Los Angeles, Belmont explained that Weisband sent the telegram to Tolin around 2:15 p.m. the day he got home, allowing no time for Tolin to respond. Even if he had returned to California by plane, he would never have made it in time. The conversation then turned in a different direction. McInerney asked if a subpoena for his appearance at a grand jury in Washington would ease the pressure on FBI surveillance. Such a step, Belmont noted, would only be "in accordance with Weisband's desires," who had "thrown down the challenge to the government." But as far as surveillance "we would like a decision as soon as possible." The question then arose about Weisband's check marks on the loyalty forms advocating the overthrow of the government. When Jones asked him about this discrepancy, he laughed, dismissing them as mere oversights made in haste. In the end it was Hoover who weighed into the debate, rejecting the idea of bringing the case to Washington. "We certainly don't want it here with usual incompetence," he wrote. "I can only hope we don't die of old age waiting. H."[27]

In this case the FBI director did not have to wait long. Ten days later on August 1, 1950, Weisband received another subpoena ordering him to return to Los Angeles for a second grand jury appearance scheduled for August 16, 1950. Once again Bill, with Mabel in tow, set out for California.

As Weisband headed west, federal prosecutors began raising new and troubling concerns. For his part, Tolin questioned the validity of prosecuting Weisband for espionage. Was it a "sound case," he wondered, and would grand jury questioning of him at this stage imperil further investigation? Another potential problem was the actual aircraft information York passed to him in 1941 and 1942. Did it constitute national defense information falling under the espionage statute? And then there was the credibility of the key witness. With all of his years of experience as a defense attorney and federal prosecutor, Tolin knew that Jones Orin York would be a less than compelling accuser of Weisband given his repeated denials of spying over the years. On the contrary, it was York who admitted his recruitment for espionage by Stanislav Shumovsky. It was York who admitted exchanging aircraft secrets with four Russian couriers for cash. It was York who admitted buying expensive Los Angeles real estate, purchasing a grand piano, and renting an upscale apartment to compose music that he was convinced would make it into major Hollywood movies. Tolin understood that Weisband's lawyer would ruthlessly attack York's desperate efforts to reconnect with Shumovsky in New York for more money and his bizarre poverty-wracked year in New Hampshire's desolate north country. And in the end, it was York who admitted lying to the FBI in 1939 and then changing his story eleven years later. Tolin needed another witness to corroborate York's testimony, but he didn't have one.

In meetings with prosecutors, Belmont insisted that the FBI was not telling the government to prosecute but did not want the Justice Department to hold off "on a basis of contemplated FBI investigation as the facts are known today." After much debate Tolin received orders on August 15 to proceed "vigorously" with his interrogation of Weisband and "not to hold off on the merits of the case if it appeared to go ahead with the prosecution." Questioning would focus on his years in California, activities in Los Angeles, and relationship with York as well as the circumstances of his first meeting with the Cubarkins.[28]

At the same time Weisband's employment with AFSA still loomed large. Six days before his scheduled testimony, it was a nervous Admiral Stone, head of AFSA, who sought assurances from the FBI that no reference of any kind would be made by prosecutors or Weisband to the jurors about the cryptologic activities underway at Arlington Hall. Jones assured Stone that FBI agents and prosecutors had been so advised.[29]

Weisband finally arrived in Los Angeles on August 14, 1950, making his first stop at the Cubarkin home at nine-thirty that night. Two days later he walked into the Los Angeles federal courthouse ready for questioning. Hours later, after testifying, he was met in the lobby by two FBI agents who interviewed him for another ninety minutes. Again, insisting that he had never committed espionage, he now admitted lying to Jones at his May 9 interview about the circumstances of his first meeting with Cubarkin. He had not met Cubarkin at the bar of the Miramar Hotel as he had claimed but rather appeared one day at his home telling him that Stan had told him to "look up" Cubarkin when he got to Los Angeles. He then denied knowing Stan, claiming instead that his brother Harold, a friend of Stan, suggested he look up Cubarkin when he got to California. The interviewing agent later reported that Weisband tried to convey the impression that there was some sort of "illicit relationship" between Harold and Stan with Bill lying to Jones in May in order to "protect the name of his brother who was killed in World War II." When asked if he would sign a statement to this effect, Weisband declined.[30]

With the conversation at an end, Weisband was arrested on contempt charges for failing to appear at the July 19 grand jury. Taken before a magistrate, he was remanded to jail and held on $1,000 bond. During routine processing an agent discovered an address book in his pocket. Upon examination two names jumped out. They were Igor Vasilyevich Chetchetkin and Konstantin Platonovich Ryzshkov—both assigned to the Russian embassy in Washington and known KGB officers.[31]

At the courthouse the press caught up with a distraught and angry Mabel, who had a few things of her own to say. She knew nothing about the nature of her husband's testimony, she assured reporters, but it had to do with his "association with an acquaintance unknown to her ten or fifteen years ago." The FBI told her he had been involved in espionage, which was a lie as they had been "unable to prove it and back it up." Bill, she said, had been treated badly and subjected to "intimidation."[32] An embittered Mabel lashing out at the FBI insisted that she was standing "one hundred percent" behind her husband and was confident of his innocence.[33]

For the next week while Bill sat in the Los Angeles County jail, Mabel struggled to raise his bail money. Some of his time was spent dealing with newspaper reporters who got very little out of him except pleas to contact the Cubarkins for financial help. At the same time Mabel hired Max Tendler, a prominent local defense attorney, to represent him. Following his arraignment and a not guilty plea, he was released on bond with a trial date set for September 26, 1950.

Now free on bail Weisband stayed in Los Angeles (probably a court-ordered requirement) rather than return to Virginia. While the FBI continued to listen, a distraught Mabel asked her husband how they could garner support for him by publicizing the facts of his case. Bill replied that he knew a newspaper that would "put out the truth." Referring to the *Daily Worker*, the Communist Party newspaper, he told her that "it is read by more people than you think, they'll put out the truth." He went on to explain that the American public was being defrauded and "that is why the Communists say they will have a revolution. You can't get those people out with votes. I don't mean a revolution by one or two or a few . . . the whole people must revolt."[34]

While Mabel looked for a job, Bill found work as a night clerk at the Ambassador Hotel. The couple also rented a cheap room. Adding to their already chaotic life were mounting problems coming at them from multiple directions. Bill's suspension in May for ninety days had ended on August 12, 1950. Unbeknownst to Weisband the process was then underway to permanently dismiss him from AFSA. The reasons offered for termination ranged from smuggling John Francis Pollock into the United States in 1938 to his "implied threats" of harm to AFSA and failure to make his scheduled July 19, 1950, grand jury appearance. On October 16, 1950, three weeks before his new trial date, he received a registered letter from the army informing him of the charges and giving him thirty days to appeal. Failure to do so would result in his termination.[35]

For Bill and Mabel, the romantic weekend getaways to New York for dinner and the latest Broadway show were now over. The sudden cutoff of KGB money meant no more evenings spent wagering at Jimmy's Place or hugging the rail at a favorite racetrack cheering home a winner. In July a gasoline credit card company began demanding the return of Bill's card for failing to pay his bills. In the hope of delaying the inevitable he appealed for an extension explaining that he had been suspended from his job pending an FBI investigation but would definitely be reinstated.[36] Next came the repossession of the new Buick Super Roadster Bill bought in Wyoming for failure to make payments. Mabel soon turned to pawning everything of value including a radio, her engagement and wedding rings, motion picture recording equipment, a portable typewriter, and anything else that could bring them a few dollars. The ultimate humiliation, however, came when Bill finally found himself reduced to begging for money. He began a desperate letter-writing campaign to dozens of friends and acquaintances at ASA pleading for help. One such letter sent to Dorothy and Arnold Buney of Arlington, Virginia, summed up his situation:

> Dear Dorothy and Arnold, You may and may not have heard some stories about me lately. So let me tell you what has taken place. Mabel and I have been suspended from work without pay for 90 days pending an investigation. The action against Mabel was taken because she is married to me. It seems that there is a question about an acquaintance long before I ever came to the Hall. I assure you that I am innocent of any wrong doing (sic) or shady activity. Now I shall ask you a little favor. All our funds are exhausted and since there is no income at all we find ourselves in dire need of help. It would be greatly appreciated if you could extend a small loan of $5, $10 or $25 or any amount you could spare. You shall be reimbursed when we get our back pay and jobs, there is a considerable amount of leave and retirement pay due us. We need this assistance immediately. A similar letter has been sent to other friends of long standing. The problem of procuring other employment is hopeless at this time. Mabel has shown excellent moral support and extreme devotion. I trust that you and your family are well and happy. Hoping to hear from you in the very near future. I am yours truly Bill Weisband.[37]

Additional emotional strain came from Mabel's family living in Del Rio. They had picked up gossip about the arrest from her brother, Wayne, still working at Arlington Hall, and probably from local newspapers containing scant details. For Mabel, the dread was that if Bill was a Russian spy her relatives would turn on both of them.

While scrambling for money to meet mounting debts, Bill's defense team was busy preparing for his trial now scheduled for November 1. One tack they were pursuing was to minimize his responsibility by pointing a finger at Bruce Mathews, the chief US Marshal, who Bill had spoken to just days after his return to Virginia on July 19. The strategy was to blame Mathews for instructing him to ignore the matter until he was contacted. When questioned by FBI agents, Mathews denied making any such statement. To make his denial a matter of record, he and a subordinate prepared affidavits attesting to the fact that they never made any such claim to him.[38]

On September 6, 1950, a conference was held between Max Tendler and prosecutors. Tendler opened the discussion by questioning the government's keen interest in pursuing Weisband. He then floated the notion that the case had to go far beyond just a simple contempt of court matter and had to be much larger in scope. He would not represent him if he was a communist, Tendler explained, and suggested that perhaps a bargain could be struck with a dismissal of the contempt case in exchange for him convincing Bill to reveal the full details of his activities. Roy Kinnison, the assistant US attorney prosecuting the case, offered no reply but interpreted Tendler's offer as a probe to get him to discuss the details of what the government knew. Belmont ordered the Los Angeles office not to discuss any details with him.[39]

For Bill the long ordeal of waiting for a trial ended on November 1, 1950. On that day, following a hearing lasting only a few short hours, Bill was convicted of contempt of court before Judge Pierson M. Hall. Twenty days later on November 21, 1950, Hall sentenced William Weisband to one year in prison.[40]

## NOTES

1. FBI interview of Edith Weisband, May 16, 18, 1950. DOC 66798767, NSA FOIPA.
2. VP Keay memorandum to Belmont, May 16, 1950, Weisband FBI file.
3. Hottel letter to Hoover, June 29, 1950, Weisband FBI file.
4. Undated memoranda entitled "Special Research Report," NSA FOIPA.
5. WFO Report, July 20, 1950, Weisband FBI file.
6. WFO teletypes to Hoover, June 20, 1950, and June 21, 1950, Weisband FBI file.
7. WFO Report, July 20, 1950, Weisband FBI file.
8. Ibid.
9. Ibid.
10. Ibid.
11. Ibid.
12. Ibid.
13. Ibid.
14. Ibid.
15. Ibid.
16. Ibid.
17. Ibid.
18. WFO Report, November 27, 1950, Weisband FBI file.
19. WFO Report, November 27, 1950, Weisband FBI file. LA teletypes, July 12, 1950, and July 14, 1950, Weisband FBI file.

20. Belmont memorandum to Ladd, July 11, 1950, Weisband FBI file.
21. Belmont memo to Hennrich, July 14, 1950, Weisband FBI file.
22. LA teletype, July 20, 1950, Weisband FBI file.
23. On the teletype Hoover wrote "Can't we speed up whatever action the Dept. is considering & also press all other angles ourselves." Ibid.
24. Hoover teletype, July 19, 1950, Weisband FBI file.
25. Hoover memorandum to McInerney, Undated, Weisband FBI file.
26. WFO Report, July 20, 1950, Weisband FBI file.
27. Belmont memorandum to Ladd, July 11, 1950, and July 20, 1950, Weisband FBI file.
28. Belmont memorandum to Ladd, August 11, 1950, Weisband FBI file.
29. DeLoach memorandum to Belmont, August 16, 1950, Weisband FBI file (III-62).
30. Los Angeles teletype, Undated, Weisband FBI file.
31. Ryzshkov departed the United States in 1949 and Chetchetkin remained until the early 1960s. Ruth Hayes memorandum to Donald Lynn, April 20, 1965, NSA FOIPA.
32. WFO Report, November 27, 1950, Weisband FBI file.
33. WFO Teletype, August 22, 1950, Weisband FBI file.
34. WFO Report, November 27, 1950, Weisband FBI file.
35. Department of Army memorandum, September 13, 1950, Weisband FBI file.
36. Baltimore Teletype, September 28, 1950, Weisband FBI file.
37. His brother-in-law, Wayne Woody, later told the FBI that he received nearly two thousand dollars in donations ($24,627 in November 2022). NSA FOIPA.
38. WFO Report, October 3, 1950, Weisband FBI file.
39. Los Angeles teletype, September 11, 1950, Weisband FBI file.
40. Los Angeles Report, November 14, 1950, Weisband FBI file.

## Chapter 34

# Aftermath

Two weeks after his sentencing, US Marshals transported Weisband more than eleven hundred miles north to the remote federal penitentiary where he would serve his time. McNeil Island is situated in southern Puget Sound near the city of Tacoma, Washington. At little more than six and a half miles wide, it is accessible only by a twenty-mile boat trip from the mainland. It was first purchased in 1860 by the federal government. Five years later a prison was built to house men convicted of federal crimes. Among its more illustrious tenants over the years were Robert Stroud, the famed "Birdman of Alcatraz," Alvin "Creepy" Karpis, the FBI's Public Enemy #1 when he was arrested in 1936, and Charles Manson, mastermind behind the murder of actress Sharon Tate, who spent five years there in the early 1960s for trying to cash forged government checks.

Mabel, now alone, returned to Virginia while her husband did his time. She soon found employment, which she told Bill she enjoyed very much. But the job came with a catch. Her new position required an insurance bond, a hurdle that would prove difficult for the bonding company because of her husband's conviction. In the hope of seeking a remedy, Mabel reached out to Agent Jones asking if the FBI could explain the charges to her boss and her lack of any involvement in them. A sympathetic Jones told her that it would be impossible and explained the provisions of the rules governing same.[1]

While the Weisbands were still in California awaiting his trial, the secretary of the army authorized the director of AFSA to suspend Weisband for an additional sixty days effective August 11, 1950. A war of letters quickly erupted on September 8, 1950, when Bill learned that effective October 4, 1950, his suspension had been extended for an "indefinite period pending an adjudication of his case." The reasons offered included his association with Victor Cubarkin, who had connections to the Communist Party and loyalty to Russia. Then there was his failure to appear at the grand jury and the John Francis Pollock episode. Weisband's response denying the claims led the army secretary to expand the charges. There was his "secret work" for an "undisclosed principle" during the 1930s, his espionage relationship with York in 1941, his "lack of discretion" following his suspension by making "implied threats as to the possibility of danger to the agency in view of your former sensitive position," and falsely listing Edith and his nephew as dependents on his federal income taxes.[2]

From his prison cell, Weisband again lashed out, denying everything. The army's accusations, he wrote, were "vague, uncertain, shadowy, illusive," making them "impossible to reply thereto." He even parsed the truth of his conviction for contempt of court noting that it was not a "criminal" offense and that after his trial a jury found it was "civil contempt—not a crime." Pleading a lack of funds to defend himself, he emphasized his inability to call witnesses including Colonel Harold Hayes then in Alaska and another officer in Arizona who could speak on his behalf. If he could not be reinstated to his old position, he argued, surely, he was still deserving of back pay from the date of his first suspension. He then went on to bemoan all of the deprivations, degradation, and humiliation the army's actions had caused him claiming that if he could not defend himself or be reinstated to his original position, his reputation would be "ruined." He should be given the opportunity to defend himself, he concluded, and to resign voluntarily.[3]

While sitting in prison he learned that a loyalty board hearing regarding his case would convene at San Francisco on March 29, 1951. Within days he demanded a delay until he could "appear in his own defense." Ignoring his appeal, the board proceeded as scheduled and unanimously found "reasonable grounds" to conclude that he was disloyal. The verdict—removal from his employment as "deemed necessary or desirable in the interest of national security." Bill was informed of the findings as well as his right of challenge within thirty days, and the fact that the appeal could be held open for sixty days following his release from jail. Then came a sinister warning: even if the appeals board reversed the original board's findings, the secretary of the army still retained the right to remove him from AFSA as a "security risk." If he decided to resign from AFSA during the proceedings, the record would still bear a notation that he "resigned pending adjudication of a loyalty board or security case whichever is appropriate."[4]

Throughout his imprisonment the FBI regularly monitored his correspondence. As Mabel knew Bill the best, Jones was still anxious to get her cooperation. The Seattle office was ordered to maintain a close watch on any mail from Mabel suggesting changes in her attitude toward Bill. Any "apathy or indifference," Jones hoped, could prove useful in approaching her for another interview. The couple exchanged three letters a week, but no evidence of marital strain was found. The FBI soon began receiving copies of the letters for analysis. At one point when he hadn't received any letters for a time, Bill became concerned about her welfare, leading the warden to permit him to make a supervised telephone call to her.[5]

Despite all their troubles, Mabel and Bill continued to express loyalty and love for each other. She kept him updated on life at home and her continued struggle with Max Tendler, his Los Angeles attorney, to pursue a writ of habeas corpus. She even went so far as to seek out a local Washington, DC, lawyer, who explained that such a petition had to originate in the jurisdiction where the trial was held. In May 1951 tragedy struck the Woody family and particularly Mabel when she received word that her brother, Wayne, had died in an automobile accident in North Carolina. Wayne had resigned from AFSA in October 1950 and returned home to attend Mars Hill College. A "grief stricken" Mabel wrote to Bill pouring out her devastation. She and Wayne were "always so close," she told her husband, and the "shock was much too great." Bill and Wayne were the only persons she ever loved.[6]

Amidst all the sorrow, Bill kept up his letter-writing campaign with Tendler demanding to know the status of his habeas corpus petition. After months of silence, he threatened to file his own. In June he made a request to the Veterans Administration to continue his schooling through a French language correspondence course. A rejection letter soon arrived citing "previous unsuccessful progress under the Veterans Administration program."

While Weisband sat in a prison cell, work was still underway by the government. In April 1951, Jones contacted Mabel for another interview and, after first agreeing, she canceled. In Los Angeles, long-distance telephone records from his residences during 1941 and 1942 were examined with little success. At one point IRS investigators arrived at the prison to interrogate him about his questionable deductions for support of Edith and other irregularities.[7]

* * *

Weisband wrote to Mabel in August 1951 expressing excitement at his upcoming release and suggesting they meet in New York City for a reunion. Instead, he flew back to Arlington on a ticket furnished by his wife, arriving home on August 26, 1951. Three days later he was back in pursuit of the loyalty board, this time telephoning Donald Garrett, executive secretary of the Loyalty Appeals Board of the Department of the Army, seeking information about procedures for appealing his discharge from AFSA.

By the end of September, his failure to apply for a new hearing led a very savvy Jones to surmise that he would never go through with the appeal process. He had a strong sense of who Weisband was, having sat across a table from him for more than nine hours of interview and leading the investigation that followed. First, he was in desperate financial straits with few funds to call witnesses and hire an attorney. "Time may be of advantageous to us—as he may be pushed for money." More importantly, however, a formal hearing would require him to appear in his own behalf and even more threatening would be having to "testify under oath," which he would be loath to do. Bill was trapped, Jones believed, because he knew that any testimony he gave would be of "estimable value" to continued FBI investigation. "Weisband is undoubtedly aware of the ramifications involved should he submit to interrogation by the board," Jones warned Belmont. To improve the Bureau's position should he decide to give testimony, Jones suggested that the FBI "feed" the board with specific questions to ask him that could elicit responses of value for any future perjury prosecution.[8] Jones impressed upon Garrett the Bureau's interest in his sworn testimony. Garrett requested a copy of his trial transcript in order to properly prepare should the issue arise. In the end, the five-member board, four civilians and one military, planned to focus on the trial transcript and his interviews by the FBI.

On October 25, 1951, Weisband finally appealed his loyalty conviction with the Department of the Army. Days later he met with Garrett to go over the appeal procedures. During their discussion he learned that a copy of the proceedings would be forwarded to the FBI. When Bill "expressed concern" he was assured by Garrett that the FBI would take no part in the hearings. Weisband then began offering Garrett a litany of woes, starting with a failure to land a job with an insurance company and being turned down for an $800 loan to "consolidate his debts." His life had been reduced to pawning jewelry to buy some luggage and a car for use in selling insurance.[9] In the end it was Garrett who shared Jones's original hunch that Weisband would not appear at any hearing over concerns that the FBI would learn the results.

Over the ensuing weeks, Garrett, having read all available material, developed concerns that the information forming the basis for Weisband's suspension from AFSA was "not conclusive." He asked for "all FBI reports clarifying the allegations" and asked Army G2 to request them. Jones recommended the preparation of a summary report making it easier for the board to understand the charges against Weisband. "It is believed" Jones observed, that "this summary is a necessary step to ensure that his suspension is upheld."[10]

On December 9, 1951, the FBI prepared a forty-four-page report for delivery to the Appeals Board incorporating everything including his personal history, allegations of espionage, the interviews of Weisband and his former girlfriend Patricia Grimes, the attempts to locate the mysterious couple living in New Jersey visited by Weisband and Grimes, the wild parties, John Francis Pollock, his fraudulent income tax returns, and other important acts. The Bureau's goal was to have the "testimony reviewed and compared with statements from Weisband under oath before the Appeals Board if he testifies."[11]

February 12, 1952, was the new date set for loyalty board hearing. A few days before, Garrett telephoned Weisband to remind him of the scheduled hearing and spoke with Mabel. She insisted that he would appear. On February 11, 1952, the day before the hearing, Weisband called Garrett and asked to meet with him that day. When they met, Bill said he had decided not to appear at the Appeals Board hearing. Instead, he wanted to submit his resignation. Garrett offered him the chance to think about it, telling him he would not accept his decision until the following day. Weisband then began ranting about the injustice of the government's actions against him. Particular venom was directed toward the FBI "persecution" of him for trying and failing to interview his wife while he was in prison. The fact that he had not been prosecuted was "ample demonstration of his innocence" because Jones produced no evidence against him. The FBI had railroaded him, he snapped, and "will ignore him only when he leaves government service." In the end he called the agents a bunch of "Boy Scouts."[12]

In a letter filed the next day, William Weisband resigned from AFSA with no admissions of guilt. It was his moment, the one he had been demanding for two years. Now was his chance to clear his name, recover his maligned reputation, and return to his old job. But instead, he was walking away. His reasons, he said, had nothing to do with "apprehensions of the consequences which might result from the hearing." Nor was he concerned about "any possible or intended deviation from the truth of any testimony" on his part. Consistent with a pattern that had become all too familiar over the years, he shifted responsibility for his decision to what he called "threatening statements made to him by members of the Justice Department."[13]

At the highest reaches of the Department of Defense and the army and the cryptologic community, huge collective sighs of relief could be heard. Their agony had ended with no public exposure of Weisband's work at Arlington Hall for five years. The thick curtain surrounding the vast worldwide Anglo-American code-breaking enterprise against the Soviet Union remained intact. Just as Admiral Stone had hoped, and Court Jones had suspected.

It was over. And now the stage was set for the final act of the William Weisband saga.

**NOTES**

1. WFO teletype, January 13, 1951, Weisband FBI file.
2. WFO Report, August 8, 1951, Weisband FBI file.
3. Ibid.
4. He charged that on December 4, 1950, after his conviction an agent told his wife, "We'll get your husband if it takes 20 years." Weisband has in the past made the same type of charges; he has insulted agents and later apologized and has attempted to embarrass investigating agents on surveillance of him. For your information insert

the Bureau's own questioning of itself regarding his claims of threats made against him. It will be informative. The report on Venona was withheld from the board and instead turned over Army G2. FBI told the Department of the Army that Weisband had "lied unhesitatingly, when it was to his advantage" and has on occasion admitted that he had lied. Ibid.

5. Seattle letter, May 18, 1951, Weisband FBI file.
6. WFO Report, August 8, 1951, Weisband FBI file.
7. WFO letter, September 29, 1951, Weisband FBI file.
8. WFO Report, August 8, 1951, Weisband FBI file.
9. WFO letter, September 29, 1951, Weisband FBI file.
10. WFO teletype, November 6, 1951, Weisband FBI file.
11. "The cover letter to this report . . . sets forth information which because of its obvious nature and/or source might if used by the Board in questioning Weisband, result in embarrassment to the Bureau and a future claim against the Government by Weisband for reinstatement in Federal service. This information has not been included in the report. The cover letter, of course, is not to be disseminated. It is believed that at the time liaison furnishes attached report, liaison should strongly urge the G2 official contacted to inform the Appeals Board that the three memoranda should not be used under any circumstance during Weisband's hearing or questioning of him. Liaison should point out that the Bureau furnished the three memoranda to AFSA on a confidential basis as it was received in order that they might be apprised of the results of our investigation of Weisband. The information was not furnished them with a view to its use in confronting Weisband." CA Heinrich memorandum to Belmont, November 27, 1951, Weisband FBI file.
12. WFO teletype, February 13, 1952. A handwritten note on the teletype says "This was expected." WFO letter, March 7, 1952, Weisband FBI file.
13. He charged that on December 4, 1950, after his conviction an agent told his wife "We'll get your husband if it takes 20 years." Venona reports were withheld from the Board and instead turned over to Army G2. The FBI told the Department of the Army that Weisband had "lied unhesitatingly, when it was to his advantage" and has on occasion admitted that he had lied. Ibid., Hoover letter to Assistant Chief of Staff, G2, Department of the Army, March 28, 1952, Weisband FBI file.

*Chapter 35*

# Endgame

Shortly after his release from prison, Bill Weisband landed a job with the Superior Life Insurance Company in Alexandria, Virginia, after answering a newspaper advertisement for a sales position. During his initial employment interview, he explained that he was "in very poor financial condition and badly needed a job." To prove it, he displayed a pawn ticket for his watch and ring. He told the interviewer that he had done "secret work" for the government in the past and had appeared before a grand jury and later served time in prison. Four weeks after hiring him a credit report confirmed it all, leading Weisband once again to complain that he was being "persecuted by the FBI as he had done nothing wrong." Despite having no previous experience in the insurance business, he performed "very well," handling current accounts and pursuing new clients "in a colored area" in nearby Arlington County. While there remained some criticism of his performance, he was closely monitored by company management, which did not wish to be "embarrassed" by the subject.[1]

Three years after his imprisonment Bill, now forty-five years old, applied for medical benefits from the Department of Veterans Affairs (VA) for conditions that he claimed started during his war years. He offered a litany of ailments starting with hypertension, hemorrhoids, varicose veins, lipoma on his upper right arm, prostatitis, and a backache. After a yearlong review the VA turned him down. With the exception of a blood pressure reading of 152/104, a physical examination found nothing wrong with him. As part of the analysis, he underwent a psychiatric exam. During questioning, a doctor noted his extreme anger toward the FBI, describing his tearful, almost weeping fury as "lachrymose" in nature. He "felt a great injustice had been done to him," the doctor reported. "He had been handicapped financially, and socially, and claimed his former friends would not have anything to do with him."[2]

Part of the evaluation process required a further exam with Bette June Hollander, a psychiatric social worker. She reviewed a psychiatric report on Bill done in January 1944 while he was still on army duty in Italy. In it he claimed that in the 1930s he did a lot of weight lifting, wrestled, played soccer, and experienced rheumatic fever in 1938. There were also difficulties with his foot, leg, and arm joints after a tonsillectomy. As a remedy he went to a spa at Saratoga Springs, New York, for a month. From 1935 to 1938, he kept an apartment in New York with a woman nine years his junior. After breaking up with her he began going steady with a "rich girl" for three years who was separated from her husband. During this period, he and his brothers had unspecified "trouble" with his father's business, which they operated together. His move to California was to get away from a married woman with whom he had quarreled. The physical report also listed his fear that he was "losing his sexual strength." In the end, the 1944 report concluded that "there is no question that this man had a psychoneurosis but insofar as this itself is concerned, could return to duty."[3]

Bill told Hollander that he had been born in Russia, not Alexandria, Egypt, as recorded on his military forms. In the 1930s he reiterated that he and his brother (not identified) had operated the family's jewelry shop following the death of the father. He claimed that his father died in 1936 and that his parents "quarreled a lot." He moved to California to get away from his brother who was causing all sorts of difficulty as well as a woman with whom he had quarreled. He attended the University of California for four years before "quitting" to join the army. Hollander recorded Bill's comments as identical to the VA physician that the FBI was "persecuting" him and that he had been "framed" by the government. Court Jones still contacts his wife and friends for information and to warn them not to associate with him. It was Jones, he claimed, who instigated his dismissal from Georgetown University language program and financially, socially, and domestically ruined his life. Employers were reluctant to hire him, and he had been "degraded" by the type of work he had been forced to take.[4]

As part of her investigation, Hollander contacted Superior Life Insurance and spoke to a manager and co-worker. He was always nervous and worrisome, they said, with a constant "chip on his shoulder." His complaints ranged from politics, the government, taxes, to the high cost of living. Fed-up co-workers told him if he was so unhappy, he should "go back to Russia if he didn't like the conditions in the United States." Bill refused to allow Hollander to speak with Mabel for her insight into his ailments. She already had her own highly nervous condition, he told her, and such questioning would only aggravate it.[5]

During this time period Bill and Mabel started a family. They eventually had five children, including twins. One overriding problem that would continually plague him was a shortage of income. With a growing family, Mabel became a full-time mother and homemaker. To help make ends meet she took in sewing. After about two years with Superior, Bill started a new sales job for Atlantic Insurance Company for a higher salary. For the next three years, he traveled daily from his home in suburban Virginia to his territory in Richmond, a distance of about sixty miles. Eventually he received a transfer to the Washington suburbs, with one manager describing him as an "excellent insurance man."[6]

As of March 1952, he was driving a twelve-year-old Buick sedan while working. Later he was forced to purchase a newer used car while his growing family continued to live in an apartment. One person from the neighborhood later remembered that the Weisbands kept to themselves, rarely having visitors except an occasional neighbor. Mabel once gave voice to the family's isolation saying that her old friends from Arlington Hall "are no longer social acquaintances" because "in view of their position with the Army Security Agency they are unable to maintain liaison with the Weisbands."[7]

When he applied for a new position with the Travelers Insurance Company, he once again felt compelled to discuss his past legal problems. This admission prompted the company to send a letter to the FBI before hiring him asking for an explanation of "his situation with your organization." A Travelers representative even visited the local FBI office to inquire about his story that he had been accused of being a "red courier," was an acquaintance of someone who had committed espionage, and had spent time in prison. Court Jones explained that no information could be offered regarding any investigation. In a letter over Hoover's signature, the FBI later replied that "the confidential nature of our files prohibits disclosure of information therein." The FBI then referred the company to the clerk of the federal district court in Los Angeles.[8] A week or so later the company notified Bill that "they could not use his services."[9]

Bill continued peddling dime insurance policies to African Americans and constantly drove around collecting monthly installments. His bosses said he was good at sales, and he was popular with his customers, booking as much as $600 a week. His yearly salary averaged $10,000 to $12,000. Yet he couldn't escape his gambling addiction, which one employer described, while another remarked on his "dire financial straits." One report concluded that he made a "fair living" but had little money left over.[10]

Adding to his growing list of worries were demands from the INS for an interview to discuss his citizenship status. When he appeared with his wife at the local Washington, DC, office, he insisted that she be present during the interview. After being turned down he learned that a stenographer would record his testimony under oath, and it would be shared with the FBI if requested. At that point he refused to go any further.[11]

Weisband's yearlong imprisonment left him embittered for the rest of his life. One person from his ASA days remembered him as a self-confident professional as well as "quite a violent tempered person" who had become "quite subdued." His jail time had been hard on Weisband, the friend noted. Since returning home his health had deteriorated, he had put on considerable weight, and his general appearance had diminished. Bill also spoke of his turbulent domestic relations noting that he and Mabel "frequently quarrel."[12]

\* \* \*

It had been three years since Bill and Court Jones had faced each other. So, it was with some concern when the FBI man telephoned Bill in June 1953 asking him for another interview. Weisband was surprisingly "cordial," Jones noted, and agreed to meet but not at his office. Bill insisted on neutral ground.[13]

On July 1, 1953, the two men met for lunch at a local restaurant. No notes were taken so he could "speak freely." Jones explained the purpose of the interview was to give him an opportunity to "clarify" his original responses.[14] At the same time Jones expressed concerns about criticisms of FBI persecution, which he hoped Bill would explain.

As the discussion got underway, discrepancies from his 1950 interviews that were either inaccurate or "deliberately misleading" were pointed out to him. He was then shown a photograph of Jones Orin York and asked if he knew him. After a moment, Weisband became visibly excited, blurting out "Yes, I know him. I've talked about him before." When told that he had never discussed York, Bill became angry, refusing to discuss him further and then demanding to see other photos. As he had made the choice not to discuss York, there was no point in showing him other photos, Jones replied. When asked if he continued to deny involvement in espionage, he replied that "he did not intend to answer that question because anything he might say would eventually be misused or misinterpreted and work a hardship on him." Throughout the lengthy back-and-forth session, Bill repeatedly railed about FBI "persecution."[15]

Jones next zeroed in on his money situation. Over the years since his release from prison, Bill had frequently been taken to court for unpaid debts. As for his wife, he said, the FBI had directly affected her and her ability to make a decent living. She had resigned from her jobs at a local clinic and as a telephone operator due to the low wages they were paying her, telling Jones that "she did not make as much as maids."[16] A puzzled Jones then wondered aloud why Mabel left even a low-paying job when he had admitted that he was still "financially embarrassed." Bill then bemoaned his own frustrations selling life insurance for Superior. He made $7,000 ($68,000 in 2020) a year, a figure that was misleading, he charged, as he was responsible for his own expenses, including gasoline totaling close to $50 a week ($487 in 2020). His customers were primarily "Negroes." On those occasions when he collected their premiums, they often lacked funds to pay, forcing him to extend credit "of a few dollars" in order to carry them over and keep the insurance policy in effect. By doing so, however, he had to absorb a loss. His salary alone covered his car payments, car repairs, rent on the apartment, family needs, as well as federal and state taxes—all of which he blamed on the FBI for forcing him to accept a job "beneath his dignity."[17]

When Jones next gently steered the conversation toward Mabel, Weisband became "excited," insisting that he did not want to discuss their relationship. When pressed about her curiosity about "Stan" (Stanislaw Shumovsky) that she voiced in May 1950 and what Bill told her about him, he claimed that he did not recall. She believed in his innocence, he retorted, and had "confidence in him when he tells her he was not involved in espionage," adding that "she is unable to understand why the FBI would still be interested in him at this late date." From his demeanor and tone of responses, Jones sensed that "all is not well between Weisband and his wife despite his insistence on their great love."[18]

For someone being "persecuted" by the FBI, it was curious when he suddenly offered his assistance to Jones. He was a "1,000 percent" loyal citizen, he said, and would be willing to work as a counterespionage agent who could "seek out and bring to justice any people committing espionage against this country." Jones rejected the offer surmising that his assistance would come with a high "price of his cooperation." As the conversation gradually drew to a close Bill asked, "What do you intend to do to me now?" Jones casually explained the importance of resolving the issue, which meant continued investigation. With that he once again became "highly excited and boisterous," returning to his persecution charges with the FBI doing everything to ruin his life.[19]

After a grueling two-and-a-half-hour back-and-forth exchange, they amicably ended their meeting with an agreement to keep in touch. Jones knew that Weisband would never talk about his spying and that Bill was well aware that doing so would place him in a "critical position."[20] The only other alternative, Jones suggested, would be forcing him to register as an agent of a foreign power.

Over the next several years, Jones's investigation continued with fewer and fewer leads being produced. Efforts to locate Pollock, whose information would have been of "inestimable value," stalled.[21] During the time they were together Bill had gifted a book of poems by Anton Checkov to Patricia Grimes. In the margins of some pages was scribbled handwriting that included the word, "Vienna." The book was submitted to the FBI laboratory in what turned out to be an unsuccessful search for evidence of secret writing or use as a codebook. Bill's life in New York City prior to his California years also remained an enigma. He had maintained several residences, kept irregular hours, and had no visible source of income after 1936, or known close associates. Any relative who could assist in the inquiry was deceased and there was a lack of evidence of Weisband's Communist Party activities. Equally frustrating for Jones was absence of any evidence that he was furnishing secrets to the Russians during his five-year employment at Arlington Hall. In the end, with all logical leads in the investigation having been run to ground, Jones closed the case with the proviso that it could resume at any time based on new information.[22]

When the new National Security Agency was created in 1952, S. Wesley Reynolds, the former FBI liaison with AFSA, resigned from the FBI to take up new duties as the new agency's chief of security. Two years later he opened an internal investigation of Weisband. It was assigned to the Special Research Unit with the mission of creating a chronological account of the case in the hope of identifying any NSA employees who might have conspired with Weisband. There is no record that this project ever went anywhere.[23]

Bill left Superior in 1957 for Citizens Home Insurance Company selling insurance door to door around the northern Virginia area. By then his health was experiencing a steady decline. In 1954, he underwent surgery for a hernia at Prince William County Hospital in Virginia that left him with blood clots in his legs. Five years later he was hospitalized again following a heart attack. While out of work recuperating, Citizens continued to pay him a full salary. His problems with blood clots and restricted blood flow continued and only worsened as the years went on. In 1964, doctors at Georgetown University Hospital were forced to amputate his leg. For months he struggled to walk with crutches until a prosthesis could be fitted. A small disability policy for a thousand dollars paid the cost of the surgery while a second policy paid his hospital expenses. While battling blood clots and learning to navigate a prosthesis, his chronic heart condition aggravated by his ballooning weight reaching 250 pounds forced him to lose 70 pounds.

For part of 1960 he worked an extra job as a night clerk at an Arlington apartment house in order to help make ends meet. His fear of the FBI was never far from his mind as evidenced by repeated warnings to employers about possible inquiries concerning him from an "investigative agency."[24] He told his boss that years earlier in California he had been "convicted of being a spy" and then just as quickly dismissed it all as a "misunderstanding."[25] On one occasion in June 1960 an NSA employee was walking out of the building one morning when Bill stopped her. He had recognized her and reminded her that they had worked together at Arlington Hall. Her report about the encounter to NSA security officials prompted concerns about his access to "her mail, her telephone conversations and even her apartment if he was so inclined." She had no plans to develop a friendship with him, she assured them, and would report any future contacts.[26] In the end the issue became moot when he was fired after someone discovered him one morning sleeping on the job.

Throughout the 1950s as his family grew, he and Mabel continued to live in the same small apartment. Having no other choice, they finally bought a house in Manassas, Virginia, at a cost of twenty thousand dollars. To cover the down payment Bill sold some stock he owned in Citizens Home Insurance Company.

\* \* \*

Christmas was rapidly approaching in 1961 when alarm bells began clanging at the CIA's station in Helsinki, Finland. A KGB major named Anatoliy Golitsyn, working undercover at Moscow's local consulate with a head full of intelligence secrets, was ready to seek asylum in the West. Along with his wife and children he was soon on a flight to Andrews Air Force Base near Washington, DC, and then to a safe house on Maryland's Eastern Shore. For the next several months the thirty-five-year-old spy sat at a table disgorging everything he knew about Russian intelligence.

One author later described him as more of a historian and a scholar than an operations officer. Much of his career had been spent at Moscow Center analyzing reports collected from KGB sources inside NATO as well as working at important think tanks such as the KGB Higher Institute, where he earned the equivalent of a "Ph.D in spying."[27]

Seven months after his arrival in America, he sat down for a debriefing with FBI Special Agents Maurice Taylor and Alexo Poptanich. He told the agents that while assigned to the Anglo-American Directorate at Moscow Center in 1952, a controversy arose between the political section and counterintelligence officials. He knew only that it involved the reactivation of an "important agent"—one that pointed directly to Weisband. During a meeting he attended, Leonid S. Krivoshein, assistant section chief for counterintelligence, discussed the agent, describing him only as having provided valuable information in 1948 that had led the KGB to secure its communications from American attack. This person was discovered by the FBI and sentenced to a term in jail. Krivoshein believed he still had potential as a valuable source. There were strong possibilities that he could reconnect with former co-workers or seek "a new job or opportunities to obtain employment of potential interest to the KGB." The fact that he had been exposed as a KGB source and imprisoned, Golitsyn explained, would not preclude KGB use of him again although "they would be wary." Golitsyn never knew the source's name, nor was he shown a photo of him. He recalled references made to his Russian background, his residing in New York and to "Alexandria, Egypt possibly in connection with birth or residence." After more thought he described the source as Jewish and married as well as references to the "West Coast." The person had worked at the 1939 World's Fair in New York City "as Soviet intelligence was very active during the World's Fair Exhibition." During World War II he supplied the Russians with "valuable data" while assigned to a "ciphering or deciphering service" working with "cryptographic material of some sort." Golitsyn then speculated that the person may have been in an organization similar to a "Cryptographic, Radio, or Security Service."[28] He had no idea where the person lived or what he was doing nor if contact was pursued but felt that "he must have had potential to cause a controversy between two sections of KGB."[29]

In March 1961, more than a decade after his release from prison, NSA's Office of Security Counterintelligence Branch launched a second inquiry into the Weisband affair. Undertaking what they referred to as "preliminary steps" to recruit Weisband as a source, they noted he was of "particular interest to NSA because he was with ASA and AFSA from 1944 to 1950." They concluded that he was with Soviet intelligence but was more than a courier as "previously supposed." He had "handled an espionage net in Los Angeles in the early 1940s" and "we have no reason to doubt that he continued his espionage work when he entered the military service in 1942."[30] They had some evidence of contact with Communist Party personalities while employed at AFSA and in the course of their work they had interviewed former co-workers along with Jones York with a view to determining the ideal approach in contacting him. "In this regard we have generally noted his strong appreciation for money, gambling, and women and his antipathy for threats and intimidation."[31] The plan called for an experienced NSA officer with a background in counterintelligence to approach him. They also discussed what an appearance before a House or Senate committee might do to his reputation, not to mention another jail sentence for contempt. "Furthermore, he does not know how much (and how little) evidence we have collected about his activities."[32] The idea was to gain his confidence and use him as a double agent back against the Russians in furtherance of the "Navaho Program," a joint NSA-military double agent program. "It is desirable that we provide such support from the very beginning of the operation" one report noted, "and that we monitor the plans in full readiness to undertake the measures as needed."[33]

At the same time that NSA was pondering the use of Weisband as a source, a very different view was unfolding in the corridors of the FBI building. By the mid-1960s, Court Jones had been assigned to the Washington Field Office for twenty years. Over those two decades, having grown considerably in experience, he was now acting as the coordinator of all the office's vast array of counterintelligence activities. Jones never gave up hope of getting Weisband to confess to his spying. Since their last meeting in 1952, however, many issues had arisen in Bill's life that had to be factored into any thought and planning for a third interview. By 1965, fifteen years after Jones's first confrontation with the Weisbands, he had concluded that nothing would be gained by another approach to Mabel as nothing had been produced suggesting that her "attitude would be different at this time." Mindful of Jones's wide-ranging interview of Weisband, consideration was given to interviewing him away from his home for improved chances of success. He would be encouraged to finally discuss his spying through appeals to his love for Mabel and the children and a "possible change of mind concerning the US form of government."[34] Next on the list of considerations was his physical condition. Jones recognized his health issues, noting that "caution should be used in approaching him." As part of the planning thought was given to obtaining an opinion from Weisband's personal physician. Jones saw it as essential to determine if Bill's "physical condition is such that an interview would not normally have an ill effect on him." Three years later the FBI still remained stymied. In the end his "present health and heart condition" made an interview inadvisable.[35]

Too many years of lying, spying, treachery, gambling, imprisonment, and struggling to support a family on a shoestring salary had finally taken its toll. After repeated ins and outs of hospitals, Bill was admitted to Virginia's Fairfax Hospital one last time after suffering a second heart attack while out driving one day with his children. The end came peacefully on May 14, 1967, with Mabel and the children at his side. Days later, following a religious service, William Weisband was laid to rest at Presbyterian Cemetery in Alexandria, Virginia. He was fifty-eight years old.[36]

## NOTES

1. Richmond Letter, November 9, 1951, Weisband FBI file.
2. WFO Report, September 16, 1954, Weisband FBI file.
3. Ibid.
4. Ibid.
5. Ibid.
6. WFO Report, November 27, 1953, Weisband FBI file.
7. (IV-335).
8. Travelers Insurance Company letter to FBI, February 24, 1953.
9. Routing Slip, March 23, 1953, Weisband FBI file, WFO Letter, March 26, 1953, Weisband FBI file.
10. Ibid.
11. WFO Report, May 5, 1953, Weisband FBI file.
12. WFO Report, October 30, 1952, Weisband FBI file.
13. WFO letter, July 30, 1953, Weisband FBI file.
14. Ibid.

15. Ibid.
16. Ibid.
17. Ibid.
18. Ibid.
19. Ibid.
20. Ibid.
21. WFO Letter, August 12, 1954, Weisband FBI file.
22. In 1941, when both were living in California, Weisband gifted a book to Patricia Grimes entitled *The Cherry Orchard/The Seagull*. The book contained notes in the margins believed to have been written by Weisband. Jones ordered Grimes to the Seattle office to request the book from Grimes for forensic examination by the FBI Laboratory. Nothing of value was discovered. Seattle letter, December 18, 1953, Weisband FBI file.
23. James A. Grooms memorandum entitled "Weisband, William Wolfe," Undated, NSA FOIPA.
24. Richmond Report, September 27, 1962, Weisband FBI file.
25. Ibid.
26. Information Report, June 14, 1960, NSA FOIPA. RH letter to Bureau, July 5, 1962, Weisband FBI file.
27. Mark Riebling, *Wedge: The Secret War between the FBI and CIA* (New York: Simon & Schuster, 2002), 181.
28. Ibid.
29. Report of SA Samuel West, September 27, 1962, FBI File 100–7813.
30. There is no evidence that the plan ever got underway and in fact Lou Benson, who wrote the history of Weisband, believes that the plan was killed by the then deputy director of NSA, Louis Tordella, a man who disliked anything to do with counterintelligence who turned down the plan in the belief that such an operation was outside the charter of the NSA and would be better handled by the FBI, which posed no objection to the idea of the Navaho approach. John Schindler by email advised on October 8, 2020, that it was a cover term, vaguely. "I believe it was a joint NSA/MIL OFCO program against the Russians. Dangles, DAs, etc. It may have been a result of the Dunlap case [which terrified NSA]. I'll try to remember more. As a DoD agency, NSA CI often worked on these sorts of OFCO projects with Military CI rather than Langley or the Bureau. Very hush-hush, obviously."

Best, memorandum entitled "The Proposed Recruitment of William W. Weisband," March 1, 1961, NSA FOIPA. Telephone interview of Robert Louis Benson, 10/5/2020. My thanks for this information go to Louis Benson, who I telephone interviewed on October 6, 2020, and Robert Hallman, interviewed via telephone on October 8, 2020.
31. Ibid.
32. Ibid.
33. Ibid.
34. The Bureau also remained concerned about his antagonistic attitude toward the FBI. In reminding Richmond Division of this fact, it noted in the past Weisband has been "antagonistic toward the Bureau and that efforts to interview him might be

utilized by him as a basis for criticism of the Bureau." Richmond Letter to Bureau, 12/12/62; Bureau letter to Richmond, December 31, 1962, Weisband FBI file. 65–5909 1965.

35. Ibid.

36. "The Spy Buried in Alexandria: Unraveling the Tale of Lieutenant William Weisband and the Impact on American Intelligence." The Presbyterian Cemetery, David Heidy, July 9, 2023. Author interview August 1, 2023.

## Chapter 36

# Epilogue

It was around midday when Oleg Kalugin slowly eased his car to a stop along the curb of a quiet street and then sat there for minutes waiting and looking around. He had parked in a residential Virginia neighborhood not far from the Russian embassy in downtown Washington. He knew that the traffic would be generally light and limited to a few local homeowners coming and going on errands and such. For the veteran KGB officer this was no ordinary day. He was on a mission ordered by his bosses in Moscow. Prompting his wariness was concern that ever-present FBI surveillance could suddenly pounce on him at any moment.

Oleg Danilovich Kalugin was born to be a spy. Born in St. Petersburg, Russia, in 1934, his father was a serving NKVD officer, the KGB's predecessor agency. After completing Leningrad University, he joined the KGB's elite First Chief Directorate, the foreign espionage arm of the service. In 1958, at age twenty-four, he earned a Fulbright scholarship to study journalism at New York's prestigious Columbia University School of Journalism. For a number of years, he posed as a radio journalist while conducting intelligence work at the United Nations. After an assignment at Moscow Center, he returned to America in 1966, again under press cover, this time at the Soviet embassy in Washington with the rank of lieutenant colonel and deputy chief of the KGB Washington station.

Among his duties was heading counterintelligence at the Washington residency, which meant responsibility for monitoring the behavior of the Russian officials and their families for any signs of deviation from the Communist principles. It also required him to hunt for sources inside US Intelligence Community agencies such as the FBI, the CIA, and the NSA. He was highly regarded by Moscow peers as a skilled officer who got things done with efficiency. Among his many successes was masterminding the capture of Nicholas Shadrin, an FBI double agent, off the streets of Vienna and the later assassination of Bulgarian dissident journalist Georgi Markov on a London sidewalk using a poisoned umbrella filled with the nerve agent Ricin.

The mission this day was no ordinary one. He was to reestablish contact after many years with Bill Weisband, who was still remembered as one of Moscow Center's finest sources. He was important to the KGB. They had quietly tracked him for years, knowing that he had fallen on hard times and believing they owed him an obligation for his service to Moscow. In the end Kalugin, who read Weisband's file while in Moscow preparing for his Washington assignment, was now ordered to find him. After finding his address, Moscow instructed him to prepare a package for delivery to Bill. As he later said, he drove around for hours one day with the package making sure that he was not under surveillance. When certainty was assured, he made his way to Bill's Manassas neighborhood and parked his car on a nearby street near his home. With package in hand, he approached the front door, rang the bell, and waited. After a few moments, Mabel answered. When Kalugin explained that he was a friend of Bill, she told him that she was his wife and that Weisband had died just a week earlier. Kalugin then expressed his condolences and quickly walked away. But not before handing her the package. She thanked him politely, closed the door, and went inside. Upon opening it she discovered forty thousand dollars ($313,350 in November 2020) in packets of crisp US currency.[1]

In the end, the KGB made good on its commitment to one of the "old masters," a faithful servant, who had done so much to ensure Russian security.

## NOTES

1. Oleg Kalugin, author interview, July 19, 2005.

# Bibliography

## CONTENTS

Records of the Federal Bureau of Investigation
Records of the US State Department
Records of the National Archives and Records Administration
Records of the National Cryptologic Museum
US Government Publications
Oral Histories
Miscellaneous
Books
Journals
Theses
Newspapers
Interviews
Videos
Music

## RECORDS OF THE FEDERAL BUREAU OF INVESTIGATION

Elizabeth Bentley 61–6328
FBI Comintern Apparatus File 100–203581
Jones Orin York FBI File 65–2223
Gregory Silvermaster 65–56402
William Weisband FBI File 65–59095

## RECORDS OF THE US STATE DEPARTMENT

US State Department Decimal File (Comintern) 800.00B

## RECORDS OF THE NATIONAL ARCHIVES AND RECORDS ADMINISTRATION

RG 46, The Center for Legislative Archives, US Special Committee Investigating the Munitions Industry 4/12/1934–1936.

RG 457, Records of the National Security Agency/Central Security Service, 1917–1993.

RG 492, US Army Forces, Mediterranean Theater of Operations.

RG 498, European Theater of Operations, World War II, Headquarters.

## RECORDS OF THE NATIONAL CRYPTOLOGIC MUSEUM

*ASA Review.* July–August 1946.

*ASA Review.* May–June 1947.

*ASA Review.* May–June 1950.

Benson, Robert Louis. *Venona.* 2 Vols. Fort Meade, MD: National Security Agency, Undated.

Burns, Thomas L. *The Origins of NSA, 1940–1952.* Fort Meade, MD: Center for Cryptologic History, National Security Agency, 1990.

*Communications Security.* Published by Authority of Joint Communications Board, Washington, DC, April 1947.

*Introductory History of Venona and Guide to Translations.* Fort Meade, MD: Center for Cryptologic History, National Security Agency, 1995.

Johnson, Clarence L., with Maggie Smith. *Kelly.* Washington, DC: Smithsonian Books, 1985.

Johnson, Thomas R. *American Cryptology during the Korean War.* Fort Meade, MD. Undated.

———. *American Cryptology during the Cold War, 1945–1960:* "Struggle for Centralization 1945–1960," Book 1. Fort Meade, MD: National Security Agency.

Kirby, Oliver. *The Origins of the Soviet Problem: A Personal View.* Fort Meade, MD: Center for Cryptologic History, National Security Agency, Undated.

Peterson, Michael L. *Before Bourbon: American and British COMINT Efforts against Russia and the Soviet Union.* Fort Meade, MD: National Security Agency, Undated.

———. Bourbon to Black Friday: The Allied Collaborative COMINT Effort against the Soviet Union, 1945–1948. Fort Meade, MD: Center for Cryptologic History, Vol. 2, Series V, National Security Agency, 1995.

*Post War Transition Period, The Army Security Agency, 1945–1948.* Prepared under the Direction of the Chief, Army Security Agency, April 7, 1952.

Rowlett, Frank. "Special Report on Bourbon Cryptography: Report on Interrogation of Corby, October 15, 1945." NCM.

*The Soviet Problem.* Fort Meade, MD: National Security Agency, Undated. DOCID 3188691.

SRH 124, *Operational History of the 849th Signal Intelligence Service, Mediterranean Theater of Operations*, US Army.
SRH 391, *American Signal Intelligence in North Africa and Western Europe.*
*Study of the Security Division, 1955.* Fort Meade, MD: National Security Agency, Undated.
*Summary Annual Report of the Army Security Agency, Fiscal Year 1946.* Prepared under the Direction of the Chief, Army Security Agency, July 31, 1947.
*Summary Annual Report of the Army Security Agency, Fiscal Year 1947.* Prepared under the Direction of the Chief, Army Security Agency, February 1950.
*Summary Annual Report of the Army Security Agency, Fiscal Year 1948.* Prepared under the Direction of the Chief, Army Security Agency, July 1950.
*Summary Annual Report Army Security Agency and Subordinate Units, July 1, 1948–June 30, 1949, Fiscal Year 1949.* Historical Section, G-2, Headquarters Army Security Agency, 1952.
Wheatley, Leroy H. *Cryptanalysis Machines in NSA.* Fort Meade, MD: National Security Agency, Undated.

## US GOVERNMENT PUBLICATIONS

Benson, Robert Louis. *A History of U.S. Communications Intelligence during World War II: Policy and Administration.* Washington, DC: Fort Meade, Maryland, Center for Cryptologic National Security Agency, Series IV, Volume 8, 1997.
Benson, Robert Louis, and Michael Warner. *Venona: Soviet Espionage and the American Response 1939–1957.* Washington, DC: National Security Agency and Central Intelligence Agency, 1996.
Benson, Robert Louis. *History of Bourbon.* Washington, DC: National Security Agency, 1990.
———. *History of Venona.* Washington, DC: National Security Agency, 1993.
Bourbon to Black Friday, The Allied Collaborative COMINT Effort against the Soviet Union, 1945–1948, 88. NSA Doc #4314635.
Davis, Carol B. *Candle in the Dark: COMINT and Soviet Industrial Secrets, 1946–1956.* Fort Meade, MD: Center for Cryptologic History, National Security Agency, 2017.
*European Axis Intelligence in World War II as Revealed by "TICOM" Investigations and by Other Prisoner of War Interrogations and Captured Materials, Particularly German.* Nine Volumes. Washington, DC: Army Security Agency, War Department, 1946.
Friedman, William. *Military Cryptanalysis: Monoalphabetic Substitution Systems*, Part I. Washington, DC: Government Printing Office, 1938.
———. *Military Cryptanalysis: Simpler Varieties of Polyalphabetic Substitution Systems*, Part II. Washington, DC: Government Printing Office, 1938.
———. *Military Cryptanalysis*, Part III. Washington, DC: Government Printing Office, 1938.

———. *Military Cryptanalysis*, Part IV. Washington, DC: Government Printing Office, 1938.

Hatch, David A., and Robert Louis Benson. *The Korean War: The SIGINT Background*. Fort Meade, MD: Center for Cryptologic History, National Security Agency, 2000.

Howe, George. *American Signal Intelligence in Northwest Africa and Western Europe*. Washington, DC: National Security Agency, 2010.

Johnson, Thomas. *American Cryptology during the Cold War, 1945–1989*. Fort Meade, MD: Center for Cryptologic History, National Security Agency, 1995.

Johnson, Thomas R. "The Sting—Enabling Codebreaking in the Twentieth Century," *Cryptologic Quarterly*, Undated, DOCID 3860890 NCM, NSA. Venona Monograph,

*Operational History of the 849th Signal Intelligence Service, July 1945*. History of the Signal Intelligence Division, Office of the Chief Signal Officer, Services of Supply, European Theater of Operations, US Army, 1942–1945, 3 Vols.

*Soviet Intelligence Targets in the United States 1946–1953*. Washington, DC: Federal Bureau of Investigation, 1953.

Wilcox, Jennifer. *Sharing the Burden: Women in Cryptology during World War II*. Fort Meade, MD: Center for Cryptologic History, National Security Agency, 1998.

## ORAL HISTORIES

Thomas Arnold Veterans History Project, Library of Congress, Washington, DC.
Oliver Kirby
Marie Meyer
Juanita Moody
Paul Neff
Selmar Norland
Frank Rowlett
John Tiltman
John Turcott Arnold, Veterans History Project, Library of Congress, Washington, DC.

## MISCELLANEOUS

Notebooks of Alexandria Vassiliev, online.
Norman H. Evans, Cullum No. 8548, List of US Military Academy Graduates.
*The Spa*. Hot Springs High School Yearbook. Hot Springs, NC, 1940–1941.
Lieutenant Dennis Campbell, "The Way We Were," Open Mike, Prince George's County Government, Undated.
"The Spy Buried in Alexandria: Unraveling the Tale of Lieutenant William Weisband and the Impact on American Intelligence." The Presbyterian Cemetery.
Christopher Popa. *Xaiver Cugat: Passion for Life*. Library.com, April 2009.

Nicole Saraniero. *The Hotel Pennsylvania's Uncertain Future.* Untapped New York, May 6, 2021.
No Author. *The Unofficial Palace.* The Towers, New York Residences, Undated.

## BOOKS

Albright, Joseph, and Marcia Kunstle. *Bombshell.* New York: Times Books, 1997.
Alvarez, David. *Secret Messages.* Lawrence: University Press of Kansas, 2000.
Anbinder, Tyler. *City of Dreams.* New York; Boston: Houghton Mifflin Harcourt, 2016.
Andrew, Christopher, and Oleg Gordievsky. *KGB: The Inside Story.* New York: HarperCollins Publishers, 1990.
Andrew, Christopher, and Vasili Mitrokhin. *The Mitrokhin Archive.* New York: Basic Books, 1999.
Andrew, Christopher. *Defend the Realm.* New York: Alfred A. Knopf, 2009.
Atkinson, Rick. *An Army at Dawn.* New York: Henry Holt and Company, 2002.
———. *Place of Battle.* New York: Henry Holt and Company, 2007.
Bamford, James. *Body of Secrets.* New York: Doubleday, 2001.
Baron, John. *Operation SOLO.* Washington, DC: Regnery Press, 1996.
Batvinis, Raymond J. *Origins of FBI Counterintelligence.* Lawrence: University Press of Kansas, 2007.
Bentley, Elizabeth. *Out of Bondage.* New York: The Devin–Adair Company, 1951.
Bird, Kai. *The Color of Truth: McGeorge Bundy and William Bundy, Brothers in Arms.* New York: Simon & Schuster, 1998.
Blum, Howard. *In the Enemies House.* New York: HarperCollins Publishers, 2018.
Blumenthal, Ralph. *Stork Club.* Boston: Little, Brown and Company, 2000.
Boyd, Carl. *Hitler's Japanese Confidant.* Lawrence: University Press of Kansas, 1991.
Bradley, Mark A. *A Very Principled Boy.* New York: Basic Books, 2014.
Brown, Anthony Cave. *Treason in the Blood.* Boston: Houghton Mifflin Company, 1994.
Budiansky, Stephen. *Battle of Wits.* New York: Simon & Schuster, 2000.
———. *Code Warriors.* New York: Alfred A. Knopf, 2016.
Chambers, Whittaker. *Witness.* Washington, DC: Regnery Gateway, 1952.
Charney, David L. *NOIR White Paper.* Self-Published, 2014.
Chirnside, Mark. *The "Big Four" of the White Star Fleet.* The Mill, Brimscombe Port, Stroud, Gloucester, England: The History Press, 2016.
Clayton, Anthony. *Three Marshals of France.* London: Brassey's UK, 1992.
Clifford, Clark M. *Counsel to the President.* New York: Random House, 1991.
Colville, John. *The Fringes of Power.* New York: W. W. Norton & Company, 1986.
Costello, John. *Mask of Treachery.* New York: William Morrow and Company, Inc., 1988.
Costello, John, and Oleg Tsarev. *Deadly Illusions.* New York: Crown Publishers, Inc., 1993.
Cressy, Paul Goalby. *The Taxi Dance Hall.* Chicago: University of Chicago Press, 1932.

DeGaulle, Charles. *The Complete War Memoirs of Charles DeGaulle.* New York: Carroll & Graff Publishers, 1998.

Deriabin, Peter, and Frank Gibney. *The Secret World.* New York: Ballantine Books, 1959.

Detzer, Dorothy. *Appointment on the Hill.* New York: Henry Holt and Company, 1948.

Fagone, Jason. *The Woman Who Smashed Codes.* New York: HarperCollins Publishers, 2017.

Feklisov, Alexander. *The Man behind the Rosenbergs.* New York: Enigma Books, 2001.

Ferris, John. *Behind the Enigma.* London: Bloomsbury Publishing, 2020.

Friedman, William. *Elements of Cryptanalysis.* Laguna Hills, CA: Aegean Press, 1979.

Gage, Beverly. *G-Man: J. Edgar Hoover and the Making of the American Century.* New York: Viking, 2022.

Gouzenko, Igor. *The Iron Curtain.* New York: E. P. Dutton & Co., Inc., 1948.

*Great Concerns of the Resident A. S. Panyushkin. Essay from the History of Russian Intelligence, Volume 4, 1941–1945.* Moscow: Federal Book Publishing Program of Russia, 1999.

Haag, Michael. *Alexandria: City of Memory.* New Haven, CT: Yale University Press, 2004.

Hagedorn, Ann. *Sleeper Agent.* New York: Simon & Schuster Paperbacks, 2021.

Halberstam, David. *The Coldest Winter.* New York: Hyperion, 2007.

Haynes, John Earl, and Harvey Klehr. *Venona: Decoding Soviet Espionage in America.* New Haven, CT: Yale University Press, 1999.

Haynes, John Earl, Harvey Klehr, and Alexander Vassiliev. *Spies: The Rise and Fall of the KGB in America.* New Haven, CT: Yale University Press, 2009.

Hermiston, Roger. *The Greatest Traitor: The Secret Lives of Agent George Blake.* London: Aurum Press Limited, 2013.

Hindley, Meredith. *Destination Casablanca.* New York: PublicAffairs, 2017.

Hornblum, Allen M. *The Invisible Harry Gold.* New Haven, CT: Yale University Press, 2010.

Ilbert, Robert. *Alexandrie 1830–1930: histoire d'une communaute, citidine,* 2vols. Le Caire: Institut Francais d' Archeologie Orientale, 1996.

Jabotinsky, Vladimir. Translated by Michael R. Katz. *The Five.* Hamilton, NY: Cornell University Press, 2005.

Jeffery, Keith. *The Secret History of MI6.* New York: Penguin Press, 2010.

Kahn, David. *The Codebreakers.* New York: Scribner, 1986.

Kalugin, Oleg. *Spymaster.* New York: Basic Books, 2009.

Kelly, Clarence L. *Kelly: More Than My Share of It All.* Washington, DC: Smithsonian Books, 1985.

Kennedy, David M. *Freedom from Fear.* New York: Oxford University Press, 1999.

Kenyon, David. *Bletchley Park and D-Day.* New Haven, CT: Yale University Press, 2019.

Kesselring, Albert. *The Memoirs of Field Marshall Albert Kesselring.* New York: Greenhill Books, 2007.

King, Charles. *Odessa.* New York: W. W. Norton & Company, 2011.

Klier, John D., and Shlomo Lambroza, ed. *The Pogrom of 1905 in Odessa: A Case Study.* Cambridge, England: Cambridge University Press, 1992.
Knight, Amy. *How the Cold War Began.* New York: Carroll & Graf Publishers, 2005.
Lamphere, Robert J. *The FBI-KGB War.* New York: Random House, 1986.
Levy, David. *Stalin's Man in Canada.* New York: Enigma Books, 2011.
Lokhova, Svetlana. *The Spy Who Changed History.* New York: Pegasus Books, 2019.
Martin, David L. *Wilderness of Mirrors.* Guilford, CT: Globe Pequot Press, 2003.
Massing, Hede. *This Deception.* New York: Duell Sloan and Pearce, 1951.
McCullough, David. *Truman.* New York: Simon & Schuster, 1991.
———. *The Wright Brothers.* New York: Simon & Schuster, 2015.
Mikolashek, Jon B. *General Mark Clark.* Philadelphia: Casemate, 2013.
Mitchell, Thomas, and Marcia Mitchell. *The Spy Who Seduced America.* Montpelier, VT: Invisible Cities Press, 2001.
Modin, Yuri. *My Five Cambridge Friends.* New York: Harpers, Strauss, Giroux, 1994. Translated by Anthony Roberts.
Mosely, Leonard. *Marshall: Hero for Our Times.* New York: Hearst Books, 1982.
Mundy, Liza. *Code Girls.* New York: Hachette Books, 2017.
Murphy, Robert. *Diplomat among Warriors.* Garden City, NY: Doubleday & Company, Inc., 1964.
Notin, Jean-Christophe. *Marechal Juin.* Paris: Tallandier, 2015.
Olmsted, Kathryn S. *Red Spy Queen.* Chapel Hill: University of North Carolina Press, 2002.
O'Sullivan, Donald. *Dealing with the Devil: Anglo-Soviet Intelligence Cooperation in the Second World War.* New York: Peter Lang Publishing, 2009.
Philby, Kim. *My Silent War.* New York: Grove Press Inc., 1968.
Rees, David. *Harry Dexter White: A Study in Paradox.* New York: MacMillan, 1973.
Riebling, Mark. *Wedge: The Secret War between the FBI and CIA.* New York: Simon & Schuster, 2002.
Roberts, Sam. *Grand Central.* New York: Grand Central Publishing, 2013.
Roll, David. *George Marshall: Defender of the Republic.* New York: Dutton/Caliber, 2019.
Romerstein, Herbert, and Eric Breindel. *The Venona Secrets.* Washington, DC: Regnery Publishing, Inc., 2000.
Rowlett, Frank. *The Story of Magic.* Laguna Hills, CA: Aegean Press, 1998.
Ruble, Mary. *Del Rio.* Newport, TN: Clifton Club, 1970.
Sakmyster, Thomas. *Red Conspirator.* Urbana: University of Illinois Press, 2011.
Schecter, Jerrold, and Leona Schecter. *Sacred Secrets.* Washington, DC: Brassey's, 2002.
Schriftgiesser, Kirk, and Oscar Tschirky. *Oscar of the Waldorf.* New York: E. P. Dutton & Co., Inc., 1943.
Shaughnessy, Dennis R. *The Business of America Is Business.* Boston, MA: Northeastern University Press, 2017.
Smith, Mary Bell. *In the Shadow of the White Rock.* Boone, NC: Minor's Publishing Company, 1979.
Smith, Michael. *The Real Special Relationship.* London: Simon & Schuster, 2022.
Spivak, John Louis. *A Man in His Time.* New York: Horizon Press, 1967.

Stafford, David. *Spies Beneath Berlin.* London: John Murray, 2002.
Straight, Michael. *After a Long Silence.* New York: Norton, 1983.
Sudoplatov, Pavel, and Anatoli Sudoplatov. *Special Tasks.* Boston: Little, Brown and Company, 1994.
Tanenhaus, Sam. *Whittaker Chambers.* New York: Random House, 1997.
Thomas, Frank, and Edward Weisband. *Secrecy and Foreign Policy.* New York: Oxford University Press, 1974.
Tuchman, Barbara. *Stillwell and the America Experience in China, 1911–1945.* New York: The MacMillan Company, 1971.
Ulam, Adam. *Stalin: The Man and His Era.* New York: Viking Press, 1973.
Vagts, Alfred. *Defense and Diplomacy.* New York: Kings Crown Press, 1956.
Vigneras, Marcel. *Rearming the French.* Washington, DC: Center of Military History, United States Army, 1989.
Weiner, Tim. *Legacy of Ashes.* New York: Doubleday, 2007.
Weinstein, Allen, and Alexander Vassiliev. *The Haunted Wood: Soviet Espionage in America—The Stalin Era.* New York: Random House, 1999.
West, Nigel. *Venona.* New York: HarperCollins, 1999.
———. *Mask.* London: Routledge, 2005.
West, Nigel, and Oleg Tsarev. *The Crown Jewels: The British Secrets at the Heart of the KGB Archives.* London: Harper/Collins, 1998.
Whalen, James. *Last of the Boom Ships.* Rockville, MD: 1st Books Library, 2000.
Wiltz, John E. *In Search of Peace.* Baton Rouge: Louisiana State University Press, 1963.

## JOURNALS

Aid, Mathew. "Stella Polaris and the Secret Code Battle in Post War Europe." *Journal of Intelligence and National Security* (September 2002): 17–86.
Callimahos, Lambros. "The Legendary William F. Friedman." *Cryptologic Spectrum*, Vol. 4, No. 1 (Winter 1974).
*Essays from the History of Russian Foreign Relations, 1941–1944*, Vol. 4. Editor: I. Rybalkin. Russian Federation State Printing Committee, International Relations Publishing House, 1997.
Feldt, Cdr. E. A. "Coast Watching in World War II." Annapolis, MD: Proceedings of the Naval Institute, 87/7/703, September 1961.
Fielding, Nick. "Britain Used Captured Nazi Code Squad to Spy on Russia." *Sunday Times of London*, 4/29/2001 VF 61–48.
Glantz, David M. "Soviet Operational and Tactical Combat in Manchuria, 1945," "Operation August Storm." London: Frank Cass Publishers, 2003.
Gonzalez, Naiomi. "William Weisband." *The Intelligencer*, Vol. 26, No. 1 (2020): 51.
"L'Affaire Weisband." *American Cryptology during the Cold War, 1945–1989, the Struggle for Centralization, 1945–1946.* NCM, NSA.
Mueller, Gordon H. "Rapallo Reexamined: A New Look at Germany's Secret Military Collaboration with Russia in 1922." *Military Affairs*, Vol. 40, No. 3 (October 1973).

Perlman, Susan McCall. "U.S. Intelligence and Communist Plots in Post War France." *Intelligence & National Security*, Vol. 3, No. 3, 376–90.
Pfeiffer, Paul N. "Breaking the German Weather Cipher in the Mediterranean, Detachment G, 849th Signal Intelligence Service." *Cryptologia*, Vol. XXII, No. 4 (October 1998).
Sullivan, Laura. "Spy's Role Linked to U.S. Failure on Korea." *Baltimore Sun*, June 29, 2000. VF 54–61.
Tarlofsky, Malcolm. "The Code War." *The Washington Post Magazine*, 5/10/1998.
Tweedie, Neil Tweedie. "Code Team Cracked Soviet Ciphers." Telegraph Co. UK., 7/17/2003.

## THESES

Atkinson, Thomas A. *The P-38 Lightning Aircraft: Lessons Learned for Future Weapon Systems Development.* MSS, 2009–2010, US Marine Corp Command and Staff College, Marine Corp University, Quantico, VA.
Fencl, Bryan J. *Adaptation to Curriculum at the Quartermasters School Officer Candidate Course during World War II.* MA&S, 2012, US Army Command and General Staff College, Fort Leavenworth, KS.

## NEWSPAPERS

*Brooklyn Daily Eagle*
*Kingsport Times*
*Los Angeles Times*
*New York Daily News*
*New York Herald Tribune*
*New York Times*
*The Newport Plain Talk*
*Orlando Sentinel*
*Princeton Alumni Weekly*
*Richmond Times Dispatch*
*Time*
*The Washington Post*
*Washington Times Herald*

## INTERVIEWS

Robert Louis Benson, September 28, 2020, October 10, 2020, June 25, 2023.
Vonda Blackwell, October 20, 2020.
William and Tanya Ciminetti, April 29, 2018.

Robert Hallman, October 8, 2020.
Ellen Haring, April 4, 1998.
David Heidy, August 3, 2023.
Courtland Jones, January 22, 2013.
Courtland Jones Jr., July 15, 2023.
Oleg Kalugin, July 19, 2005.
John Schindler, September 9, 2020.
Katherine Scott, June 3, 2018.
Donald Walters, January 25, 2013.

## VIDEOS

*What Makes Traitors Tick.* David Charney YouTube: Presentation International Spy Museum/Smithsonian, Spy Seminar Series, Undated.
*Secrets, Lies, and Atomic Spies.* Tug Yourgrau, Powderhouse Productions, NOVA, 2002.
*The Codebreaker: Wife, Mother, and Secret American Hero.* Woman in History, American Experience, Public Broadcasting, 4/29/2023.
*A Man Who Aligned Japan with the Nazis.* NHK World Prime, Japan, 2021. YouTube.
*Station X: The War of the Machines.* United Kingdom, 1999. YouTube.
Youngren, Tug. *Secret Lies and Atomic Spies.* NOVA, Public Broadcasting Corporation, 2002.

## MUSIC

Postalmuseum.si.edu/airmail/resources.html
Music by Dorothy Mayhew, words by Joy York.
Hollywood, California, Dorothy Mayhew, 1937.
"I am a Knight of the Open Way," Dedicated to the Conquerors of the Sky.

# About the Author

**Raymond J. Batvinis** is an author, lecturer, historian, retired FBI agent, and former professional lecturer at George Washington University. He holds a doctorate from The Catholic University of America and is the author of two previous books on the history of the FBI's counterintelligence program.

Milton Keynes UK
Ingram Content Group UK Ltd.
UKHW051826160424
441261UK00004B/25

9 781538 184899